Restoring Dignity

Responding to
Child Abuse in
Canadian Institutions

LAW COMMISSION OF CANADA
COMMISSION DU DROIT DU CANADA

An Executive Summary of this Report is available under separate cover
(ISBN: 0-662-64474-3 and CAT: JL2-7/2000-1)

This Report is available in French: *La dignité retrouvée : La réparation des
sévices infligés aux enfants dans les établissements canadiens* (ISBN: 0-662-
83999-4 & CAT: JL2-7/2000-2F)

The Law Commission of Canada has also produced a video to
accompany this Report: *Just Children* (ISBN: 0-662-28386-4 & CAT: JL2-8/
2000E for video) – Running time: 24 minutes

The Report and an Executive Summary are also available online at
<http://www.lcc.gc.ca>

Canadä

ISBN: 0-662-28154-3
CAT: JL2-7/2000-2E

The Honourable A. Anne McLellan,
Minister of Justice,
Justice Building,
Wellington Street,
Ottawa,
K1A 0H8

Dear Minister,

Pursuant to your request under section 5(1)(b) of the *Law Commission of Canada Act*, and in accordance with section 5(1)(c) of that Act, we are pleased to submit the Report of the Law Commission of Canada on processes for dealing with institutional child abuse.

Yours sincerely,

Roderick A. Macdonald,
President

Nathalie Des Rosiers,
Vice president

Gwen Boniface,
Commissioner

Stephen Owen,
Commissioner

Alan Buchanan,
Commissioner

Summary of Contents

Preface xiii

Acknowledgements xv

Part I – Issues 1

   A. Why a Report on Institutional Child Abuse? 1
   B. What Children Experienced 21
   C. Residential Schools for Aboriginal Children 51
   D. Needs Identified 71

Part II – Responses 105

   A. Criteria of Assessment, Approaches to Redress
      and Guiding Principles 105
   B. The Criminal Justice Process 115
   C. Civil Actions 145
   D. Criminal Injuries Compensation Programs 193
   E. *Ex Gratia* Payments 207
   F. Ombudsman Offices 223
   G. Children's Advocates and Commissions 239
   H. Public Inquiries 249
   I. Truth Commissions and Similar Processes
      to Address Systemic Human Rights Abuses 267
   J. Community Initiatives 283
   K. Redress Programs 303
   L. Maintaining A Diversity of Approaches to
      Providing Redress 343

Part III – Commitments 347

   A. Prevention 347
   B. Reflections 383

Recommendations 401

Appendix A: Minister's Letter 425

Appendix B: Bibliography 427

Table of Contents

Letter of Transmittal i

Summary of Contents. iii

Table of Contents v

Preface xiii

Acknowledgements xv

Part I – Issues 1

   A. Why a Report on Institutional Child Abuse? 1

      1. The Question From the Minister of Justice. 1
      2. Why Do We Have Institutions for Children?. 2
      3. Why Did Abuse Occur in Institutions for Children? 4
      4. Why Institutional Child Abuse is an Important
         Issue Today. 6
      5. How the Commission Responded to the
         Minister's Question 7
      6. The Commission's Research Program 10
      7. Outline of This Report. 12
      8. Learning From the Past 14
      Endnotes 15

   B. What Children Experienced 21

      1. Why Children are in Institutions 21
      2. Life in a Total Institution. 22
         a. Disconnection 23
         b. Degradation. 25
         c. Powerlessness. 26
      3. Types of Total Institutions for Children 27
         a. Goals of total institutions 30
         b. Resistance 32
      4. Types of Abuse Suffered. 35
         a. Physical abuse 35
         b. Sexual abuse 39
         c. Other types of abuse 41

5. The Effects of Child Sexual and Physical Abuse
on Adult Survivors. 45
Endnotes 46

C. Residential Schools for Aboriginal Children 51

1. A Brief Historical Background. 51
a. Chronology of the residential school system. 52
b. Official policy governing the residential
school system 55
2. The Experience of Residential Schools 57
a. The experiences of children 57
b. The experience of families and communities 64
3. The Legacy of Residential Schools 66
Endnotes 67

D. Needs Identified. 71

1. Values. 71
a. Respect and engagement. 72
b. Information and support 73
2. Needs of Survivors. 74
a. Establishing an historical record; remembrance 75
b. Acknowledgement 80
c. Apology 83
d. Accountability. 87
e. Access to therapy or counselling 89
f. Access to education or training. 91
g. Financial compensation 92
h. Prevention and public awareness. 95
3. Needs of Families. 96
4. Needs of Communities 97
5. Particular Needs of Aboriginal Communities
and Peoples 98
6. Societal Needs: Prevention and Public Education 100
Endnotes 100

Part II – Responses. 105

**A. Criteria of Assessment, Approaches to Redress
and Guiding Principles**. 105

1. Criteria for Assessing Redress Processes 105
2. Approaches to Redress. 107

3. Guiding Principles 109
4. Organisation of this Part of the Report 113

B. The Criminal Justice Process 115

1. Introduction 115
2. Description 115
   a. Complaints and investigations 115
   b. Pre-trial processes 117
   c. The trial 118
   d. Sentencing 120
3. Assessment 121
   Overview 121
   a. Respect, engagement and informed choice 122
   b. Fact-finding 125
   c. Accountability 127
   d. Fairness 128
   e. Acknowledgment, apology and reconciliation 131
   f. Compensation, counselling and education 132
   g. Needs of families, communities and peoples 133
   h. Prevention and public education 133
4. Conclusion 134
   Recommendations 135
   Endnotes 138

C. Civil Actions 145

1. Introduction 145
2. Description 145
   a. Wrongful conduct 145
   b. Who may sue? 147
   c. Group actions and class actions 147
   d. Who may be sued? 149
   e. How long after abuse can one sue? 151
   f. The process 153
   g. Remedies 155
   h. Settlements and alternative dispute resolution 157
3. Assessment 161
   Overview 161
   a. Respect, engagement and informed choice 162
   b. Fact-finding 164
   c. Accountability 166
   d. Fairness 167
   e. Acknowledgment, apology and reconciliation 168

f. Compensation, counselling and education 169
g. Needs of families, communities and peoples. 171
h. Prevention and public education. 172
4. Conclusion. 174
Recommendations. 176
Endnotes 180

D. Criminal Injuries Compensation Programs 193

1. Introduction. 193
2. Description. 193
a. Underlying principles 194
b. Eligibility criteria. 194
c. Application process. 195
d. Benefits available. 195
e. Limitation periods. 197
3. Assessment. 197
Overview 197
a. Respect, engagement and informed choice 198
b. Fact-finding. 199
c. Accountability 199
d. Fairness 200
e. Acknowledgment, apology and reconciliation 200
f. Compensation, counselling and education 201
g. Needs of families, communities and peoples. 201
h. Prevention and public education. 202
4. Conclusion. 202
Recommendations. 203
Endnotes 203

E. *Ex Gratia* Payments 207

1. Introduction. 207
2. Description. 208
3. Assessment. 210
Overview 210
a. Respect, engagement and informed choice 211
b. Fact-finding. 211
c. Accountability 213
d. Fairness 213
e. Acknowledgment, apology and reconciliation 214
f. Compensation, counselling and education 214
g. Needs of families, communities and peoples. 214
h. Prevention and public education. 215

4. Conclusion. 216
Recommendations. 217
Endnotes 217

F. Ombudsman Offices. 223

1. Introduction. 223
2. Description. 223
   a. Triggering an ombudsman investigation 224
   b. Jurisdiction and authority to investigate 225
   c. Investigatory powers 226
   d. Power to report and recommend action 226
3. Assessment. 227
   Overview 227
   a. Respect, engagement and informed choice 228
   b. Fact-finding. 229
   c. Accountability 230
   d. Fairness 230
   e. Acknowledgment, apology and reconciliation 231
   f. Compensation, counselling and education 231
   g. Needs of families, communities and peoples. 232
   h. Prevention and public education. 232
4. Conclusion. 232
Recommendations. 234
Endnotes 234

G. Children's Advocates and Commissions. 239

1. Introduction. 239
2. Description. 239
   a. Informing and advocating 240
   b. Helping to resolve problems and investigating
      complaints. 240
   c. Making recommendations 241
   d. Conducting research and public education. 241
3. Assessment. 242
   a. Informing and advocating 242
   b. Helping to resolve problems and investigating
      complaints. 243
   c. Making recommendations 243
   d. Conducting research and public education. 243
4. Conclusion. 244
Recommendations. 245
Endnotes 245

H. Public Inquiries 249

   1. Introduction. 249
   2. Description. 250
     a. Mandate. 250
     b. Procedures 251
   3. Assessment. 251
     Overview 251
     a. Respect, engagement and informed choice 252
     b. Fact-finding. 253
     c. Accountability. 254
     d. Fairness 254
     e. Acknowledgement, apology and reconciliation 255
     f. Compensation, counselling and education 256
     g. Needs of families, communities and peoples. 256
     h. Prevention and public education. 257
   4. Conclusion. 257
   Recommendations. 259
   Endnotes 260

**I. Truth Commissions and Similar Processes
to Address Systemic Human Rights Abuses** 267

   1. Introduction. 267
   2. Description. 268
     a. The establishment of truth commissions. 268
     b. Mandate and powers of truth commissions 269
     c. Structure and process of truth commissions 270
   3. Assessment. 271
     Overview 271
     a. Respect, engagement and informed choice 272
     b. Fact-finding. 273
     c. Accountability. 273
     d. Fairness 274
     e. Acknowledgment, apology and reconciliation 275
     f. Compensation, counselling and education 275
     g. Needs of families, communities and peoples. 276
     h. Prevention and public education. 277
   4. Conclusion. 278
   Recommendations. 279
   Endnotes 279

J. Community Initiatives 283

  1. Introduction 283
  2. Description 283
      a. Initiatives based in non-Aboriginal communities 284
      b. Initiatives based in Aboriginal communities 286
      c. Funds and programs committed to helping
         survivors of abuse 287
  3. Assessment 293
      Overview 293
      a. Respect, engagement and informed choice 293
      b. Fact-finding 294
      c. Accountability 294
      d. Fairness 295
      e. Acknowledgement, apology and reconciliation 295
      f. Compensation, counselling and education 296
      g. Needs of families, communities and peoples 296
      h. Prevention and public education 296
  4. Conclusion 297
  Recommendations 298
  Endnotes 298

K. Redress Programs 303

  1. Introduction 303
  2. Description 305
      a. Input 307
      b. Beneficiaries 308
      c. Harms 309
      d. Redress 310
      e. Validation 316
      f. Outreach 320
      g. Duration 321
      h. Administration 323
  3. Assessment 324
      Overview 324
      a. Respect, engagement and informed choice 326
      b. Fact-finding 327
      c. Accountability 328
      d. Fairness 329
      e. Acknowledgement, apology and reconciliation 330
      f. Compensation, counselling and education 331
      g. Needs of families, communities and peoples 332
      h. Prevention and public education 333

4. Conclusion. 334
Recommendations. 335
Endnotes 339

**L. Maintaining A Diversity of Approaches to
Providing Redress**. 343

Part III – Commitments. 347

A. Prevention. 347

1. The Information Base 348
2. Frameworks and Strategies for Preventing
   Institutional Child Abuse 352
   a. Values and principles 353
   b. Proactive responses. 356
   c. Reactive responses. 362
Recommendations. 369
Endnotes 370

B. Reflections. 383

1. The Recommended Approaches 383
2. Situating Responses to Institutional Child
   Abuse: Redress and Prevention 393
3. A Continuing Agenda of Law Reform 398

Recommendations. 401

Appendix A: Minister's Letter 425

Appendix B: Bibliography 427

Preface

In November 1997, the Minister of Justice asked the Law Commission of Canada to assess processes for redressing the harm of physical and sexual abuse inflicted on children who lived in institutions that were run or funded by government. This Report draws together the research and consultations conducted by the Law Commission in response to that request.

The Commission has attempted to analyse the social and legal issues involved in institutional child abuse and to evaluate a variety of approaches to redress. It has also made several specific recommendations for action. The Law Commission hopes that this Report will provide governments with a framework of analysis and a blueprint for actions that must be taken to meet the needs of those whose childhood was destroyed by physical and sexual abuse.

Although this Report was written for the Minister of Justice, it is addressed to a broader public audience, not just to governments. The Law Commission hopes that the Report will:

- enable Canadians to learn more about why children were placed in institutions, what happened to them there, and the enormous harm some of them suffered;

- help Canadians learn what types of redress have been made available to survivors, assess their adequacy, and consider how we can repair the damage that has been done to these survivors, their families and their communities;

- support Canadians who want their governments to address this painful issue by negotiating adequate redress directly with survivors; and

- encourage Canadians not to view this issue as a problem of the past, and support efforts to have their governments commit themselves to effective strategies to prevent child abuse in various situations of out-of-home care.

This is by no means a final report. It is an invitation to reflect upon the issues that the Law Commission was asked to address and a call to help transform this Report's recommendations into an agenda for action.

We welcome your comments and ideas.

By mail:	The Law Commission of Canada,
	473 Albert Street,
	Ottawa, ON K1A 0H8
	Canada
By fax:	(613) 946-8988
Via the Internet:	http://www.lcc.gc.ca.

Acknowledgements

The Law Commission wishes to acknowledge the contribution of several people to this Report. It has benefitted enormously from the counsel and insight of members of its two Study Panels, which met three times each. The Commission has also received much help from many scholars who produced research reports: Ronda Bessner, SAGE (Ronda Claes and Deborah Clifton), Mark Gannage, and Rick Morris and his colleagues at the Institute for Human Resource Development.

In addition, Beverley Jacobs, Diane Corbière and David Nahwegahbow, Lila Duffy, Carol Hansen and Trygve Lee provided studies on the violation of Aboriginal laws. Linda Hill submitted a report on the facilitated discussion group with members of the Deaf community.

A number of law professors contributed research into particular areas of law. The Commission owes thanks to Nicholas Bala, Anne-Marie Boisvert, Bruce Feldthusen, Louise Langevin, Susan Miklas and Kent Roach. Members of the practising bar – including defence and Crown counsel, and lawyers for plaintiffs and defendants in civil matters – provided thoughtful comments on these academic pieces. We gratefully acknowledge the assistance of: John Briggs, John Brooks, Peter Burns, Ron Caza, Hubert Poulin, Isabel Schurman, Anne-Marie Veilleux and Susan Vella.

Within the Commission, research officers Susan Alter and Dennis Cooley researched and contributed drafts of sections of the Report. They also worked tirelessly on the innumerable and often tedious aspects of putting together a report of this magnitude. In addition, Susan Alter wrote a separate paper on apologies, that is published as a background paper.

The work of full-time staff was capably supplemented by a number of part-time researchers. Invaluable help was provided by Hélène Sioui-Trudel, and by Harry Gousopoulos and Karen Gorby, co-op students from the University of Victoria and Salim Fakirani, the Commission's articling student. Goldie Shea wrote background pieces on civil and criminal cases, as well as descriptions of redress programs. In addition, the Law Commission benefitted from the research assistance of

Natalie L'Heureux, Bill Riley, Stuart Herbert and Chantal Plamondon, each of whom played an important role in assembling statistics and verifying references.

The Law Commission owes an enormous debt of gratitude to Susan Zimmerman, Director of Research, who designed, administered and organised the entire project. She wrote the Interim Report, the Discussion Paper, and a large portion of this Report. She also integrated the many pieces of research that others prepared for the Commission and wove the various sections of this Report together.

The final product is a joint effort of the staff and Commissioners.

List of Study Panel members:

Study Panel on Residential Schools

Gerard BELLEFEUILLE
Manitoba

James BOBBISH
Quebec

Carol BRZEZICKI
Alberta

Cecilia EAGLE
Ontario

Jim EAGLE
Ontario

Ron GEORGE
Ontario

Joan GLODE
Nova Scotia

Carol HANSEN
Saskatchewan

Susan HARE
Ontario

Monica ITTUSARDJUAT
Nunavut

Allan LONGJOHN
Saskatchewan

Irma MURDOCK
Saskatchewan

Bill MUSSELL
British Columbia

Gene RHEAUME
Ontario

Marius TUNGILIK
Nunavut

Lydya ASSAYAG
  Quebec

Gerard BELLEFEUILLE
  Manitoba

Cecil O.D. BRANSON, Q.C.
  British Columbia

Cosette CHAFE
  Ontario

David C. DAY, Q.C.
  Newfoundland

Mary Lou DICKIE
  Ontario

Emerson DOUYON
  Quebec

Megan R. ELLIS
  British Columbia

Monica ITTUSARDJUAT
  Nunavut

Brenda KNIGHT
  British Columbia

Donna LEE
  Ontario

Beverley MANN
  Ontario

Bill MUSSELL
  British Columbia

Lorne SIPLE
  Ontario

Pamela SLEETH
  British Columbia

Part I – Issues

A.   Why a Report on Institutional Child Abuse?

It is often said that children are our future. How we treat our children and how we allow them to be treated reveal much about ourselves and about our values as a society.

Over the past ten to fifteen years, child abuse has surfaced as a painful issue for Canadians. With greater public discussion has come greater awareness that children have been abused not only in their homes and communities, but also in institutions where they were placed for their education, welfare, rehabilitation or even protection. Many of these institutions were run by, or on behalf of, federal, provincial and territorial governments. As increasing numbers of survivors of institutional child abuse[1] reach adulthood and achieve a clear understanding of the harm done to them, they are finding a public voice to describe their experiences, to express the pain they have suffered, and to seek an accounting from those who they claim are responsible.

The scope and seriousness of the allegations have caused governments, and religious and other organisations to ask how best to respond. Classical legal processes – criminal prosecutions of wrongdoers and civil actions to recover damages – seem inadequate to fully address the consequences of past institutional child abuse. It has become clear that other approaches must also be considered.

1.   The Question From the Minister of Justice

On November 14, 1997, the Minister of Justice, the Honourable A. Anne McLellan, wrote to the Law Commission of Canada requesting it to prepare "a report addressing processes for dealing with institutional child physical and sexual abuse".[2] In framing this request [hereinafter the Reference], the Minister charged the Commission with the task of furnishing "governments, and Canadians generally, with an inventory and comparative assessment of approaches available" for providing redress for adult survivors.

The Reference was meant to examine abuse that took place in residential schools for Aboriginal children and in institutions such as orphanages, schools for the Deaf, long-term mental health care facilities, sanitoria and training schools. According to the Minister, the goal of the Reference was to identify "what types of processes would best address wrongdoing, while affording appropriate remedies, and promoting reconciliation, fairness and healing".

Early on, the Commission decided to frame its research by asking how those adults who had been abused as children understood their needs. The idea was to begin by identifying the full dimensions of the social situation being studied and then work towards possible responses, rather than to undertake a conceptual legal analysis and then seek to apply that analysis to the issue under study. The Commission also decided that to properly address the needs being expressed by survivors, it could not look solely at the processes meant only to redress physical and sexual abuse. It would have to evaluate how well the current processes dealt with all the related types of abuse to which children may have been subjected in institutions, including emotional, psychological, cultural, racial and spiritual abuse.

Many difficult decisions confronted the Commission in determining how best to respond to the Minister's question. One issue, however, was not in doubt. In Canada, our history of institutional child abuse has been a tragedy of enormous proportion. It is not, sadly, only an issue of the past. Understanding the nature and settings of historical child abuse and what we can do to provide appropriate redress for survivors is a priority, both because justice demands that we act, and because it helps us to see how we, as a society, can take steps to root out child abuse of all types today.

2.   Why Do We Have Institutions for Children?

When societies plan and establish institutions for children, they do so with a beneficial purpose in mind. Some of the purposes that lay behind the creation of those institutions where abuse occurred, or is alleged to have occurred, continue to be valued. Providing a nurturing environment to meet the special educational needs of children with disabilities is one of these. Other rationales have become completely discredited.

The attempt to assimilate Aboriginal children by separating them from their families and their cultures is a striking example.

Residential institutions for children were conceived because, collectively, we concluded that they were an appropriate response to what we saw and described as problems. In some cases, such as residences run by religious orders and schools for children with special needs, parents sent their children willingly. In other cases, the institutions cared for children who had been abandoned or whose parents felt unable to look after them. In cases where children were found to be neglected or abused, or were judged to be "unmanageable" or truant, the law required that they be placed in institutions.[3] In short, disability and special needs, Aboriginal origin, poverty, illegitimacy and ungovernability were seen as sufficient reasons for taking children out of their homes and placing them in residential facilities.

It is not within the Commission's mandate in this Reference, nor is it the Commission's desire, to put policies and decisions of the past on trial by applying to them current knowledge, current sensibilities and current standards of behaviour. But the profound long-term effects of institutional child abuse are now much better understood. As a society, we cannot simply accept without question and comment the choices made in the past, and leave it to those who suffered to get on with their lives as best they can. We must confront the consequences of those choices and do what is necessary to rectify the wrongs that were done to innocent children – our children.

The Commission acknowledges that the institutions under such close scrutiny today were intended to improve the lives of the children placed in them. It recognises that they contributed significantly to doing so, and that many children acquired an education and life skills that have served them well as adults. It believes that the organisations that sponsored these institutions acted with the best of motives and often made considerable sacrifices to establish and maintain them. The Commission also acknowledges that most of the people who worked in these institutions did their very best to fulfil their roles as educators, caregivers and guardians, often with inadequate resources and support.

However, to explore appropriate responses to past child abuse in institutions, as the Commission has been asked to do, the focus must necessarily be on what went wrong, not on what worked. Without wishing to present a distorted picture of these institutions, the Commission feels obliged to emphasise that wrongdoings were pervasive enough, both within certain institutions and across a significant enough number of institutions,[4] that the recent and ongoing revelations of child abuse cannot be dismissed as isolated episodes. These revelations paint a picture of wide-ranging and serious inadequacies in the design of these institutions, their recruitment and training processes, their supervisory and management procedures, and their child placement decisions.

3.   Why Did Abuse Occur in Institutions for Children?

It is undeniable that significant harm was done to children in many institutions that were designed for their benefit. This fact leads some to suggest that all children's institutions should be closed. But a policy of simply abolishing institutions is not the answer. However much we may wish to find alternative means for caring for children in need, it is likely that some residential institutions will always be necessary. In any event, getting rid of institutions is no guarantee that physical and sexual abuse will end. The evidence is quite otherwise. So the goal must be to understand the situations that may give rise to abusive behaviour, and what combination of circumstances and attitudes may permit such behaviour to flourish. If, as a society, we shy away from these inquiries, the same mistakes will continue to be made, but in different contexts and under different guises.

What have we learned? Three lessons are clear. First, we must recognise which children are normally placed in institutions. Generally, they come from groups or communities that are now referred to as "marginalised". This means that they are members of society's most powerless groups; those who have neither the financial resources nor the political clout to make themselves heard and to exercise control over the course of their lives. It is no surprise, therefore, that the majority of children who were placed in institutions came from racial and ethnic minorities, and from families who suffered an economic disadvantage. It is, as well, no surprise that residential institutions were seen as appropriate environments for children who did not fall within what society considered the norm: children with developmental and physical disabilities, those with mental disorders, orphans, and even those who were simply born outside marriage.

The very factors that caused society to view residential institutions as a response to the perceived needs of these children, contributed to their vulnerability. These same factors also made it easier for officials to discount, disbelieve or deny the children's complaints of the treatment they received or witnessed. They also made it easier for society in general to regard these complaints as unimportant.

Second, we must recognise the enormous power imbalance that existed between the children within an institution and the officials who ran the institution.[5] To date, allegations of child abuse have invariably arisen in connection with residential institutions that were run by governments, and by churches and their lay orders.[6] These organisations wield significant social power and are potent symbols of authority today. They were even more potent symbols of authority in previous decades, when much of the child abuse under consideration took place.[7]

Two or three generations ago, citizens would have found it hard to believe – incredible in fact – that public officials might fail to ensure the welfare of children they had taken under their care, or might fail to respond quickly and effectively to plausible complaints of abuse. For many communities, the idea that ministers, deacons, priests, nuns, or members of lay orders could commit acts of physical and sexual child abuse was unthinkable. Even today, to accept the extent of the abuse that was committed, and the failure of those in charge to prevent or stop it, is to have one's faith in governments and churches seriously undermined. Many would rather believe that the abuse did not occur, or that the reports have been wildly exaggerated. The extent of the deference accorded to governments and churches made it difficult for anyone to effectively challenge the policies and acts of officials at the time.[8] The dynamic thus created within residential institutions – a group of vulnerable children placed under the control of caregivers whose authority was virtually unquestioned – was a recipe for the abuse of power by predators.

The third lesson relates to the societal visibility of residential institutions. When children are placed in institutions, they enter a different world; for those who are not part of that world, it is often a case of "out of sight, out of mind". Because society does not see these children, it needs to ensure that others see them. Effective external and independent oversight can serve as a check on those who would abuse children. Too often, however, there was little oversight of any kind brought to bear on the daily activities, the level of discipline and the quality of care that children received.[9] In some cases, an institution or its sponsor responded to documented evidence of abuse by simply transferring or dismissing the employee,[10] without seeking the involvement of police, offering counselling to the children or even seriously reviewing its hiring and supervisory policies.

Once society places children in institutions, it seems largely content to assume that this is the end of its direct responsibility to look after them. But brick and mortar institutions, or anywhere else we choose to place children "for their own good", are not solutions in and of themselves. They can be solutions when they provide services and care that meet the needs of children; when they do not, they become part of the problem. Children, *all* children, require ongoing care, attention, respect and love. Where parental responsibility is replaced by institutional care, external vigilance is essential. This is especially true when the parents themselves have proved neglectful or inadequate, because it means that their children will usually lack effective natural advocates outside the institution. Society's responsibility for vigilance through oversight and advocacy operates whatever the nature of the institution and whatever the reason for the placement.

4.   Why Institutional Child Abuse is an Important Issue Today

In seeking to redress the wrongs of the past, society must not become complacent and assume that these problems no longer exist. One reason why institutional child abuse that took place many years ago is a current issue is the recognition that child abuse continues today. Settings may have changed somewhat, but the vulnerability of children remains. This is true not only for children with special needs for whom residential institutions remain an appropriate option, but also for children now being placed in settings such as group care facilities and foster homes that have been developed, in part, as substitutes for some larger institutions. Survivors of past abuse feel a deep need to ensure that child abuse is stopped. They want to see education and prevention made a societal priority, for they know first-hand where abuse lurks and how it occurs.

Another reason why historical child abuse cannot be treated simply as an issue of the past is that its effects are passed on from generation to generation. Those who grew up in sterile institutional environments with harsh discipline and little nurturing, and who experienced physical or sexual abuse while there, are at great risk of being harsh and non-nurturing with their own children.[11] These intergenerational impacts make it all the more critical for society to help survivors and their families to confront the abuse and to heal. Only in this way can we hope to prevent another generation of children from suffering as their parents suffered.

Finding appropriate responses to past institutional child abuse is, consequently, a current and urgent concern. We must come to terms with history and deal with the wrongs committed. At the same time, we must scrutinise the situation of children currently in care outside their homes to ensure that we are not repeating the complacency that allowed previous generations to ignore or to discount complaints of abuse.

5.   How the Commission Responded to the Minister's Question

The Commission's initial task, in responding to the Minister's question, was to decide how to organise its research. Almost from the beginning, it concluded that it could not limit itself to considering only physical and sexual abuse. While such types of abuse are certainly the focal point of concern about institutional child abuse, they cannot be viewed in isolation. Children who are physically or sexually abused suffer emotionally as well. Similarly, emotional and psychological harm is done to children who are not physically or sexually abused themselves, but who witness abuse. Certain groups of children may also have been subjected to racial and cultural abuse.[12] To ignore or discount these other types of abuse would be to take the problem of historical physical and sexual

Paternalism and sexism are very much in evidence, the [Archdiocesan] Commission was told, among both young and old priests in the Archdiocese. Many who spoke and presented briefs to the Commission described an alarming lack of awareness and insensitivity in the use of patriarchal language and imagery in worship, and in preaching and teaching throughout the Archdiocese. In some situations the inability to separate power from clerical position, combined with an institutionally conditioned reticence toward women, has been so pronounced that parish councils at times have been rendered ineffective.

Many have argued that patriarchal thinking is one of the contributing factors to the sexual abuse of children within the Archdiocese because of the power and position it confers upon the members of the patriarchal establishment, in particular the ordained clergy. In our culture this has been linked to the power over women and children which males have traditionally exercised. Such arbitrary assignment of authority, whether to men generally in a male-dominated society, or to priests specifically in a patriarchal church, can preclude freedom of insight and liberty of action.

The Report of the Archdiocesan Commission of Enquiry into the
Sexual Abuse of Children by Members of the Clergy, Volume One, at pp.93-94

abuse of children in institutions out of the larger contexts within which it occurred.

Of equal importance, the Commission resolved to keep the perspectives of survivors foremost. It is the concerns survivors identify, the outcomes they seek, and the effect of any redress processes on them that have been the Commission's primary, though not sole, ways of evaluating the desirability of particular redress measures. This does not mean that the Commission has adopted an approach that is closed to the perspectives of others. Governments, churches, charitable organisations, as well as unions and religious orders whose members staffed these institutions, and those who themselves worked in these institutions – all have a direct and significant stake in how allegations of abuse and claims for redress are handled. To be fair and balanced in its analysis, the Commission has sought to address the legitimate concerns and interests of all parties in its assessment of the strengths and weaknesses of the different approaches to redress it examines.

Finally, in exploring the dimensions of institutional child abuse, the Commission was struck by the variety of out-of-home settings in which children are placed, and in which they are abused. Given recent revelations, Canadians know that abuse can and does occur, for example, in foster homes, group homes, day schools and summer camps, and on educational field trips and sports and exchange programs. Because the Minister's specific concern was with institutions that were run, funded or sponsored by government, the Commission limited its research to institutions that met these criteria. Within that category, it has attempted to be as inclusive as possible. The Commission recognises, however, that abuse also occurs in many other less formal government-sponsored settings. It hopes that its observations and recommendations may be useful in dealing with child abuse in out-of-home situations generally, despite the narrower scope of this Report.

6.   The Commission's Research Program

The Commission received the Minister's letter establishing the Reference in November 1997. As a first official step in developing a response, it issued an Interim Report in February 1998.[13] The Interim Report set out the issues that the Commission felt needed to be addressed in order for it to be able to assess properly what were "fair and reasonable ways" to respond to adult survivors of institutional child abuse. It reviewed the state of knowledge in the field and described the further research that would have to be undertaken.

Based on the issues identified in the Interim Report, the Commission asked four teams of researchers to produce papers looking at four key aspects of the question posed by the Minister. One paper was an inventory and description of institutions where abuse is alleged or has been proven to have occurred.[14] A second paper provided an analysis of the needs of survivors of residential schools for Aboriginal children,[15] and a third paper reviewed the needs of survivors from other types of children's institutions.[16] A fourth research paper examined the experience of other countries in dealing with state-sanctioned and long-standing abuse of sectors of the population.[17]

To obtain advice and input from those closely connected with the issues it was studying, the Commission established contact with a number of Aboriginal organisations. In February of 1998, the Commission made a presentation to the leadership of the six main national Aboriginal organisations. Members of a number of Aboriginal organisations were then invited to a series of meetings where the Commission reported on the progress of its work.[18] The purpose of these meetings was not only to keep these organisations up to date on the Commission's activities but also to provide them with an opportunity to comment informally on the research. The Commission notes, however, that these information-sharing meetings were neither intended nor understood as formal consultations with Aboriginal leaders or their organisations.

The Commission is authorised by the *Law Commission of Canada Act* to establish volunteer study panels to advise it on specific research projects. Given the scope of the Reference, the Commission felt it important to have a study panel which included survivors of institutional abuse, therapists who have counselled survivors, lawyers who have acted on their behalf, prosecuted alleged perpetrators, and those who have participated in commissions of inquiry, as well as some representatives from government and from affected communities. At the suggestion of the information-sharing group of Aboriginal organisations, the Commission decided to establish, in fact, two study panels. One panel was specifically concerned with abuse in residential schools for Aboriginal children, and was composed entirely of Aboriginal members. The other, which also contained members from the residential schools study panel, was concerned with abuse in all other types of institutions.[19]

These study panels each met three times. The panels were convened in July and September of 1998 to review drafts of the research papers and to offer advice about other studies to undertake. As a result of suggestions from the residential schools study panel, further research was commissioned to determine how traditional Aboriginal law was violated in residential schools. Case studies were completed in four communities.[20] The study panels also met in January 1999 to consider a Discussion Paper released by the Commission in December 1998.[21] This Discussion Paper drew together the results of the research studies prepared in connection with the Reference, and set out various policy options. Over 2,000 copies of the Discussion Paper were circulated, and the Internet site on which it was posted recorded more than 20,000 visits.

During the winter and spring of 1998–1999, the Commission organised or participated in several meetings, round-tables and colloquia to obtain feedback about the Discussion Paper. The executive summary was translated into three Aboriginal languages and a Braille version was also produced. The entire Discussion Paper was made available on audio tape. A special two-day consultation was held with the Deaf community. In addition, the Traditional Indigenous Healers of Canada held a workshop with the Commission on the impact of residential schools.

Two Internet "chat rooms" (one in English and one in French) were also launched and conversations were carried on for many weeks.

The Commission is grateful to all those who participated in its feedback processes. The extent of agreement it heard, and the key points upon which members of the study panels and those who responded to the discussion paper disagreed, have sharpened the Commission's perspective and have been very helpful in the preparation of this Report. Nonetheless, the Report should be taken as reflecting only the Commission's own perspective and conclusions.

7. Outline of This Report

This Report has been written so as to respond to the Minister's letter by addressing the following questions:

- How do those who were abused understand and live their experience today?

- What are the needs of adult survivors of child abuse in institutions, their families and their communities?

- What (or who) are the major obstacles to meeting these various needs?

- What can the formal, established processes for redress actually deliver by way of remedies and how well do these remedies respond to the needs identified?

- Are there steps that can be taken to improve each of these processes for survivors?

- Might there be better ways of meeting the full range of their needs in a manner that promotes reconciliation, fairness and healing?

- What parties should or must be involved in developing responses to past abuse?

The first part of this Report frames the issues. It describes the circumstances in which children who are placed in residential institutions generally find themselves. It seeks to explain why the Commission approached the Reference as it did, and to offer a snapshot of "institutional life" as experienced by children. This overview is completed by a survey of the types of abuse – physical, sexual, emotional, racial and cultural – that children actually suffered. Part I also provides a focussed discussion of the situation of Aboriginal children who were abused in residential schools, and of the impact of that abuse on their families and communities. In the last section of Part I, the Commission sets out a list of the needs that adult survivors may have as individuals, as members of communities and as peoples. The scale and scope of the needs identified reveal the deep and long-lasting impact of childhood physical and sexual abuse, and the wide range of responses that must be imagined in order to provide appropriate redress today.

Part II of this Report addresses possible responses. It begins by listing eight criteria against which the Commission believes that the various processes now available for redressing the harms caused by institutional child abuse should be evaluated. In its inventory of these processes, the Commission has tried to be as inclusive as possible. It begins with the existing legal approaches, involving courts, administrative tribunals and *ad hoc* executive processes, assessing all of them in their many contemporary variations. The Commission then investigates and analyses several other approaches that it believes could offer some measure of redress for survivors. In doing so, it considers approaches tried both in Canada and in other countries. It also looks at responses initiated by governments as well as those developed by non-governmental organisations such as churches, community groups and local social service agencies.

Each approach to redress is examined from two different perspectives. First, the internal dynamic of the process: How, in practice, does it work? What are its assumptions about fact-finding, for example? What does it require of the parties involved? How does it treat these parties? Second, the outcomes produced by the process: What type of sanction or burden can it place on those who committed or tolerated the physical and sexual abuse of children? What type of benefits can it confer on those who were subjected to physical or sexual abuse? How well do these benefits respond to the needs identified?

Confronting the past and attempting to redress the wrongs done is only a beginning. Many issues relating to child abuse remain an ongoing challenge for Canadians and their governments. Therefore, in Part III, a variety of understandings of and approaches to public education and prevention are outlined. It bears repeating that a culture of abuse requires an enabling environment within which to flourish. Identifying and isolating attitudes that protect people who physically and sexually abuse children is a key step in the prevention of child abuse. Another is to carefully investigate the settings in which abuse has thrived. This means gaining a clearer understanding of why certain types of institutions have been revealed as more likely to attract child abusers. Much of the prevention process entails putting into place systems and procedures that will limit the opportunities for abuse. The Commission believes that there are important lessons to be shared by survivors of past abuse about the conditions in institutions where abuse took place, and about how these institutions were organised and managed.

8. Learning From the Past

The Minister asked the Law Commission of Canada to comment on which processes may best respond to the needs of survivors of institutional child abuse. This task is not, however, just about how to compensate people for the wrongs of the past, and it is not just about law. It is about understanding how our society views its children and how it allows them to be treated. It is about attitudes in Canada toward Aboriginal peoples and the lack of respect accorded to Aboriginal values. It is about facing up to some unpleasant truths, not only about abuse of power and the pedophiles in our midst, but about how the people who are charged with the care and protection of children can fail, and in some cases deliberately refuse, to protect them from those in whose custody they are placed. It is about our faith in certain institutions, and how misplaced that faith can sometimes be. It is about wrenching families and communities apart through misplaced notions of cultural superiority. Above all, it is about our own failure, even today, to fully acknowledge the harm that was done and to take adequate steps to address that harm.

There is a real danger that we have not learned enough from the wrongs of the past. There are children today who suffer abuse at the hands of adults who have the responsibility of caring for them.

Even though children are no longer forcibly removed from their homes in order to attend school, for example, we have no cause for complacency. Many children who formerly would have been placed in institutions are now placed in other settings, where the treatment they receive may not be easily monitored. Resources are needed so that more children are able to live at home, in security. When this is not possible, we must not hesitate to invest in programs to select, train, supervise or monitor the foster families or staff at any non-institutional setting where these children may live. Other children, such as some of those with special needs, continue to require residential facilities for their care or education; as such, they may still be vulnerable to institutional abuse. If we choose to turn the same blind eye, refuse to discharge our obligations, or persist in denying our responsibility, there is every chance that another group of survivors will be coming forward in 10, 15 or 20 years from now.

The fact that physical and sexual abuse was common in many institutions intended to protect, nurture and educate young people reflects a tragic breach of trust by those who were abusers. It is an indictment of the supervisory processes in place at those institutions. And it is a damning commentary on the casual attitude that we took towards the children we placed in residential facilities. Each one of us is damaged when we permit our children to be abused in the institutions that our governments have established, or supported, to care for them. Understanding how that damage occurred, how it may be redressed, and how we may prevent it from recurring is the challenge we face, and must meet.

---

[1] "Institutional child abuse" in this report means abuse inflicted on a child residing in an institution, as distinguished from abuse occurring at home, or "domestic child abuse". The term does not imply that child abuse is an integral feature of all institutions for children, or that it has become "institutionalised".

[2] Letter from the Honourable A. Anne McLellan, Minister of Justice and Attorney General of Canada, to Roderick Macdonald, President, Law Commission of Canada (14 November 1997). For the full text of the letter, see Appendix A.

[3] For example, child welfare laws required provincial authorities to remove children from homes where they were judged to be suffering from neglect or abuse; juvenile delinquency laws (as they were then known) required the placement of youths in correctional facilities for a wide variety of offences, including some now considered too minor for incarceration; and the *Indian Act* authorized agents of the federal government to remove Aboriginal children from their home communities for placement in residential schools, if they had not been attending school. See for example, *Youth Protection Act*, as am. by 8-9 Eliz. II, c. 42, R.S.Q. 1964, c. 220, s. 15: children could be brought before a judge when they were children "whose parents, tutors or guardians are deemed unworthy, orphans with neither father nor mother and cared for by nobody, abandoned illegitimate or adulterine children, those particularly exposed to delinquency by their environment, unmanageable children generally showing pre-delinquency traits, as well as those exhibiting serious character disturbances." See also for example *Indian Act*, R.S.C. 1906, c. 81, ss. 9, 10, 11, as am. by S.C. 1919–20, c. 50, s.1.

[4] The Commission has compiled charts of civil and criminal cases involving allegations or findings of institutional child abuse. The charts are not meant to be an exhaustive list, but simply to give an idea of the volume of these types of cases. The charts are published as a companion to the report. They are by no means complete or final, as actions continue to be launched. See Law Commission of Canada, *Institutional Child Abuse in Canada – Civil Cases* by G. Shea (Ottawa: Law Commission of Canada, 1999) and Law Commission of Canada, *Institutional Child Abuse in Canada – Criminal Cases* by G. Shea (Ottawa: Law Commission of Canada, 1999). Both are available in hard copy from the Law Commission of Canada and online: <http://www.lcc.gc.ca>.

[5] While power imbalances continue to exist in institutional settings and are unavoidable when dealing with children and adults in any setting, the harshest effects of these imbalances have been softened to a great degree by increased independent oversight, better training of staff, fewer institutions and greater awareness on the part of child protection authorities.

[6] See for example the defendants in the cases cited in *Institutional Child Abuse in Canada – Civil Cases, supra* note 4.

[7] See E.Z. Friedenberg, *Deference to Authority: The Case of Canada* (Toronto: Random House, 1980) for a discussion of traditional Canadian attitudes towards institutions like governments and churches.

8   There is, however, some evidence that Canadians are becoming less willing to accept without question the authority of institutions. See N. Nevitte, *The Decline of Deference* (Peterborough, Ont.: Broadview Press, 1996).

9   B.C. Hoffman, *The Search for Healing, Reconciliation and the Promise of Prevention, The Recorder's Report Concerning Physical and Sexual Abuse at St. Joseph's and St. John's Training Schools for Boys*, a report prepared for the Reconciliation Process Implementation Committee, Ontario (place of publication unknown: Concorde Inc., 30 September 1995); J.R. Miller, *Shingwauk's Vision: A History of Native Residential Schools* (Toronto: University of Toronto Press, 1996); L. Hill, "Enough is Enough – Report on a Facilitated Discussion Group Involving the Deaf Community Responding to the Minister's Reference on Institutional Child Abuse" (March 1999) [unpublished research report archived at the Law Commission of Canada]; British Columbia, *Public Report No. 38: Righting the Wrong: The Confinement of the Sons of Freedom Doukhobor Children* (Victoria: British Columbia Ombudsman, 8 April 1999), online: <http://www.ombud.gov.bc.ca/publications/reports/righting_the_wrong/index.html> (date accessed: 16 November 1999).

10 Examples of a failure to respond adequately to allegations of abuse include the case against Karl Toft, a former employee of the New Brunswick Training School at Kingsclear and the case against John Critchley, the former proprietor of a facility for juvenile boys in British Columbia. See *C.A. v. Critchley*, [1997] B.C.J. No. 1020 (S.C.), online: QL.

11 R.K. Oates, "The Effects of Child Sexual Abuse" (1992) 66:4 A.L.J. 186 at 186-193; C. Alksnis & D. Robinson, *Childhood Victimization and Violent Behaviour Among Adult Offenders* (Ottawa: Correctional Service of Canada, Research Branch, 1995) at 16; J.C. Johnston, *Aboriginal Offender Survey: Case Files and Interview Sample* (Ottawa: Correctional Service of Canada, Research Branch, 1997).

12 By cultural abuse, the Commission is referring to abuse of individuals that denigrates a customary way of life, set of ideas and values, language or world view. Examples of cultural abuse include forbidding Aboriginal children in residential schools to speak their language or wear their traditional clothing; forbidding Doukhobor children in the New Denver residential school to practise their religion; and structuring an educational environment for the Deaf based on the assumptions of the hearing community about what is best for them. Other examples of cultural abuse are given in Parts I-B and C of this Report.

13 Law Commission of Canada, *Minister's Reference on Institutional Child Abuse [:] Interim Report* (Ottawa: Law Commission of Canada, 16 February 1998). Available in hard copy from the Law Commission of Canada and online: <http://www.lcc.gc.ca>.

[14] R. Bessner, *Institutional Child Abuse in Canada* (Ottawa: Law Commission of Canada, October 1998). Available in hard copy from the Law Commission of Canada and online: <http://www.lcc.gc.ca>.

[15] R. Claes & D. Clifton (SAGE), *Needs and Expectations for Redress of Victims of Abuse at Residential Schools* (Ottawa: Law Commission of Canada, October 1998). Available in hard copy from the Law Commission of Canada and online: <http://www.lcc.gc.ca>.

[16] Institute for Human Resource Development, *Review of the Needs of Victims of Institutional Child Abuse* (Ottawa: Law Commission of Canada October 1998). Available in hard copy from the Law Commission of Canada and online: <http://www.lcc.gc.ca>.

[17] M. Gannage, *A Review And Analysis Of Approaches To Addressing Past Institutional Or Systemic Abuse In Selected Countries* (Ottawa: Law Commission of Canada October 1998). Available in hard copy from the Law Commission of Canada and online: <http://www.lcc.gc.ca>.

[18] Aboriginal Healing Foundation; Aboriginal Nurses Association of Canada; Assembly of First Nations; Canadian Aboriginal AIDS Networks; Congress of Aboriginal Peoples; Indigenous Bar Association; Inuit Tapirisat of Canada; Métis National Council; National Association of Cultural Education Centres; National Association of Friendship Centres; National Indian and Inuit Community Health Resources Organization; Native Women's Association of Canada; Pauktuutit; Survivor Tasiuqtit; Tunngasuvivingat Inuit; Wunska (a network of First Nations social work and social science educators in Canada).

[19] Each panel had approximately 14 members (there were some withdrawals and additions in the course of the work). Three Aboriginal members agreed to sit on both panels. Members of these study panels deserve special recognition for their contributions to the Commission's work. While the Commission alone is responsible for the positions taken in this document, members of the study panels provided invaluable guidance. Each of them contributed well beyond attending three weekend meetings. They all gave freely of their time, responding to the requests of Commission researchers and staff, providing links to their home or professional communities, passing on written materials, reviewing drafts and spreading the word about this work. The Commission wishes to publicly acknowledge the tremendous efforts and enormous value of the entirely volunteer group of people, whose only interest was to ensure that the work of the Commission have the greatest possible impact in improving the way our society addresses this issue.

20 B.K. Jacobs, "Rekindled Spirit" (23 December 1998) [unpublished research report archived at the Law Commission of Canada]; D. Corbière & D. Nahwegahbow, "The Mitchikanibikok Inik Experiences" (4 January 1999) [unpublished research report archived at the Law Commission of Canada]; L. Duffy, "Report on the Violation of Ojibwe Laws: The Residential School Experience of Members of The Wabigoon Lake First Nations" (9 February, 1999) [unpublished research report archived at the Law Commission of Canada]; C. Hansen & T. Lee, "The Impact of Residential Schools and Other Institutions on the Métis People of Saskatchewan: Cultural Genocide, Systemic Abuse and Child Abuse" (March 1999) [unpublished research report archived at the Law Commission of Canada].

21 Law Commission of Canada, *Minister's Reference on Institutional Child Abuse [:] Discussion Paper* (Ottawa: Law Commission of Canada, December 1998). Available in hard copy from the Law Commission of Canada and online: <http://www.lcc.gc.ca>.

B.   What Children Experienced

1.   Why Children are in Institutions

Children do not decide to live in institutions. It is, rather, their parents, legal guardians, the courts and others with legal control over them who are responsible for sending children to residential institutions. The reasons may range from the desire to provide special facilities for education (as in the case of children with disabilities), to a government policy of assimilation (as in the case of Aboriginal children), to detention for often minor offences or behavioural problems, to name a few. Earlier in this century, parents of limited means sometimes chose to place children in boarding schools run by religious orders in order to give their children access to what they believed would be a better material quality of life or a superior education.

The Commission has not been asked to judge the legislative policies that resulted in large numbers of children being placed in institutions. Nor has it been asked to review the reasons for doing so offered by courts, social welfare agencies and, in some cases, parents. It is, however, impossible to address the effects of institutional child abuse without taking note of the general attitudes, beliefs and values that condemned so many children to live in places where so much harm was done to them. Issues of race, class, ability and gender were never far from the surface in decisions about which children would wind up in institutions.

Of course, these decisions must be considered within the particular contexts in which they were taken. While some of the motives and objectives being pursued stand the test of time, not all do. Debate continues about now abandoned practices and policies. Some Canadians view them as simply a reflection of the values and standards of the era in which they were in force. Others see the harsh discipline often practiced, even in facilities for young offenders, as excessive by any standards.

No matter how one characterises the various motives for placing children in institutions, the stark fact remains: these children went through a major, involuntary change in their lives, and many suffered terribly in the very places that were intended to educate and protect them.

2.   Life in a Total Institution

To fully understand the impact of past institutional child abuse, it is crucial to investigate the nature of life in those settings at the time the abuse took place. Although children lived in a wide variety of institutions, designed for different purposes, serving different communities, and located in different regions of the country, all can be described as *total institutions*. This term refers to institutions that seek to re-socialise people by instilling them with new roles, skills or values. Such institutions break down the barriers that ordinarily separate three spheres of life: work, play and sleep. Once a child enters, willingly or not, almost every aspect of his or her life is determined and controlled by the institution.

> First, all aspects of life are conducted in the same place and under the same single authority. Second, each phase of the member's daily activity is carried on in the immediate company of a large batch of others, all of whom are treated alike and required to do the same thing together. Third, all phases of the day's activities are tightly scheduled, with one activity leading at a prearranged time into the next, the whole sequence of activities being imposed from above by a system of explicit formal rulings and a body of officials. Finally, the various enforced activities are brought together into a single rational plan purportedly designed to fulfil the official aims of the institution.[1]

Total institutions are not simply places to live; each is a world unto itself. In this world, those who are in charge hold all formal power. Rules govern almost every aspect of daily life and residents have little say about how these rules are administered. More dangerously, life in such institutions may at times be governed more by arbitrary and unpredictable orders than by established rules. In such a situation, the possibility of effective protests or appeals is inhibited. During the period in which the abuse under consideration took place,[2] there was little effective external oversight and usually no independent procedure for handling complaints from children. Contact with the outside world – family, friends, community – was tightly controlled and infrequent.

Residential schools for Aboriginal children, reformatories, schools for the Deaf and blind, orphanages, training schools and mental institutions tended, as total institutions, to impose the following conditions on their residents: disconnection; degradation; and powerlessness. While all children in all institutions did not necessarily experience them, each condition played a part in facilitating and perpetuating the infliction of abuse.

a.   Disconnection

Disconnection means experiencing a sense of both physical and psychological isolation. Aboriginal children, for example, were often taken to residential schools far removed from their home communities. Many did not see their families during the entire school year; they returned home only in the summer. The Royal Commission on Aboriginal Peoples summarised the effects of disconnection on the family life and culture of Aboriginal peoples in the following manner:

> Residential schools did the greatest damage. Children as young as 6 years old were removed from their families for 10 months of the year or longer. They were forbidden to speak the only languages they knew and taught to reject their homes, their heritage and, by extension, themselves. Most were subjected to physical deprivation, and some experienced abuse. We heard from a few people who are grateful for what they learned at these schools, but we heard from more who described deep scars – not least in their inability to give and receive love.[3]

The Royal Commission went on to note that many of the problems encountered in Aboriginal communities today – violence, alcoholism and loss of pride and spirituality – can be traced back to the sense of disconnection that children experienced as a result of being sent to a residential school.

Psychological isolation is equally alienating. When mail is censored, outside visits are strictly controlled and telephones are non-existent or are located only in public areas, children have no ability to convey their concerns in a meaningful way. They have no one in whom they can confide without fear of reprisal.

Life in a total institution is a world cut off from family and community – a world where there is virtually no one to question the actions of staff or to challenge the way is which authority is misused and abused. Here is how one former student described the institution he attended:

> ... I learned that there is a prison that occupies no physical space. This prison is a form of solitary confinement that when expertly inflicted upon you, can hold you in check for decades. For lack of a better name for this prison I will call it FEAR.[4]

The experience of disconnection can be particularly acute for children with disabilities. They are more likely to be placed in an institution and, because their needs are greater, they are more likely to rely on adults for care and attention. This reliance makes them especially vulnerable. They may not resist abuse or expose an abuser because they do not want to jeopardise the care they are receiving. This was the case for a student attending a school for the Deaf:

> Hall [the student's teacher] was driving her home and he indicated that he wanted to stop at his home as he had forgotten something. He invited P.N. into his home and took her to the lower bedroom where he removed her clothing and after removing his clothing, pushed her on the bed and had sexual intercourse with her. She claims that she did not consent to having intercourse with the accused. She did not wish to have intercourse with him and claims that the accused was controlling her and she had to respect him because he was a man, a teacher and as a hearing person, had the power. She had sexual relations with the accused at his house as she was afraid of him. She went into his house because he asked her to go in and she felt that she had to do what Hall said. She always listened to her teachers and did what she was told. She indicated that Hall was a teacher and she had to do what he said.[5]

Children with intellectual disabilities may have difficulty interpreting the difference between appropriate and inappropriate behaviour. They may be easily tricked, bribed, scolded or coerced by an abuser. Children with communication disabilities may experience additional barriers to disclosing incidents of abuse. These factors increase the disconnection of children with disabilities and heighten their position of vulnerability. They then become even more accessible targets for abusers.

b.   Degradation

Degradation is another characteristic feature of life in a total institution. It can occur in both subtle and obvious ways. Gross physical punishment and beatings are only one form of degradation. Humiliation, discrimination, the constant message that "you're no good and will never amount to anything" – all contribute to what is commonly referred to as "low self-esteem". This term is used to describe the harsh reality of months or years of being emotionally beaten down and having one's self-confidence and pride continually undermined, with little or no opportunity for nurturing, support or encouragement. Consider this example from the Mount Cashel inquiry:

> [One boy] frequently wet his dormitory bedsheet. On each such occasion the moistened portion of the sheet was cut away by a Brother. When, one night, nothing remained of the bedsheet, save its hem, the resident was ordered out of his cot by a Brother and required to remove his underpants, the only article of clothing he was then wearing. He was given a canvas suitcase containing his few worldly goods and marched, while wearing nothing and bearing his suitcase, through his dormitory and all the others. He was required to shake hands with and say goodbye to all of the 90 or so residents then at Mount Cashel; having been told by the Brother escorting him that he would not be seeing his Orphanage chums again because his bedwetting required him to be exiled from Mount Cashel. Having bid his farewells he was led out onto the Orphanage grounds, then out through its gates, while some of his friends watched from the dormitory windows. It was a cool autumn night, about 10:30 p.m. The gates were secured and the doors of the Orphanage closed. He stood, naked, holding his suitcase on a public road in St. John's. Within half an hour he was repatriated by the Brother with his Orphanage comrades and furnished a fresh blanket under threat of future punishment if he wet his bed again.[6]

The scars of such treatment may not be visible, but the damage is as real as in the cases of physical and sexual abuse.

c.   Powerlessness

Powerlessness, some might say, is a natural condition of childhood. There is a critical difference, however, between respect for, or obedience to adult authority, and lack of control over the fundamental aspects of one's life. There is a critical difference between accepting the directions of another in a context of parental love and affection and being roughly and coldly ordered around. Children can learn and understand that there are rules of behaviour that must be followed within a home, a school or an institution. Most children can accept that misbehaviour will lead to punishment or other consequences.

Power in an institution, however, is not reflected in the equitable enforcement of fair and explicit rules. It is reflected in the infliction of suffering on arbitrary grounds, the meting out of punishment disproportionate to the misconduct, or the imposition of rigid and overly harsh rules that make compliance a hardship and punishment a virtual certainty. For example:

> At the Hearing the applicant testified that on his first night at the Training Schools, he was in the bathroom and admitted that he and another student were fooling around squirting tooth paste. A [Christian] Brother came from behind and punched him on the side of the head, striking his head on the wall. He was made to stand in front of the clock with his hands behind his back. He was very scared and [had] tears in his eyes. The Brother struck him with a closed fist on his shoulder, he fell on one knee and he was punched. Later on the Brother came and took him to another Brother's where he was sexually assaulted and buggered by both Brothers. Thereafter this would occur on a regular basis two or three times a week, sometimes he was subjected to sexual assault by a single Brother, but most of the time it was with the two Brothers. At times, instruments would be inserted in his rectum.[7]

A psychologist's report produced for the court summarised the abuse of an eleven-year-old male resident of a Protestant orphanage as follows:

> He stated the abuse consisted of frequent beatings with a stick, hair pulled, thrown in the 'hole' for extended periods of time and on one occasion a female staff attempted to drown him in the bathtub.[8]

These examples of punishment go so far beyond any reasonable bounds of how one would expect a caregiver to discipline a child that they cannot in any way be explained or excused.

The fear of arbitrary or excessive punishment generally relates to physical abuse. Added to this may also be the fear of a form of abuse that has nothing to do with rules and discipline, but everything to do with the arbitrary exercise of power: sexual abuse. It is an intensely private form of abuse, and a singularly potent expression of power and domination that totally undermines a person's autonomy.

Once that sense of the unchecked power of those in authority is firmly established, an atmosphere of insecurity and fear pervades an institution. Children do not have to experience arbitrary or excessive punishment to want to avoid it – they just have to witness enough of it to understand that they could be next.

3.   Types of Total Institutions for Children

The Commission has grouped the various total institutions that housed children into four broad categories: special needs schools; child welfare facilities; youth detention facilities; and residential schools for Aboriginal children. Each had a slightly different purpose, a slightly different character, and a slightly different record of abuse. All, however, were places where children suffered and were harmed.

Special needs institutions were established for children with special physical or developmental needs. These children can be even more vulnerable to abuse than other children. Isolation and powerlessness are more marked in their case, because the disability itself may cause or contribute to those conditions. Thus the very characteristic that makes institutionalisation more necessary for children with disabilities also makes them easier targets for abuse once they are there.

Deaf children are a case in point. In the past, a language barrier compounded the physical separation of Deaf children from their families. Many parents were not familiar with American Sign Language or the Langue des signes québécoise. As a result, even in the two months of the year when the children were at home, they could not properly communicate instances of abuse to their parents. Deaf children lost even

I am 11 years old ... I have been at Mount Cashel Orphanage for about five years. I am happy at the orphanage except for Brother Burke, Brother Ralph and Brother English. I don't like Brother Burke because he beats me for every little thing he beats me across my bare backside with a stick about three days ago Brother Burke took me into a closet and made me pull down my pants he hit me five or six times across my back side with a stick. He beat me because I threw a after shave tin into the garbage can it made a noise and Brother Burke was watching T.V. both Brother Ralph and Brother English on seven or eight times have caught a hold of me and have felt my legs and felt my bird. Sometimes this has happened when I have been in bed. Brother Ralph would sit down on the bed and feel my bird inside my pyjama pants. Most times Brother English would feel my bird when I was in the dining Hall he would do it sometimes when I was in bed.

Statement of Gregory Connors, Hughes Inquiry Appendix C Vol. 2: at p.31

... Comprehensive regulations on the acceptable means and limits to punishments were never issued, despite requests by more junior departmental employees, and thus principals and staff behaved largely as they saw fit. Children were frequently beaten severely with whips, rods and fists, chained and shackled, bound hands and foot and locked in closets, basements and bathrooms, and had their heads shaved or closely cropped.

Report of the Royal Commission on Aboriginal Peoples at p.369 this safe family haven to turn to for protection. For many, this has caused serious, perhaps irreparable damage to their relationships with their parents. The parents, in turn, suffer tremendous guilt for not having been aware of the abuse endured in schools to which they returned their children year after year.

Children placed in child welfare facilities were deemed to be "in need of protection" as defined in provincial child welfare legislation. This is an example of the State (through its child welfare agencies) using its statutory authority to step into the role of the child's parents. Such action may be taken, for example, because the parents are deceased, ill or imprisoned, or because the child has been abused, seriously neglected or abandoned. In all of this, of course, the child is an innocent victim.

Unfortunately, the very reasons such children were placed in these facilities also made them more vulnerable to abuse within those settings. When selecting child victims, in virtually every setting perpetrators choose those who have been afforded the least protection in the form of caring adults. By definition, these children lacked a family that could be counted on to look after their interests or even inquire about their welfare. Thus they were obvious targets for physically abusive or sexually predatory staff.

Children in youth detention facilities carried, in addition to the vulnerabilities of other children, the stigma of a conviction. Already earmarked by society as meriting punishment, they were viewed as obvious targets for degradation and rough treatment, which, in certain cases, spilled over into physical, emotional and sexual abuse. Their problems were exacerbated by the fact that their credibility as complainants may have been tarnished by their association with those types of institutions.

What is particularly disturbing about youth detention facilities is that many children who were incarcerated in them should never have been incarcerated at all. Minor offences such as truancy were sufficient to land a child in one of these facilities. Girls were often placed there for behaviour that was considered difficult or socially unacceptable. In other words, many children were made to feel like criminals, and were treated like criminals, for behaviour that should not have been judged so harshly.

Residential schools for Aboriginal children were established by the Canadian government, and run by churches and governments, to provide for the education of Aboriginal children. This education was to be based on the language, religion and culture of those who ran the schools, not those of the children. Children – sometimes as young as six years of age – were removed from their parents and communities. Once in the schools, siblings were often not permitted to speak with one another. Children were normally only permitted to speak English or French and were made to practice Christianity to the exclusion of their own spiritual customs and beliefs.[9]

Therefore, Aboriginal children in residential schools suffered a special and especially damaging form of abuse. They were deprived of their language, their culture, their families and their communities. In short, they were deprived of any emotional and support resources that could have assisted them in resisting physical and sexual abuse. It cannot be emphasised too strongly that, for all the elements of similarity with abuse in other types of institutions, Aboriginal children suffered in a unique way in residential schools. For this reason, the experience in residential schools will be treated more fully in a separate section of this Report.

a. Goals of total institutions

In many instances, total institutions were designed to control a race or a class of people. Indeed, institutions of this type could only effectively fulfil their designated role by being total institutions. Residential schools for Aboriginal children were an example. From the religious and vocational training they received to the rules forbidding the use of their language and cultural practices, Aboriginal children experienced residential schools as an effort to assimilate them into European culture. Mary Carpenter, an Inuit writer, described how the school system attempted to control the Inuit people:

> After a lifetime of beatings, going hungry, standing in a corner on one leg, and walking in the snow with no shoes for speaking Inuvialuktun, and having a stinging paste rubbed on my face, which they did to stop us from expressing our Eskimo custom of raising our eyebrows for 'yes'

and wrinkling our noses for 'no', I soon lost the ability to speak my mother tongue. When a language dies, the world dies, the world it was generated from breaks down too.[10]

The following is a recollection of the childhood school experiences of a member of the Dene Nation:

> We were given a number and were called by that number. Our heads were shaved bald and we were all dressed the same. Our daily schedule included rounds of prayer and French Canadian songs. Our mail was read and censored. We were strapped for speaking our own languages and humiliated for any natural act. To a person who actually went through the residential school experience itself, any study on the subject hardly serves to convey the reality to the reader. It was a process we were put through, like animals to the slaughter, only the process was slower, a daily agony. I am one of the survivors of that colonialist experience, still recovering in a different age. I can still remember the day in September of 1959, being taken from our fish camp along with my little sister, to be led off, hundreds of miles away to school. My grandma standing on the shore, getting smaller.[11]

In the 1950s, up to 170 children of Sons of Freedom Doukhobors were removed from their homes by police and placed in the New Denver residential school. According to the Government of British Columbia, the rationale was that the students were truants. The underlying motive, however, had more to do with influencing the political and religious beliefs of their parents. According to the British Columbia Ombudsman's report on the New Denver incident:

> These children were victims of a situation not of their making nor within their control. They were caught in a web of conflicting values and political turmoil involving their parents, religious leaders, police and government.[12]

The basic intent of these actions by the B.C. government was not lost on the Doukhobor leadership:

> They want to wipe us out – faith, religion and all. Education was chosen as the issue because it's the easiest way to do it.[13]

A total institution for children was simply an effective method of controlling and influencing a large group of people.

Total institutions are also frequently oriented towards minority populations and the socio-economically disadvantaged. Residents of youth correctional facilities today are disproportionately drawn from these groups or other marginalised populations, as were residents of reformatories, training schools and orphanages in the past. A report by the Canadian Welfare Council in 1967 concluded that "statistical data on the number of people of Indian ancestry in correctional institutions is shocking...."[14] A study from the mid-1980s made the following comparison between the residential school system and correctional facilities:

> Placed in an historical context, the prison has become for many young native people the contemporary equivalent of what the Indian residential school represented for their parents.[15]

Aboriginal men, women and children continue to be over-represented in correctional facilities in the 1990s.[16]

Because socio-economically disadvantaged children are more likely to reside in a total institution than middle- and upper-class children, abuse in institutions tends to fall disproportionately on them. Many adults have recounted how their childhood vulnerability was used by their abusers to manipulate and coerce them into compliance. An example from Mount Cashel shows how an abuser can prey upon a child's marginalised status:

> J.L. testified that some weeks before the first incident of sexual abuse by Kenny, the latter read the boy's family file to him. It referred to how the boy had been put in the orphanage because none of his relatives wanted him. J.L. stated that at one point in time Kenny told him he was a piece of garbage and that nobody wanted him. The boy said that at that point he felt exactly like a piece of garbage. The incidents started not long after that.[17]

b. Resistance

Although power in total institutions was overwhelmingly in the hands of those in authority, children, on occasion, courageously resisted the exercise of that power. There are many examples of how children and parents struggled against the power of those who were in control.

Some children directly confronted authorities. By disobeying rules, ridiculing those in charge and fighting back against those who physically and sexually abused them, even when they knew that this type of resistance would expose them to more discipline, they asserted their will to retain some control over their lives.

Many children also engaged in formal protests. Doukhobor children held nude demonstrations and hunger strikes and refused to take their seats in schools. Aboriginal children continued to partake in their cultural practices, even in the face of strict rules forbidding such activities and stern punishment for being caught. Parents of Aboriginal students, who often encouraged acts of resistance on the part of their children, petitioned school administrators to improve the quality of their children's education, formally appealed to the federal government for effective oversight of the schools[18], and, as early as 1914, sued residential schools for the mistreatment of their children.[19]

Some Aboriginal students resorted to the most extreme and desperate form of resistance: suicide. A woman who attended a residential school in the 1950s recalls the depth of emotion that school life brought on:

> I started to think, 'Well, twelve years here. I don't want to be here for twelve years.' By the time I was in grade five, they used to let us go for walks…. I decided … to go down to the Thompson River … [It] was really high; it was spring time, I guess and you could see that the water was deep and I don't know how many times … I used to think of drowning myself. I would be standing there and I would think 'Gee, life can't continue like this.'[20]

By far the most common method of resistance by Aboriginal students was running away. Truancy was a chronic problem for school administrators. Unsanitary conditions, strict discipline, missing their families and communities, and physical, sexual and psychological abuse were among the reasons why children ran away from residential schools. It is remarkable that the truancy persisted, given the severe punishment for being caught.

> At Birtle school two boys were beaten by the Principal leaving "marks all over the boys bodies, back, front genitals etcetera." … [the] … regional inspector of schools for Manitoba, conceded only that such punishment had "overstepped the mark a little" but as the boys had been caught trying to run away "he had to make an example of them."[21]

The most tragic consequence of truancy was that there were students who died while running away.

> On the 10th of February, 1902, just as it was getting dark, Johnny Sticks viewed the body of his eight-year-old son, Duncan, dead from exposure having fled from the William's Lake Industrial School. He lay, Mr. Sticks recalled for the coroner, "75 yards off the road in the snow – he was quite dead but not frozen." Duncan's blood-stained hat was laying about one yard away, and "he had marks of blood on his nose and forehead – the left side of his face had been partially eaten by some animal." Sticks took his son home in a sleigh regretting all the while that the school had not notified him immediately that his son had run off for "I should have gone at once and looked for him – he ran away from the Mission about one o'clock on Saturday and must have been dead for nearly two days when found."[22]

Deaths from exposure, drowning, and other accidents suffered by children while running away from residential schools continued into the 1970s.[23]

These acts of courage and desperation demonstrate the will of Aboriginal children to resist what they perceived to be the injustice of their lives in a total institution. In their own way, they are testaments to their strength of character and inventiveness in the face of degradation and dehumanisation. In some instances, the efforts of students and parents had tangible results. Abuse was exposed, policies were changed and individuals were held accountable.[24]

Individual acts of resistance were not, of course, sufficient to change the overall organisation and structure of these institutions. They did, however, have a lasting impact on the children who resisted. Many of the Aboriginal leaders who struggled to end the residential school system were former students in that system.

All of the residential schools for Aboriginal children are now closed. Many of the policies that led to other children being inappropriately placed in institutions have been reversed. In addition, many of the objectionable features of those types of institutions in which children still reside have been altered. There is a much higher level of public oversight, accountability and community involvement in these institutions. Family, volunteers and social service agencies have much greater access to children who live in institutions of all kinds. Nevertheless, there continues to be a risk that the characteristics of total institutions – disconnection, degradation, and powerlessness – have not been expunged from residential institutions for children. It is, therefore, necessary to remain vigilant in order to prevent their emergence. All children who are placed in institutions deserve to have a safe and secure environment in which to grow.

4.   Types of Abuse Suffered

a.   Physical abuse

Determining the point at which physical punishment crosses the line from discipline to abuse is not easy. Reasonable people differ as to whether physical punishment is a necessary disciplinary tool and, if so, what the appropriate amount is, and how it should be administered. Whatever divergent views people may have on the subject of physical discipline, however, one thing should be clear. If physical punishment in an institutional setting is to be tolerated at all, it must be a regulated, moderate, measured form of response, used only to discipline serious behaviour that is in clear breach of an established code of conduct. In theory, this approach to physical punishment has long been official policy. For example, the 1957 regulations on corporal punishment issued by the Director of Training Schools in Ontario explicitly provided:

1.   Corporal punishment may only be awarded (or authorised) by the Superintendent, or in his absence, by a responsible official in charge of the school.

2.   Where corporal punishment is authorised, it shall be applied on the palms of the hands only – it must not be administered by the person laying the complaint.

3.   It must be witnessed by a member of staff.

4.   The strap used is to be of the same dimensions and material as is used in Public Schools – no handle is to be added.

5.   Corporal punishment must not be administered in the presence of other pupils.

After release? Violent and abusive at home with my family; blame my mother for putting me there. I've never been able to hold a job; on welfare now; stay away from people; don't want to hurt them; never had a girlfriend; no one wants to be around me – 1 watch TV; less than a grade 9 education; in counselling now; tried to kill myself three years ago; the only reason I don't blow my brains out now is because of my mother – she has suffered a lot through this.

St. John's student, 1974, Hoffman, The search for healing..., at p.189

Boy's first involvement with Father Bromley was during a period of counselling and/or confession. At Father Bromley's request, the boy was encouraged to expose his person and show the scars that were present from various operations he had to attempt to alleviate his handicap. Bromley encouraged the boy to undress, masturbate, and touch himself in front of the priest. This ultimately led to masturbation by Bromley on the boy as well as oral sex being performed by him.

R. v. Bromley, Supreme Court of Newfoundland, 1998

6. Punishment must be recorded in a Punishment Book, and signed by the person who awards the punishment and by the witness. The record must show the number of slaps on each palm and the reason for the punishment.

7. It must be recorded on the Daily Log with details as to the reason, number of slaps administered, and witness.

8. Corporal punishment must not be administered if it is known that the pupil is mentally abnormal, or has at any time been a patient in a mental hospital....

   a. In each Training School under the supervision of this department, cases will occur in which certain pupils display extreme rebellion, violence, disobedience and insolence to supervisory staff.

   b. When such a situation arises it sometimes happens that Staff concerned may respond in kind and there have been instances in which they have resorted to slapping, punching, kicking, "giving the knee", roughing, shaking, shoving against the wall, "interviews" in an adjacent room, *etc.*

   c. It is emphasised that punishments as listed in (b) above are unauthorised: That if they occur, the staff member concerned is to be taken off duty pending official enquiry, the findings of which would determine the advisability of more drastic action being taken. Such cases are to be reported by telephone to the department.

   d. It is understandable that a staff member may have to defend himself against assaultive conduct on the part of the pupil and in such a case he will take such restraint measures as are necessary.[25]

These detailed guidelines regulating when and how to administer discipline are a clear indication that authorities recognised the need to set limits on physical punishment; discipline was not to be administered randomly or in an overly zealous manner. In other words, past actions are not being judged as abusive by only today's standard of conduct. They can also be judged as inappropriate by the standards that were in place at the time. Unfortunately, as widespread incidents of abuse attest, it is not enough to simply develop policies or publish guidelines; they must be put into practice. Failure to do so sends a message to the perpetrators that excessive and arbitrary use of force is acceptable or at least tolerated. It enables abusive behaviour to continue unchecked and unpunished. It also sends a message to children that they have no reliable authority to appeal to for protection.

The need for effective enforcement is demonstrated when the Ontario training school regulations cited above are contrasted with the abuse that some children experienced, both at these training schools and at other institutions. As a punishment for trying to run away, an adult remembered experiencing the following discipline:

> He [a Christian Brother] stripped my clothes off, made me lie across his bunk. He took a leather strap – maybe a foot long or a little more – one side was flat, the other side had lumps on it.... To me, being young, I thought he was really big. I looked around once and saw him reach the ceiling with the strap. God I thought he was big. I cried, yelled, screamed – the pain. I think he used both sides of the belt. On the one dresser there was a salt shaker, he would stand there, you could feel him staring – I begged him not to use the salt – I knew I was bleeding because I reached around and felt the blood, but he just kept pouring the salt on me. The pain – God the pain.[26]

The failure to enforce regulations can lead to a culture of abuse in which physical assault becomes a normal way of disciplining a child:

> Slapping, kicking, striking, was considered everyday normal. It was when they punched someone in the face, or used weapons – that was when it was unusual, even for the day. The primary weapon was the sawed off goalie stick. Some kids were stripped down. I got it three times. It would knock you right over. I was balling [sic] my eyes out and he still made me get up and he hit me – I remember it vividly.[27]

In a residential setting, such brutality, even if engaged in by only a small minority of staff members, can set a tone of fear and repression throughout an institution. This is particularly the case when their activities go unchecked by those who are responsible for managing the institution. An institution run by force and by fear is not a well-run institution. Far from teaching children to respect authority, it teaches them to distrust it.

b.   Sexual abuse

Sexual abuse of children is a topic that was not openly acknowledged or discussed until relatively recently. Now society is much more aware of the prevalence of child sexual abuse. Personal disclosures, public inquiries, criminal prosecutions and civil actions have revealed that sexual abuse of children can take place virtually anywhere – in homes, day schools, sports and recreation programs, summer camps and, as we now know, in residential institutions.

Both girls and boys are targets of sexual abuse. The abuse ranges from sexual touching to penetration and intercourse. While some children were subjected to violent rapes, others had sexual favours cajoled out of them in return for treats, privileges, or for the promise of withholding physical abuse. Some experienced the perversion of what begins as an affectionate and trusting relationship with a person in authority, to one where sex is eventually introduced and demanded.

The following synopsis describes how one school counsellor abused his position of authority and trust. G.R. was fourteen years of age when she first came to the Nova Scotia School for Girls. Her mother had died when she was ten. She had come from a home where her father and his common-law wife had a tumultuous relationship, including considerable drinking and fighting. As a result, she spent time on the streets before she was apprehended. While she was in the School she had no visitors, received no mail from her family or otherwise. She was lonely, naïve and vulnerable and therefore easy prey for Hollett, a male counsellor working at the School.

> Hollett initially presented himself to the plaintiff [G.R.] as an understanding fatherly figure. He shared with the plaintiff feelings about losing his own mother. Using his position as counsellor and the plaintiff's vulnerability, he began his seduction.[28]

The counsellor went on to demand sexual relations with the girl.

Sexual abuse is a secret and intensely private form of abuse. It increases the power of the abuser because, for the most part, there are no witnesses. The stigma attached to sexual abuse and the moral authority of the adults who run residential institutions mean that a child who complains is subject to disbelief and to punishment for making the complaint. Such reactions illustrate the absence of control that children or youths in total institutions have over their lives. The autonomy of the child is doubly undermined by sexual abuse – first, by the infliction of the abuse itself, and second, because the fact of its occurrence is questioned by those in authority.

Understanding the relationship between power and abuse is particularly relevant in the case of abuse involving girls.[29] Violence against women and children is often rooted in an unequal distribution of power between males and females. It is one method of control and can be used to maintain the female's subordinate position. Children, particularly girls, are often socialised not to question the authority of adult males. This makes them vulnerable to unwanted and inappropriate sexual advances. The following example illustrates how one adolescent girl reacted to a male abuser:

> [He] would pat her behind or grab her elsewhere and would make suggestive comments. She was so certain that he respected her that she did not know how to respond.... She tried to ignore the actions or pass them off because the Club was important to her.... [W]hen she was fourteen, he invited her and her girlfriend to his residence. He took her to his bedroom and showed her pictures in men's magazines. He pulled down her clothing, tried to stimulate her vagina orally and put his hands all over her body, including on her vagina. He then penetrated her and had intercourse without her consent. She had been a virgin. She did not assist and did not resist. She was scared and confused. He had been a mentor to her and had seemed almost god-like and because of that she had thought that it must be okay.[30]

While abuse may occasionally be committed by a female, sexual abuse perpetrated against young girls by men is largely about the use of physical force, intimidation, and emotional and spiritual degradation by men to bring girls under their control and domination.

Boys are also most likely to be sexually abused by men. As a result, some boys have expressed a reluctance to report abuse because they fear they will be stigmatised or their sexual identity will be called into question. For example, the following passage recounts how abuse threatened the self-image of one young boy:

He said he felt fear and helplessness during the assault, afterwards he felt ashamed and bad. He thought he had done something wrong. He became concerned about his masculinity and wondered if he might have attracted homosexual attention. He did not go back to the Club after the first time and kept to himself. He even kept himself apart from his family and friends to some extent. He told no one for some 10 years....[31]

Because the effects of childhood sexual assault often carry forward into adulthood, many survivors of childhood abuse report difficulties in developing caring and nurturing relationships with others.

c.   Other types of abuse

Physical and sexual abuse are at the centre of the Minister's Reference because these are the categories of abuse which are unquestionably a basis for legal liability, whether civil or criminal. Other types of abuse described by survivors – emotional, psychological, spiritual, racial, cultural – are less clearly compensable in legal proceedings, particularly if they are not tied to instances of either physical or sexual abuse.

Nonetheless, in order to understand the real impact of the experience of some children and to assess the adequacy of redress options, it is necessary to view the institutional experience as the children viewed it. They lived their experiences as a whole, undifferentiated by the categories imposed by the law. Children who have been beaten and know they are vulnerable to further beatings for any infraction at any time live in fear every day, not just at the precise moments when the beatings are taking place. Children who have been sexually assaulted by someone who has authority over them, and who cannot turn to anyone to protect them from further assaults, must live with the horror of being under the power of their abuser every minute of every day.

Similarly, some children lived in an atmosphere where they were frequently demeaned and psychologically degraded, and where their upbringing, spiritual practices and culture were scorned and repressed. Some children were exposed to these conditions for years on end. The effects of such suffering can be as enduring as those of physical and sexual abuse. Minds and spirits can be damaged as deeply as bodies, and in a wide variety of ways.

The case of J.H., who spent three years at the Woodlands Institution for the Mentally Handicapped in British Columbia, is an example of the psychological strain that can be placed on children in institutions:

> Soon after the plaintiff had settled into Woodlands it became apparent that he had a normal range of intelligence and he was seen to be amongst the brightest at the school, despite his behavioural problems persisting largely unabated. As time progressed, it was accepted by the staff who knew him that he had been misplaced and did not belong in an institution for the mentally retarded.[32]

> There cannot have been very much more devastating to a troubled boy of fourteen who had no home – no one in the world to turn to – than to be placed on a ward at Woodlands where, despite having been told that his time in the institution would be temporary, it soon became very evident to him he would remain there, to be subjected to what he referred to as the "horrors" of his confinement, indefinitely.[33]

> Punishment for misbehaviour meant a loss of privileges. At Woodlands everything was a privilege including regular food, wearing something other than pajamas, and any measure of freedom. Offenders were locked up, sometimes for days, in an empty room with nothing but a sheet on the floor and fed purée (baby) food, or they were made to sit on a hard chair for long periods of time in a common room on the ward. Heavy doses of subduing medication were frequently used…. It hardly need be said that he hated the institution and wanted only to get out of it the whole time he was there.[34]

The pain of being separated from family and familiar surroundings was often very difficult on some Aboriginal children. An Aboriginal woman recalls her childhood residential school experience as follows:

> I knew I couldn't stay home. I knew that. But the times that really, really gets to the bottom of my soul: the first day back [after being home for the summer holidays]…. You're feeling pretty lonesome, suddenly go to bed and in the morning, you wake up and you see this white ceiling. You may as well have a knife and stab me through the heart…. You know where you are and you got to survive and you just cover it over, seal it up for ten months.[35]

This pain of separation was not restricted to Aboriginal children. Deaf children, blind children, and children in reformatories, orphanages and other residential institutions experienced similar levels of psychological harm from living in an alien environment.

During the 1950s, Inuit children with tuberculosis who were taken to hospitals in the south for treatment were separated from their parents because no formal method was established to maintain contact with relatives. Some children were kept in the south without their parents' consent. These "lost" children were brought up in non-Inuit, southern families.[36] Identification tags and personal records were often lost, making it impossible to locate families in the event of a patient's death. Often, relatives were not informed of the deaths until years later and many Inuit were buried in the south without notice being given to, or consent obtained from, their relatives.[37] During the 1980s, the Government of the Northwest Territories established a program to trace tuberculosis patients who went missing following treatment during the period of 1940–1975. Relatives were informed of the cause of death and the burial site of their missing family members.[38]

In some institutions, emotional abuse flowed from a dissociation between what were held out to be the purposes of the institution and its actual practices. Some institutions treated their charges with a disdain bordering on neglect. They offered very little in the way of services or support for their residents. British Columbia's Arden Park Youth Ranch, for example, housed young offenders. The purpose of the ranch was to instruct boys in woodcraft, ecology, camping and other skills to broaden self-respect and self-esteem. The program actually offered at the ranch was substantially different:

> The boys spent their days engaged in physical labour. Some of the boys described cutting firewood at the time. Others recalled shovelling snow for no apparent reason and otherwise sitting around doing nothing. At times, the boys worked long days on Critchley's forestry contracts planting trees and seeding grass. Critchley told them they would be paid but generally they were not.
>
> After dinner there was little to do. The boys simply sat in their cabins which were very cold in the winter. There were virtually no sports, crafts

Many girls were incarcerated in training schools as a form of social control, rather than for criminal behavior. Studies of training school admissions from 1967 to 1969 show that 75% of females were incarcerated for truancy, unmanageability and sexual impropriety. Girls who came from low income, single parent, substance abusing homes were more likely to be incarcerated than boys coming from the same background. Incarceration for these girls was seen as a form of social control and protection from their own behavior.

Until Someone Listens by Laura Sky & Verne Sparks

Because I was deaf, I was treated as mentally retarded. I was put in the kitchen, then on the farm. They didn't think I was too mentally retarded to work their equipment. Afterwards I told a lawyer, who is now a judge, how I had been sexually abused and he wouldn't believe me.

The Vision to Reconcile: Process Report on the Helpline Reconciliation Model Agreement by Doug Roche and Ben Hoffman or skills. Some boys described playing cards, chess and other board games. One of the boys recalled swimming in the lake once in a while, one hunting trip with Critchley, and a single football game with social workers and sheriffs. For the first couple of years, the boys were not allowed visits or telephone calls. The only telephone was only a radio phone in Critchley's truck. Critchley censored their mail ... For at least the first two years, there was no formal schooling at Arden Park.[39]

5. The Effects of Child Sexual and Physical Abuse on Adult Survivors

There are a number of factors that may mitigate the effects of childhood abuse at the time it is experienced: having close attachments to family, the ability to disclose abuse in a safe and supportive environment and having access to services to respond to the abuse. Unfortunately, the very fact of an institution being a total institution works against the development of these mitigating factors.[40]

The experience of abuse does not end when the actual abuse stops; the effects of abuse in childhood can continue into adulthood. The recovery process for adult survivors of abuse is unique to each individual. For some, the effects of abuse may be less pronounced, while for others they may be more pervasive. The effects vary according to a number of circumstances, most of which have nothing to do with the victim. They include: the duration and frequency of the abuse, the type of abuse, the age of the victim when the abuse occurred, the relationship of the abuser to the victim and the response to the incident once it was reported or disclosed.

There are several common physical symptoms that both male and female survivors may experience as adults. They include sleep disturbances, nightmares, fear of public spaces, anxiety, and other fears.[41] Adults with a history of childhood abuse may also develop physical conditions such as heart disease, cancer, chronic bronchitis and emphysema. These conditions may be attributable to, or made worse by, the prior experience of abuse.[42] In addition to these physical conditions, survivors may experience feelings of shame, isolation and low self-esteem. These emotions may trigger blackouts and flashbacks as events in their adult lives cue memories of childhood abuse. Some adult survivors find it difficult to cope with the emotional and psychological conditions that result from childhood victimisation.[43]

The relationship between gender and the effects of childhood abuse during adulthood is complex. There is some evidence to suggest that childhood abuse affects male and female adult survivors differently. [Women may be more likely to internalise the effects of their abuse,[44] while men may be more likely to externalise it by venting their anger verbally and physically.]

While gender differences deserve further study, this key point should not be lost: [the effects of child abuse do not end when the abuse stops.] Abuse during childhood – whether it occurs in an institution or not – can have long-lasting detrimental effects on adult survivors. Not only can it prevent them from living productive lives and reaching their potential as adults, it is also sometimes associated with their engaging in violent behaviour, including sexual abuse, themselves.[45] Understanding the childhood experiences and current needs of adult survivors of institutional abuse is important not only to do justice to the survivors, but also to end the cycle of abuse.

---

[1] E. Goffman, *Asylums, Essays on the Social Situation of Mental Patients and Other Inmates* (Garden City, N.Y.: Anchor Books, 1961) at 6.

[2] Most of the allegations of abuse now emerging cover the period from roughly the 1930s to the 1970s, although there are allegations up to the early 1990s as well.

[3] Canada, Royal Commission on Aboriginal Peoples, *People to People, Nation to Nation: Highlights From the Report of the Royal Commission on Aboriginal Peoples* (Ottawa: Libraxus Inc., CD-ROM, 1997) at record 537.

[4] From a victim impact statement written by a former student of St. Joseph's Training School, Alfred, Ontario (name withheld).

[5] *R. v. Hall*, [1993] O.J. No. 3344 (Gen. Div.) at para. 48, online: QL.

[6] D.C. Day, Q.C., "Power and Vainglory: Lessons from Mistreatment of Children at Mount Cashel Orphanage and Other Institutional Settings in Newfoundland" (Civil Liability for Sexual Assault in an Institutional Setting, Canadian Institute Conference, Toronto, 30 September 1993) [unpublished].

7   B.C. Hoffman, *The Search for Healing, Reconciliation and the Promise of Prevention,
     The Recorder's Report Concerning Physical and Sexual Abuse at St. Joseph's and
     St. John's Training Schools for Boys*, a report prepared for the Reconciliation
     Process Implementation Committee, Ontario (Place of publication unknown:
     Concorde Inc., 30 September 1995) at 142 [hereinafter *Recorder's Report –
     St. Joseph's and St. John's Training Schools*].

8   *T.S. v. New Brunswick Protestant Orphans' Home*, [1998] N.B.J. No. 109 (Q.B.),
     online: QL.

9   For an inventory of sources where these features of residential schools are
     recounted, see Claes, R & D. Clifton (SAGE), *Needs and Expectations for Redness
     of Victims of Abuse at Residential Schools* (Ottawa: Law Commission of Canada,
     October 1998). Available in hard copy from the Law Commission of Canada and
     online: <http://www.lcc.gc.ca>.

10   M. Carpenter, "Recollections and Comments: No More Denials Please"
     (Inuktitut, 74:56-61, 1991, record 93741) as quoted at record 93741 in J.S. Milloy
     " 'Suffer the Little Children': A History of the Residential School System, 1830-
     1993", a research paper submitted to The Royal Commission on Aboriginal
     Peoples (Canada), *For Seven Generations, Pour sept générations* (Ottawa: Libraxus
     Inc., CD-ROM, 1997) at records 92370 to 122566.

11   A. Mountain & S. Quirk, "Dene Nation: An Analysis, A Report to the Royal
     Commission on Aboriginal Peoples, Part Two – Key Events in Dene Nation's
     History, Beginnings", *For Seven Generations, Pour sept générations, supra* note 10
     at record 103783.

12   British Columbia Ombudsman, *Public Report No. 38: Righting the Wrong – The
     Confinement of the Sons of Freedom Doukhobor Children* (Victoria: B.C.
     Ombudsman, 8 April 1999), online: <http://www.ombud.gov.bc.ca/publications/
     reports/righting_the_wrong/index> (date accessed: 16 November 1999). In that
     report the B.C. Ombudsman noted that Sons of Freedom Doukhobor
     children were singled out because of the religious and political views of their
     parents, which underlay their refusal to send their children to public schools.
     From 1953-1959, children were taken from their homes by the RCMP, on the
     orders of the British Columbia government, and placed in a residential school.
     The B.C. Ombudsman reviews the circumstances under which children were
     removed and the conditions in which they lived. The Ombudsman recom-
     mends that the B.C. government acknowledge its wrongdoing, provide a full
     explanation, an unconditional apology, and consult with complainants as to
     appropriate compensation.

[13] S. Katz, "The Lost Children of British Columbia" *Maclean's Magazine* (11 May 1957) 17.

[14] Canadian Welfare Council, *Indians and the Law, a survey prepared for the Hon. A. Laing* (Ottawa: Canadian Welfare Council, August 1967) at 42.

[15] M. Jackson, "Locking Up Natives in Canada" (1988-89) 23:1 U.B.C. L. Rev. 216.

[16] While Aboriginal people represented 2% of the general adult population in Canada, they accounted for 15% of the individuals placed in custody in provincial and territorial institutions in 1997/98, see Statistics Canada, "Prison population and costs, 1997/98" *The Daily* (6 April 1999), online: <http://www.statscan.ca:80/Daily/English/990406/d990406.htm> (date accessed: 16 November 1999). For a review of Aboriginal over-representation in the criminal justice system see *Justice On Trial: The Report of the Task Force on the Criminal Justice System and Its Impact on the Indian and Métis People of Alberta* (Edmonton: 1991); Manitoba, Report of the Aboriginal Justice Inquiry of Manitoba: *The Justice System and Aboriginal People*, Vol. 1 (Winnipeg: Queen's Printer, 1991) (Co-chairs: A.C. Hamilton and C.M. Sinclair); Canada, Indian Justice Review Committee, *Report of the Saskatchewan Indian Justice Review Committee* (Regina: 1992); C. LaPrairie, *Examining Aboriginal Corrections in Canada*, (Canada: Ministry of the Solicitor General, 1996); Canada, Royal Commission on Aboriginal Peoples, *Bridging the Cultural Divide: A Report on Aboriginal People and Criminal Justice in Canada* (Ottawa: Canada Communication Group, 1996).

[17] *R. v. Kenny*, [1992] N.J. No.118 (NFLD.S.C.), online: QL.

[18] Milloy, *supra* note 10 at record 93 / 162.

[19] J.R. Miller, *Shingwauk's Vision: A History of Native Residential Schools* (Toronto: University of Toronto Press, 1996) at 357.

[20] C. Haig-Brown, *Resistance and Renewal* (Vancouver: Tillacum Library, 1988) at 123.

[21] Milloy, *supra* note 10 at record 93788 citing R.F. Davey correspondence (INAC File 501/25-1-064, Vol. 1, 19 November 1953).

[22] Milloy, *ibid.* at record 93108.

[23] Milloy, *ibid.*; Miller, *supra* note 19 at c. 12.

[24] Haig-Brown, *supra* note 20 at c. 4 "The Resistance".

[25] Letter from A.R. Virgin, Director of Training Schools, Ontario, to St John's and St Joseph's Training Schools, November 28, 1957, as reproduced in *Recorder's Report – St. Joseph's and St. John's Training Schools, supra* note 7 at 86-7.

26 *Ibid.* at 201-202 [profile of a former resident of St. John's School, 1951].

27 *Ibid.* at 139.

28 *G.B.R.* v. *Hollet,* [1995] N.S.J. No. 328 at para. 11 (S.C.), online: QL.

29 See The Alliance of Five Research Centres on Violence, *Violence Prevention and the Girl Child: Final Report* (Ottawa: Status of Women Canada, February 1999); The Alliance of Five Research Centres on Violence, *Violence Prevention and the Girl Child: Literature Reviews of Select Areas – Appendix I* (Ottawa: Status of Women Canada, November 1998).

30 *G.J.* v. *Griffiths,* [1995] B.C.J. No. 2370 at para. 12 (S.C.), online: QL.

31 *Ibid.* at para. 10.

32 *J.H.* v. *British Columbia,* [1998] B.C.J. No. 2926 at para. 80 (S.C.), online: QL.

33 *Ibid.* at para. 82.

34 *Ibid.* at para. 17.

35 Haig-Brown, *supra* note 20 at 95.

36 P. Sandiford Grygier, *A Long Way From Home: The Tuberculosis Epidemic Among the Inuit* (Montreal: McGill-Queen's University Press, 1994) at 126.

37 R. LaPointe, "TB treatment left 'lost' Inuit tracing their roots" *The Globe and Mail* (27 September 1986) A1.

38 Ministry of Health, *Medical Patient Search Project: Summary: Final Report* (Yellowknife: Northwest Territories, 1991).

39 *C.A.* v. *Critchley,* [1997] B.C.J. No. 1020 at paras. 17, 19 and 20 (S.C.), online: QL.

40 J.M. Chandry, R.W. Blum & M.D. Resnick, "Female Adolescents with a history of sexual abuse: Risk, outcome and protective factors" *Journal of Interpersonal Violence* 11:4 (December 1996) at 503-518.

41 F. Mathews, *The Invisible Boy: Revisioning the Victimization of Male Children and Teens* (Ottawa: Health Canada, 1996) at 37.

42 C. Kilgore, "Abused Children Often Grow Into Sick Adults" *Pediatric News* 32:7 (July 1998), online: <http://www.medscape.com/IMNG/PediatricNews/1998/v.32.n07/pn3207.10.01.html> (date accessed: 16 November 1999).

43 J.G. Johnson, P. Cohen, J. Brown, E.M. Smailes & D.P. Bernstein, "Childhood Maltreatment Increases Risk for Personality Disorders During Early Adulthood" *Archives of General Psychiatry* (July 1999) online: <http://archpsyc.ama-assn.org/issues/v56n7/full/yoa8212.html> (date accessed 16 November 1999).

44 J. Flemming, P.E. Mullen, B. Sibthorpe & G. Bammer, "The long-term impact of childhood sexual abuse in Australian women" *Child Abuse and Neglect* 23:2 (1999), 145-160; J. McCauley, D.E. Kern, K. Kolodner, L. Dill, A.F. Schroeder, H.K. DeChant, J. Ryden, L.R. Derogatis & E.B. Bass, "Clinical Characteristics of Women With a History of Childhood Abuse: Unhealed Wounds" *Journal of the American Medical Association* 277:17 (7 May 1997).

45 C. Widom, "Victims of Childhood Sexual Abuse – Later Criminal Consequences" (National Institute of Justice, March 1995), online: <http://www.ncjrs.org/ txtfiles/abuse.txt> (date accessed: 16 November 1999). R.K. Oates, "The Effects of Child Sexual Abuse" (1992) 66:4 A.L.J. 186-193; C. Alksnis & D. Robinson, *Childhood Victimization and Violent Behaviour Among Adult Offenders* (Ottawa: Correctional Service of Canada, Research Branch 1995) at 16 (FV-06); J.C. Johnston, *Aboriginal Offender Survey: Case Files and Interview Sample* (Ottawa: Correctional Service of Canada, Research Branch, 1997).

C. Residential Schools for Aboriginal Children

1. A Brief Historical Background

Although abuse of any kind in any type of institution is extremely damaging and should never be tolerated, the stories of abuse suffered by Aboriginal children who attended residential schools are especially poignant. What distinguishes residential schools for Aboriginal children is that they were part of a policy of assimilation that was sustained for many decades: the residential school experience influenced the lives of several generations of people. To focus only on the harm done to individual survivors is, therefore, to ignore the damage done to families, communities and Aboriginal peoples generally – all of whom are also, in this context, survivors.

A complete explanation of the forces that created and shaped the residential school system would require an exhaustive study comprising substantial empirical and archival research. Like the Royal Commission on Aboriginal Peoples, the Law Commission believes that such a sociological and historical study should be undertaken. But even in the absence of comprehensive research, enough is known about the effects of the residential school system to understand its social and historical significance. In responding to the questions directed to it by the Minister of Justice, the Law Commission takes this existing knowledge as a key element in its assessment of the different approaches for responding to the abuse suffered by Aboriginal children in institutions.

The importance of a holistic approach to redress and healing for Aboriginal survivors and their communities is a direct consequence of the policies and practices that lay behind the residential school system. For it was these policies and practices that disrupted children's lives and tore so many communities apart. Consequently, this section begins by sketching the social history of residential schools. It then considers the ways in which the residential school system adversely affected the lives of individuals and the stability of communities, drawing upon specific examples as illustrations.

The Commission's review of the growing body of information on residential schools for Aboriginal children has led it to three conclusions. First, racial attitudes about the backwardness and inferiority of Aboriginal peoples fuelled the maltreatment and abuse experienced by children at residential schools. Sadly, these attitudes have not been entirely overcome. Second, the affronts to the collective dignity, self-respect and identity of Aboriginal peoples that occurred in residential schools are closely linked to the nature and scope of the redress individuals and communities now seek. Third, there remains today a significant need for public education. All Canadians must be offered the opportunity to understand the destructive influence of the residential school system and to appreciate why the federal government is morally obliged to take significant steps to help survivors and their communities.

a.   Chronology of the residential school system

Much has already been written about the system of residential schools for Aboriginal children. The following few pages offer a chronology of key events, compiled from a variety of sources, that outline the evolution of that system.[1] The aim is to show the pervasiveness of the idea of residential schools over time, and to trace the way in which the changing government policies with regard to such schools shaped their design and operation.

The history of residential schools in Canada begins shortly after European colonisation.[2] From the outset, the educational and missionary vocations of residential schools were closely intertwined. In 1620, the Récollets, an order of Franciscans, established the first known boarding school for Aboriginal children in New France. The school closed in 1629 when the friars left the colony. Following the cession of New France to England 150 years later, various Protestant denominations began to establish residential schools. In 1787, for example, the New England Company, a non-sectarian Protestant missionary organisation, established boarding schools or "Indian colleges" for "Native children" in British North America. The schools were set up in New Brunswick, and included a farm apprenticeship system.

In the early 19th century, officials in Upper Canada embarked upon the establishment of a residential school system. In 1820, the Governor of Upper Canada submitted a proposal to the Colonial Office "for ameliorating the condition of the Indians in the neighbourhood of our settlements".[3]

By 1844, the Bagot Commission of the United Province of Canada, which was set up to examine Aboriginal education, recommended training students in

'as many manual labour or Industrial schools' as possible.... In such schools ... isolated 'from the influence of their parents' pupils would 'imperceptibly acquire the manners, habits and customs of civilized life.'[4]

The Commission also recommended the continuation of common schools on reserves, such as the Mohawk Institute that had been established in 1829 by The New England Company. The Superintendent of Education for Upper Canada, the Reverend Egerton Ryerson, reported that the objectives of the manual labour schools for Aboriginal children were

'to give a plain English education adapted to the working farmer and mechanic,' and ... that the 'animating and controlling spirit of each industrial school establishment should ... be a religious one.'[5]

These schools were planned on the "half-day system", whereby students would spend one half of their day in the classroom and the other half-day learning skills for living in the Euro-Canadian economy.

At the time of Confederation in 1867, the *British North America Act* made "Indians, and Lands reserved for the Indians" a federal responsibility in the new Dominion of Canada.[6] For the next few decades, the Government of Canada embarked on treaty-making processes with Aboriginals in the West. Aboriginal peoples wanted assurances that the treaties would include measures, such as the provision of adequate schooling, to assist them in making the transition from a hunting economy to a farming economy. In 1876, the *Indian Act* made all Aboriginal people wards of the federal government.[7] Shortly thereafter, following a report from Nicholas Davin, a Member of Parliament from Regina, Saskatchewan, the government embarked upon a program of creating church-run, off-reserve, industrial boarding schools.

Although a handful of residential schools already existed in Ontario at the time, Davin's report may be credited with fuelling the rapid growth of industrial and boarding schools.

By the turn of the century, some 18 industrial schools and 36 boarding schools for Aboriginal children were in operation. While Métis and non-status Indians had been admitted to these schools until the mid-1890s, thereafter the official policy was to admit only status Indians. Per capita funding for industrial schools was introduced in 1892,[8] with the result that many schools used student labour to help offset costs. In 1911, the federal government established formal contracts with the churches that clearly outlined their responsibilities in operating the boarding schools. That year, the government decided to end the industrial school program.[9] There were then 54 boarding schools and 20 industrial schools in operation with enrolments of 2,229 and 1,612 students respectively. In addition, the Department of Indian Affairs was responsible for 241 day schools that served 6,784 students.[10] Shortly after, the Department of Indian Affairs – which had previously avoided making school attendance compulsory for Aboriginal children – concluded that the system of voluntary recruitment was not effective. The *Indian Act* was amended to make attendance compulsory for every child between the ages of seven and fifteen. Sixteen industrial and 55 boarding schools were operating across Canada, except in the Maritimes and Quebec; 5,347 Aboriginal children resided in these schools.

The number of residential schools reached its peak in 1931. At that time there were 80 schools: one in Nova Scotia, 13 in Ontario, 10 in Manitoba, 14 in Saskatchewan, 20 in Alberta, 16 in British Columbia, four in the Northwest Territories, and two in the Yukon. In addition, two schools were then being planned in Quebec. During the 1940s, various reports recommended that the system of segregated, residential education for Aboriginal children should be replaced by integrating Aboriginal children into provincial day schools. In 1951, the federal government began what became a four-decade long process of shutting down residential schools for Aboriginal children. The *Indian Act* was again amended to enable Aboriginal children to attend provincial schools.[11]

In 1969, the federal government formally ended its partnership with the churches in Aboriginal education, allowing it to accelerate the rate of residential school closures. Sixty per cent of Aboriginal students were then enrolled in provincial day schools, but fifty-two residential schools still remained in operation. The following year, control of the Blue Quills residential school, near Saint Paul, Alberta, was turned over to the Blue Quills Native Education Council, the first school in Canada to be officially administered by Aboriginal people. In 1973, the federal government agreed to shift control of the administration of Aboriginal education programs to band councils or their delegated education authorities. The last government-funded residential school for Aboriginal children was closed in 1986.[12]

b.   Official policy governing the residential school system

The preceding chronology of the development of residential schools reveals that for over 350 years, the operation of these schools was part of official government policy. In particular, from the mid-1800s until the 1970s, these policies were a central component of the educational system for Aboriginal children. According to the Assembly of First Nations,[13] the policy of the federal government on educating Aboriginal children evolved through four stages:

1840s – 1910: Assimilation
Teach Indian children the skills needed to participate as labourers in the mainstream Euro-Canadian economy, so that they would become "amalgamated with the white population" and "self-supporting members" of society.

1911 – 1951: Segregation
Teach Aboriginal children, separated from their communities, about the civilised ways of white society, so that they would return to their own communities as "good Indians".

1951 – 1970: Integration

Educate Aboriginal children in the same schools as other Canadian children, since this approach offered "the best hope of giving the Indians [and other Aboriginal People] an equal chance with other Canadian citizens to improve their lot and to become fully self-respecting".[14]

1971 – present: Self-determination

As part of the movement toward Aboriginal self-government, Aboriginal peoples assume control over the education of their children.

Social and legislative judgements about race, class, gender and ability made some children more likely to be institutionalised, and more vulnerable to abuse within institutions, than others. Those same factors of vulnerability were frequently compounded in the case of Aboriginal children. In addition, Aboriginal children were the only children in Canadian history who, over an extended period of time, were statutorily designated to live in institutions primarily because of their race. Large numbers of school-aged Aboriginal children, at times up to one-third of them, were sent to residential schools. In some communities, this institutionalisation continued for decades, and affected many generations.

For these reasons – the racial attitudes underpinning residential schools, their mission to re-socialise children, the large number of schools and the lengthy period they were in operation – the Law Commission believes that the impact of the abuse suffered by individual Aboriginal children can only be totally understood when it is placed within its larger social context: families and communities have been profoundly harmed. Nor is it enough to look at possible redresses as if it were only necessary to redress physical and sexual abuse, although that is a priority. Developing an understanding of the link between the degradation and disconnection caused by physical and sexual abuse and the context within which it took place requires approaches that also address emotional, psychological and spiritual harm. In other words, the adequacy of any redress mechanism must be evaluated according to how well it addresses the full range of harms experienced by individuals, families and communities.

2.   The Experience of Residential Schools

What Aboriginal children experienced in residential schools, and what Aboriginal families and communities experienced because their children went to these schools, are widely known. These experiences have, however, not yet been comprehensively and systematically documented. Aboriginal communities, church-sponsored conferences, the Royal Commission on Aboriginal Peoples, public inquiries into the over-involvement of Aboriginal people with the criminal justice system and social scientists and historians have begun the process of recording and evaluating the experience of residential schools.[15]

The Law Commission sees this documentation process as an important complement to its own primary task. This process will provide further confirmation of the Commission's summary conclusions, about the character of residential schools. It will, in turn, shed further light on the needs for redress that Aboriginal people are expressing as well as help to clarify why these needs must, and how they can, be addressed.

The Commission recognises the uniqueness of each child's experience at a residential school. It also acknowledges that the impact the schools had on each community is different. For these reasons, it believes that the words of Aboriginal people themselves can best describe their experiences with residential schools.

a.   The experiences of children

In this Report, residential institutions for children have been described as "total institutions". This characterisation is especially apt in the case of residential schools for Aboriginal children. Here is how one text describes these schools:

> Regardless of shifts in naming – industrial, boarding or residential – all residential schools were "total institutions". The residential school was a place where a large number of people lived and worked together cut off from both the wider First Nation and mainstream societies. In contrast to "day schools" where children came and went on a daily basis, residential school separated children from their families and communities for extended periods of time, in some instances for years.

Further evidence of residential schools as total institutions is attested to by the fact that they were places within which all activities of the children – eating, sleeping, playing, working, speaking – were subject to set time tables and to regulations determined by staff comprised of supervisors and teachers who, for the most part, belonged to a variety of Christian denominations. Residential schools, in a way not unlike other total institutions such as penitentiaries, were places where two distinct groups of people lived and worked – children and adult staff – and where one group (the staff), had the power to determine on a daily basis, the conduct of behaviour for the second group, the First Nations children.[16]

A number of features distinguish the experience of Aboriginal children in residential schools from the experience of other institutionalised children. Many officials well understood that the residential school system was intended to undermine a culture. It was one component in a loosely integrated set of statutes and programs aimed at controlling and reorienting Aboriginal behaviour. The aim of the general policy adopted by the federal government was to elevate Aboriginal people from a 'savage' state to a state of self-reliant 'civilisation'. In 1920, Duncan Campbell Scott, Deputy Superintendent-General of the Department of Indian Affairs, expressed this policy as one of forced assimilation:

> I want to get rid of the Indian problem. I do not think as a matter of fact, that this country ought to continuously protect a class of people who are able to stand alone.... Our object is to continue until there is not a single Indian in Canada that has not been absorbed into the body politic and there is no Indian question, and no Indian Department.[17]

A particularly odious feature of the residential school system was that it was deliberately aimed at children, the most vulnerable and least powerful members of society. The link between children's education and assimilation was clearly stated during the establishment of the school system. In a letter to the Prime Minister written in 1887, Lawrence Vankoughnet, Deputy Superintendent-General of the Department of Indian Affairs, proclaimed:

> Give me the children and you may have the parents, or words to that effect, were uttered by a zealous divine in his anxiety to add to the number of whom his Church called her children. And the principle laid down

by that astute reasoner is an excellent one on which to act in working out that most difficult problem – the intellectual emancipation of the Indian, and its natural sequel, his elevation to a status equal to that of his white brother. This can only be done through education.... Only by a persistent continuance in a thoroughly systematic course of educating (using the word in its fullest and most practical sense) the children, will the final hoped and long striven for result be attained....[18]

Church officials who ran residential schools recognised that the school system had a larger role to play than just educating students. The following statement in the late 19th century by the Reverend Alexander Sutherland, General Secretary of the Methodist Church of Canada, indicates the degree to which the assimilationist policy was supported by some religious orders.

Experience convinces us that the only way in which the Indians of the country can be permanently elevated and thoroughly civilized is by removing the children from the surroundings of Indian home life, and keeping them separated long enough to form those habits of order, industry, and systematic effort, which they will never learn at home. [The department should] fix the term of residency at five years for girls and six for boys, and make attendance for this term compulsory. The return of children to their houses, even temporarily, has a bad effect, while their permanent removal after one or two years' residence results in the loss of all that they have gained.[19]

Individual acts of physical and sexual abuse cannot be attributed to the general government policy of assimilation. Nonetheless, the policy did set the framework within which the schools operated. This framework was used to denigrate and erase all aspects of Aboriginal heritage and justify a number of harmful practices that were undertaken in the name of instilling non-Aboriginal values in Aboriginal children.

Upon entering a residential school, children were stripped of their personal belongings and artefacts of their culture. Their hair was cut (a seriously demeaning act for many Aboriginal people), their clothes were taken away and replaced with those from the institution, and they were separated from other family members. To facilitate cultural assimilation, Aboriginal students were generally forbidden to speak their languages or practice their cultural traditions. While there is some

It is not too late for the government of Canada to do the right thing where residential school abuse is concerned. It should drop its legalistic case-by-case technique, which simply re-abuses Aboriginal people, and take immediate and large-scale steps, after consultation with the national Aboriginal groups, to provide appropriate redress for these many generations of destructive racism.

Marilyn Buffalo, President, Native Women's Association of Canada

My kids are being hurt by my recycling all this stuff now. I had it blocked out of my mind for 29-30 years. I take it out on my wife.

Quoted in The Vision to Reconcile: Process Report on the Helpline Reconciliation Model Agreement by Doug Roche and Ben Hoffman, at p.21

I see a lot of money, big money, going into process machine. When do we get our needs addressed?

Quoted in The Vision to Reconcile: Process Report on the Helpline Reconciliation Model Agreement by Doug Roche and Ben Hoffman, at p.22 debate regarding the extent to which individual schools permitted the use of native languages,[20] there is little doubt that the overall effect of this policy was to engender a sense of cultural and spiritual alienation among the children.

In any situation, an imposed prohibition against children speaking their mother tongue can be destructive to their sense of identity. Such a prohibition is particularly damaging, however, in oral cultures. Language is the basic medium through which culture is expressed. It helps create and sustain a world view. Removing children from their families, preventing them from speaking their mother tongue and denying them occasions to express their culture through language and associated rituals is a powerful attack on the personal and cultural identity of members of an Aboriginal community.

> ... [P]eople in the circle recognised the importance of being able to speak one's language as a way of expressing and having access to one's Aboriginal identity. People spoke of their feelings of great hurt and loss because they felt their rites of passage were incomplete without their language. For example, one man told the group that in his nation it is the role of the eldest son to speak at the burial of a parent. This man was noticeably sombre and his voice barely audible as he told the group how he experienced great shame when, at his father's funeral, he could not fulfil this role because he could not speak his language well enough.[21]

The denial of language, and the cultural loss that ensued, typically led to psychological disorientation and spiritual crises among Aboriginal children. Many were left unable to assume responsible positions as mothers, fathers and community members – a persisting legacy.

Chronic underfunding and official indifference, common themes that ran through the investigations into residential schools in the 1940s and 1950s, meant that Aboriginal children were usually placed in institutions with substandard living conditions. Some children who had been used to a varied diet of fish, waterfowl or other game were often given food that was seen as unappetising and bland ("mush" for example), or worse, a diet seriously deficient for sustaining a growing body. Several studies conducted by health practitioners during the 1940s and 1950s confirmed children's accounts of substandard and rotten food and unsanitary food preparation practices.[22] In many cases, children were simply malnourished. According to one report:

> The Children were lean and anaemic and T.B. glands were running in many cases. Energy was at its lowest ebb. Five minutes leap frog was the most I could get out of the boys at once. In examining the Bill of Fare I found that here lay a great deal of the trouble in the health and welfare of the children. They were not getting enough to eat....[23]

The quality and quantity of the food was not the only health issue at residential schools. As early as 1897, reports from medical officers noted unsanitary conditions, poor ventilation, improper clothing, unsafe drinking water and crowded living quarters. These conditions exacerbated the tuberculosis epidemic that cut though the Aboriginal population during the first half of this century, and made Aboriginal children particularly susceptible to influenza and other infectious diseases.

Underfunding of residential schools also meant that children were needed as labourers. The half-day system of work and study was in effect until the 1950s. Children tended crops and livestock, cleaned, did laundry and mending, and engaged in carpentry and blacksmithing. As a result, many students received an education that was not even remotely like the one given to their non-Aboriginal contemporaries. Some received even less than half-a-day's instruction. One former student recalls her experience as follows:

> The other thing I think I was denied was school. They put me in the kitchen all the time. I would go six weeks without seeing a classroom, I would be in the kitchen. I spent a lot of time in the kitchen [laundry and sewing]. And ... when the exam came I didn't know what was going on. I didn't do very good and I told the sister I didn't learn it because I didn't go to school for six weeks and she'd say," Don't worry about it, we'll fix it." [24]

Frequently, the farm produce resulting from students' labour in dairies, gardens and hatcheries and in tending livestock was sold to the general public rather than being consumed by the children at the school.[25] There is little evidence that this work experience was designed to teach modern agricultural skills to the students or that the revenues generated were regularly funnelled back to the residential school.

Underfunding also had an impact on the staff at residential schools. The schools were frequently short-staffed and the working conditions were less than adequate. This situation contributed to a climate of indifference and neglect. Churches often had difficulty recruiting qualified teachers because of low pay, remote locations, a lack of teaching equipment, inhospitable living conditions and few opportunities for professional development. Staff turnover was a constant problem. Lack of resources also made it difficult for school administrators to attract professionals such as dietitians, cooks and nurses or qualified groundskeepers and maintenance personnel. One historian described how these working conditions affected the lives of children:

> Working conditions for staff which destroyed their morale and drove them to opposition and resignation and the failure of Principals, whether it was due to incompetence or to overwhelming odds, could in no way benefit the children. Nor could the fact that the schools were not peaceful, rewarding places to work, not havens of civilisation. Rather, they were sites of struggle against poverty, the result of underfunding, and, of course, against cultural difference and, therefore, against the children themselves.[26]

The pool of often under-qualified applicants for positions contained some who were abusers and who saw residential schools as places where they could more readily abuse children. Earlier in this century, many screening processes now in place to safeguard children – police record reviews, for example – were not available to school administrators.

The institutional form of the residential school, its avowed aims, and some of the staff it attracted, together generated a climate in which many children did not flourish. However dedicated most of those who managed individual schools may have been, and however noble the motives of the sponsoring organisations, a flawed governmental policy, poorly funded and administered, led to an educational experience that did not well serve many Aboriginal children, and that exposed some to terrible acts of physical and sexual abuse.

b. The experience of families and communities

Denial of access to family and culture and other forms of emotional abuse, including, for some students, physical and sexual assaults, characterised the experience of Aboriginal children at residential schools. The effects on their mental and physical health were both immediate and long-lasting. Even today, many former residents are still coming to terms with their childhood experiences. But any assessment of the impact of residential schools would be incomplete if it did not examine how they affected the lives of families and the functioning of communities. A long-term program aimed at re-socialisation, even if not ultimately successful, will produce reactions and responses that, over time, can have a negative socio-cultural impact.

In Aboriginal cultures, the family is a focal point for the transmission of spiritual values from one generation to the next. The organisation of communities along kinship lines reinforces those responsibilities of each member that serve to connect the individual to the larger group. An oral tradition grounded in the transmission of stories and fables reinforces this social bond. Grandparents play a key role in teaching children their place within the community. A former student described his life before entering residential school as follows:

> If I did something wrong, my grandfather would tell me a long story, and I would figure out for myself its meaning and what it told me about what I had done.... [My grandmother] was always teaching. She'd cook wonderful things and tell me why it was so important to have respect for everything on earth that feeds us.[27]

The residential school system undercut and devalued this type of educational experience. The teaching of basic subjects such as reading, writing and arithmetic is an important contribution that residential schools made to Aboriginal children. But when situated in an educational context that also devalues traditional knowledge, and when provided in a physical setting where children are separated from their parents, siblings and extended family, this knowledge creates deep conflicts for many students. Their formal education should have complemented and reinforced the learning first encountered at home within the family. Instead, it weakened or severed the relationships among family members and the kinship organisation of many Aboriginal communities.

By removing students from their families, the residential school system also disrupted the transmission of cultural values and practices. Residential school students were less able to learn these values and practices from their elders than those who attended day schools. Whatever they did learn prior to going off to residential school or during the summer months at home, they were forbidden to practice while at school. The demands of child rearing and the abilities needed to be effective parents are learned at home and in the community. Residential institutions of any kind – boarding schools, orphanages, training schools – remove children from this source of learning. By definition, students at residential schools were deprived of the chance to live as a family and to learn the skills of effective parenting within their culture.

Without the tangible aspects of their culture – their languages, customary clothing, cultural traditions, religion, traditional meals – many Aboriginal children lost touch with their traditional world view. Students were often made to feel ashamed of their cultural heritage. Many former students recall that, upon leaving residential school, they had little knowledge of what it meant to be Aboriginal. Over time, this loss of culture and connection came to devastate many Aboriginal communities. Without the support of an internalised culture, the capacity for social cooperation, governance and mutual aid is severely diminished. This diminished capacity is reflected in a number of social problems experienced by Aboriginal communities today – substance abuse, violence and crime, domestic abuse, family breakdown – as has been documented by the Royal Commission on Aboriginal Peoples.[28]

Not every community whose children attended a residential school has experienced these problems acutely, and some communities whose children only attended day schools experienced them nonetheless. But the general pattern is apparent. Because childhood experiences deeply influence later behaviour, many students who had a negative experience at a residential school have suffered problems in their adult lives. In turn, their own personal problems have often created problems for their families and communities.

Persons who attended these schools continue to struggle with their identity after years of being taught to hate themselves and their culture. The
residential school led to a disruption in the transference of parenting
skills from one generation to the next. Without these skills, many survivors had had difficulties in raising their own children. In residential
schools they learned that adults often exert power and control through
abuse. The lessons learned in childhood are often repeated in adulthood
with the result that many survivors of the residential school system often
inflict abuse on their own children. These children in turn use the same
tools on their own children.[29]

The large number of Aboriginal people currently in prison – another
form of non-community based institutional life – is a concrete reminder
of how negative childhood experiences can have an impact that
reaches beyond the individual and spills over, in the form of anti-social
behaviour, into the individual's own family and community.

3.   The Legacy of Residential Schools

The effect of residential schools on Aboriginal families and communities has been so pervasive that some believe the school system could
only have been part of a larger campaign of genocide.[30] They contend
that the actions of the federal government and the churches that ran
the residential schools violated Article II(c) of the Convention on
Genocide. That Article defines genocide as acts committed with the
intent to destroy a national, ethical, racial or religious group by such
means as: "Deliberately inflicting upon the group conditions of life calculated to bring about its physical destruction in whole or in part".[31]

The 1997 Royal Commission on Aboriginal Peoples was clear and
unequivocal in its conclusions regarding the residential school system.
In commenting on the response of the federal government to the legal
issues concerning abuse, the Royal Commission stated that the government's focus was on individual acts and that "there was no
consideration that the system itself constituted a 'crime' ".[32] It also
underlined that acknowledging the full extent of the harms of the past
is critical to building a better relationship between Aboriginal and
non-Aboriginal communities:

The government has refused to apologize or to institute a special public inquiry and instead wishes to concentrate on the 'now' of the problem, the 'savage' sick and in need of psychological salvation. This is an attempt to efface the 'then', the history of the system, which, if it were considered, would inevitably turn the light of inquiry back onto the source of that contagion – on the 'civilized' – on Canadian society and Christian evangelism and on the racist policies of its institutional expressions in church, government and bureaucracy. Those are the sites that produced the residential school system. In thought and deed this system was an act of profound cruelty, rooted in non-Aboriginal pride and intolerance and in the certitude and insularity of purported cultural superiority.[33]

The task of the Law Commission in this Reference is to investigate and evaluate processes of redress for those who suffered physical and sexual abuse in government-run or sponsored institutions when they were children. Residential schools for Aboriginal children were among these institutions. The Commission believes that it is fundamentally important to redress the harms that were visited upon residential school students by this abuse. It also believes that the residential school system itself produced harm for these former students, and that this harm has flowed outwards to their family members and the communities in which they live. This is one of the enduring legacies of the residential school system. Whatever approaches to redress are imagined, therefore, they must have the capacity to deal appropriately with this broader range of harms and this broader range of persons suffering these harms.

---

1   Canada, *Report of the Royal Commission on Aboriginal Peoples: Looking Forward, Looking Back*, Vol.1 (Ottawa: Canada Communication Group, 1996) c.10 "Residential Schools" at 344, also available in CD-ROM (Ottawa: Libraxus Inc., CD-ROM, 1997) at record 1710 [hereinafter *Looking Forward, Looking Back*]; J.R. Miller, *Shingwauk's Vision: A History of Native Residential Schools* (Toronto: University of Toronto Press, 1996); J.S. Milloy, " 'Suffer the Little Children': A History of the Residential School System, 1830–1993", a research paper submitted to The Royal Commission on Aboriginal Peoples (Canada), *For Seven Generations, Pour sept générations* (Ottawa: Libraxus Inc., CD-ROM 1997) records 92370 to 122566 at record 92439.

2   Miller, *supra* note 1 at 39.

3   Milloy, *supra* note 1 at record 92439.

4   *Ibid.* at record 92435 quoting from the Bagot Commission.

5   *Ibid.* at record 92443 quoting from R.F. Davey, *Residential Schools Past and Future* (INAC file 601/25-2, Vol. 2, 8 March 1968).

6   *Constitution Act, 1867* (U.K.), 30 & 31 Vict., c. 3, s. 24, reprinted in R.S.C. 1985, App. II, No. 5.

7   *An Act to amend and consolidate the laws respecting Indians*, S.C. 1876, c. 18.

8   Miller, *supra* note 1 at 126.

9   *Ibid.* at 129; *An Act to Further Amend "The Indian Act"*, S.C. 1894, c. 32, 57-58 Vict., s. 11 (amending ss. 137-139 of the Act).

10 Milloy, *supra* note 1 at record 92716.

11 Miller, *supra* note 1 at 141.

12 *Looking Forward, Looking Back*, *supra* note 1 at 351, CD-ROM at record 1798.

13 *Breaking the Silence: An Interpretive Study of Residential School Impact and Healing as Illustrated by the Stories of First Nation Individuals* (Ottawa: Assembly of First Nations, 1994) at 13-20 [hereinafter *Breaking the Silence*].

14 Milloy, *supra* note 1 at record 92589.

15 *Looking Forward, Looking Back*, *supra* note 1; Milloy, *supra* note 1; Miller, *supra* note 1; Manitoba, *Report of the Aboriginal Justice Inquiry of Manitoba: The Justice System and Aboriginal People*, vol. 1 (Winnipeg: Queen's Printer, 1991); E. Graham, *The Ninth Hole: Life at Two Indian Residential Schools* (Waterloo, Ont.: Heffle Publishing, 1997); N. Dyck, *Differing Visions – Administering Indian Residential School in Prince Albert, 1867–1995* (Halifax: Fernwood Publishing, 1997); Assembly of First Nations, *Breaking The Silence – An Interpretive Study of Residential School Impact and Healing as Illustrated by the Stories of First Nations Individuals* (Ottawa: Assembly of First Nations, 1994); Canadian Conference of Catholic Bishops, *Let Justice Flow Like a Mighty River* (Ottawa: Canadian Conference of Catholic Bishops, 1995) at 16-17; The Anglican Church of Canada, *Residential Schools – Legacy and Response*, "Summary of Projects – 1999", "Summary of Projects – 1996–1998" and "Summary of Projects – 1992–1995", <http://www.anglican.ca> (date accessed: 16 November 1999).

16 *Breaking the Silence*, *supra* note 13 at 3-4.

[17] Duncan Campbell Scott, Deputy Superintendent-General, Department of Indian Affairs, testifying before a Special Committee of the House of Commons in 1920, in R. Chrisjohn & S. Young, *The Circle Game – Shadows and Substance in the Indian Residential School Experience in Canada* (Penticton: Theytus Books, 1997) at 42; *The Historical Development of the Indian Act* (Ottawa: Department of Indian Affairs, 1978) at 114.

[18] Milloy, *supra* note 1 at records 92415-92416.

[19] See Thalassa Research, "Nation to Nation: Indian Nation-Crown Relations in Canada", a research paper prepared for The Royal Commission on Aboriginal Peoples (Canada) in *For Seven Generations, Pour sept générations, supra* note 1 records 59182 to 61027, at record 60281.

[20] "The policies respecting the use of one's own language and the enforcement against it were set by individual administrators resulting in a patchwork of differing approaches." See Milloy, *supra* note 1 at record 93284.

[21] K. Absolon & T. Winchester, "Cultural Identity for Urban Aboriginal Peoples Learning Circles Synthesis Report" a research paper submitted to The Royal Commission on Aboriginal Peoples (Canada) in *For Seven Generations, Pour sept générations, supra* note 1, records 110353 to 110945 at record 110543.

[22] Milloy, *supra* note 1 at records 93635-93679.

[23] Milloy, *supra* note 1 at record 92865 [footnote 460, Report from Rev. A. Lett to the New England Company, 10 April 1923].

[24] Absolon & Winchester, *supra* note 21 at record 110791.

[25] Miller, *supra* note 1 at c. 3.

[26] Milloy, *supra* note 1 at record 93050.

[27] R. Claes & D. Clifton (SAGE), *Needs and Expectations for Redress of Victims of Abuse at Residential Schools* (Ottawa: Law Commission of Canada, October 1998) at 22. Available in hard copy from the Law Commission of Canada and online: <http://www.lcc.gc.ca>.

[28] *Looking Forward, Looking Back, supra* note 1 at 376-382, CD-ROM at records 196-215.

[29] Milloy, *supra* note 1 at record 93826 [footnote 1408].

[30] See Chrisjohn & Young, *supra* note 17; A. Grant, *No End of Grief: Indian Residential Schools in Canada* (Winnipeg: Pemmican Publishing, 1996).

[31] Article II (c) of the *Convention on the Prevention and Punishment of the Crime of Genocide* (GA Res. 260A(111) (9 December 1948): "In the present Convention, genocide means any of the following acts committed with intent to destroy, in whole or in part, a national, ethnic, racial or religious group, as such: .... (c) Deliberately inflicting on the group conditions of life calculated to bring about its physical destruction in whole or in part...".

[32] *Looking Forward, Looking Back, supra* note 1 at record 1925.

[33] *Looking Forward, Looking Back, ibid.* at record 1926. Since the Royal Commission Report from which this quotation is taken was issued, the federal government has issued its Statement of Reconciliation. See "Statement of Reconciliation" included in an Address by the Honourable Jane Stewart, Minister of Indian Affairs and Northern Development on the occasion of the unveiling of *Gathering Strength – Canada's Aboriginal Action Plan* (Ottawa: Department of Indian Affairs and Northern Development, 7 January 1998), online: <http://www.inac.gc.ca/info/speeches/jan98/action.html> (date accessed: 16 November 1999).

D. Needs Identified

From the outset, the Law Commission decided that its report should acknowledge the perspectives of those adults who suffered physical and sexual abuse as children. It resolved to keep the interests of survivors foremost for three reasons. First, the needs of survivors are the necessary starting point for assessing the adequacy of redress. After all, it is they who have suffered harm and they who are best able to articulate that harm. Second, of all the parties involved in allegations of institutional child abuse, survivors have by far the weakest voice. They often lack the resources, the organisation and the expertise to make their case strongly and convincingly. Third, too often the needs of survivors have been seen as incidental to other concerns, such as punishing perpetrators. By focussing on survivors, the Commission hopes to change the way responses to abuse are developed and assessed.

1. Values

This attention to the perspective of survivors has enabled the Commission to identify two overarching values that are reflected in the way survivors themselves have expressed their needs. A primary value is to respect and engage survivors. This might seem self-evident. In practice it is difficult to put this value into practice. In the desire to help, there is a temptation to tell people what is best for them, ignoring or overriding their own wishes and needs. Professionals are particularly susceptible to such behaviour. For example, lawyers may be convinced they know what is best for their clients and may weight their advice accordingly. Other professionals may seek to counsel or provide therapy to survivors on the same basis. Still others may feel the need to offer both legal and therapeutic advice although they lack the appropriate qualifications and experience.

The second value is to ensure that survivors have the information and support to express the needs they feel and to make considered choices about how they wish to deal with those needs. Again, this might seem self-evident. But again, in practice, it is easier said than done. Both legal and therapeutic professionals already approach issues through the lens of their professional training. Survivors need comprehensive information from disinterested parties in order to understand and assess the professional advice being presented. This disinterested information must be followed by support from professionals and from those who have themselves experienced abuse.

Many survivors are at their most vulnerable when they are discussing the abuse they suffered as children. They are particularly susceptible to manipulation and exploitation when seeking advice as to their options. This is why the Commission emphasises the two values that it feels should govern all dealings with those who have experienced child abuse.

a. Respect and engagement

Children who live in an institutional setting generally feel powerless and unable to exert any influence over the most important aspects of their lives. When a child's physical and emotional integrity is respected, an institution can indeed be a place of learning, a haven and a home. However, when a child faces abuse in an institution, the sense of powerlessness and isolation inherent in any instance of child abuse is heightened by the child's limited access to help from outside the institution.

This experience of profound powerlessness is what makes it so important to fully engage former residents of institutions for children in any process aimed at overcoming the consequences of abuse they have suffered. The involvement may be as simple as having the chance to exercise real choice about what redress options to pursue, and about strategic decisions – for example, concerning the conduct of litigation. Imposing "solutions" on survivors without consulting them as to their needs or taking account of those needs can be as offensive as refusing to offer redress altogether. In such cases, once again, others who have more power are making important decisions affecting their lives.

Engaging survivors as much as possible in any approach to redress is a clear way to demonstrate respect for them. It is a public acknowledgement that they know what is needed in order to undo the harm done to them. Engagement may also mean full consultation on the design and implementation of any programs of redress directed to particular groups of survivors.

b.   Information and support

Another aspect of asserting control over one's life is having options, and the information necessary to choose among them. Those who experienced abuse in institutions do not often have many options for redress. Their choices may be limited by financial considerations – not being able to afford a civil action, for example. They may also be limited by time – having to choose whether to join in a compensation program by a cut-off date, which may have passed by the time they hear about it.

Even if there is only one redress process still open to them, it is important that survivors have enough information to enable them to understand the process available and to make decisions they feel are best about how to proceed. For example, they may want to understand what a criminal trial is like before voluntarily agreeing to appear as a witness for the Crown. Knowledge is power, and too often survivors feel they lack the knowledge necessary to make wise choices. The source of the information is also important. Given that the harms were, for the most part, inflicted by individuals in positions of authority, it is understandable that survivors often have difficulty trusting authority figures. It is important that they are given the opportunity to also receive the information necessary to make an informed decision from non-official sources such as survivors' groups.

Many survivors express a strong need for support during any process of redress. Very often they feel disconnected from the environment within which redress is sought. Testifying at a criminal trial can be stressful and traumatic. The uncertainty of ongoing civil litigation can wear on one's capacity to function. Confronting daily an abusive past is a reminder of just how disempowered one was and how disempowered one may still feel. Meaningful support for individual survivors, families and communities is, therefore, essential.

2. Needs of Survivors

Each person who was abused as a child experienced it differently, coped with it differently and suffered different consequences. The effects of childhood abuse depend not only on the duration of the abuse, but also on its nature, its intensity, the institutional context within which it occurred, the particular psychological make-up of the child and the subsequent support that child received, among other factors. It follows that the needs of survivors are as unique and varied as are the survivors themselves.

The types of needs set out in the pages that follow are neither a prescription for every survivor nor a checklist for any particular group of survivors. Rather, together they describe the primary areas of needs identified by survivors in the course of the Commission's research and consultations. They are:

a.   Establishing an historical record; remembrance

b.   Acknowledgement

c.   Apology

d.   Accountability

e.   Access to therapy or counselling

f.   Access to education or training

g.   Financial compensation

h.   Prevention and public awareness

This list is not, of course, exhaustive. Moreover, not all of these eight needs are priorities for all survivors. It is equally important to note that most of these needs are felt not only by individuals but also by families and communities. The Commission offers this list of very broad categories of needs as a starting point only, and perhaps as a springboard for imagining how these needs can be fulfilled in ways specifically suited to certain individuals or groups. It also hopes that the list may assist in identifying further needs of survivors.

a. Establishing an historical record; remembrance

When a problem begins in silence and denial, its resolution must involve acknowledgement and publicity. But acknowledgement is insufficient if there is no permanent public record of it. The maxim that those who forget history are doomed to repeat it is all too relevant here. Child abuse – particularly sexual abuse – is by its nature a secret phenomenon. The secrecy is enhanced in an institutional setting, because children have so few opportunities to disclose the harm to people outside the institution. Thus, even forms of abuse that were carried out openly within an institution are often not known or fully understood on the outside. Survivors feel a strong need to ensure that their experiences are not forgotten – not only the actual instances of abuse, but also the failure of adults, in many cases, to protect them.

Many survivors wish to see some memorial created so that their experiences, once acknowledged, will not be forgotten. Some envision a memorial as a physical structure – a statue, a plaque, the preservation of the building where they lived – that would serve as a concrete reminder of what they endured, both individually and collectively.

Others, however, are strongly opposed to the idea of a physical memorial. For them, the preservation of an institution or the erection of a monument would serve as an unwelcome, even a harmful, reminder of a painful past.

A memorial need not be a physical structure, however. It can serve an active, educational role – a place where survivors could record their experiences, or those of friends or family members no longer alive, to ensure that future generations will know how they lived and what they endured. Such a memorial would relieve survivors of the burden of having to bear witness alone for the rest of their lives. In this sense, the memorial would serve as a reminder and an ongoing caution.

Above all, any kind of memorial should be a testament to the children of the institutions: those who disclosed what they went through and those did who not; those who survived and those who died; those who have healed and who help to heal others. Appropriate memorials give survivors an assurance that history will not perpetuate denial.

The following is a list of various kinds of memorials that have been established, both in relation to abuse in institutions for children and other tragic or historic situations. They are meant to illustrate the range of approaches that can be taken to promote remembrance.

i. *Plaque named in honour of Charlie Wenjack*

In 1966, twelve-year-old Charlie Wenjack ran away from a residential school, bound for his home community. He collapsed and died of hunger shortly thereafter. A theatre was named in his honour at Trent University, in Peterborough, Ontario. Outside of the hall is a plaque with the following inscription:

NAMED IN MEMORY OF CHARLIE WENJACK

An Ojibwa Indian attending residential school in Kenora, Ontario separated from his home and family, he became lonely and ran away. He died trying to walk the four hundred miles between Kenora and the Martin Falls Reserve, his home in northwestern Ontario.

Born 19th of January 1954 died 22 October 1966.

ii. *Commemoration of the tuberculosis epidemic among the Inuit*

In the 1950s, many Inuit children travelled south to receive treatment for tuberculosis. These children ended up being permanently separated from their parents. In 1990, a cairn was erected at St. Albert's Aboriginal Cemetery in Edmonton, Alberta to commemorate the Aboriginal and Inuit children who died in Charles Camsell Indian Hospital between 1946 and 1966. The memorial lists the names, places of birth and dates of death of 98 Inuit, Aboriginal and Métis patients. A movement is also underway to establish a granite monument at Woodland Cemetery in Hamilton, Ontario, to commemorate 33 Inuit patients who died in that city. Citizens of The Pas, Manitoba, are seeking to mark, with individual stones, the graves of patients who died at the Clearwater Lake Sanatorium.

iii. *The Survivor Monument project*

This is a project dedicated to designing, developing and establishing a bronze monument that acknowledges both the harm done by child abuse and the victories won by survivors. Founded by a therapist and sculptor, Dr. Michael C. Irving, who works with survivors of child abuse, the project includes public education campaigns and travelling exhibitions that display artwork and poetry created by children. The project is sponsored by the Canadian Centre for Abuse Awareness, a registered charity.[1]

   iv.   *Grosse Île and the Irish Memorial National Historical Site*

In the early 19th century, Grosse Île, Quebec, was used as a quarantine station for immigrant arrivals, as many were feared to, and did in fact carry infectious diseases from mainland Europe. Devastated by the Great Famine, large numbers of Irish people immigrated to Canada between 1845 and 1849. Thousands died at sea, thousands were buried at Grosse Île, and thousands died in Quebec, Montreal and Kingston. In 1984, the federal government recognised the island as a National Historic Site.

There are three memorials at the site. The first, the Celtic Cross, was built in 1909. This monument honours the memory of the Irish immigrants who died in 1847–48. Its trilingual inscription (English, French and Gaelic) tells the tale of the first Irish immigrants to Canada. The second memorial is a monument honouring the physicians who sacrificed their lives to help the immigrants. It too bears witness to the tragic events of 1847. The third memorial is the Irish Cemetery, which holds 6,000 of the island's over 7,000 burial plots.[2]

   v.   *Halifax Harbour Pier 21*

In recognition of the immigrants who arrived in Canada between 1928 and 1971, Pier 21 on Nova Scotia's Halifax Harbour has been designated an historic site. A commemorative plaque was unveiled there on August 17, 1999. The federal government (through the Atlantic Canada Opportunities Agency), the province of Nova Scotia, and the Halifax Regional Municipality have provided $4.5 million, with a matching $4.5 million raised from the private sector, to preserve this point of entry for thousands of immigrants and to develop an interpretive centre.

The Avoidance of Scandal

The [Archdiocesan] Commission is persuaded that the need to avoid scandal has played a part in the thinking of senior Archdiocesan administrators over the past generation or so. While such a policy may not be always and everywhere inappropriate it can lead to serious abuse. The original Greek word from which the English word "scandal" derives means something which causes people "to stumble". The traditional cultural and ecclesiastical concern for avoiding the spread of scandal is based on the view that if people see their leaders and those they admire doing evil things the tendency will be "to stumble" either by direct imitation of those evil actions or by being shocked into turning away from the good that may be associated even with those who do evil.

This traditional view, however, which gives priority to preventing the spread of scandal as a way to protect people and their children against failing into evil, has two fundamental fallacies if inappropriately employed. It is a further example of the kind of patriarchal thinking that robs people of their own authority and their right to judge for themselves.

The Report of the Archdiocesan Commission of Enquiry into the
Sexual Abuse of Children by Members of the Clergy, Volume One, at p.112

vi.   *National Film Board projects*

The National Film Board has produced an "internment and exile" film package. The films include *Shepherd's Pie and Sushi*, the story of the internment of Canadians of Japanese ancestry during World War II and *Freedom Had a Price*, the story of Ukrainian immigrants who suffered from discriminatory and repressive measures at the outbreak of World War I. The latter does so by means of archival footage, vintage photographs, survivor testimonials and historical commentary.

vii.   *Shoah Visual History Foundation record of survivors*

The mission of this foundation is to chronicle first-hand accounts of Holocaust survivors and eyewitnesses. More than 50,000 unedited statements have been taken, comprising over 100,000 hours of testimony. The multimedia archive is to be used as an educational and research tool, intended to be accessible to universities worldwide and through travelling exhibits. In addition, it's been designed with an eye to the development of scholarly curricula, educational CD-ROMs and study guides, as well as documentaries.[3]

viii.   *FreeToBe's*

FreeToBe's is the name of a website where survivors of abuse can post their stories of hardship so that others can read and learn about their experiences.[4]

ix.   *Banff National Park*

Parks Canada has installed interpretive panels at the Cave and Basin National Historic Site in Banff National Park, in Alberta, to highlight the contribution made to the park by Ukrainian internees who were forced to do hard labour in national parks during World War I.[5]

x.   *Museum of Afro-American History*

The Museum of Afro-American History in Boston, Massachusetts, is a not-for-profit institution dedicated to preserving, conserving and accurately interpreting the contribution of African-Americans to the New England area. It collects and exhibits significant artefacts, and maintains physical structures and sites that relate to the history of the African-American. It has preserved the African Meeting House on Beacon Hill, the oldest black church in the United States, built by free African-American artisans; the Abiel Smith School on Beacon Hill, the first publicly funded grammar school for black children in the country; and the Black Heritage Trail, a walking tour encompassing a collection of historic sites relating to the life of the free African-American community prior to the Civil War.[6]

xi.   Black Archives of Mid-America

The Black Archives, located in a firehouse in Kansas City, Missouri, is a non-profit organisation that serves as an educational resource and repository of African-American culture. It was created to collect and preserve the history of African-Americans in the Midwest. Along with sponsoring travelling exhibits, the organisation specialises in presenting research and in a critical examination of the culture of African-Americans, offering educational programs, research services and special projects of interest to the public.[7]

b.   Acknowledgement

One of the enduring harms of child abuse is that many who lived through it do not feel they can freely tell others of their experiences. They are afraid of the responses they might get: disbelief; blame; indifference; irritation; and the advice that they should forget the past and get on with their lives. Some recall the denial they faced and even the punishment they received when they tried to complain about abuse when it was happening; they also remember how these responses accentuated their feeling of powerlessness and isolation, effectively silencing them.

For these reasons, many survivors try hard to bury the past and move on. They do not share this part of their lives with partners, parents, or children. Often, they do not recognise the profound effect that abuse in childhood has had on them for years after the abuse has ended. But they must live daily with the harm they suffered and the silence that surrounds its cause. A small number of survivors do simply accept the past. They are able to talk about their experiences openly, and rebuild their lives. Yet they too, express a need to have the abuse they endured publicly acknowledged.

Against this backdrop, it is not hard to understand why those who experienced institutional child abuse want that abuse and the harms it caused to be publicly acknowledged. What is acknowledgement? It is naming the acts done and admitting that they were wrong. In effect, those seeking acknowledgement are, above all, "asking the wrongdoers to admit … that they know they violated moral standards".[8] To be complete, an acknowledgement must have three other features. It must be specific, not general, and forthright, not reticent; nothing less than a detailed and candid description of persons, places and acts is required. Second, it must demonstrate an understanding of the impact of the harms done; acknowledgement requires recognition of the consequences of the acts perpetrated. Third, it must also make clear that those who experienced the abuse were in no way responsible for it; acknowledgement means there can be no shifting of blame on to survivors.

An acknowledgement can cover all kinds of abuse. It may come from many sources. It can be directed to a specific person or to a more general audience. It can be given by a specific person, as when a perpetrator acknowledges to a former victim the wrongness of the physical or sexual abuse committed. It can also be given on behalf of a group, as when those responsible for an institution acknowledge what occurred there. So, for example, Aboriginal peoples want a collective acknowledgement that the residential school system was culturally abusive in its very conception. A number of statements from governments and churches do in fact contain such acknowledgements, often as part of an apology.

The Minister of Indian Affairs and Northern Development made the following observations in the federal government's Statement of Reconciliation:

> Sadly, our history with respect to the treatment of Aboriginal people is not something in which we can take pride. Attitudes of racial and cultural superiority led to a suppression of Aboriginal culture and values. As a country, we are burdened by past actions that resulted in weakening the identity of Aboriginal peoples, suppressing their languages and cultures, and outlawing spiritual practices. We must recognise the impact of these actions on the once self-sustaining nations that were

disaggregated, disrupted, limited or even destroyed by the dispossession of traditional territory, by the relocation of Aboriginal people, and by some provisions of the Indian Act. We must acknowledge that the result of these actions was the erosion of the political, economic and social systems of Aboriginal people and nations.[9]

In addition, an apology of the Oblate Conference of Canada to the First Nations of Canada included the following recognition:

> We apologize for the part we played in the cultural, ethnic, linguistic, and religious imperialism that was part of the mentality with which the peoples of Europe first met the Aboriginal peoples and which consistently has lurked behind the way the Native peoples of Canada have been treated by civil governments and by the churches. We were, naively, part of this mentality and were, in fact, often a key player in its implementation. We recognise that this mentality has, from the beginning, and ever since, continually threatened the cultural, linguistic, and religious traditions of the Native peoples.
>
> We recognise that many of the problems that beset Native communities today – high unemployment, alcoholism, family breakdown, domestic violence, spiraling suicide rates, lack of healthy self-esteem – are not so much the result of centuries of personal failure as they are the result of centuries of systemic imperialism. Any people stripped of its traditions as well as of its pride falls victim to precisely these social ills. For the part that we played, however inadvertent and naïve that participation might have been, in the setting up and maintaining of a system that stripped others of not only their lands but also of their cultural, linguistic, and religious traditions we sincerely apologize.[10]

A significant segment of the Deaf community also feels even today that full acknowledgement has not been forthcoming. They believe that their members have been (and are) subject to abuse because of the assumptions the hearing community has made about what is best for them. They classify being forced to vocalise rather than being educated in American Sign Language (or Langue des signes québecoise) as a form of education abuse. Similarly, they classify the staffing of schools with teachers and dormitory personnel who cannot sign as a form of abuse. For them, a first step is to acknowledge the harm caused by these assumptions. These views were summarised in a report of discussions that members of the Deaf community had with the Law Commission.

> Participants discussed how abuse of Deaf Children begins from the time of diagnosis and affects information given to parents, access to ASL, and access to education.

>> "And I'm just worried that they're not teaching children in an appropriate way."

>> "The focus was on the oral skills, and I wanted to read."

>> "We need to be really adamant that teachers are well qualified in the language of the Deaf community, that they're competent and fluent in the language and instruction".[11]

c. Apology

Acknowledging a wrong may imply apology for that wrong, but it is only one element of a meaningful apology. While not all survivors want an apology, especially if it is offered in lieu of other forms of redress, many identify receiving an apology as one of their highest priorities. What survivors seek from an apology is not a mechanical "I'm sorry that I hurt you" or "We're sorry that you suffered". The elements necessary for a meaningful apology have been described as follows:

- Acknowledgement of the wrong done;

- Accepting responsibility for the wrong that was done;

- The expression of sincere regret or remorse;

- Assurance that the wrong will not recur, and

- Reparation through concrete measures.

An apology reminds the wrongdoer of community norms because the apologiser admits to having violated them.

> By retelling the wrong and seeking acceptance, the apologiser assumes a position of vulnerability before not only the victims but also the larger community of literal or figurative witnesses.... Equally important is the adoption of a stance that grants power to the victims, power to accept, refuse, or ignore the apology.[12]

Criticism is frequently levelled at the call for apologies. Some say one cannot rewrite history by apologising for actions that, in their time, were considered legitimate. This is often said, for example, in connection with the assimilationist policy behind residential schools for Aboriginal children. Others say these wrongs occurred in the past, and if we were to apologise and compensate for every historic wrong there would be no end to the apologies and reparations.[13] Finally, some say that an apology is equivalent to an admission of legal liability and therefore cannot be risked. These are spurious arguments.

First, the assertion that we should not apologise for conduct that was acceptable at the time it occurred misconceives the character of the wrongs committed. In most cases, the actions for which an apology is being sought now are, and always have been, unambiguously wrong. Violent physical assaults and sexual abuse were never acceptable in institutions. Moreover, there is a difference between apologising for a specific harm that is and always has been wrong, and apologising for a policy that is now seen to have been misguided. The nature of the apology for the second should in no way diminish the content and the force of an apology for the first.

Second, apologies do not rewrite history – quite the contrary. They aim to facilitate reconciliation and healing by honestly facing up to the harms of the past. And while the harms may, in some cases, be historically distant, their effects are a fact of life that survivors and those around them continue to live with daily. The sad truth is that, as a society, we are living with the fallout from the abuse of children in institutions: through the intergenerational effects of poor parenting or domestic violence; the low educational levels and diminished life skills of many survivors; and the disproportionate numbers of survivors who spend time in correctional facilities. An apology is a step in the healing process, and should be understood as a move towards a better future, rather than as a fruitless hearkening back to an unhappy but unchangeable past.

Third, whether or not an apology is an admission of liability depends on the nature of the apology. Certainly, an apology could be entered as evidence in a court proceeding. But the weight that it will be given depends on how specific it is with respect to particular acts of wrong-doing.[14] An apology is not, of itself, an admission of legal liability.

Where an apology is more than just a spontaneous utterance but is meant to be an attempt, in good faith, to respond to the needs of the recipient or recipients, those offering it should keep the following factors in mind. The apology should, if at all possible, be based on first-hand knowledge and involve an explicit naming of the harms suffered by an individual or a group. It should be in the form that the person or group desires (*e.g.*, private, personalised, written, public). It should be delivered by the person the recipients believe is the most appropriate one to do so. A one-on-one apology may be most effective when it comes from the actual perpetrator. An apology delivered in a representative capacity on behalf of an organisation or government is best coming from the highest level. The higher the stature or authority of the person apologising is, the greater the credibility of the apology.

Apologies must be delivered in a timely way, keeping in mind that many survivors have been waiting many years, even decades, since the wrongdoing took place. Years of denial are no excuse for not apologising. An apology can still be meaningful, even when years have elapsed.

Apologies must also be culturally sensitive and otherwise appropriate to the person or group to whom they are addressed. So, for example, where a Christian church delivers an apology to its own members, references to Christian values and beliefs are entirely appropriate. Where it addresses an apology to an Aboriginal community whose members may not be predominantly Christian, references to values and beliefs would more appropriately draw on native spirituality or other, more universal references. In this situation, the apology must at the same time express confession and contrition in a language that commits the person or group apologising to a moral position within their own framework of belief, while also committing them to a moral position within the spiritual context of those who are receiving the apology.

Finally, it is not up to the person delivering the apology to decide what should be the appropriate reaction of the person to whom the apology is offered. Survivors express the need for an apology; they alone are able to determine if it is meaningful and if it will be accepted. A true

On another occasion, four or five boys walked three or four miles into town along the railroad tracks. Critchley caught them about midnight. He made them strip naked and run back to the home without clothes or shoes in the headlights of Critchley's truck. The next day, Critchley came into L.K.'s cabin and told him it was his fault they had ran away. When L.K. complained that the soles of his feet were numb, Critchley grabbed his feet and placed them on the woodstove. Mrs. Critchley later brought L.K. some spray for his feet because they were burned so badly he was unable to walk on them.

C.A. v. Critchley Supreme Court of British Columbia, 1997

Critchley took the boy to Vancouver to do some Christmas shopping. After visiting C.A.'s parents briefly, Critchley took the boy to the Holiday Inn in Vancouver where he told the boy to represent himself as Critchley's son. When they got to their room, he told the boy that unless he did everything he was told, Critchley would throw him out the window and say that he had tried to escape. Critchley inflicted oral and anal sex upon the boy repeatedly over three or four days. Critchley told him that he loved him but that if C.A. told anyone, he would kill the boy and Critchley would go to jail. On the way back, about a mile from Arden Park, he made C.A. perform oral sex in the truck. C.A. said after that, Critchley forced sex on him every day.

C.A. v. Critchley, Supreme Court of British Columbia, 1997 apology comprises a complex set of elements that, together, can succeed in shifting the power between the parties, restoring the dignity of the survivor, and opening the way to reconciliation.[15]

d.   Accountability

Acknowledgement and apology are important to survivors because they affirm the truth of what survivors experienced as children in an institution. It is possible, however, to acknowledge that a specific harm was done without identifying who actually committed the harm. The same holds true with an apology. Acknowledgement and apology may be sufficient for some who experienced abuse. Others need to see individual people held to account; this is true whether or not the perpetrator of the abuse is still alive.

The desire for explicit accountability is not only directed at those who actually inflicted the injuries and abuse. It extends to those (for example, co-workers) who chose to protect the abuser or the institution, rather than the children in their care. It extends to those (for example, supervisors or heads of institutions) who did not investigate the complaints of children in their care because they could not, or would not believe them. And it extends to those (for example, boards of directors and government officials) who permitted institutions to operate without adequate processes of internal oversight in place.

Accountability should not necessarily be seen as synonymous with punishment or the imposition of liability. Some survivors may be satisfied just to see the record set straight and the perpetrators identified; at a minimum, this would expose the disbelief and denial of those in authority at the time the abuse took place. There is, in other words, value in making findings of accountability, even if legal liability is not attached to those findings. In fact, there are times when the law is powerless to impose civil liability despite the acknowledgement of personal responsibility; this happens, for example, when a claim for damages is barred by a statute of limitations.

In certain circumstances it is worthwhile to cease the pursuit of punishment, simply in order to arrive at the truth. This may be necessary or useful in cases where those who are potentially liable also hold most of the detailed information required to establish accountability. The rationale for a number of truth and reconciliation commissions lies in this realisation.[16] Where the model of accountability without liability is chosen, care must be taken to ensure that clear criteria are used to establish accountability. This is because people falsely or unjustly linked to child abuse will suffer the serious social stigma of those accusations, even if they are never exposed to legal liability.

There is, of course, a strong desire on the part of many survivors to see those who abused them brought to justice through a criminal prosecution. A finding of criminal guilt is one of society's most powerful mechanisms for holding people to account for their actions. Moreover, some survivors believe that explicit punishment of abusers is a necessary part of their own healing process. They therefore seek direct input into the process of determining what punishment would be appropriate for convicted abusers – for example, by submitting victim impact statements.

Survivors also want to identify and hold accountable those who have remained nameless and faceless. Who were the officials in the ministries of child welfare or social services who were responsible for monitoring the conditions in the training schools, schools for the Deaf or the blind, residential schools and health care facilities? Who were the superiors in the religious orders that moved Brothers or priests from place to place but continued to allow them to work with children? In these cases, a criminal prosecution may not be possible. But administrative hearings and sanctions – both for public and religious officials – usually are, and they too are explicit processes for holding those in authority accountable for their negligence or willful blindness.

The need of survivors for accountability is more than just a desire for revenge through the punishment of perpetrators. Indeed, revenge is a motive mentioned by only a few survivors. Rather, they seek the public denunciation of perpetrators and of the whole network of people who made it possible for abusive situations to develop, and to continue for several years or even decades.

e. Access to therapy or counselling

The trauma of child abuse often has profound consequences for survivors. The nature and seriousness of these consequences depend on many factors, including: the type of abuse; the age when it began; its duration; the relationship of the perpetrator to the child; the age when the abuse was disclosed; the reaction of others to the disclosure; *etc.* Coming to understand the connections between one's experience of use as a child and one's behaviour as an adult can be a lengthy and complex process.

Survivors need help to make that journey, once they are ready to embark on it. The help must come from a person or persons that they trust. It could be a health care professional, or a traditional Aboriginal healer. It could be a community worker, or even a survivor who has gone through a similar experience. While professional qualifications are important, they are not always the primary consideration. In a submission to the Commission, members of the Deaf community expressed this idea in the following way:

> Maybe Deaf people don't want to go through an interpreter, they'd rather have one-on-one therapy with a therapist they feel comfortable with, and who signs.

> Deaf people often have more life experience and have the experience of living as a Deaf person, and may not have a piece of paper to be credible in the Hearing society's eyes.

> So we have to look at our own community. I guess, in other words, we're the doctors, we're the professionals, we're the ones that know that information.[17]

The need for therapy or counselling has two dimensions: immediate support and long-term support. Events sometimes thrust survivors into a direct confrontation with their past for which they may not be ready, as when a police investigator unexpectedly arrives at their doorstep, or when they are called to testify at a criminal trial. In such circumstances, survivors may need access to immediate and ongoing support to deal with the memories triggered by the investigation, by a public inquiry, or by facing an abuser in court and being cross-examined about the abuse. Support is necessary from the moment survivors are drawn into an investigation or inquiry. It cannot await the outcome of a judicial proceeding or the conclusion of negotiations for a compensation package.

This support may consist of assistance in organising and running a mutual aid group for those who attended a particular institution. It may involve providing victim service coordinators to help those called on to testify in criminal proceedings. What is important is that when survivors are encouraged or compelled to disclose experiences of past abuse, they must not be left on their own to deal with the personal stresses that may develop after their participation.

In addition to these situational needs for therapy, survivors need access to long-term therapy and counselling in order to work through the emotional, psychological and other consequences of child abuse. This need is not necessarily linked to or triggered by any legal proceeding or redress program. It is simply part of the healing that survivors require in order to overcome the harm caused by the abuse. Some may require help in conquering addictions to alcohol and drugs before they can even begin to tackle their emotional and psychological problems. Some may have become abusers themselves. These kinds of problems are not easily resolved, nor are the behaviours that sustain them easily changed.

No one can dictate when people should seek therapy and no one can dictate when it must end. Individuals must have the time that they require to heal. This is not to say that all survivors need or want therapy. Some have been able to surmount the effects of abuse on their own. Others wish to forget the past, and cannot, or will not speak of it. But many need to understand their experiences and the impact of those experiences on them, in order to achieve greater peace in their lives. For them, therapy or counselling is likely to be a necessary part of the healing process.

f.   Access to education or training

In certain cases, one consequence of institutional abuse is that some children did not receive an adequate education. This situation is not a comment on the quality of education offered, but on the lost educational opportunities directly linked to abuse of some kind. Many who suffered physical or sexual abuse found it hard to concentrate in class or to study. Others were poorly educated because they were misplaced. In the case of the "Children of Duplessis", for example, loss of education was due to their being placed in a psychiatric facility rather than an orphanage or a school. In the case of certain residential schools for Aboriginal children, loss of education was due to the amount of time allotted to manual or other labour rather than to studies. Even if the abuse itself did not restrict a child's access to classes, it may well have undermined his or her ability to learn.

Whatever the cause, certain survivors of institutional child abuse entered adulthood with little education and very poor vocational skills. Younger survivors, in particular, want the opportunity to upgrade their education; for example, by obtaining a high school diploma or a vocational certificate. Many survivors see education as a significant step toward asserting greater control over their lives. Improved qualifications or new vocational skills open the way to financial independence, perhaps for the first time. The increased autonomy, and opportunity to make real choices that is provided by an education, can be an important step in overcoming some of the harm caused by abuse.

Returning to school as an adult can be a difficult experience. It is likely to be especially stressful if the setting is reminiscent of the settings of one's abuse as a child. Low self-esteem may also make it hard for survivors to believe they can handle further education. Special care must be taken to ensure that survivors are made aware of the educational opportunities open to them, and of the various support services available in the educational facilities offering these opportunities.

Some survivors desire access to education not for vocational reasons, but for cultural ones. For example, Aboriginal survivors may wish to learn their native languages and spiritual practices from Elders. Deaf survivors may wish to improve their ability in American Sign Language or Langue des signes québécoise in order to feel more at home in the Deaf community. It should be for survivors themselves to determine how best to recover the education of which they were deprived as children.

g. Financial compensation

Some descriptions of the current needs of survivors will downplay the importance of financial compensation, emphasising instead acknowledgement, apology, accountability, therapy and education. There is no reason to do so. Money is the way the Canadian legal system compensates people for injuries wrongfully caused by others. Of course, survivors must be able to demonstrate, according to the standards set by whatever judicial or extra-judicial process is being invoked, that they were injured by the wrongs committed against them. But once they have fulfilled that obligation, they are entitled to compensation, just like all other victims of a crime or a civil wrong.

Financial compensation is, in some ways, the most basic material need of survivors, because it has the potential to provide for a range of other needs, such as therapy and education. It is also one of the most contentious needs. Fear of the potential size of valid claims for compensation by survivors of institutional child abuse is one of the main barriers to resolving these claims. It explains, at least in part, the caution with which governments, church organisations and others have reacted to the wave of civil actions launched over the last few years.[18]

It is not easy to establish the right amount of compensation for injuries that cannot be compensated by money, in any true sense. Yet courts perform these calculations every day in ordinary civil actions for damages. What is fair and reasonable as financial compensation for the abuse experienced by children in institutions will vary depending on the redress process adopted and the jurisdiction in which it takes place. While the Supreme Court of Canada has provided certain broad guidelines for damage awards in civil cases,[19] judges still have a broad discretion in assessing damages.[20]

Consistency in the amounts awarded to survivors is difficult to achieve. Differences in the cost of living and the value of lost wages in different provinces are among the factors that can lead to discrepancies in awards. Conversely, attempting to achieve consistency by putting a monetary value on the different kinds or degrees of abuse can dehumanise survivors by subjecting them to formulae or tables for compensation that do not really reflect their unique experience.

The judicial assessment of damages for personal injury has become a fine art in which consistency is, at best, relative. For this reason, one cannot expect absolute consistency in non-judicial processes, such as when claims are settled prior to judgement. In these situations, the parties are not bound by any fixed criteria or amounts, and information on settlements reached in similar cases is usually confidential. Consistency can be even more elusive in the case of payments made through non-court based compensation processes where neither the criteria for the decision nor the amount of the awards is disclosed. What is certain, however, is that judicial assessments of damages are almost always significantly higher that those awarded under administrative compensation programs.

Finding the most appropriate framework for paying compensation has also proved difficult. Some survivors see no reason why they should not receive money in a lump sum, just like anyone else who is awarded damages for a harm suffered. Others may feel that this unduly exposes them to requests from friends and neighbours to share the award. They would prefer to receive money on a periodic basis in smaller amounts. Whatever method of payment is adopted, survivors also have a need to receive appropriate information and financial counselling about savings and investment options open to them.

Survivors justly feel that they deserve to be compensated for the injuries they have suffered. In giving expression to this need, they wish to see their claims validated by the legal system in the same way as other claims for compensation for injuries. This may in fact be more important to them than concerns about possible discrepancies in awards among themselves, and the manner in which the awards are paid.

> I have a good job. I don't need the money. It's for my grandchildren. I don't want them to suffer the way I did.
>
> *Quoted in The Vision to Reconcile: Process Report on the Helpline Reconciliation Model Agreement by Doug Roche and Ben Hoffman, at p.21*

> Reconciliation is a great human quality. One of the more important. Those with power know it can be neglected, abased, deformed, ridiculed in the name of various emotional or financial imperatives. Reconciliation is the most difficult of human states to defend. It is dependent on an acceptance of the idea of the public good. It invariably stands in the way of power, narrow self-interest and self-righteousness.
>
> *– John Ralston Saul,*
> *Reflections of a Siamese Twin – Canada at the End of the Twentieth Century, at p.289*

h.   Prevention and public awareness

Many adult survivors who shared with the Law Commission their views about how best to respond to the harm they suffered underscored the importance of ensuring that new generations of children are spared from abuse – whether committed in an institution or elsewhere. Participants in a discussion group involving members of the Deaf community, for instance, were very concerned about the safety of Deaf children attending residential schools at the present time, and in the future.[21] They said, for example: "I hope that these things will never happen to our Deaf children in the future"; "I want the cycle to end here"; and "It's got to stop".[22]

Some survivors have translated their concerns into specific actions, such as helping to increase public knowledge and promoting prevention. A number of survivors of the Grandview training school for girls in Ontario, for example, collaborated in the production of the video "Until Someone Listens" to raise community awareness of the continuing danger of institutional abuse. The discussion guide accompanying the video states that: "The Grandview survivors themselves hope their experiences can be instrumental in the prevention of hurt and abuse to other children."[23]

Advocating and sometimes becoming actively engaged in developing strategies and measures to prevent institutional child abuse are important to many survivors. Helping to educate others to ensure that better preventive practices are put in place may even contribute to an individual's personal healing. Judith Herman, a doctor who has written about trauma and recovery, observes that survivors of a personal trauma often become involved in social action and make it their "mission" to raise public awareness. She notes that such activities can have significant therapeutic effects:

> "Survivors undertake to speak about the unspeakable in public in the belief that this will help others.... Although giving to others is the essence of the survivor mission, those who practice it recognise that they do so for their own healing."[24]

Increasing public knowledge of institutional child abuse as a continuing social problem meets a need felt by many survivors. Believing that there is the societal will to prevent further harm is an important part of survivors' everyday struggle to overcome the damage done to them.[25]

3. Needs of Families

There are many ways in which members of a survivor's family can be affected by institutional child abuse. Some parents, particularly those whose children had special needs, sent their children away to school willingly, believing it was in the child's best interests to do so. In many instances, these parents did not discover until years later that their children had been abused. Some Deaf children with hearing parents believed that their parents knew of the abuse that was taking place at school, but sent them back anyway. As a result, these children became alienated from their parents and blamed them for the abuse they suffered. Their parents, in turn, now feel guilty for having failed to protect their children. In some cases the families are able to reconcile, but not always.

For Aboriginal parents who may have felt they had no choice but to send their children to residential schools, the guilt may be compounded. Often, the parents themselves had been residential school students. Therefore, they knew what experiences might await their children. However, where no schooling was available locally, and where there was a threat of fine or imprisonment for failure to surrender their children, parents may not have been in a position to resist.

Children who were physically and sexually abused while away from home frequently brought the effects of that abuse back to their families. Some abused children became abusers themselves, directing their violent behaviour at parents, siblings, partners and even their own children. Family members may suffer without even being aware of the abuser's own previous abuse in residential institutions.

In addition to experiencing the effects of physical and sexual abuse, the families of Aboriginal survivors also suffered the alienation of children who lost their language and their cultural heritage at residential schools. For these reasons, survivors and their family members share many of the same needs. Spiritually, they would benefit from an acknowledgement of the consequences of abuse, and an apology. Counselling to better understand and cope with the behaviour of survivors and to deal with harms survivors may have caused them is also a key need felt by many family members. Finally, because they have lived first-hand the spill-over effects of abuse, members of survivors' families are especially attuned to the need to see preventive measures and public awareness campaigns put into effect.

4.   Needs of Communities

The damage caused by institutional child abuse, particularly abuse that has continued over a period of years or through more than one generation, extends beyond the individual survivors and their families: it affects entire communities. Communities are groups of people who live in a particular area or who identify with each other on the basis of common interests or common characteristics. In this sense, the idea of community would include, for example, a neighbourhood, an Inuit village, an Aboriginal nation, the Deaf community, or the community known as the "Children of Duplessis".

A community can be affected by institutional child abuse in profound and subtle ways, directly and indirectly. The difficulties experienced by the Deaf community, for instance, have been significant. They are exacerbated by the relative isolation of community members from resources, such as therapy, that are available in the hearing community. In a community where virtually all members have passed through the same institution, and many have been subjected to serious levels of abuse, in particular sexual abuse, it is hard to locate where an effective healing process might begin.

Small or tightly-knit communities are especially vulnerable to the ripple effects of institutional child abuse. They must integrate victims back into a community that may already contain victim-offenders. Even when the survivor's destructive behaviour is turned inward, communities will have to cope with the consequences. They must rebuild a sense of confidence in the community as a safe place for disclosure and healing. They must repair the rifts that have been caused by recriminations among community members where some survivors have themselves become perpetrators of abuse. They must replace (in the case of Aboriginal communities) or reform (in the case of the Deaf community) the institutions where the abuse took place, because the educational function performed by those institutions remains necessary and important.

A population disproportionately prone to substance abuse and exhibiting suicidal tendencies puts enormous pressure on the healing resources of small, close-knit or isolated communities. Because many survivors simply do not have the education or life skills to become self-sufficient, this, in turn, places additional economic stress on the community.

Small or close-knit communities have needs much like those of families. Remembrance and acknowledgement of their ongoing suffering is a first step to their empowerment. They may also need financial assistance to hire community workers and therapists to provide the support services and programs necessary to overcome the social and economic side effects of child abuse. These programs can also increase public awareness and promote prevention as a community goal.

5.   Particular Needs of Aboriginal Communities and Peoples

Aboriginal communities and peoples have special needs in their efforts to deal with the aftermath of institutional child abuse. Some Aboriginal children were physically and sexually abused in day schools; some were abused in training schools, orphanages and sanitoria; however, the abuse that occurred in residential schools presents a unique challenge. There, many Aboriginal children were physically and sexually abused. There, they also suffered emotionally and psychologically from being abused or from witnessing abuse. But the extent of the harm done was even broader than this. Because the residential school system was designed to "civilise" and to assimilate the Aboriginal population, it amounted to nothing less than an attack on Aboriginal people as a whole. For this reason, it is important to recognise and respond to the special needs of Aboriginal communities and peoples.

When Aboriginal children were removed from their families and placed in residential schools, a crucial link in the transmission of cultural values and practices was weakened. Those who were forced to speak in only English or French sometimes lost their ability to communicate effectively with their parents. These children were no longer able to learn from their parents and extended families. This situation of intergenerational disconnection has contributed to poverty, substance abuse, lack of parenting skills, spiritual and cultural alienation, psychological and emotional problems, and violence and crime in Aboriginal communities. It has also diminished the capacity of Aboriginal communities to heal those who were physically and sexually abused.

What type of assistance and support do Aboriginal communities need to address the fallout from residential schools? Of course, each community has to determine its own needs, but some general points can be made. One legacy of the residential school experience is that Aboriginal children are disproportionately represented even today in foster homes and youth detention facilities. The rebuilding of cultural traditions is a key step to overcoming this problem. This process of rebuilding will require that resources be made available directly to Aboriginal communities so that they can develop language, cultural, spiritual and educational programs. In the more immediate context, however, communities need counsellors and therapists who can work with Aboriginal children and adults in a culturally appropriate manner.

Aboriginal peoples, as a whole, also have needs that come out of the residential school experience. As the Royal Commission on Aboriginal Peoples noted, acknowledgement, apologies and the creation of memorials are important elements of healing. A memorial could be achieved through the institution of a national repository that would act as a clearinghouse of information for researchers and educators. Ideally, it would have the power to conduct independent research, collect an oral history of the experiences of former residents, and to conduct public education programs on the history and effects of residential schools. This repository would also document cases of physical and sexual abuse, both at residential and day schools. The more Canadians learn of the full range of abuse Aboriginal children suffered, the more they will understand the destructive influence of the residential school system. This, in turn, will lead to a better appreciation of why significant steps must now be taken to help survivors and their communities.

6.   Societal Needs: Prevention and Public Education

The abuse of children in institutions or out-of-home care has adversely affected not only the children involved, their families and communities, but also Canadian society in general.

Society's main needs today are for greater public awareness of the risk of abuse that children in out-of-home care face, and for better strategies to prevent this abuse. While Canadians are familiar with the most notorious occurrences of institutional child abuse, they tend to see it as a pathology of the past and as the result of the actions of a few "bad apples", rather than as continuing and a systemic problem. Public perceptions need to change.

Rix Rogers, formerly special adviser to the Minister of National Health and Welfare on the issue of child sexual abuse, noted in 1990 that Canadians were not prepared to endorse a national strategy to heighten awareness of the issue. He did, however, recommend government support for other forms of public awareness programs such as training films and documentaries.[26]

Canada is a signatory to the United Nations *Convention on the Rights of the Child*, and played a leading role in convening the 1990 World Summit for Children.[27] Yet our lack of information about child abuse in institutional and out-of-home care settings indicates that we may not be managing the risks of abuse as well as we could. Education and prevention are goals that will benefit not only the children of today and in the future, but also yesterday's children, whom society failed to protect from this abuse. This is a key societal need that must be met if we are to now do justice to adult survivors of institutional child abuse.

---

[1]   Online: The Survivor Monument Project <http://www.childabusemonument.org> (date accessed: 9 November 1999).

[2]   Online: Parks Canada-National Historic Sites <http://parcscanada.risq.qc.ca/grosse_ile> (date accessed: 9 November 1999).

3   Online: Survivors of the Shoah Visual History Foundation <http://www.vhf.org/> (date accessed: 9 November 1999).

4   Online: Free To Be's <www.geocities.com/HotSprings/1124/index.html> (date accessed: 9 November 1999).

5   Online: Parks Canada <http://www.worldweb.com/ParksCanada-Banff/ intern.html> (date accessed: 9 November 1999).

6   Online: Museum of Afro American History <http://www.afroammuseum.org/ about.htm> (date accessed: 9 November 1999).

7   Online: Black Archives of Mid-America <http://www.blackarchives.org/> (date accessed: 9 November 1999).

8   See Law Commission of Canada, *Apologising for Serious Wrongdoing: Social, Psychological and Legal Considerations* by S. Alter (Ottawa: Law Commission of Canada, 1999) at the sections entitled "Acknowledgement of the Wrong Done" and "Accepting Responsibility for the Wrong Done". Available in hard copy from the Law Commission of Canada and online: <http://www.lcc.gc.ca>.

9   "Statement of Reconciliation" included in an Address by the Honourable Jane Stewart, Minister of Indian Affairs and Northern Development on the occasion of the unveiling of *Gathering Strength – Canada's Aboriginal Action Plan* (Ottawa: Department of Indian Affairs and Northern Development, 7 January 1998), online: Indian and Northern Affairs Canada <http://www.inac.gc.ca/info/ speeches/jan98/action.html> (date accessed: 16 November 1999) [hereinafter "Statement of Reconciliation"].

10 The Missionary Oblates of Mary Immaculate (1991) – Apology from the President of the Oblate Conference of Canada, the Reverend Doug Crosby, on behalf of the 1200 Catholic Missionary Oblates of Mary Immaculate living and ministering in Canada, for the role played by the Oblates in running Native Residential Schools. See Reverend D. Crosby OMI, "An Apology to the First Nations of Canada by the Oblate Conference of Canada" (Edmonton: Oblate Conference of Canada, 1991). For excerpts of this apology see Assembly of First Nations Health Secretariat, *Residential Schools Update* (Ottawa: Assembly of First Nations, March 1998) at 20.

11 L. Hill, "Enough is Enough – Report on a Facilitated Discussion Group Involving the Deaf Community Responding to the Minister's Reference on Institutuional Child Abuse" (March 1999) [unpublished research report archived at the Law Commission of Canada] at 25, 27.

12 M. Minow, *Between Vengeance and Forgiveness – Facing History after Genocide and Mass Violence* (Boston: Beacon Press, 1998) at 114-115.

[13] Examples of this attitude were displayed in the press when Premier Lucien Bouchard offered to provide money to the Duplessis Orphans in March of 1999. See J. Simpson, "The Trouble with Trying to Compensate Groups for Historical Wrongs" *The Globe and Mail* (14 June 1990) A16. In a similar vein, see L. Gagnon, "Le protecteur des 'orphelins' " *La Presse* (11 March 1999) B3.

[14] For a more detailed discussion of the legal implications of apology, see Alter, *supra* note 8, "Apologising for Serious Wrongdoing: Social, Psychological and Legal Considerations" in the section that compares apologies made through court based and non-court based processes.

[15] A careful analysis of the forms and meaning of apologies is presented in N. Tavuchis, *Mea Culpa – A Sociology of Apology and Reconciliation* (Stanford: Stanford University Press, 1991)

[16] See M. Gannage, *An International Perspective: A Review And Analysis Of Approaches To Addressing Past Institutional Or Systemic Abuse In Selected Countries* (Ottawa: Law Commission of Canada, 1998). Available in hard copy from the Law Commission of Canada and online: <http://www.lcc.gc.ca>.

[17] Hill, *supra* note 11 at 39 and 48.

[18] For an idea of the range of damage awards in cases of child abuse in institutions, see Law Commission of Canada, *Institutional Child Abuse in Canada – Civil Cases* by G. Shea (Ottawa: Law Commission of Canada, 1999). Available in hard copy from the Law Commission of Canada and online: <http://www.lcc.gc.ca>.

[19] For example, as it did in the case of the "trilogy": *Andrews* v. *Grand & Toy Alberta Ltd.*, [1978] 2 S.C.R. 229; *Arnold* v. *Teno*, [1978] 2 S.C.R. 287; and *Thornton* v. *Board of School Trustees of School District No. 57 (Prince George)*, [1978] 2 S.C.R. 267.

[20] Shea, *supra* note 18.

[21] Hill, *supra* note 11 at 45.

[22] *Ibid.* at 46.

[23] L. Sky & V. Sparks, *Until Someone Listens* (Work Book) (Toronto: Skyworks Charitable Foundation,1999) at 7 [hereinafter Until Someone Listens draft discussion guide]. See also *Until Someone Listens – Recovering from Institutional Child Abuse* produced for the Grandview Survivors' Support Group (Toronto: Laura Sky and Skyworks Charitable Foundation, 1999) 120 min.

[24] J. Lewis Herman, *Trauma and Recovery* (NY: Harper Collins, 1992) at 208 and 209.

[25] *Until Someone Listens* draft discussion guide, *supra* note 23 at 17.

26 R. Rogers, *The Report of the Special Advisor to the Minister of National Health and Welfare on Child Sexual Abuse in Canada – Reaching for Solutions* (Ottawa: Canada Communication Group, 1990) at 47.

27 United Nations Committee on the Rights of the Child, *Consideration of Reports Submitted by States Parties Under Article 44 of the Convention – Concluding Observations of the Committee on the Rights of the Child: Canada* (9 June 1995) at 1, online: Department of Canadian Heritage, The Human Rights Directorate <http://www.pch.gc.ca/ddp-hrd/english/rotc/concobs.htm> (date accessed: 9 November 1999).

Part II – Responses

A. Criteria of Assessment, Approaches to Redress and Guiding Principles

The Commission believes that to properly assess possible responses to past institutional child abuse, it must begin by examining the various objectives and purposes to be pursued. First among these is addressing the needs of survivors. Only with a clear understanding of these needs, expressed by survivors themselves, can the Commission evaluate different responses with any confidence.

Survivors have a broad range of needs. Of course, not all needs are common to all survivors – healing is a highly individual experience. But all needs must be accounted for. In addition, many families and communities have been profoundly damaged by institutional child abuse. It is important to recognise the harm suffered by these families and communities, and by Aboriginal peoples, in order to address their distinct needs. Finally, Canadian society itself has suffered from the scourge of institutional child abuse and has its own needs.

The discussion in Part I.D of this Report highlights the values that should underpin attempts to redress the harm that has been done to survivors. It also identifies the types of needs that must be met to further both the individual and the collective healing process – for survivors, their families and their communities.

1. Criteria for Assessing Redress Processes

The Commission sees the needs set out in Part I.D as the foundation for its assessment of the various approaches to redress that can be made available to survivors. However, it is not sufficient to evaluate a process solely according to how well it meets the needs of survivors, their families and communities. The Minister asked the Commission to make suggestions for addressing the issue in a "responsible and fair way". A key concern is also to find or create appropriate remedies that will promote reconciliation and healing. Other considerations that must be built into the assessment process include equity and procedural fairness for everyone involved in allegations of abuse, as well as public acceptability, fiscal responsibility, and goals of prevention and public education.

With all these considerations in mind, the Commission developed eight general criteria for evaluating existing and potential redress processes for survivors of institutional child abuse. These criteria give concrete expression to the two values that the Commission believes must infuse all approaches to redress: respect and engagement; and information and support.

The following are the criteria that the Commission sees as providing an appropriate analytical grid for its comparative assessment of redress processes.

- **Respect, engagement and informed choice** – Does the process satisfy the values of respect and engagement? Does it offer the information necessary for survivors to make an informed decision about participating in the process?

- **Fact-finding** – Can the process uncover all the important facts to validate whether abuse took place? Does it help establish an understanding of how the abuse occurred?

- **Accountability** – Do those administering the process have the authority to hold people and organisations to account for their conduct?

- **Fairness** – Is the process fair to all parties directly and indirectly affected by it – whether as claimants, defendants, witnesses or in some other capacity?

- **Acknowledgement, apology and reconciliation** – Does the process promote acknowledgement, apology and reconciliation in cases where abuse has occurred?

- **Compensation, counselling and education** – Can the process lead to outcomes that address the needs of survivors for financial compensation, counselling, therapy, education and training?

- **Needs of families, communities and peoples** – Can the process meet the needs of the families of those who were abused as children as well as the needs of communities and peoples?

- **Prevention and public education** – Does the process promote public education about institutional child abuse and contribute to prevention?

2. Approaches to Redress

The Minister's letter gave the Commission a broad discretion to select the approaches to redress that it would examine and assess. For this reason, the Commission did not feel constrained to look just at existing judicial processes. Part II surveys a range of current approaches that could be used to provide some form of redress for those who were harmed. It also considers models of redress that have not, to date, been generally applied to cases of institutional child abuse.

The Commission begins by assessing the two classic legal responses for righting a wrong through the courts: the criminal justice process, which focusses on the accountability of wrongdoers; and the civil justice system, through which injured persons can obtain financial compensation. Both these processes are not specifically meant to meet the needs of survivors of institutional child abuse. They are designed to cover all types of criminal and civil wrongs. Their common feature is that they are adversarial processes designed to establish wrongdoing or fault.

The Commission then considers two alternative, non-judicial responses: criminal injuries compensation programs, and *ex gratia* payments. These are, respectively, an administrative and an executive process. Their fundamental goal is to compensate people for harm suffered. Entitlement to receive compensation does not depend on a finding of guilt or liability against an alleged wrongdoer.

Next, the Commission examines a third kind of approach: processes in which public officials have, or are given, authority to investigate allegations of abuse. Ombudsman offices, provincial children's advocates or commissioners, commissions of inquiry, and truth and reconciliation-type commissions have no authority to establish guilt and punish wrongdoers, to pronounce on legal liability, or even to provide compensation. However, they do have extensive investigatory and advisory powers that enable them to determine whether and why harm occurred and to make systemic recommendations about how to prevent its continuation or recurrence. Most also have the authority to recommend the payment of compensation or some other form of redress when they feel that this is appropriate.

Not all approaches need to be established, administered and funded by the government or to involve the courts. The Commission explores a number of community-based alternatives that can complement official processes. These grass-roots initiatives are usually designed to address the impact of institutional child abuse in particular communities or in relation to particular institutions. They lack the formal structure and support of the State-run processes just noted, although they may receive some government or private funding. Their focus tends to be on providing redress through healing and community building.

After considering this spectrum of responses, the Commission concludes by reviewing a broad range of redress programs. For the purposes of this Report, redress programs are *ad hoc* responses developed specifically to address the claims of survivors of institutional child abuse. They may originate within the executive or the legislative branch of government, although they almost always involve negotiations with survivors or their representatives. The Commission begins by describing what has already been accomplished through redress programs and ends by imagining what else might be done. It sees redress programs as an opportunity to draw on those features of other approaches that appear most effective in meeting the needs of survivors, their families and their communities while respecting the other parties directly or indirectly affected. In this sense, redress programs can be individually crafted for specific situations in a manner that meets all the considerations mentioned by the Minister of Justice.

3.   Guiding Principles

The Commission's assessment of the different approaches available for responding to survivors has led it to formulate five general principles to govern the manner in which cases of institutional child abuse should be handled. These principles are intended to apply to all approaches, and are addressed to everyone who is involved in attempts to respond to institutional child abuse. They are directed not only to governments and to courts, but also speak to professional associations and their members, to religious organisations, to survivors and their families, and to the groups that represent them. Finally, they are meant for the public, whose support and understanding are vital to assuring that survivors receive appropriate and adequate redress.

These principles recur in the discussion of each approach that the Commission considers in this Part of the Report. They serve as a constant reminder that the central goal of any approach, whatever else it accomplishes, is to redress the harm suffered by survivors of institutional child abuse.

- Former residents of institutions should have the information they need to make informed decisions about which redress options to participate in.

Survivors seeking redress need information in order to select the option(s) best suited to their particular needs and desires. They must have some understanding of the criminal and civil justice systems, the mandate and purposes of other official processes such as criminal injuries compensation programs, ombudsman investigations and public inquiries, and the procedural mechanisms of any redress programs available to them. This information needs to be provided in a timely and impartial fashion, before survivors are required to choose how to proceed, or even whether to proceed. Two equally important types of information are required.

The first is detailed legal information. Because most approaches to redress involve the legal system – directly or indirectly – survivors need to know exactly what proceeding through civil and criminal justice processes involves, what remedies these processes offer, the costs they entail, and the time they take. This information, and answers to any other questions survivors might have, needs to be presented in an understandable, comprehensive, and impartial manner. Therefore, the information should not be provided by someone who has a personal professional stake in representing these potential plaintiffs in a civil action, who relies on them as witnesses in a criminal prosecution, or who counsels them as private clients in a therapeutic setting. Ideally, existing public agencies that offer services to victims (for example, sexual assault centres) could be used as vehicles for dispensing this information.

The second need is for contextual information. Former residents require information about how different approaches are likely to affect them personally. They should have the opportunity to hear from others who have gone through one or more of these processes. Understanding what the actual experience is like for a survivor is valuable information for someone trying to decide what redress option(s) to pursue.

- Former residents need support through the course of any process.

Confronting a difficult, in some cases traumatic, past is never an easy experience. Survivors seeking personal redress, or assisting the State by testifying in a criminal prosecution, may need psychological and emotional support so that their participation in a process does not unduly exacerbate the harm they have already suffered.

In the case of those who perform a civic duty by testifying at a criminal trial or by providing information to an Ombudsman or a public inquiry, the public interest in discovering wrongdoing and prosecuting the guilty more than justifies providing this support. In a civil action for damages, an administrative compensation program or an *ad hoc* redress program, the public interest in validating claims requires a degree of intrusiveness into a personal and painful past that, for survivors, can only be justified if they are properly supported.

- Those involved in conducting or administering different processes must have sufficient training to ensure that they understand the circumstances of survivors of institutional child abuse.

One assumes that officials involved in judicial processes – whether criminal or civil – will have the legal expertise to ensure that justice is done according to law. Necessarily, the police, prosecutors, lawyers and their investigators, clerks and judges will focus on the legal dimensions of their roles. Judicial processes rest on the assumption that any other persons involved – victims and witnesses, for example – will look after their own needs. This is, however, not a realistic assumption in the case of child abuse, especially for survivors. To the extent that officials are able to understand the needs of survivors, they can help to reduce the negative impacts of adversarial judicial proceedings or the inquisitorial processes of other types of inquiries and investigations.

It is not just those officials involved in traditional State-run processes who must be aware of the circumstances of survivors. Any community-based initiative or *ad hoc* redress program will draw on the knowledge, expertise and services of a wide range of persons. Not all will have specialized training in law or in the health and social service professions. Like everyone else, they will need training for awareness of the particular situation and needs of survivors.

- The response to institutional child abuse must be integrated, coordinated and subject to ongoing assessment and improvement.

Confronting the legacy of child abuse, and the harm it continues to cause, generates a sense of urgency. Such reactions are often translated into single path proposals, such as setting up a Claims Commissioner or a take-it-or-leave-it redress program. However commendable the desire to act, this desire must be translated into action across the entire range of legal and social services systems. On the other hand, inaction cannot be excused by characterising a problem as *social*, not *legal*, or *legal*, not *social*. Those involved in providing redress must co-ordinate their efforts to meet all the needs of survivors. They should draw on and support existing services or programs that may be able to respond to any of these needs.

Furthermore, one should not assume that different approaches to redress (no matter how innovative they may seem) can be perfectly designed in a single moment. Experience with existing approaches, or with the administration of new approaches, will provide insight into what works and what does not. This insight must then be used to improve existing processes and to develop new and even better *ad hoc* redress programs.

- Every effort must be made to minimise the potential harm of redress processes themselves.

In view of the pain already suffered by survivors, it is imperative that every process for providing redress or pursuing wrongdoers is carefully scrutinised to avoid compounding the harm done. Legal processes must be examined to determine whether present practices and procedures are unduly prejudicial to survivors for very little gain in the protection of the rights of alleged abusers. All processes involve a balancing of interests. Recognising the specific context of historical child abuse may lead to the conclusion that the balance needs to be restruck, and that these processes should be reformed, either in the specific context of past child abuse, or more generally.

When designing new processes, care must be taken not to repeat harmful aspects of existing processes simply through a failure of imagination. All efforts to establish new approaches must be undertaken with full acknowledgement that every redress process will profoundly affect the people caught up in it. To achieve this goal it is necessary to attend to the substantive values of respect, engagement, information and support for survivors, as well as to the complementary process values of choice, inclusiveness, equity, flexibility, appropriateness, and comprehensiveness.

4.   Organisation of this Part of the Report

This Part is written to provide an outline and assessment of different approaches to redress. Each approach is discussed by first offering a description of its main substantive and procedural features. This description is meant to provide the background for the Commission's assessment of the various approaches by reference to the eight criteria just elaborated.

The primary concern of the Commission in this Part is not to make comparative assessments of these approaches as against each other. The goal is, rather, to assess them on their own terms against a common standard. Only after this has been done is it possible to clarify the assumptions upon which each rests and to make comparative recommendations about their effectiveness in meeting needs of survivors while respecting the values reflected in the other criteria of assessment.

Each section of this Part concludes with a brief summary of how well the process under consideration meets the eight criteria. This summary is followed by specific recommendations intended to improve the way in which the process functions as a means for providing redress to survivors of institutional child abuse.

B. The Criminal Justice Process

1. Introduction

The primary goal of the Canadian criminal justice system is to provide a public forum for the recognition and punishment of wrongful conduct defined by Parliament as a crime. Its processes are designed to ensure a fair trial, to minimise the chances of an unjust conviction, and to impose an appropriate punishment upon individuals who have been convicted.

Historically, the criminal justice system was developed to forestall blood feuds and private retribution. Today, the criminal law is also viewed as a statement of society's core values. The State takes on the role of prosecutor and is responsible for proving that the accused has committed a crime. In the criminal justice process, the victim is not a party to the proceedings.

Accused persons are. Because their liberty is at stake, they have much to lose. Fairness requires that strict safeguards be put into place to balance the power of the State as prosecutor with the rights of those who are accused. Detailed procedural rules about the conduct of criminal investigations and prosecutions, many entrenched in the *Canadian Charter of Rights and Freedoms*, are intended to maintain this balance.[1]

2. Description

a. Complaints and investigations

Usually the criminal process starts when a citizen files a complaint with the police. The police then screen and investigate the complaint, laying charges where appropriate.[2] The person filing the complaint[3] is not an actual participant in the process. Rather, the complainant is just a potential witness who may be asked to provide his or her version of the facts at a trial. Once an initial complaint and statement are made to the police, the complainant is no longer involved in the investigation, except at the request of the police.

The goals of a police investigation are to determine whether there are reasonable grounds to believe that an offence has been committed, to gather evidence, and to identify the alleged offender. One of the main tools in a police investigation is the statement the police obtain from any individual who may have knowledge of the events being investigated. No one is obliged, in law, to cooperate with a police investigation. The police are not entitled to use anything stronger than persuasion to encourage potential witnesses to make statements. Given the evidentiary requirements of a criminal trial, and the requirement that the prosecution establish guilt beyond a reasonable doubt, the police may sometimes conclude that they do not have sufficient evidence to justify laying a charge even in cases where they believe the complainant.

In deciding what charges to lay, criminal justice officials may consider only what constituted an offense at the time the event took place. For example, in 1983, Canada's *Criminal Code* created a new offence of sexual assault. This offence is defined as an assault of a sexual nature committed by a person of either sex on another person of either sex. This offence would cover most cases of sexual abuse. But prior to 1983, the *Criminal Code* set out only offences like rape, attempted rape and indecent assault. Since the definition of rape in the *Criminal Code* did not include assaults by a male on another male, the sexual abuse of a male prior to 1983 would even today have to be prosecuted not as a sexual assault, but as an indecent assault, buggery or gross indecency, according to the facts.

In cases where the police decide not to lay charges, or recommend that the Crown not lay charges,[4] a citizen may initiate a prosecution after obtaining the authorisation of a justice of the peace.[5] This right to prosecute privately is said to be the ultimate safeguard against government inaction, bias, incompetence or corruption.[6] However, the State does retain a broad discretion to intervene. It can take over private prosecutions. It can also stop (or stay) a private prosecution when it determines that there is not a reasonable likelihood of obtaining a conviction, or that it is not in the public interest to proceed. In practice, a private citizen rarely conducts prosecutions.

A person suspected of having committed an offence, if arrested or detained, has the right to remain silent.[7] During the investigation, the police can look for material evidence. Citizens are protected from illegal entry, searches, and seizures. The police must first obtain judicial authorisation for a search warrant. The warrant can be issued only if there are reasonable and probable grounds to believe that an offence has been committed. Evidence obtained by an illegal search, entry or seizure can be excluded from the trial if its admission would bring the administration of justice into disrepute.[8]

b. Pre-trial processes

The judicial stage of the criminal justice process begins with an information sworn before a judge or justice of the peace;[9] this is how a charge is laid. At this point, control of the prosecutorial process passes directly to the Crown attorney. The Crown attorney is discharging a public duty and is not the victim's advocate.

After a charge is laid, accused persons must appear in court to have the charge read, and in some cases, to choose how they wish to be tried.[10] Prior to making that decision, the defence will generally request the Crown to disclose the evidence it has gathered. Accused persons can be held in custody or released while awaiting trial. They are presumed innocent and cannot be ordered detained unless the Crown establishes that detention is necessary. Detention might be deemed necessary to ensure that an accused person appears in court for trial or other proceedings, to ensure the protection or safety of the public,[11] or because releasing the accused would undermine public confidence in the administration of justice. While most accused persons are released simply upon signing a promise that they will appear in court, some are required to "post bail" to be released.

In many cases, a preliminary inquiry is the next step in the process. This is a hearing before a judicial officer to determine if the accused should stand trial on the charges that have been laid. At this hearing, the Crown generally presents evidence of the offence committed. Evidence consists of the testimony of key witnesses and the submission of documents or other material. The presiding officer only has to determine if there is some evidence upon which a jury could convict the accused. If there is, the accused is committed to stand trial. If not, he or she is discharged and the criminal justice process ends.

The preliminary inquiry provides the Crown and the defence an opportunity to evaluate the strength of the case against the accused, and to assess the behaviour and credibility of selected Crown witnesses. Preliminary inquiries are not always held, although in cases of sexual assault dating back many years,[12] they are more common. The defence will want to hear and evaluate testimony from victims and to cross-examine them because their credibility is often the crucial issue in a trial. The obligation to testify at the preliminary inquiry and the obligation to testify at the trial may mean that the victim has to submit to cross-examination on a painful subject twice. This is one of the reasons why the federal government has contemplated reforms to the preliminary inquiry.[13]

As noted, there is no client-lawyer relationship between the victim and the Crown attorney. The Crown's obligation to disclose all its evidence to the defence includes disclosing statements made by the victim as well as any information or documents that the victim has provided.[14] The Crown's evidence does not belong either to the prosecutor, or to the victim, but to the public. As such, confidential documents held by third parties such as therapists or sexual assault centres may be subject to disclosure. In 1995, the Supreme Court of Canada established ground rules to be followed when an accused seeks disclosure of a complainant's therapeutic records for the purposes of preparing his or her defence.[15] Subsequently, Parliament amended the *Criminal Code* specifically to deal with disclosure of these records.[16]

When the accused is committed for trial after the preliminary inquiry, the Crown prepares an indictment specifying each charge being laid. The accused is required to appear in court to enter a plea to the charges in the indictment. A guilty plea is a legal admission of guilt and makes the holding of a trial unnecessary. If the accused pleads not guilty, a trial will follow.

c.   The trial

All the evidence that will form what is known as the court record must be presented during the trial. This means that witnesses who testified at a preliminary inquiry may have to do so again.[17] The presumption of innocence means, among other things, that the prosecutor must present all the evidence necessary to satisfy the burden of proof before the accused is required to offer any evidence.[18] The rules of evidence govern what evidence is admissible. Their purpose is to ensure a fair trial. For example, some evidence cannot be presented because its reliability is in doubt. This is usually the case with second-hand evidence, such as a statement about what someone else is supposed to have said to another person. Other evidence, such as evidence of the reputation or habits of the accused, may not be admissible because its value as evidence is greatly outweighed by the prejudice to the accused that may flow from it.

The rules governing "similar fact evidence" are a good example of how these principles work. Because the purpose of the trial is to determine whether the accused committed a specific offence at a fixed moment in time, there is a rule that evidence presented to establish that the accused committed a similar offence at another time is not admissible. This rule is difficult to apply when a single trial involves several offences committed against several persons, which is often the case in allegations of institutional child abuse.[19] Under section 24(2) of the *Canadian Charter of Rights and Freedoms*, relevant evidence may also be excluded during the trial if its admission would bring the administration of justice into disrepute. For example, admissions obtained by the police in violation of the right of the accused to consult a lawyer may be inadmissible.[20]

In cases involving physical or sexual assault committed in an institution years before the trial, material or documentary evidence may be rare. The prosecutor's evidence will consist mainly of testimony of witnesses recounting events of which they have personal knowledge. In some situations, a person alleging that he or she was a victim of physical or sexual assault is the Crown's key, if not only, witness. The outcome of the trial may therefore largely turn on the questioning (or examination-in-chief) of the complainant by the Crown and the cross-examination by the defence.

The defence has a right to cross-examine all witnesses presented by the Crown immediately after the Crown completes its own questions. The Crown has a corresponding right to cross-examine any witnesses presented by the defence. Cross-examination has two important purposes. It serves:

- to bring out the elements of the testimony of a witness that will corroborate the version of the events which the party asserts; and

- to show inconsistencies or contradictions in the witness's version of the events, sufficient to permit the court to conclude either that the witness is not truthful or that he or she is honest, but mistaken.

In a sexual offence trial, where the victim is the Crown's key witness and the accused's defence is denial, the credibility of witnesses is almost always the key issue. Often, cross-examination is the only way for an accused to exercise the right to make a full answer and defence. Therefore, cross-examination of Crown witnesses may be intense and the judge will not intervene or interfere unless it is abusive. Once the trial is over, if there is a reasonable doubt as to the guilt of the accused, there must be an acquittal.

An important goal of the criminal justice system is to prevent the conviction of innocent persons. Its concern is neither the acknowledgement of victimisation nor restitution for that victimisation as such, but with ensuring that accused persons are convicted only in accordance with due process of law. Therefore, a verdict of "not guilty" is not a moral pronouncement on guilt or innocence. Unless victims clearly understand that an acquittal does not necessarily mean the assault never happened, they risk disappointment and disillusionment on an acquittal.

d. Sentencing

If an accused person pleads guilty or is found guilty, the next step is sentencing. The *Criminal Code* sets out the maximum sentence that can be imposed for an offence, but courts will only impose maximum sentences in exceptional cases. There is normally a significant difference between maximum stipulated sentences and those imposed in institutional abuse cases.

The fundamental principle in sentencing is that the punishment should fit the crime and the offender. Among the factors to be considered are the accused's character, his or her admissions, the existence of underlying psychological problems that have been or may be treated in therapy, and the lifestyle and activities of the accused since the events that formed the subject matter of the complaint. Based on their analysis of these factors, the Crown and the defence make arguments to the court about the appropriate sentence to pass. The aim is to impose a sentence that achieves a balance between the goals of denunciation, prevention, deterrence, retribution and rehabilitation of the offender.[21]

Victims have an opportunity to express their views on sentencing by making a victim impact statement. The judge is directed by the *Criminal Code* to consider victim impact statements when sentencing offenders,[22] but the judge alone decides what weight will be given to them. The statements are a means for the victim to describe not just the actions of the offender but also the physical and psychological impacts of those actions. In June 1999, the *Criminal Code* was amended to provide:

> The court shall, on the request of a victim, permit the victim to read a [victim impact] statement prepared and filed in accordance with subsection (2), or to present the statement in any other manner that the court considers appropriate.[23]

3. Assessment

Overview

Those involved in the criminal justice process – police, Crown, defence counsel and judges – are likely to treat complainants and witnesses with respect, especially if they have an understanding of the effect institutional child abuse may have on survivors. However, the process itself has certain formal constraints that make it difficult to really engage complainants and witnesses.

Adequate information is required, both before the process begins and throughout its duration, to enable survivors to exercise real choice about their participation. As a fact-finding and accountability exercise, the criminal justice process is well-suited to identifying individual perpetrators and holding them liable. It is less well-suited to uncovering any systemic problems that may have allowed the abuse to occur or to continue for a lengthy period.

In terms of fairness, the main concern of the criminal justice system is to balance the power of the State against the rights of the accused. Particularly in cases involving allegations of sexual abuse, this leaves some areas where complainants or witnesses may feel that the system does not always treat them fairly.

While there is a growing trend toward restorative justice in the criminal justice system, the process is not inherently one that promotes acknowledgement, apology and reconciliation. It also can only provide for a relatively narrow range of survivors' needs and does not respond at all to the distinctive needs of their families, communities or peoples. Finally, the publicity of a criminal conviction may serve to enhance public awareness of institutional child abuse, but it does little in the realm of prevention.

a.   Respect, engagement and informed choice

The criminal justice process is a public process involving the State and the accused. Complainants and witnesses are not parties to a criminal proceeding even though their cooperation and participation are essential to it. As a result, survivors may often be compelled to participate in the criminal justice process without feeling fully engaged in or fully respected by it.[24] Each major decision made by the police and the Crown presents an opportunity to demonstrate respect for survivors or a failure to do so.

In cases where a significant number of years have passed since the offence was committed, there may be problems obtaining sufficient and reliable evidence. The Crown also may decide not to prosecute some offences if there is no reasonable likelihood of conviction.[25] Courts cannot review the Crown's decision not to proceed unless there is evidence of bad faith.[26] Victims may perceive these various decisions not to pursue a complaint as a rejection of the truth of their allegations, and as trivialising their suffering or re-victimising them. The police, the Crown or other officials should be respectful of complainants and carefully explain such decisions to them. This is especially important given the infrequency with which private prosecutions are launched.[27]

The Crown attorney is responsible for making all strategic decisions concerning his or her cases and is under no obligation to consult the victim before withdrawing a charge or entering into a plea bargain.[28] Crown prosecutors have recently become increasingly sensitised to the importance of fully informing victims of the process and including them in key decisions. In dealing with sexual abuse complainants, many prosecution services in Canada now have specific policies or strategies in relation to:

- withdrawing or staying charges and plea bargaining;

- preparation for court and referral to victim services; and

- advising on the status of the case and developments.

Because of the importance of a complainant's testimony, one measure of the Crown's respect for and engagement of complainants will be how thoroughly they are prepared for testifying, both at the preliminary inquiry and at trial. The Crown decides the manner in which it will question complainants. Witnesses who have been properly prepared will understand this and will know what areas the Crown's questions will cover. Cross-examination by the defence is rarely easy on the victims of abuse, particularly sexual assault. They have described it as a second victimisation, or even a third, in cases where complainants have also testified at the preliminary inquiry. The decision to file a complaint, originally perceived as an opportunity to obtain justice, may subsequently be regretted if survivors are not prepared for an attack on their credibility.

The emergence of victim/witness assistance programs reflects a greater respect for victims and an awareness of their needs. Every province has some form of victim/witness assistance program. They are generally part of a larger victims' assistance program run by the provincial Ministry of the Attorney General, the federal Solicitor

Graham, then an inspector of Indian agencies, reported that Principal McWhinney had, when retrieving a number of runaway boys, "tied ropes about their arms and made them run behind the buggy from their houses to the school." Referring the matter to a senior member of the Presbyterian Church, the department suggested that the principal be dismissed. The church refused, for its investigation had found no reason to fault the principal's action: he had, it was claimed, tied the boys to the wagon only because there was no room inside; the distance was only some eight miles, and the boys did not have to run the whole way, as "the horses trotted slowly when they did trot and they walked a considerable part of the way."

In 1919, Graham forwarded reports to the department from a local agent and a police constable describing the case of a runaway from the Anglican Old Sun's School. On being brought back, the boy had been shackled to a bed, had his hands tied and was "most brutally and unmercifully beaten with a horse quirt until his back was bleeding".

Report of the Royal Commission on Aboriginal Peoples at p.369

General, or federal Department of Justice. These programs offer some or all of the following services:

- information about the court process in general;

- specific information about the progress of the case, including updates on trial scheduling, sentencing and post-sentencing;

- emotional support before and during court proceedings;

- accompaniment to court;

- court preparation and orientation – including tours, pamphlets and books, children's resources and logistical support;

- assistance with victim impact statements and criminal injuries compensation programs;

- interpreters;

- short-term counselling;

- referrals to community groups and agencies that can provide specialised and ongoing support and counselling; and

- public outreach and education.

Ontario developed a specific protocol for assisting victim/witnesses in cases involving allegations of abuse in institutions – and more generally, allegations involving multiple perpetrators and victims – following its experience with the prosecution of abusers at the Grandview, St. John's and St. Joseph's schools.[29] Nonetheless, victims of an offence remain merely witnesses with no special status as a party.[30] Although required to participate in a process they have initiated or been drawn into as witnesses, victims are not always given adequate information about the process – and in any event, have no control over it.

b.   Fact-finding

The evidentiary goals of the criminal justice process are to determine whether an offence has been committed and to identify the offender. The process is not an inquiry aimed at understanding the larger context in which abuse took place or uncovering all the evidence about other offences that were committed. Therefore, evidence about conditions in institutions that facilitate abuse may not be relevant for the purposes of a criminal trial. Moreover, the ,accused will usually have critical information for understanding the abuse that the court may never obtain because of his or her right to remain silent.

While the criminal justice process is not specifically concerned with understanding the factors that contribute to the commission of an offence, contextual evidence is important, particularly in sexual abuse cases. This includes discovering:

- the nature of the crime;

- why the victim did not report the abuse;

- whether the same accused committed other similar offences;

- how the accused had the opportunity to commit the crimes and go undetected;

- in cases of allegations of physical abuse, whether the actions were an appropriate form of discipline for the time or were unreasonable; and

- the relationship of trust between accused and victim.

Although it is a fact-finding exercise, the criminal justice process has strict rules governing the relevancy of evidence and a narrowly defined scope, which means that it cannot satisfy a desire to paint the overall picture of life at the institution. Furthermore, while a conviction may provide closure, an acquittal may make closure more difficult to achieve. An acquittal means only that, in law, the guilt of the accused was not established beyond a reasonable doubt. This legal conclusion may not reflect reality and many victims perceive an acquittal as a rejection of their story by the legal system. Survivors who expect the criminal justice system to uncover all the facts and to validate their testimony will be disappointed unless they have a solid grasp of its nature and purposes.

c.   Accountability

The *Criminal Code* does not make all morally reprehensible conduct – such as all forms of abuse in institutions – a criminal offence. Physical and sexual abuse are criminal offences. Psychological abuse[31] and cultural abuse[32] – however connected to physical and sexual abuse and however relevant in understanding the context and circumstances of that abuse – are not criminal offences.

It bears repeating that accused persons can be convicted only if the admissible evidence establishes their guilt beyond a reasonable doubt. In principle, a person is only criminally responsible if he or she personally committed or was involved in the commission of an offence. Responsibility by association, save for two exceptions,[33] is not recognised in Canadian law. For example, an employer cannot be held criminally responsible for an offence committed by an employee if the employer did not personally participate in the commission of the offence. An institution or organisation can be found guilty of an offence only if the individuals constituting the core of the organisation (for example, members of the Board of Directors) knowingly allowed or participated in the offence.[34] Carelessness, negligence or even a certain tolerance of criminal conduct by an organisation is not sufficient. Indifference to a criminal situation does not constitute a crime.[35]

A criminal conviction is an effective form of accountability, both at the point of conviction and in sentencing. Courts may now consider "evidence that the offender, in committing the offence, abused a position of trust or authority in relation to the victim".[36] This is directly relevant to situations of institutional child abuse. As well, since 1997, where an offender has been convicted of multiple offences, the court may impose consecutive sentences for each offence.[37] However, maximum sentences are only imposed in rare cases. In addition, courts are now directed to consider all available sanctions other than imprisonment that are reasonable in the circumstances for all offenders, with particular attention to the circumstances of Aboriginal offenders.[38]

Some victims may be dissatisfied with sentences they view as lenient when compared to the long-term harm they have suffered. Nevertheless, the criminal justice system is first and foremost an accountability process that operates by convicting offenders. Punishment is only a secondary part of accountability.

d. Fairness

The criminal justice process is designed to ensure, to the greatest extent possible, that no person is convicted of an offence that he or she did not commit. Fairness in the criminal justice process focusses on the relationship between the Crown and the accused. Fairness to others who are not parties to the proceedings is less important. It is not surprising, therefore, that victims and witnesses, particularly survivors of child abuse, often perceive some aspects of the criminal justice process as unfair to them. But many proposed protections or privileges accorded to victims to make the process more responsive to their needs are opposed by defence lawyers who fear that these may undermine the ability of accused persons to make full answer and defence.

i. Impact of the preliminary inquiry

There are differing views on the purposes and usefulness of the preliminary inquiry.[39] Survivors of child abuse generally object to the preliminary inquiry because it forces them to undergo an additional round of testifying and cross-examination. One judge has criticised preliminary inquiries in the following terms:

> ... the preliminary hearing or preliminary inquiry has been turned into a nightmarish experience for many Provincial Court judges. Rules with respect to relevancy have been widened beyond recognition. Cross-examination at a preliminary inquiry now seems to have no limits. Attempts by Provincial Court judges to limit cross-examination have been perceived by some superior courts as a breach of the accused's right to fundamental justice, a breach of his or her ability to be able to make full answer and defence.[40]

A preliminary inquiry probably seems an unnecessary burden to anyone who has already given a statement in a police investigation and who will have to testify at a trial. It is more than a burden in sexual offence cases where cross-examination can be harsh and persist-ent.[41] The requirement to testify more than once is not, itself, obviously unfair to the complainant. It may show a lack of respect for survivors, be inconvenient and upsetting, even traumatic. But it does not com-promise the complainant's rights, nor does it favour the accused so as to render the criminal justice process unfair. However, given that the purpose of the preliminary inquiry is simply to determine if the Crown has some evidence upon which a jury could convict, it is unclear why an extensive and harsh cross-examination of a complainant is allowed at this stage.

ii.   *Restrictions on conversations among witnesses prior*
        to testifying

Those who will testify in a criminal proceeding are warned by the police not to discuss, among themselves, the events that are the subject of the trial. This warning is based on the view that victims who have had dis-cussions might coordinate their evidence in such a way as to strengthen their case. While not a formal rule of evidence, this precautionary prac-tice has almost taken on the character of a prohibition that begins when the charge is laid.[42]

The practice of requiring witnesses not to discuss the trial issues deserves to be reconsidered in the context of historical institutional child abuse. It may mean, both unfairly and unrealistically, that friends, former classmates and even siblings cannot discuss with each other some of the most significant shaping events of their lives – possibly for a period of years. This imposes a particular hardship on survivors, who may be coming together and revealing their experiences for the first time since they were children. Mutual support and sharing are vital coping mechanisms for confronting a troubled or traumatic past. A hard-and-fast rule prohibiting discussions among complainant-witnesses is, in this light, excessive. The judge or jury is capable of determining whether any such discussion coloured the witness's testimony, and subsequently making an evaluation of credibility based on more objective factors (such as how well witnesses stand up to cross-examination).

iii. Cross-examination of complainants with respect to other sexual activity

In 1993, the *Criminal Code* was amended to make evidence of the complainant's history of sexual activity inadmissible in cases involving specified sexual offences – namely all sexual offences created by the 1983 amendments.[43] In two cases, judges have interpreted this provision to mean that complainants alleging a sexual offence that occurred prior to 1983 are still subject to cross-examination on their other sexual activity.[44] This strict interpretation is not in keeping with the remedial nature of the 1983 amendments. It unfairly subjects those who are alleging historical sexual abuse to a line of questioning that Parliament has ruled inadmissible in post-1983 cases.

iv. Breach of complainants' privacy

Although some procedural rules protect the complainant's privacy and dignity, the fact remains that his or her medical,[45] therapeutic and personal files are not automatically confidential. The trial judge may allow disclosure of these files if the accused can establish that they are relevant to an issue at trial or to the competence of a witness to testify.[46] The judge weighs the complainant's right to privacy against the right of the accused to full answer and defence. In cases of accusations that date back many years, defence access to these records may be quite important. But the rules governing the process for obtaining disclosure can be unfair to complainants. Where the accused makes a disclosure application, the Crown cannot act as counsel for the complainants. Complainants must normally hire their own lawyer to argue for maintaining the confidentiality of their medical or therapy records.[47]

v. Delay in parole

Since 1995, courts have the discretion to delay an offender's parole eligibility for any sentences received after November 1, 1992.[48] Rather than being eligible after serving one-third of their sentence, offenders may now be required to serve at least one-half their sentence (or ten years, whichever is less) before applying for parole. This provision covers sentences for sexual offences, but not those offenses set out in the *Criminal Code* prior to 1970. Consequently, perpetrators convicted of sexual offences that took place prior to 1970 cannot have their parole ineligibility extended to one-half their sentence. This might be seen as unfair to survivors of institutional child abuse that occurred prior to 1970.

e. Acknowledgement, apology and reconciliation

The criminal process does not promote voluntary acknowledgement of responsibility because the State must establish the guilt of an accused person beyond a reasonable doubt, and because an accused person (presumed innocent) has the right to silence and cannot be compelled by the Crown to testify. Other features of the process that encourage accused persons to avoid voluntarily acknowledging their guilt are the adversarial nature of the process and the fact that a term in prison may follow a conviction.

In the 1995 amendments to the *Criminal Code*, one of the stated objectives of sentencing was "to promote a sense of responsibility in offenders, and acknowledgement of the harm done to victims and to the community".[49] The ability of sentencing to effect this objective is limited unless other elements of the process are also modified.[50] Some offenders contritely plead guilty, which is a verbal acknowledgement of their responsibility. Others, however, may plead guilty as a strategic move to achieve a more lenient sentence. This has little to do with real acknowledgement.

Many Aboriginal communities have implemented programs that allow for acknowledgement of responsibility by the offender, apology, and ultimately, reconciliation. As well, certain judges have taken the initiative and created sentencing circles to determine an appropriate sentence. This type of procedure has had some success in cases where the offender is a member of a community, has committed an offence in that community, and will be required to live there.[51] There is no single procedural model to follow for sentencing circles and the *Criminal Code* only stipulates some conditions for their use.[52] It is up to local authorities, with the consent and participation of the community, to implement mechanisms intended to involve the community and the offender in establishing a sentence.

To date, there is no experience as to whether these alternative measures can work in cases of historical institutional child abuse. Even when an attempt at acknowledgement, apology and reconciliation is made within a criminal justice proceeding, its results are not always greeted with enthusiasm. In the case of Bishop Hugh O'Connor, for example, the trial and various appeals went on for years. When a new trial was ordered,[53] the complainants requested that Bishop O'Connor participate in an Aboriginal healing-circle in their community. He agreed. The original complainants were satisfied with the healing-circle, but some others in the community expressed concern that the accused did not take full responsibility or apologise for the acts he acknowledged having committed.[54] This case shows how difficult it can sometimes be to fix a sentence that meets the needs of both survivors and communities.

f.   Compensation, counselling, and education

For victims, the main benefit of the criminal justice process is that they can recount, in a public forum, the wrongs that were done to them and, in that way, assist in seeing that justice is done. This is a basic need for many survivors and may provide a certain closure, even where the trial does not result in a conviction. However, the criminal justice process can do little to satisfy the needs of survivors for compensation, counselling and education.

Since 1995, courts may order offenders to pay restitution for offences involving bodily harm.[55] These provisions do not provide victims of past abuse with much in the way of compensation. The criminal justice process is not a vehicle for the recovery of civil damages.[56] In addition, restitution can only be ordered to compensate for physical harm and financial losses such as loss of income or support. Psychological damages are not mentioned in the *Criminal Code*. Furthermore, in practice, courts rarely order restitution. Finally, even if restitution is ordered, the victim cannot count on the criminal justice system to ensure compliance. The victim must apply to a civil court to enforce a restitution order.

The other needs identified by survivors, such as therapy, counselling and education, are even more remote from the objectives of the criminal justice system. It simply does not address them.

g.   Needs of families, communities and peoples

Since the primary objective of the criminal justice system is to bring the perpetrator of an offence to justice, the distinctive needs and interests of families, communities and peoples are not a major concern. They are not even considered "victims". At the very most, their needs may be given consideration during the sentencing process. Vindication of a community interest as opposed to a general societal interest may be achieved in a restorative justice process, but this community interest is not normally a consideration in the criminal justice process. In some cases, an offender may be ordered, as part of the terms of probation, to pay a certain amount of money to a victim-assistance agency. If directed at agencies that serve the survivor's own community, such orders may assist in responding to that community's needs.

h.   Prevention and public education

The public nature of the criminal justice process and the stigma of a guilty verdict – particularly in the case of assaults on children or vulnerable individuals – can be powerful tools for affirming collective values. The publicity generated by these cases is a reminder of the unacceptability of abusive behaviour toward children, especially by persons in a position of trust. In this sense, the criminal justice process may serve an educative function.

Although general and collective discouragement from committing offences is an objective of criminal law, the actual preventive effect of the criminal justice process is difficult to measure. Social scientists have not yet identified all the factors that cause, let alone prevent, crime – particularly sexual crimes. Of course, convicted perpetrators of institutional child abuse may follow and benefit from therapy programs offered in certain penitentiaries. This might help to reduce recidivism and may therefore be considered a form of prevention.

However, more general strategies of prevention – directed to the redesign of institutions and their processes – are neither an objective, nor a likely outcome, of the criminal justice process. At best, prosecutions and convictions for institutional child abuse point to areas where prevention strategies are most required.

4.   Conclusion

The criminal justice system seeks to achieve a balance between the rights of the accused and the power of the State. The system requires the cooperation of victims in order to achieve its aims. This cooperation comes at a personal cost to victims, however willing they may be to assist.

Despite the emergence of restorative justice as a way of responding to criminal conduct, the criminal justice process is still essentially adversarial, reactive and punitive. Some changes have been made to facilitate the participation of victims in the process. These include procedural changes relating to the manner in which police investigate, prosecutors involve and prepare victims, and judges conduct trials. But the central goals of the system have not been, and likely will not be, modified in the near future. The criminal justice process offers a good, although narrow, fact-finding capacity, and does produce accountability – at least upon a guilty plea or a conviction.

Fundamentally, the criminal justice system is designed to ensure a fair trial for accused persons and to punish those who have been properly convicted. It does not provide an instrument for victims to exact vengeance or to achieve redress that meets their other needs. Achieving a balance between the rights of the accused and the desire to bring wrongdoers to justice is particularly difficult when accusations date back 20, 30 or 40 years. Survivors of institutional child abuse must have realistic expectations as to which of their needs can be met through the criminal justice system, and which cannot.

Recommendations

PEOPLE BRINGING COMPLAINTS TO THE POLICE should be fully informed at the outset of how the criminal justice process works and their role in it.

Considerations:

Governments should prepare, in consultation with interested parties, pamphlets and information kits that describe the character of the criminal process as it affects adult complainants alleging institutional child abuse.

Community service agencies, survivors' groups and other non-governmental organisations should also be given resources to develop their own information kits and pamphlets about how the criminal justice process works when there are allegations of institutional child abuse.

These various information kits should be available at all police stations, social service agencies, hospitals and the offices of health care professionals.

Police, social service agencies, hospitals and the offices of health care professionals should have access to literature or help-line numbers to which they may refer those who may disclose experiences of child abuse.

THOSE INVOLVED IN investigating, prosecuting, defending and judging allegations of institutional child abuse should have special training, expertise or experience and should have access to survivor-sensitive protocols that have been developed for this purpose.

Considerations:

Protocols have been developed to deal with investigations of multi-victim institutional child abuse. Any police force embarking on such an investigation should consult these protocols or those who have developed them.

When approaching potential witnesses, particularly for the first time, there must be respect for the privacy of former residents of institutions.

As a rule, the first substantive interview in an investigation should be conducted by a person with whom a survivor feels comfortable, and this option should be presented to survivors. Where possible, former residents of institutions should have follow-up interviews by an officer with whom they feel comfortable (*e.g.* a female officer or an Aboriginal officer).

Complainants should, however, be informed at the outset that it may not be possible, over long and complex proceedings, to ensure that the witness or complainants will always be able to deal with the same officials.

All major decisions about how the police intend to proceed should be explained fully to the complainant(s), especially any decision not to lay charges or to terminate an investigation.

PEER, PROFESSIONAL AND PRACTICAL SUPPORT for survivors should be available from the commencement of a criminal investigation throughout the trial and beyond.

Considerations:

Those involved in victim witness support programs should receive training or education with respect to the particular needs of survivors of institutional child abuse.

Wherever possible, witnesses for the prosecution should have access to a private area while waiting to testify, so they do not have to wait with the accused.

Support should include access to both peer and professional counselling during a criminal investigation and prosecution.

Financial support should be available to permit a family member or friend of the complainant to attend the trial or to provide the services of a therapist or peer counsellor.

Considerations:

Devices to protect witnesses, such as screens in front of the witness box, closed-circuit television and videotaped evidence should be available, in appropriate circumstances, to adult witnesses. Currently, such devices are available only to witnesses under the age of 18, and only where they are complainants in cases involving sexual abuse.

Crown attorneys should have the resources necessary to fully prepare survivors for testifying. Crown counsel who undertake prosecutions of historical child sexual abuse should have the resources to explain issues such as: how the process works, possible outcomes, the role of the complainant, the duration of the process, *etc.*

Efforts should be made to avoid subjecting witnesses to multiple examinations in the course of one criminal proceeding. Such a procedure would require the support and collaboration of the Crown and defence bars. The testimony would have to be videotaped, so that those relying on it and not present when it was taped could assess the demeanour of the witness.

If preliminary inquiries are not abolished, cross-examinations within them should be time-limited, as determined on a case-by-case basis, subject to an extension where this is justified.

The *Criminal Code* should be amended to ensure that all victims of child abuse benefit from the same procedural protections as those who are covered by the 1983 amendments to the sexual assault provisions.

Witnesses' testimony should not automatically be discredited solely because they have spoken together. There should be no presumption that such as evidence is tainted. Defence counsel who wish to establish that testimony is not reliable should have the burden to do so as in other ordinary challenges to evidence.

THE SENTENCING PROCESS should be inclusive and restorative wherever possible.

Considerations:

Defence counsel should exercise discretion and restraint in cross-examining persons who have submitted a victim impact statement.

Family members should be entitled to provide victim impact statements to illustrate the lifelong effect of child abuse and how it affects the relationships of victims with their families.

---

[1] See D. M. Paciocco, *Charter Principles And Proof In Criminal Cases* (Toronto: Carswell, 1987) at 3-11.

[2] There are significant variations among the provinces in this respect. In some provinces, the police have a large degree of independence in the decision whether or not to start an investigation and when to continue it. In others, for example Quebec, the State supervises the exercise of that power. Nova Scotia has an independent director of public prosecutions. However, in all cases, a decision on whether to prosecute is made by the Crown.

[3] A complainant need not be the person who actually claims to be a victim of an offence. He or she could be a bystander or someone who suspects a crime has been committed, *e.g.* an emergency room physician who has examined a severely bruised baby. Most often, however, in the context of child abuse cases, the adult who lays the complaint is the person who alleges he or she was the victim of abuse.

[4] In British Columbia, charges only proceed where the Crown so decides (*Crown Counsel Act*, R.S.B.C. 1996, c. 87, s. 2).

[5] *Criminal Code*, R.S.C. 1985, c. C-46, ss. 504-508.

[6] See B. Hodge, "Private Prosecutions: Access to Justice" (1998) 4 New Zealand Law Journal 145 at 145.

7   This right to silence means that a person may choose whether or not to speak to the authorities or respond to questions. The police may attempt to persuade a person to talk, but cannot for example, use force or subterfuge to obtain a statement. In part to protect the right to silence, there is a rule of evidence that statements or admissions made to the police by the suspect are admissible at trial only if they have been obtained voluntarily (that is, without any promises or threats).

8   Section 24(2) of the *Canadian Charter of Rights and Freedoms*, Part I of the *Constitution Act, 1982*, being Schedule B to the *Canada Act* 1982 (U.K.), 1982, c. 11 [hereinafter *Charter*]. Increasingly, however, courts are distinguishing between real evidence (evidence which would have existed notwithstanding the breach of *Charter* protections) and conscriptive evidence (where the accused has been conscripted to provide evidence against him or herself, *e.g.* through a confession or a blood sample). See *R. Stillman*, [1997] 1 S.C.R. 607. Real evidence is rarely excluded, even if obtained in violation of the *Charter*.

9   Based on the offence in question, once an information is sworn, the procedure can vary. For the purposes of this paper, and given the nature of the offences we are addressing, we will assume the most complex and lengthy procedure will be followed, *i.e.*, indictment.

10 The *Criminal Code* provides that an accused may be tried by a superior court judge sitting without a jury, by a superior court judge sitting with a jury or by a provincial court judge sitting alone, depending on the nature of the charge. For example, in certain cases the accused may elect how to be tried (*supra* note 5, s. 536(2)).

11 For example, if there is a clear possibility of the accused committing an offence while free.

12 For current complaints involving physical and sexual violence, the preliminary inquiry is much less common. Preliminary inquiries cannot be held where the Crown decides to choose a form of trial called a "summary proceeding". Many offences relating to physical and sexual assault may be prosecuted by a summary process. But since such proceedings must be taken within six months, where the alleged offence took place many years previously the Crown will have to proceed by following a more complex proceeding involving an indictment, and usually, a preliminary inquiry.

13 The federal government is considering amendments to the *Criminal Code* that would reduce the number of preliminary inquiries by classifying all offences in the *Criminal Code* with a maximum penalty of 10 years imprisonment or less, as hybrid offences. This means Crowns would have the option of proceeding either by way of indictment (where a preliminary inquiry is generally available) or by way of summary conviction (which does not include a preliminary inquiry). See "Criminal Code Changes Could Mean Fewer Juries " *National Post* (16 August 1999) A4. See also Department of Justice, *A Survey of the Preliminary Inquiry in Canada* (Working Paper) by D. Pomerant & G. Gilmour (Ottawa: Department of Justice, 1993).

14 The Crown must inform the defence of documents provided to the Crown by the complainant, such as medical or therapeutical files, but their disclosure to the defence is not automatic.

15 *R. O'Connor*, [1995] 4 S.C.R. 411.

16 *Criminal Code*, *supra* note 5, ss. 278.1-278.91. The constitutionality of these provisions was challenged, principally on the basis that they infringe the right of an accused person to make full answer and defence. In the case of *R. Mills*, [1997] S.C.C.A. No. 624, online: QL, which it decided on November 25, 1999, the Supreme Court of Canada upheld the constitutionality of these provisions regarding the production of confidential records to the accused, thus supporting the legislative balance between the rights of the accused and the complainant's rights.

17 Recent judicial decisions (*e.g. R. v. K.G.B.*, [1993] 1 S.C.R. 740) make it possible (though exceptional) to file a statement of a witness, if taken in circumstances that guarantee its reliability, in certain special cases where the witness will not testify at trial.

18 The defence need not present any evidence if it believes that the Crown's evidence is not sufficient to support a conviction. The accused does not present any evidence until all the Crown's evidence is presented. Once the accused has responded, the Crown cannot present any additional evidence except to counter evidence presented by the defence that could not have been anticipated during the Crown's case.

19 The rules regarding the admissibility of similar fact evidence have evolved over the last several years. While the law is not entirely settled, some similar fact evidence may now be available in trials involving several complaints against a single accused. See *R. v. Arp*, [1998] 3 S.C.R. 339.

20 See *R. v. Feeney*, [1997] 2 S.C.R. 13; *R. v. Burlingham*, [1995] 2 S.C.R. 206 and *Charter*, *supra* note 8.

21 *Criminal Code, supra* note 5, s. 718. For a discussion of these goals of sentencing see Canadian Sentencing Commission, *Sentencing Reform: A Canadian Approach* (Ottawa: The Commission, 1987) c. 6 and Ruby, C. *Sentencing* (5th ed.) (Toronto: Butterworths, 1999).

22 *Criminal Code, supra* note 5, s. 722. It is only as a result of amendments to the *Criminal Code* in 1995 that judges are required to take the statements into account (S.C. 1995, c. 22, s. 6).

23 *An Act to amend the Criminal Code (Victims of Crime) and Another Act in Consequence*, S.C. 1999, c. 25, s. 17(1). This Act came into effect on December 1, 1999.

24 Recognizing this, efforts have been made to develop protocols about how the different stages of the process should engage survivors. For example, British Columbia has two protocols for responding to allegations of abuse in respect of the Jericho Hill School and Indian Residential Schools. P*rotocol for Jericho Hill Intervention* (undated), *Protocol for Indian Residential School Abuse Support Service*, Between: Provincial and Federal Governments and Aboriginal Representatives (21 June 1995). Both were developed through a process of negotiation involving the affected communities, representatives of various ministries of the provincial government and, in the case of the Residential School protocol, representatives of the federal government. The RCMP has also developed a guide for the investigation of sexual offences (A. Szabo et al., *Investigative Guide for Sexual Offences* (Ottawa: RCMP, 1997)).

25 For a discussion of the effect of delay in charging and prosecuting an individual see *R. v. L.(W.K.)* [1991], S.C.J. No. 40 (S.C.C.), online: QL. Note also the decision not to prosecute in connection with the Westray mine disaster, due to insufficient evidence of criminal conduct. See "Westray Investigation was Botched, Former Prosecutor Argues in Memo" The Ottawa Citizen (17 December 1998), online: <http://www.geocities.com/Athens/3116/commen45.html> (date accessed: 16 November 1999).

26 *Campbell* v. *Ontario* (A.G.) (1987), 58 O.R. (2d) 209 (H.C.J.).

27 A private prosecution was launched in Quebec by one of the Duplessis Orphans. The prosecution was successful (*R. v. Burton* (29 February 1996), Montreal 500-01-016545-946 (C.Q.)).

28 A plea bargain is an informal procedure where an agreement is reached by the Crown and the defence as to the plea and possible sentence.

29 *Protocol for the Development and Implementation of a Victim/Witness Assistance Program in Multi-Victim Multi-Perpetrator Prosecutions* (January 1996).

30 Certain provisions of the *Criminal Code* do differentiate between the complainant and other witnesses or provide special consideration for victims. See for example those provisions dealing with issues such as evidence of the complainant's sexual activity (*supra* note 5, s. 276-276.4); restitution orders for victims of offences (*ibid.*, s. 738); and the use of victim impact statements (*ibid.*, s. 722).

31 Psychological trauma may, however, be included in the *Criminal Code* definition of bodily harm, see *R. v. McCraw*, [1991] 3 S.C.R. 72.

32 For a discussion of cultural abuse see Part IA., above at n. 12. Some argue that the residential school system for Aboriginal children was a form of genocide, as defined in international law. See R.D. Chrisjohn & S. Young, *The Circle Game* (Penticton, B.C.: Theytus Books, 1997). Genocide is a criminal offence in Canada (*supra* note 5, s. 318).

33 The two exceptions are: a party to an offence (*Criminal Code, supra* note 5, s. 21) and conspiracy or counselling offences (*ibid.*, ss. 463, 464).

34 See *Canadian Dredge & Dock Co. v. The Queen*, [1985] 1 S.C.R. 662.

35 The duty to report actual or suspected child abuse is contained in provincial child welfare legislation. Failure to report is therefore a statutory provincial offence rather than a criminal offence. See for example *Child and Family Services Act*, R.S.O. 1990, c. C-11, s. 72.

36 *Criminal Code, supra* note 5, s. 718.2(a)(iii).

37 *Ibid.*, s. 718.3(4). Previously, a court could only impose concurrent sentences when an accused was being sentenced for multiple offences at one time.

38 *Criminal Code, supra* note 5, s. 718.2(e). Note that this provision, which has elicited a certain amount of controversy, was considered in an appeal motion on July 7, 1999 in *R. v. Akan*, [1999] B.C.C.A. 452, online: <http://www.courts.gov.bc.ca> (date accessed: 16 November 1999).

39 See *R. v. Dawson*, [1997] O.J. No. 2188 (Gen. Div.), online: QL (aff'd (1998), 39 O.R. (3d) 436 (C.A.)) for a review of the purposes of a preliminary inquiry.

40 *R. v. Darby*, [1994] B.C.J. No. 814 (Prov. Ct.), online: QL, mentioned with approval in *R. v. O'Connor*, [1995] 4 S.C.R. 411 and *R. v. Dawson*, [1997] O.J. No. 2188, online: QL.

41 An Ottawa lawyer was apparently the first to use the expression "whacking the complainant" in 1988 to refer to how a criminal defence lawyer might employ access to private therapeutic records. See C. Schmitz, " "Whack" sex assault complainant at preliminary hearing" *The Lawyer's Weekly* 8:5 (27 May 1988) 22; M. Blanchfield, "Courtroom Warrior Goes to Battle for Accused" *The Lawyer's Weekly* 15:35 (26 January 1996) 1 at 6:

> In 1988, Mr. Edelson laid out his philosophy for winning a sex assault case in a seminar for Ottawa-area lawyers … "Whack the complainant hard" at the preliminary hearing, he advised. "Generally, if you destroy the complainant in a prosecution," he said, "you destroy the head. You cut off the head of the Crown's case and the case is dead… "You've got to attack the complainant hard with all you've got so that he or she will say: 'I'm not coming back in front of 12 good citizens to repeat this bullshit story that I've just told the judge". Four years later, Toronto Star columnist Michele Landsberg was still critical. "More and more defence lawyers are enthusiastically following Edelson's blueprint," she wrote.

42 In trials, it is also common to exclude other witnesses from the courtroom when one is testifying. This is done so that later testimony will not be influenced by what has already been said. The court can also order witnesses not to talk to each other about any matter related to the trial or their testimony.

43 *Supra* note 5, s. 276.

44 In *R. v. Lawlor* (28 January 1999), St.John's (Nfld. S.C: (T.D.)) [unreported], and in *R. v. Lasik*, [1999] N.J. No. 55 (Nfld. S.C. (T.D.)), online: QL, (oral rulings during trial), ruled that in pre-1983 cases defence counsel were permitted to question complainants on previous sexual activity.

45 In cases of sexual assaults which took place prior to 1970, there is some issue as to whether the *Criminal Code* provisions restricting access to a complainant's medical records (*supra* note 5, s. 278.2) apply. See *R. v. Lasik, ibid.*

46 *Criminal Code, ibid.*, ss. 278.1-278.91

47 British Columbia will pay for these legal fees. In Newfoundland, the decision to cover these fees is made by the province on a case by case basis.

48 *Criminal Code, supra* note 5, s. 743.6(1) reads:

> Notwithstanding subsection 120(1) of the *Corrections and Conditional Release Act*, where an offender receives, on or after November 1, 1992, a sentence of imprisonment of two years or more, including a sentence of imprisonment for life imposed otherwise than as a minimum punishment, on conviction for an offence set out in Schedule I or II to that Act that was prosecuted by way of indictment, the court may, if satisfied, having regard to the circumstances of the commission of the offence and the character and circumstances of the offender, that the expression of society's denunciation of the offence or the objective of specific or general deterrence so requires, order that the portion of the sentence that must be served before the offender may be released on full parole is one half of the sentence or ten years, whichever is less.

49 *Ibid.*, s. 718.

50 It is recognition of the close relationship between sentencing and other aspects of the criminal justice process that lies behind the movement to "restorative justice". See, for example, Correctional Service of Canada, *A Framework Paper on Restorative Justice and the Correctional Service of Canada* (Ottawa: Correctional Service of Canada, 1998), and Law Commission of Canada, *From Restorative Justice to Transformative Justice [:] Discussion Paper* (Ottawa: Law Commission of Canada, 1999). Available in hard copy from the Law Commission of Canada and online: <http://lcc/gc/ca>.

51 See Canada, Department of Justice, *Building Community Justice Partnerships: Community Peacemaking Circles* (Ottawa: Minister of Public Works and Government Services Canada, 1997).

52 *Criminal Code, supra* note 5, s. 717(1).

53 See *R* v. *O'Connor*, [1998] B.C.J. No. 649, online: QL.

54 See <http://www.islandnet.com/bcasvacp/oconnor.html> (date accessed: 16 November 1999) on the website for B.C. Association of Specialized Victim Assistance and Counselling Programs.

55 *Criminal Code, supra* note 5, s. 738(1)(b). Prior to 1995, when this section was enacted, restitution was only available for damage to property.

56 Constitutionally, criminal law is under federal legislative jurisdiction: *Constitution Act, 1867* (U.K.), 30 & 31 Vict., c. 3, s. 91(27), reprinted in R.S.C. 1985, App. II, No. 5, and the general civil law, including damages for wrongful behaviour, is under provincial legislative jurisdiction, *ibid.*, s. 92(13).

C. Civil Actions

1. Introduction

Most forms of physical and sexual abuse constitute crimes under the *Criminal Code*, but an even broader range of wrongful conduct can give rise to a civil action.[1] If one person causes harm to another intentionally, or even unintentionally, that harm may constitute a civil wrong. In the common law, a civil wrong is called a tort, and under the civil law of Quebec it engages that person's extra-contractual responsibility. To obtain compensation (usually monetary), persons who have been harmed have the right to sue the person or persons they believe to be responsible for the harm done.

Although both may deal with the same events, a civil action operates independently of the criminal justice process. It may be commenced whether or not there has been a criminal investigation or prosecution. A person may be convicted in a criminal trial and found liable at a civil trial for the same misconduct. It is also possible to succeed in a civil action even though the defendant has been acquitted in a criminal trial. This occurs partly because different facts may be put into evidence at each trial, and partly because the plaintiff need only prove the civil case "on the balance of probabilities" and not "beyond a reasonable doubt". Finally, a defendant may be held civilly liable for wrongful conduct that is not a crime.

2. Description

a. Wrongful conduct

The basic premise of a civil action is that people are responsible for the injuries they cause to others.[2] Under both the common law and the civil law of Quebec, a plaintiff must prove three basic elements in order to succeed: the fault of the defendant, the injury to the victim, and a causal connection between the fault and the injury. Physical, psychological or sexual violence constitutes a civil wrong.

Quebec civil law does not distinguish between different categories of wrongful conduct. The principles of liability are the same regardless of the type of fault alleged. In addition, people subjected to physical violence may also bring a claim under the Quebec *Charter of Human Rights and Freedoms*[3] for a violation of their fundamental rights (security, liberty, dignity, *etc.*). Even though victims can invoke both the *Civil Code of Québec* and the Quebec *Charter of Human Rights and Freedoms*, as a basis for claiming damages from a wrongdoer, they are not entitled to double compensation.[4]

In the common law, a plaintiff is required to establish that the facts complained about fit into a defined civil wrong, or "cause of action". Depending on the facts, allegations of physical and sexual abuse can satisfy the definitions of several causes of action. The plaintiff is permitted to allege and prove that the same factual allegations constitute more than one recognised civil wrong.

In common law provinces, most of the civil actions available for physical and sexual abuse are torts. It is also possible to bring an action for "breach of fiduciary duty" where the defendant held a position of power and trust over the plaintiff. The torts most commonly alleged against perpetrators of child abuse are assault and battery. A battery is defined as intentional physical contact with the person of another without that person's consent.[5] Battery covers corporal punishment and any sexual contact. Regarding physical discipline, parents and teachers are permitted to defend against a battery claim by proving they used only reasonable force by way of correction.[6] Assault is the intentional creation of the expectation of physical contact without consent. Psychological abuse might be actionable as an assault[7] – if, for example, the perpetrator intentionally causes fear of imminent sexual battery.

The action for breach of fiduciary duty is also available in the common law where a plaintiff alleges that a person has abused his or her power for personal benefit. It is not a tort action, although there are many similarities.[8] It might lie against a doctor, teacher, priest, or step-parent who took advantage of the relationship to secure sexual favours. It might also lie against the institution itself for failing to ensure that the employees did not abuse their positions of trust.[9] While conduct that constitutes breach of fiduciary duty in sexual and physical assault cases will generally also constitute a tort,[10] there may be advantages to the fiduciary action, such as the possibility of recovering a larger amount of damages.[11]

In both the common law and civil law systems, civil actions may be brought against persons other than the direct perpetrator, and against responsible institutions. The principle of liability for negligence means, for example, that schools and other institutions must take reasonable care in hiring and supervision to prevent their employees from causing harm to students. It could be negligent to have inadequate security at an institution, or to have no appropriate disciplinary procedure policy for staff. The defendant's conduct is judged against what could be expected of the reasonable person or institution in a similar position to that of the defendant.

b.   Who may sue?

A civil action is initiated, controlled and financed by the plaintiff – that is, the person who chooses to commence it. In cases of institutional child abuse, the plaintiff is usually the direct or immediate victim. In Ontario, others such as members of the survivor's family who did not experience the abuse but who suffered the consequences can also bring an action as indirect victims.[12] However, usually damages will be awarded only to the spouse at the time of the abuse and children who were born at that time, thereby excluding most family members of a survivor of institutional child abuse.[13]

If an immediate or an indirect victim dies before bringing a lawsuit, his or her heirs can act on his or her behalf, initiating the action that the deceased victim could have brought. Often, an heir and an indirect victim are one and the same person, and as a result, can obtain dual compensation: firstly as the heir and secondly as the indirect victim.

c.   Group actions and class actions

A number of people who have suffered similar harm at the hands of the same person or persons may wish to sue together. A representative action occurs when a group of plaintiffs asserts a common right through one individual or a small number acting as their agent. These actions are intended to avoid having a large number of plaintiffs make the same proof of the same fault in a large number of very similar lawsuits. This allows them to save on costs, such as lawyer's preparation time or hiring of expert witnesses.

Provincial rules of procedure governing group actions are largely similar. These rules require only that prospective plaintiffs have "the same interest". But courts have been cautious in their interpretation of this requirement. As a result, very few multiple-plaintiff actions have been authorised to proceed.[14]

Three provinces – Quebec, Ontario and British Columbia – have also tried to simplify some types of multiple-plaintiff proceedings by enacting class action legislation.[15] In addition, both Ontario and Quebec have mechanisms to provide funding to support class actions.[16] While the composition of the class is at first defined by those initiating the action, the courts must "certify" the class before the action may proceed. The certification decision is based on criteria such as:

- there is an identifiable class of two or more persons;

- the claims of the class members raise common issues; and

- a class proceeding would be the preferable procedure for the fair and efficient resolution of the common issues.

Procedures exist to allow persons to opt out of a class action. Members who remain in the class action usually are not active participants in the litigation, but they share in the damages awarded if it is successful. Class action statutes do not necessarily make it any easier for survivors of institutional abuse to join in bringing a civil action. An attempt by the "children of Duplessis"[17] to launch a class action was unsuccessful. The court found that the class action was not an appropriate procedure due to the diversity of individual claims. Certification was initially denied to survivors of the Jericho Hill School[18] in part because the judge was of the opinion that:

> the class action will inevitably break down into substantial individual trials … and does not promote judicial economy or improve access to justice.[19]

The British Columbia Court of Appeal disagreed. It allowed certification for the class, which it defined as:

> students at the Jericho Hill School between 1950 and 1992 who reside in British Columbia and claim to have suffered injury, loss or damage as a result of misconduct of a sexual nature occurring at the school.[20]

In both cases, the suit was against a provincial government. The allegations related to the policies, practices and state of knowledge generally within the government that may have contributed to abuse. If the Quebec court had adopted a more liberal interpretation of the law, those common issues could have enabled the certification of a class action.

d.   Who may be sued?

The primary defendant in a civil action will be the person alleged to have committed the abuse, or if that person dies before the lawsuit, his or her heirs. But there is a risk that, if found liable, the perpetrator will be unable to pay damages. This leaves the plaintiff with a symbolic victory, but no money.[21] Therefore, it may be important for the plaintiff to sue other parties as well.[22] For example, where a defendant is insured, plaintiffs will allege causes of action for which the defendant has insurance coverage. Again, if more than one defendant committed the harm, the plaintiff may sue them all. If successful, the plaintiff can choose from which defendant or defendants to collect the full amount of damages.

In common law provinces, the perpetrators' employers can be held liable in their own right for negligence. An institution may be found liable in negligence where, for example, it failed to screen employees before hiring them, or failed to supervise them adequately.[23] An employer (such as a training school or a residential school) can also be found liable where there is no direct liability – that is, where it has committed no fault. This form of legal responsibility is known as vicarious liability. If the act falls within the ambit of the risk that the employer's enterprise creates or exacerbates, employers may justly be held liable even for the unauthorised act of an employee.

In one recent case, *Bazley*,[24] a child placed in a residential facility was sexually abused by the man responsible for his care. This man had the responsibilities of a parent, including bathing the child and tucking him in at night. The Supreme Court of Canada set out principles governing vicarious liability in the following terms:

> The test for vicarious liability for an employee's sexual abuse of a client should focus on whether the employer's enterprise and empowerment of the employee materially increased the risk of sexual assault and hence the harm.[25]

It concluded that the employer was vicariously liable. In a companion case, *Griffiths*,[26] an employee of a non-residential children's organisation carried out the abuse and the assault occurred at the employee's home. The Court held that there was not a sufficient connection between the risk created by the employment and the assaults. The employer was therefore not held vicariously liable.

In both cases, the defendants argued that charitable or non-profit organisations should be exempt from vicarious liability. They argued, in part, that unlike commercial enterprises, they cannot pass on the costs of this no-fault liability to their customers, and the potential costs of vicarious liability might force them to stop providing the important social services that they offer. The Court rejected this argument.[27] These decisions have clear implications for the liability of both governments and churches in respect of institutions where their employees committed acts of sexual and physical abuse on children in their care. In general, the circumstances of institutional child abuse are more closely analogous to the *Bazley* case, where the employer was held vicariously liable, than to the *Griffiths* case where it was not.[28]

In addition to the person who actually perpetrated the abuse, plaintiffs may also sue others who may have had a duty to control or supervise the perpetrators or otherwise prevent the abuse. This is most frequently done through actions in negligence or breach of fiduciary duty. For example, co-workers of the abuser may have had a duty to report the abuse to superiors. Management is required to take reasonable care to prevent the abuse once it knows, or ought to know, about it. Health care professionals, police, teachers and social workers have special obligations to report abuse when they are aware of it. Their failure to do so may result in civil liability.

In the civil law of Quebec, the wrongdoer's employer, such as the government or a religious community, can be held personally liable for negligence under article 1457 C.C.Q. Some examples of negligence include hiring the employee, not providing training, and not immediately firing the employee.[29] In addition, under article 1463 C.C.Q., employers may be held vicariously responsible for the fault committed by their employees in the performance of their duties. As in the common law, vicarious liability does not involve proving the fault of the employer, but rather, proving that the employee's offences were committed in "the performance of his or her duties". For example, when the violent acts were committed during the employee's working hours or within the institution, there is a strong possibility that the employee committed those offences "in the performance of his or her duties" and the employer will automatically be held responsible. Finally, under article 1457 C.C.Q., the offenders' co-workers or supervisors who failed to report could be held liable for failing to have exercised the care of a reasonable person in the circumstances.

e.   How long after abuse can one sue?

The law limits the time within which victims can sue after they have been injured. Once the applicable time limit, known as a "limitation period" in the common law and "prescription" in the civil law of Quebec, has expired, the action cannot proceed.[30] The delay within which a person must commence a civil action is usually between two to six years after the misconduct occurred.[31] Special rules apply to minors who have been injured. The limitation period is suspended, and does not begin to run until the minor has reached the age of majority. Even so, limitation periods can be a significant barrier to those who suffered abuse, particularly sexual abuse, as children. It may take years, even after reaching adulthood, for survivors to recognise the connection between the harm they suffered and the psychological impact of that harm.

The common law has begun to acknowledge this difficulty. In 1992, the Supreme Court of Canada ruled that the limitation period in a case of incest does not begin to run until the victim becomes conscious of the damage suffered and its probable cause.[32] This "delayed discoverability" rule has been applied to actions for sexual abuse against those who had fiduciary relationships with the victim – for example, teachers, priests and doctors. It is not yet clear, however, whether the "delayed discoverability" rule also applies to cases involving physical abuse of children.[33]

The *Civil Code of Québec* provides that where it is physically or psychologically impossible for a victim to commence an action, prescription begins to run only when the impossibility ends.[34] Ignorance of the law or lack of financial resources does not constitute impossibility to act. The courts have traditionally given a narrow interpretation of the impossibility to act as a reason to suspend prescription.[35] However, the Supreme Court of Canada recently changed direction in *Gauthier* v. *Beaumont*,[36] where the plaintiff was tortured by police in an effort to obtain an admission, and waited over six years before bringing an action against them. The Supreme Court recognised the plaintiff's psychological impossibility to act,[37] and suspended prescription. In addition, although *M.(K.)* v. *M.(H.)* is a common law decision, two recent Quebec decisions[38] have expressed approval for the principles it states.

Some common law provinces have recently amended their limitations legislation to make it clear that actions alleging sexual misconduct are not subject to the usual limitation periods.[39] Others have simply enacted the principle set out in *M.(K.)* v. *M.(H.)*.[40] The Northwest Territories and Newfoundland statutes explicitly recognise that the dependent nature of the relationship between the offender and the victim is a relevant consideration in deciding whether the extended limitation period will apply in cases involving allegations of sexual misconduct. In Saskatchewan, the dependent nature of the relationship is a distinct basis for extending the limitation period for a broader range of offences, such as trespass to the person, assault or battery.

f. The process

The plaintiff is responsible for managing the action, as well as the investigation and gathering of evidence to support the claim. The typical civil action proceeds through the following stages. A prospective plaintiff visits a lawyer to explain the damage suffered. Should the lawyer conclude that a cause of action exists, normally the first step is to write the potential defendant requesting payment of damages or some other remedy. If that person refuses, legal proceedings will be formally commenced. The procedure for doing so varies slightly from province to province.

Next comes the stage of collecting evidence, including a process where the lawyers for each side may question potential witnesses, called an "examination for discovery". During this process, applications may have to be made to the court in order to settle differences between lawyers. The examination for discovery resembles a preliminary inquiry in a criminal trial, with the result that many claimants find it quite unsettling.

After these pre-trial processes, the case can proceed to trial. The proceedings are adversarial, with each party entitled to conduct the case as it sees fit. This includes making decisions about what evidence to present and whether to have the plaintiff and defendant testify. If the plaintiff decides to testify, he or she will be subjected to cross-examination. While cross-examination in a civil trial may not always be as rigorous as in a criminal trial it can still be a revictimising experience for claimants.

The plaintiff enjoys a great deal of control over the proceedings, at least in theory. Defendants are also in a position to control the pace of the process, and may choose to move them along at a more rapid pace than the plaintiff desires. Similarly, defendants may prolong the proceedings if that better suits their purposes. For this reason, many provinces have begun to experiment with allowing judges a greater power to control civil actions. This idea, called case management, is one way for the court to control the pace of a lawsuit.[41]

Social workers, teachers, and foster Parents always told me, "You can do it." But my peers in the network PROVED that I could do it. Teaching by example, my peers showed me that someone from the same background as me can take control of their life, help themselves and their peers, heal, and experience "life after the system".

– National Youth in Care Network – "Tools for Change"
a conference sponsored by the Department of Justice Canada,
"Working Together for Children", September 27, 1999.

I still felt guilt, shame, and self-hatred because of the abuse I'd experienced. It was the network that taught me to love myself and want to live – before I joined the network, I only wanted to die.

Really my success Is much like a loaf of bread; My agency gave me the flour, eggs, and other ingredients that form the dough. But dough alone doesn't make a loaf. It was the network that provided the yeast: the care, support, and motivation that gave life to the dough and allowed me to rise.

– National Youth in Care Network – "Tools for Change"
a conference sponsored by the Department of Justice Canada,
"Working Together for Children", September 27, 1999.

The plaintiff normally bears the expenses of preparing and conducting the litigation.[42] Usually a successful plaintiff will receive an "order of costs" from the court that will help meet some, but by no means all, of these expenses. In sexual assault cases in some common law provinces, plaintiffs have a good chance of receiving an award for costs that covers a significantly higher proportion of their actual expenses.[43] On the other hand, where a plaintiff is unsuccessful in his or her action, he or she may have to pay a good part of the defendant's legal costs. The possibility of an adverse ruling and liability to pay the defendant's is a serious financial risk for the plaintiff.

At any time during a civil action, the plaintiff may put an end to the proceeding by abandoning the lawsuit. Similarly, the defendant may choose simply to pay the defendant the amount asked for and avoid the trial. More commonly, however, trials are avoided by an agreement between the plantiff and the defendant. Lawyers for the parties negotiate a settlement, in which each compromises slightly in order to resolve the dispute privately without the need for a trial. These settlements can be reached right up until the moment the judge renders a decision.[44]

g.   Remedies

The remedy generally available to a successful plaintiff in a civil action is an order of the court directing one or more defendants to pay the plaintiff a sum of money (damages). Damages are of three types: pecuniary (or special), non-pecuniary (or general), and punitive. The first two categories are intended to compensate plaintiffs for their loss.[45] Pecuniary damages cover actual expenses already incurred,[46] as well as the anticipated costs of future expenses. They also cover the lost income and lost earning capacity of the plaintiff. For example, physical and sexual abuse of children may impair the ability of survivors to do well in school, and consequently prevent them from earning as much as they could have otherwise. This lost earning capacity is estimated on the basis of actuarial and personal evidence presented at trial. All such claims must be proven, often requiring testimony from experts.[47]

Non-pecuniary damages – also referred to as general or moral damages – are intended to compensate for pain, suffering, and loss of enjoyment of life, in short, for the psychological and emotional harm caused.[48] Moral damages cannot be quantified as readily as pecuniary damages. However, courts will consider the nature and duration of the injury suffered and its effects on the victim when assessing this amount.

Punitive damages may be awarded to punish the defendant for conduct that was particularly outrageous. An award of punitive damages is intended to demonstrate society's rejection of the defendant's acts.[49] In determining whether to make a punitive award, the court considers the conduct itself, how much the defendant has already been ordered to pay in compensation, and any prior criminal penalties that may have been imposed for the same wrong.[50] In Quebec, punitive damages may be awarded only where the law expressly provides for them.[51]

Indirect victims, such as parents, can also be entitled to monetary compensation for injuries sustained.[52] Pecuniary damages might include past and future costs of therapy and medication, and loss of past and future income. Non-pecuniary damages might include the loss of affection and support that they personally sustain as a result of injuries to the immediate victim. Indirect victims are rarely awarded punitive damages.

Damages are usually awarded as a lump sum, that is, a single, final amount.[53] If the survivor's condition deteriorates, he or she cannot return to court to claim additional compensation.[54] Similarly, if the victim's condition improves, the defendant cannot request that the matter be reopened. Damages to cover future needs are based on aggregate data – for example the average life expectancy for people of that age.

Plaintiffs may elect to receive their damages in the form of periodic payments. Generally, they cannot be compelled to do so.[55] However, courts in Manitoba and Ontario have authority to order that damages be paid in instalments.[56] As with the case of lump sum awards, quantification of the amount of periodic payments is also fixed in advance, and cannot afterwards be varied to take account of actual future need.

It remains the plaintiff's responsibility to enforce a civil court order. Where a defendant does not, or cannot, pay cash a plantiff will normally hire a bailiff to seize the defendant's property, sell it by public auction and hand over the net proceeds of the sale. Sometimes, rather than use this regular process for collecting a judgement, plaintiffs will sell the judgement (usually at a large discount) to a collection agency, to immediately receive cash. Other plaintiffs may transfer their right to receive periodic payments in the future in exchange for goods and services provided immediately. In most provinces there is no regulation of when and how these transactions are undertaken.

Insolvent defendants or defendants who are incarcerated will probably never pay the damages awarded against them.[57] Nonetheless, some plaintiffs in sexual abuse cases bring civil actions for the purpose of vindication, even though there is no reasonable prospect of actually collecting any financial compensation.[58] Others may seek non-monetary remedies in the form of injunctions ordering the defendant to do, or to refrain from doing something. When these orders are directed to reforming an institution's procedures or practices, they are usually referred to as structural injunctions.[59] In certain cases, structural injunctions can prove quite useful in countering the systemic conditions that may give rise to institutional abuse.[60]

h.   Settlements and alternative dispute resolution

Because a civil action is a private proceeding between a plaintiff and a defendant, the State normally has no formal role in the process. This is true even when there are several plaintiffs as in a class action, or several defendants (for example, when the perpetrator and his or her employer are sued together). For this reason, either the plaintiff or the defendant may end the action at any time before the judge renders a decision.[61] As noted, the plaintiff may simply abandon the action and withdraw the suit. Likewise, the defendant may choose to pay the plaintiff. More often, however, the plaintiff and the defendant come to an agreement, in which both parties compromise slightly in order to resolve the dispute privately. In the common law, this type of agreement is referred to as a settlement, and in the civil law as a transaction. A settlement may occur at any time. It may happen right after the document initiating the action is filed; it may be reached after the "pre-trial discoveries" have been held (but before the trial); it may be negotiated during the trial; or even after the trial is over and the judge is still deliberating. In cases involving institutional child abuse, one example of this type of proceeding is the settlements concluded in Alberta with approximately 900 victims of forced sexual sterilisation.[62]

Settlements are binding upon the parties in the same way as a judgement would be. Occasionally, the plaintiff and defendant ask the judge to publicly record their settlement in a judgement.[63] Unlike a judgement, however, the details of the settlement need not be made public. A judgement that incorporates a settlement may contain features that the court itself could not order. For example, the defendant may agree to apologise to the plaintiff, contribute money to establish a therapeutic program, found a community centre or pay for a memorial or a documentary archive. Even where the agreement is strictly about money, the parties have a great deal of flexibility in determining how that money should be paid: payment can made in a lump sum, in periodic payments, or as part of what is called a "structured settlement".[64] Some believe that there is a public side to civil actions and that all settlements should be filed in court as a matter of public record.[65] This would provide other potential claimants with detailed information about the amount of the settlement and help to ensure that a certain consistency between different claimants is maintained. No province has yet required that negotiated settlements be made public.

As a matter of course, most cases do settle rather than proceed to trial.[66] But the settlement will always be negotiated in the shadow of the judicial process, and under the threat of the court's decision. Many provinces have experimented with adjustments to the civil justice system to make it more effective, expeditious and accessible, and to better regulate the settlement process.[67] A common adjustment is to assign a judge to the case as soon as it is filed and to give him or her responsibility for managing the pace of the litigation. In other cases, provinces have imposed mandatory mediation as a precondition to a trial for certain types of lawsuit. As well, to assist in negotiating a settlement, courts can appoint experts to give the parties an early evaluation of the strength of their case ("early neutral assessment"). Still other provinces offer plaintiffs and defendants the chance to opt for a "mini-trial" in which a judge holds an expedited hearing with limited evidence being presented.[68]

All of the above adjustments to the civil justice system presuppose that a civil action has been commenced in the ordinary way. They are designed to deflect cases from the regular system of litigation: they are meant to make the civil action less costly, less time consuming, and less complex.[69] These adjustments have the added advantage of encouraging the settlement process and avoiding adversarial proceedings. Where plaintiffs may be reluctant to expose themselves to rigorous cross-examination, or may wish to obtain closure on a case, they offer an attractive alternative to the full-blown civil action previously discussed.

Concern for cost, delay and complexity in the civil justice system has also led to a wide variety of proposals to establish distinctive alternatives to it.[70] These "alternative dispute resolution" processes are of two main types: those that provide alternative models for the adversarial adjudication of disputes, and those that provide the means to resolve disputes in a non-adversarial and non-adjudicative manner. As noted, both approaches have been taken by provinces seeking to make minor adjustments to the regular civil justice process.

These other dispute resolution techniques are also common as free-standing approaches to resolving conflict. For example, in many contractual disputes, parties agree that rather than launch a civil action, they will refer any conflicts to an arbitrator or to an arbitration panel. The chosen arbitrators will then have whatever authority the parties delegate to them. They may be authorised to run the process as they wish, to hear what evidence they wish, to apply whatever standards of judgement they wish, and to award whatever type of remedy they think is appropriate. The process followed could well be simply the mirror (in a private setting) of an ordinary judicial trial. Or it could be a process that is neither adversarial nor an adjudication: a mediation; a facilitated negotiation; or a conciliation process, for example.

In situations that can give rise to regular civil actions for damages caused by wrongful conduct, the parties obviously do not have the opportunity to negotiate a dispute resolution process before the harm is caused. Whatever alternatives are chosen, this choice will be taken after the event that may give rise to a lawsuit has occurred. It may or may not be negotiated prior to the lawsuit being launched. However, these are not like cases where a term of a contract requires private arbitration or some other dispute resolution mechanism. In cases involving potential civil actions for damages, the parties themselves are free to negotiate not only the character of the dispute resolution process, but also whether or not to opt into one. Once again, the advantage of many of these processes is that they are usually less costly, less time consuming, and less complex than a civil action.

Most alternative dispute resolution processes have the advantage of encouraging the settlement process and avoiding adversarial proceedings. As in pre-negotiated arbitration agreements, parties can decide how to run the hearing process (for example, to limit cross-examination) and what types of evidence can be presented (for example, to admit second-hand evidence). It is also possible to negotiate what kinds of claims may be raised (for example, whether only recognised civil wrongs shall be heard), which standards of judgement are to be applied (for example, whether to take into account "equity" between the parties) and which degree of proof will be required (for example, whether the standard of proof and validation will be the same as in a civil trial). In addition, parties may negotiate the range of remedies that will be available if a finding is made in favour of the plaintiff (monetary damages in lump sums or periodic payments; apologies; therapeutic programs; and so on). Finally, these alternative dispute resolution processes permit plaintiffs to aggregate their claims, in a manner like a class action proceeding. Parties may negotiate a process to be made available to a whole category of potential plaintiffs.[71] Where an alternative dispute resolution process incorporates a wide variety of the non-standard elements just noted, it begins to take on the character of a redress program – a set of approaches that are discussed in greater detail at the end of this part.

Only the needs and imaginations of plaintiffs and defendants limit the types of dispute resolution processes that may be negotiated and put into place. When negotiated in a manner respectful of all potential parties to a lawsuit, they offer attractive alternatives to the full-blown civil action as a means of obtaining accessible, inexpensive, efficient and expeditious civil justice, and as a means of obtaining closure on a conflict in a non-adversarial setting.

3.   Assessment

Overview

The civil litigation process is consistent with the principles of respect and engagement because it is a process that, in theory at least, is initiated and shaped by survivors of institutional child abuse themselves. Survivors are, moreover, key participants in it. The extent to which they have access to the civil justice system and can truly direct the course of their action depends, of course, on the resources and information available to them. As well, it depends upon the conduct of the other actors in the process: the defendants, the lawyers (including their own lawyer) and the judge.

One strength of the civil litigation process is its fact-finding capacity. The requirement of proof in an adversarial setting promotes (although it does not guarantee) the emergence of all the facts relating to the particular wrongs alleged. The rules of evidence do, however, mean that broader questions about the design of children's institutions and the general contexts of child abuse will not be raised.

A judgement in favour of the plaintiff in a civil action is a very effective means for holding defendants accountable. The judgement and the amount of damages awarded are a matter of public record. Resolution of a civil action through an out-of-court settlement or some form of alternative dispute resolution may not achieve a similar type of clear and public accountability. The procedural rules of the civil justice system are designed to be fair to all parties. In practice, significant differences in financial and other resources may strain this balance and leave at least a perception that the process is not entirely fair.

As an adversarial process, the civil action is an unlikely forum for the promotion of acknowledgement, apology and reconciliation. It is, of course, quite effective at responding to the financial claims of survivors, but less so at meeting their other needs and the needs of their families. To date, it has not shown itself to be effective in responding directly to the needs of communities and peoples. By contrast, however, a settlement or an alternative dispute resolution process may include an apology and the provision of therapy – something the civil process does not provide. Finally, the public nature of a civil action means that it can serve both a preventive and an educational role, as can alternative processes when they lead to outcomes that are made public.

a.   Respect, engagement and informed choice

On the surface, a civil action offers great potential for survivors to engage meaningfully in the process designed to redress their grievances. They decide whether or not to initiate a civil action. They usually choose their own lawyers, and in theory, instruct their lawyers about who to sue, which experts and witnesses to call, the amounts claimed, and so on. They may testify in their own words about what happened to them. They participate in settlement negotiations and it is their decision whether or not to settle. This offers survivors an opportunity for control and decision making – key aspects of respect and engagement. This opportunity must, however, be placed in context. There are issues of access, control and decision making that make the reality of civil actions somewhat less attractive to survivors than its theory would suggest.

i.   Access

Survivors are not necessarily well-informed about the claims they may have against those who abused them and against the institutions where they resided. The actual or perceived cost of consulting or retaining a lawyer may prevent some from seeking the information they need to determine whether they wish to proceed with an action. Survivors may be deterred for psychological as well as financial reasons. They may lack confidence in the legal system. They may not be prepared to open up perhaps the most sensitive and private parts of their lives for scrutiny in the adversarial setting of a courtroom.[72] Survivors may also not know where to turn to find a lawyer who has the special legal training or experience necessary to deal effectively with a case involving institutional child abuse. These cases present particular difficulties of proof, as well as the challenge of dealing with clients who are likely to be psychologically fragile. Lawyers must also be willing to work with therapists and others who support survivors.[73]

Most lawyers who represent abuse survivors are sensitive to the special needs of their clients. This includes the need to keep them fully informed and to otherwise treat clients with respect.[74] Some, however, may see the emerging cases involving institutional abuse more as an opportunity to increase their volume of business. Concern over the aggressive solicitation of Aboriginal plaintiffs for group actions arising out of their residential school experiences[75] led the Grand Chief of the Assembly of First Nations to write a cautionary letter in October 1998 to law societies across the country.[76] The Law Society of Saskatchewan responded by clarifying a rule of conduct in its professional code of ethics to provide further protection to victims of physical and sexual abuse.[77]

Apart from a survivor's potential vulnerability to exploitation, civil litigation can also be expensive.[78] A survivor must have the financial resources not only to initiate an action, but also to see it through. Some provinces permit what are called contingency fee arrangements.[79] This means that the client will pay a fairly high percentage of the amount recovered if the action is successful. If the action is unsuccessful, the lawyer receives no fees. Contingency fee arrangements facilitate access by permitting those without funds to proceed with a lawsuit.[80] They also present the possibility for exploitation, particularly of survivors of institutional child abuse who may not be in a position to negotiate for a reasonable percentage.

A class action will normally not be commenced, nor a contingency agreement reached unless, in the lawyer's opinion, the client stands a good chance of actually collecting damages from a solvent defendant. Similarly, legal aid plans are unlikely to fund actions with little prospect of realising on a judgement. Survivors, on the other hand, may wish to litigate to obtain public vindication whether or not they actually recover any money. In these cases, a civil action is not a real option unless they have the funds to finance it themselves.

ii. Control over and tone of proceedings

While survivors decide whether to commence an action or to participate in a class action, their control over the process is reduced once the action is commenced. [81] Plaintiffs must rely on their lawyers for legal and strategic advice. It may be difficult for lawyers to take instructions from more than a representative group of plaintiffs in group or class actions. Therefore, other plaintiffs may feel they have only limited control over their claim. Even where the plaintiffs are open to a settlement, the terms are often more a matter of negotiation between the lawyers, with the plaintiffs given the opportunity only to accept or refuse. Furthermore, although survivors have initiated the process, they are not the only people involved; defendants and the judge also have a role to play. Research shows that most trial judges do treat survivors with respect. It also indicates how devastating it can be when judges are perceived as disrespectful, or worse.[82]

Civil litigation is by definition adversarial. It is generally in the interest of the defence to discredit the plaintiff and to minimise the loss suffered. Cross-examination of the plaintiff in a civil action, as in a criminal prosecution, is a stressful experience.[83] The defendant who is sued on the basis that he or she physically or sexually abused a child faces an enormous social stigma and the potential loss of family, friends and employment. In this context, a thorough cross-examination of the plaintiff should not be seen as disrespectful (unpleasant though it may be for the plaintiff) but rather as necessary to ensure fairness for defendants.

In practice, whether the civil litigation process promotes active engagement, respect, and informed choice by survivors depends largely on the competence and sensitivity of the plaintiff's lawyer and the judge,[84] the conduct of defence counsel, and the availability of support systems such as therapy and peer support. Although the civil action appears to accord greater respect and control to the plaintiff and allows for greater participation by the plaintiff than a criminal trial, the plaintiff does not always have the financial, psychological or other resources to fully benefit from the opportunities it presents.

b.   Fact-finding

In a civil case, each side is entitled to marshall and present its own evidence. Even when a case involves complex legal issues, most lawyers believe that the outcome of a civil action turns on the facts, as proven at trial. The fact-finding goal of a civil action is to determine whether there is fault and, if so, to assess the injury sustained. Obviously, a civil trial does not necessarily shed light on all the facts the plaintiff may believe are important. Moreover, some evidence, although factually accurate, will be excluded because of its tenuous relevance to the actual claim being made.[85]

The plaintiff and the defendant each have the right to testify about the facts as they perceive them and to challenge each other's version by cross-examination. It is assumed that this is the most just fact-finding process that can be employed to resolve a dispute between two or more persons. Nevertheless, when the events occurred several years previously, evidence may be hard to collect.[86] Some evidence may have disappeared, particularly files kept by institutions. Key witnesses may have died. Memories of details fade. The passage of time thus works against a survivor trying to shed light on the facts.

Furthermore, the intimidating atmosphere of the courtroom may not make it the best milieu for eliciting the full range of facts from survivors and their witnesses. The plaintiff may not feel comfortable, and may wish to suppress relevant facts so as not to divulge information on certain periods of his or her life.[87] Some events, which are significant for the survivor, may be ignored or not given great weight by the court. This can suggest to survivors that the court is neither truly listening to them, nor attempting to understand their situation.[88] Finally, given that its goal is to discover facts about events which have affected a single victim and his or her family, the civil process does not seek to establish an overall picture of past events in a given institution.

Fact-finding in a civil action is the plaintiff's responsibility. This poses two challenges. First, where the action is against the institution as well as the individual perpetrator, it pits the financial resources of an individual or group of individuals against those of an institution or government. Second, it requires access to records, many of which are within the control of the institution. The plaintiff's disadvantage is mitigated somewhat by the laws of pre-trial discovery that require parties to the lawsuit to produce relevant documents in their possession to the other side. But this works both ways. Survivors may be required to produce private medical, counselling and other intimate records for inspection by the defendant.[89] Undoubtedly, some of this material provides a factual basis for a fair trial. But defence lawyers may also use it to intimidate survivors.

Whether cross-examination promotes fact-finding by exposing untruths and uncertainties in direct evidence, or suppresses truth by intimidating, confusing and otherwise discrediting accurate testimony, is a matter of opinion. The answer no doubt varies from case to case. Testimony about abuse experienced by children, many years ago, in private, and at the hands of apparently reputable defendants, may be easier to discredit than other testimony, even where it is true. It is also likely that the personal characteristics of many survivors may make them more vulnerable to being discredited despite the truth of their testimony. For example, survivors often exhibit low self-esteem, a quality that may weaken their credibility on the stand. Where judges are attuned to the effects of child abuse, these characteristics may not undermine credibility so much as they may seem to substantiate the allegation of abuse.[90]

Race and gender discrimination (conscious and unconscious), and simple cultural differences (such as whether it is polite to look another person in the eye, or to contradict someone in authority) also influence perceptions of credibility.[91] These perceptions are especially important when the plaintiff and the defendant offer dramatically different accounts of events that transpired without any other corroborating evidence.[92]

c.   Accountability

Civil actions are well-suited to holding defendants accountable: there is a finding of liability followed by an award of damages.[93] This public determination and pronouncement of the defendant's personal responsibility for wrongful conduct may also have a punitive effect, particularly if punitive damages are awarded. A successful civil action can also assign responsibility without fault to the perpetrator's employers through their vicarious liability.[94] The judgement constitutes official recognition of the liability of defendants, even if they refuse to acknowledge that responsibility.

While even a large damage award may not carry as great a social stigma as a criminal conviction or imprisonment, it may have a significant impact on a defendant. Some churches and charitable or non-profit organisations fear that the impact of potential vicarious liability awards may drive them into bankruptcy.[95] Others have stated that they are considering ending their involvement in residential programs for children (for example, summer camps). If this proves to be the case, the effect of a civil judgement may be more permanent or more publicly noticeable than the imprisonment of an individual perpetrator. When cases settle out of court, the terms of settlement are usually confidential, thereby diminishing the public punitive effect of the payment damages. Most multi-plaintiff alternative dispute resolution processes do, however, have a component of public recognition.

Little is known about the consequences for the survivor who is unsuccessful in a civil action. There may be a perception that an unsuccessful action means that the plaintiffs were responsible for their own misfortune or worse, that they did not even suffer abuse. Plaintiffs may feel that dismissal of their claim is a dismissal of the truth of their experience. This can be devastating. But accountability flows in both directions. Defendants sometimes commence their own civil actions against the plaintiff for defamation. Alleged perpetrators have succeeded in obtaining awards of damages against plaintiffs who have been unable to prove their allegations were true.[96]

d.   Fairness

The procedural rules of a civil trial are designed to treat everyone fairly. Each side has an opportunity to present his or her case and to challenge the case presented by the other. Each must follow the same rules of evidence. The trial is public. An impartial tribunal decides the case and gives reasons for its decision. Nonetheless, because individual plaintiffs are less well-off financially, and less well-informed than institutional defendants, they may be less able to mount their case. Litigation is also a highly personal matter for most survivors, a process in which they have a huge emotional and psychological stake. This is not true of institutional defendants, whatever their financial and reputational stake in the litigation. One example of the difference is the impact of delay. For the plaintiff, delay in adjudication can be stressful and psychologically damaging.[97] A pressing need for closure, or for funds, can lead a plaintiff to settle a case for a lower amount than would likely be achieved if he or she could bear delay as well as an institutional defendant.

Beyond the issue of actual fairness, there is a question of perception. On the one hand, survivors of abuse in institutions may not trust institutions, including courts, to treat them fairly. They may believe, rightly or wrongly, that the dice are loaded and that the courts are predisposed in favour of institutional defendants. Economic disparity between the two parties may also contribute to their feeling that the process is not fair. On the other hand, public sympathy may favour survivors who allege that they suffered abuse. Institutional defendants may perceive that this predisposes courts against them. Thus, the question of whether the civil process is equitable goes beyond the trial itself and touches on perceptions of the legal system, accessibility, and public opinion.[98]

e.   Acknowledgement, apology and reconciliation

A drawback to civil litigation is its tendency to discourage defendants from acknowledging their wrongdoing, apologising, and reconciling with their victims. This shortcoming is inherent in the adversarial process. The mere possibility of litigation is enough to inhibit defendants (especially legally astute institutional defendants) from taking any step that might later be construed as an admission of liability. Once an action has commenced, defendants may decide to take an aggressive stance, responding with personal allegations against the plaintiffs. An adversarial system initially encourages litigants to move further apart, not closer together; it encourages defendants to deny, not acknowledge responsibility.[99] Even a negotiated settlement does not necessarily include an acknowledgement of responsibility. The parties may eventually agree on financial compensation without any voluntary acceptance of responsibility.[100]

A court can impose judgement, but it cannot order an apology or force a defendant to assume responsibility. Seeking to resolve conflict through adversarial litigation, particularly if the defendant has initiated numerous proceedings and has been uncooperative, can therefore be a major barrier to apology and reconciliation. This suggests that alternatives to traditional civil justice regimes that do not produce winners and losers – for example mediation and conciliation processes – are needed to accommodate those who seek acknowledgement, apology and reconciliation, and those who might be willing to provide it. Litigation is better left to those who seek public attribution of responsibility or who require it in order to obtain financial compensation.

f. Compensation, counselling and education

Civil actions centre on the financial needs of plaintiffs. But survivors of institutional child abuse have a range of other needs. Civil actions can also meet many of these, which may help plaintiffs turn the page and move on in their lives.[101] Some refer to this as the "therapeutic" effect of the civil action.[102]

i. *Financial needs*

The civil justice system offers an opportunity to fully respond to the needs of those seeking financial compensation.[103] A properly quantified damage award should provide sums sufficient to meet all needs for past and future care brought about by the abuse. The manner of payment may, however, cause problems. Typically, in abuse cases, the majority of the award will be calculated to meet future needs. This entails making predictions about the future: for example, how long the plaintiff will live, what the state of his or her health will be over that period, and what she or he would have earned, if not for the injuries suffered. Given that the survivors were children or adolescents at the time of the assaults, it is difficult to restore them to their initial state, or imagine what they would have become had the assaults not occurred. In these cases, the courts rely on statistical averages. Where statistics show low levels of education and income for particular populations, courts assume that individuals from those populations would not have earned much even if they had not been abused. Therefore, damages for lost income are calculated accordingly. This approach contributes to maintaining discrimination against such groups, which include women, Aboriginal persons and persons with disabilities.[104]

Another difficulty is the cap placed on general damages. Some years ago, the Supreme Court of Canada set a maximum amount that could be awarded for general damages[105] in the context of cases involving massive physical injuries, where the vast majority of the damages awarded were for the cost of future care. In the case of survivors of physical and sexual abuse, however, it is the psychological, not the physical damage that is the most significant. Limiting the general damage awards of survivors of institutional child abuse may prevent them from receiving an award that adequately compensates for the damages they have suffered.[106]

Awarding plaintiffs large lump sums of money gives them the power to control their financial future through prudent investment. Not all are prudent investors, however. For this reason, some suggest that mandatory periodic payments would save some plaintiffs from the danger of dissipating their damage awards. Periodic payments could also protect them, to some extent, from the claims of family, friends and others. Nonetheless, it is not clear that urging survivors to accept periodic payments is a better approach than providing them with independent financial advice about the comparative advantages and disadvantages of lump sum and periodic payments, and about investment strategies for handling any money received.

In any event, it is less the form in which a payment is made than the circumstances surrounding the payment that can cause additional harm to survivors. Making payments available as part of a more general program of redress that offers financial counselling, therapy or other services allows survivors themselves to choose how they wish to receive, and to view, the monetary compensation awarded.

Some survivors prefer to be compensated by direct entitlement to specific services rather than by receiving money to purchase the service.[107] Courts could order defendants to fund the provision of services by a third party (for example, a group of therapists or a firm of financial advisers). In general, however, this has not been the pattern for civil damage awards. The civil action is not of direct assistance to survivors wishing to receive counselling, educational opportunities and vocational training.

ii.   Therapeutic needs

Survivors of abuse also use civil actions to meet non-financial goals. These include obtaining public affirmation that they have been wronged; seeking justice; obtaining closure; securing an apology; and taking revenge. A civil action is one way in which survivors can give voice to their experiences. This in itself may prove therapeutic, even if survivors are not always successful in their claims.

It is difficult to generalise about how well expectations of survivors are satisfied.[108] For some, the stress of litigation outweighs the gains. Most abuse survivors report that they become physically or emotionally ill during the process. Litigation seems to work best for plaintiffs who have already confronted the consequences of their abuse and are well along the path of recovery or for those who have a strong support system.[109] To maximise the amount of compensation they stand to recover, survivors must emphasise the seriousness of their injuries and present the most extensive list of needs possible. It is questionable whether creating this "damaged" profile encourages and assists in the healing process. The stress of a civil action (cross-examination, delay, publicity) coupled with need to present a negative self-portrait may produce the opposite effect.

g.   Needs of families, communities and peoples

In some provinces, the civil trial can take into account the needs of both immediate and indirect victims. The spouse and children of a survivor may bring an action for their own losses suffered in consequence of the abuse sustained by the survivor.[110] In addition to meeting the basic financial needs of families, the civil process can provide them with a "therapeutic" effect, as it can for survivors themselves. But this is not always the case. The majority of survivors report being heavily dependent on family and friends during the process, and many feel that pursuing the action actually damaged their relationships with these supporters.

In some cases, particular communities may have suffered from widespread institutional abuse. These include members of the Deaf community, or in the case of residential schools, Aboriginal people. An argument can be made that a community suffers a different kind of damage from that experienced by survivors and their families. To date, the civil justice system has not recognised separate group claims.[111] It is possible, however, that groups of Aboriginal people might one day succeed collectively in obtaining damages for breach of the fiduciary duty that Canadian governments owe to them.[112]

h. Prevention and public education

The civil action indirectly plays a role in educating the public. The trial and judgement are public, and may be reported in the media. By creating public awareness of the issue, civil actions can serve to encourage others to initiate civil actions and help prevent future institutional abuse.

i. Prevention

Deterrence is generally regarded as one of the main purposes of the law of civil wrongs. Since individual perpetrators already face the likelihood of criminal liability, public censure and dismissal from employment, the deterrent effect of civil liability is hard to gauge. If the conduct of perpetrators is due more to personality disorders rather than rational calculation, they are unlikely to be deterred by the prospect of civil liability.

Once again in theory, liability should encourage employers to design their institutions, programs for hiring, training and supervision to minimise the chances of abuse by their employees. The recent Supreme Court decisions on vicarious liability make it clear that those in charge of residential institutions for children can be held responsible for abuse perpetrated by their employees. Governments and organisations that run or fund such institutions were already aware of their potential responsibility to ensure the safety of those in their care. While the *Bazley*[113] decision clarified that responsibility, it might discourage some organisations from continuing with residential programs instead of encouraging them to take additional preventive efforts. Much will depend on how the insurance industry responds. If it continues to provide coverage for institutional employers and simply raises premiums across the board, this may reduce the deterrent impact of liability. On the other hand, insurers may contribute to better prevention if premiums are adjusted to take into account better recruitment and training programs, performance ratings, and so on.

Although there is much to be said for the idea that potential civil liability does a better job of discovering and publicising wrongdoing than it does of correcting and preventing it, the two go hand-in-hand. A judgement will spell out in detail precisely what acts or omissions constituted the basis for liability. This information educates insurers and lawyers. In turn, they advise potential defendants (including institutional defendants) about how to improve their practices. In this sense, civil judgements can be said to promote prevention. Of course, in cases where settlements remain confidential, and where alternative dispute resolution processes themselves are not well known, the preventive effect is less pronounced.

ii. Public education

Physical and sexual abuse, especially when perpetrated on children, is newsworthy. The involvement of major political and social institutions in institutional abuse is also newsworthy. Civil trials are open to the public, and the press often covers trials of this sort. The documents initiating the action, and the supporting documentation, are also public, and frequently the subject of press coverage. There is no doubt that civil litigation can reveal sordid details long hidden and otherwise suppressed. Many Canadians have learned a great deal from these court cases about the manner in which governments, some leading churches and other institutions allowed children to be treated in institutions designed for their benefit. Without the prospect of civil litigation, much of this would have remained secret. Even when the threat of a civil trial is transformed into a settlement or an alternative dispute resolution process, public education can be one of the outcomes. This is especially the case where the agreement expressly provides for programs of public education.

4. Conclusion

The civil litigation process is, in theory, well-suited to meeting most of the needs of survivors, while respecting other concerns such as fairness, responsibility, prevention and public education. It is a public, neutral process initiated by survivors that is consistent with the principles of respect and engagement. The requirement of proof in an adversarial setting promotes, although it does not guarantee, the emergence of all the facts relating to the particular wrongs alleged. This fact-finding capacity is an acknowledged strength of the civil litigation process. A judgement in favour of the plaintiff in a civil action is also an effective means for holding defendants accountable since the judgement and the amount of damages awarded are on the public record.

The procedural rules of the civil justice system ensure that the formal process is fair to all parties. As an adversarial process, however, the civil action is an unlikely forum for the promotion of acknowledgement, apology and reconciliation. It is, of course, quite effective at responding to the financial claims of survivors, but is less suited to meeting their other needs, or the needs of families, communities and peoples. Finally, the public nature of a civil action means that it can serve both a preventive and an educational role.

The principal difficulties with the civil action relate to access to justice issues, and to incidental consequences of the adversarial system. Many survivors do not have the financial resources to mount a successful civil action. Others do not have the emotional resources, or the support systems in place that would enable them to pursue an action successfully without being revictimised. These significant differences in financial and other resources of victims and defendants can lead to a perception that the civil justice process is not entirely fair.

When survivors settle a pending lawsuit or opt into an alternative dispute resolution process, a different evaluation of the civil justice system must be undertaken. The goals of respect, engagement and informed choice will usually be met, although the extent to which the facts are revealed depends on the nature of the process adopted. Since the alternative process will be negotiated, it is likely to be fair to all parties. Whether a form of alternative dispute resolution achieves clear and public accountability depends on the terms of the agreement. These may not speak to acknowledgement, or conversely, may provide for both acknowledgement and apology. The same is true of remedies. The amount of financial compensation is likely to be less in a settlement or alternative process. However, other remedies like therapy and education can be included in the agreement. Finally, alternative dispute resolution processes can serve both a preventive and an educational role if they lead to public settlements or explicit preventive and educational programs.

Recommendations

PROSPECTIVE PLAINTIFFS should have access to basic information about civil actions at no cost.

Considerations:

> Provincial governments, Law Societies, professional organisations and law faculties should continue to develop basic public legal information programmes that provide accessible information about legal options available to survivors of institutional child abuse.

> This information should relate to matters such as how to contact a lawyer, the procedure, costs, possible outcomes, and the length of the process.

> Community service agencies, survivors' groups and other non-governmental organisations should also be given resources to develop their own information kits and pamphlets on the same topics.

> Access to information about the experience of pursuing a civil claim involving institutional child abuse should also be available, and social service agencies or others who work with survivors should set up programs that enable former residents to share their experiences with potential plaintiffs.

PROSPECTIVE PLAINTIFFS should have access to support services to assist them in coping with the stress of civil litigation.

Considerations:

> Social service agencies should develop and promote support networks composed of survivors with experience in civil litigation and related processes for seeking redress. They should also compile and publicise a list of community organisations that have experience in assisting survivors. Emotional and psychological support should be available throughout the litigation process.

> Professional associations should compile a roster of therapists experienced in working with abuse survivors.

LAW SOCIETIES AND BAR ASSOCIATIONS should continue to organise professional development programs on how to conduct cases involving allegations of past institutional child abuse.

Considerations:

Law Societies may also wish to consider adding civil litigation dealing with child sexual and physical abuse to the list of specialties that may be certified.

Certification should require not only expertise in litigation, but also training in how abuse affects survivors, and the implications for the desirability and conduct of the litigation.

Certification lists should be promoted in appropriate communities, including within therapeutic communities.

LAW SOCIETIES SHOULD REVIEW their *Codes of Professional Conduct* to ensure that appropriate rules are in place to safeguard against the exploitation of survivors of institutional child abuse, especially with respect to recruitment of clients and fee arrangements.

Considerations:

The recent revisions to rule 1602.1 of the *Code of Professional Conduct* made by the Law Society of Saskatchewan could serve as a model.

The potential for exploitation inherent in contingency fees for class actions involving survivors of institutional abuse could also be minimised or eliminated through a variety of means:

- Establishment of a provincially-run class action fund to cover initial disbursements.

- Mandatory taxation of contingency accounts, or a requirement of prior judicial approval of contingency fee arrangements.

- Governments or other institutional defendants could refuse to negotiate settlements where the contingency fee is inflated.

THE NATIONAL JUDICIAL INSTITUTE and other judicial education bodies should promote judicial education programs about the circumstances and consequences of physical and sexual abuse of children in institutions.

Considerations:

These programs should provide judges with basic information about survivor litigants, including:

- information about how survivor symptoms may manifest themselves during litigation, and how they might be misinterpreted.

- information about racial and cultural differences that may manifest themselves in testifying.

- information about the non-financial expectations shared by many abuse survivors, and how the judicial role and the conduct of the litigation may assist survivors to obtain these goals without impeding any other requirements of justice.

LEGISLATURES SHOULD REVISE the principles governing limitation periods in cases of institutional child abuse, and governments should refrain from relying on limitation periods as a defence in such cases.

Considerations:

Provincial legislatures should consider the extension of limitation periods for child sexual abuse through such means as:

- amending legislation so that the limitation period does not begin to run, in the case of certain types of sexual offences in particular those that occurred during childhood or adolescence, until the plaintiff becomes aware of the connection between her or his injuries and the harm inflicted; and

- increasing the limitation period whenever the action is based on misconduct committed in the context of a relationship of dependency.

The federal government should take the lead in adopting a policy that it will not rely solely on a limitation period defence in cases relating to institutional child abuse.

COURTS SHOULD GENERALLY RESPECT the requests of plaintiffs to preserve their privacy over the course of a trial.

Considerations:

In a few recent decisions involving compensation to victims of sexual violence, the courts have respected the victims' wish to protect their privacy by granting a request for authorization to use a pseudonym or initials, seal the file, obtain a temporary order preventing the publication of any information that could identify the victim, or holding the proceedings *in camera*.

Where legislation now protects the anonymity of the parties by requiring civil proceedings in family matters to be held in camera but does not apply to civil proceedings relating to institutional child abuse, it should be amended so that it encompasses any proceedings relating to matters, such as institutional violence, that directly or indirectly affect the family.

GOVERNMENTS SHOULD NOT IMPOSE confidentiality provisions on settlements with survivors of institutional child abuse, or on awards granted pursuant to any alternative dispute resolution process.

Considerations:

It should be up to the plaintiff to decide whether he or she wishes to keep the terms of an agreement confidential.

Settlement agreements that are not confidential could be recorded in the register of the superior court where the case was launched.

Where plaintiffs wish to preserve the confidentiality of their settlement agreements, governments (and other institutional defendants) should nevertheless publish aggregate data about settlements in respect of institutional child abuse cases, so long as the data cannot identify any plaintiff.

WHERE COURTS APPLY statistical data in order to determine lost income for survivors of institutions, they should use the statistics for the Canadian public as a whole, rather than those specific to the population that attended the particular institution.

Considerations:

Statistical averages drawn from among those who were survivors of institutional child abuse offer only a partial indication of how any particular individual would have succeeded had he or she not suffered abuse.

---

[1] An inventory of civil actions relating specifically to institutional child abuse in Canada appears in Law Commission of Canada, *Institutional Child Abuse – Civil Cases* by G. Shea (Ottawa: Law Commission of Canada, 1999). Available in hard copy from the Law Commission of Canada and online: <http://www.lcc.gc.ca>.

[2] See A.M. Linden, *Canadian Tort Law*, 6th ed. (Toronto: Butterworths, 1997) at c. 1 for a discussion of the situation in common law provinces. In Quebec, article 1457 of the *Civil Code of Québec* [hereinafter C.C.Q.] establishes this principle. For a discussion see J.L. Baudouin & P. Deslauriers, *La responsabilité civile*, 5th ed. (Cowansville: Yvon Blais, 1998) at 75ff.

[3] R.S.Q. c. C-12.

[4] See *Béliveau Saint-Jacques* v. *F.E.E.S.P.*, [1996] 2 S.C.R. 345.

[5] It seems odd to apply the same definition to years of institutional child abuse. This was one reason why L'Heureux-Dubé and McLachlin JJ. preferred to impose liability instead under the action for breach of fiduciary duty in *Norberg* v. *Wynrib*, [1992] 2 S.C.R. 226 [hereinafter *Norberg*].

[6] Such a right has been recognised at common law. See *Murdock* v. *Richards*, [1954] 1 D.L.R. 766 (N.S.T.D.) and *Vance (Next friend of)* v. *Coulter*, [1977] O.J. No. 121 (Co. Ct.), online: QL. Tort law generally adopts provisions in the *Criminal Code* and other legislation as defences based on the assertion of lawful authority. In this context, it is s. 43 of the *Criminal Code*, R.S.C. 1985, c. C-46 which permits the use of reasonable force to discipline a child.

[7] Several other actions in intentional tort might also apply in a given case of institutional abuse. It is tortious to intentionally cause nervous shock to another, where the injury actually manifests itself in physiological symptoms. This includes injuries that manifest themselves as a mental disorder. False imprisonment consists of the intentional and total restraint of the plaintiff without lawful authority.

[8] Where "...one party has an obligation to act for the benefit of another, and that obligation carries with it a discretionary power, the party thus empowered becomes a fiduciary. Equity will then supervise the relationship by holding him to the fiduciary's strict standard of conduct" (*M.(K.)* v. *M.(H.),* [1992] 3 S.C.R. 6 at 62, per La Forest J. quoting Dickson J. in *Guerin* v. *Canada,* [1984] 2 S.C.R. 335 at 384.

[9] This point is not yet settled, but there are a number of current actions where it has been alleged or litigated. See *F.S.M.* v. *Clarke,* [1999] B.C.J. No. 1973 (S.C.), online: QL.

[10] This is made most clear in *Norberg, supra* note 5, where the majority proceeds in tort and the minority in breach of fiduciary duty.

[11] This was the view expressed in the minority judgment of McLachlin J. in *Norberg, ibid.* and again in *M.(K.)* v. *M.(H.), supra* note 8. Damages will be discussed below under "Remedies".

[12] For example, the sexual assault of a child can disrupt the lives of the parents, who seek therapy. They can thus be compensated for personal injury caused to them, separate from the injury to the victim. See *Family Law Act,* R.S.O. 1990, c. F-3, s. 61. as am. by S.O. 1992, c. 32, S.O. 1997, c. 20, S.O. 1998, c. 26.

[13] Children, spouses, parents and grandparents may recover for defined out of pocket expenses, services provided for the immediate victim, and for loss of "guidance, care, and companionship".

[14] See Manitoba, *Report on Class Proceedings* (Winnipeg: Manitoba Law Reform Commission, 1999).

[15] See *Class Proceedings Act,* 1992, S.O. 1992, c. 6; *Class Proceedings Act,* R.S.B.C. 1996 c. 50, as am. by S.B.C. 1998, c. 9, s. 96; and Book IX of the *Code of Civil Procedure* (arts. 999-1051) [hereinafter C.C.P.]. For example, class actions have been permitted in British Columbia, Ontario and Quebec on behalf of purchasers of breast implants against Dow-Corning and other defendants. See *Harrington, as Representative Plaintiff* v. *Dow Corning Corp.,* [1999] B.C.J. No. 321(S.C.), online: QL.

16 *Law Society Amendment Act (Class Proceedings Funding)*, R.S.O. 1992, c. 7; and *Loi sur le recours collectif*, R.S.Q. c. R-2.1. However, in the "Orphelins de Duplessis" matter, which has similarities with the issue we are exploring, financial assistance was refused because the court held that the action did not raise identical, similar or related issues in law or in fact (art. 1003 (a) C.C.P.). According to the administrators of the Quebec *Fonds d'aide aux recours collectifs*, each orphan presented an individual situation. The nature and duration of the battery, the age of the children, *etc.*, varied, preventing a class action. See *Bertrand* v. *Fonds d'aide aux recours collectifs* (25 January 1994), Montreal 500-02-030332-931 J.E. 94-311 (C.Q.).

17 *Kelly* v. *Communauté des Soeurs de la Charité* (1 October 1995), Quebec 200-06-000001-936 J.E. 95-1875 (Sup. Ct.), online: QL [hereinafter *Kelly*; appeal abandoned February 8, 1996].

18 *L.R.* v. *British Columbia*, [1998] B.C.J. No. 2588 (B.C.S.C.), online: QL.

19 *L.R.* v. *British Columbia*, *ibid.* at para. 74.

20 *Rumley* v. *British Columbia* [1999], B.C.C.A. 689, at para. 51, online: <http://www.courts.gov.bc.ca> (date accessed: 17 January 2000).

21 It would appear that many of the decided actions for civil sexual abuse were brought against judgement-proof defendants. See B. Feldthusen, "The Civil Action for Sexual Battery: Therapeutic Jurisprudence?" (1994) 25 Ottawa L. Rev. 203 [hereinafter "The Civil Action"]. As discussed below, it would also appear that many plaintiffs brought these actions to achieve non-monetary goals.

22 There are, of course, valid reasons to pursue persons or institutions other than the direct perpetrator liable. Arguably, moral responsibility for institutional abuse rests with institutional management at the highest level, not only with individual perpetrators.

23 See for example *W.K.* v. *Pornbacher* (1997), 32 B.C.L.R. (3d) 360 (S.C.), [1997] B.C.J. No. 57, online: QL.

24 *Bazley* v. *Curry*, [1999] S.C.J. No. 35 (S.C.C.), online: QL [hereinafter *Bazley*].

25 *Bazley*, *ibid.* at para. 46.

26 *Jacobi* v. *Griffiths*, [1999] S.C.J. No. 36 (S.C.C.), online: QL [hereinafter *Griffiths*].

27 *Bazley*, *supra* note 24 at paras. 47-56.

28 See *W.R.B.* v. *Plint* (1998), 161 D.L.R. (4th) 538, [1999] 1 W.W.R. 389 (B.C.S.C.) in which both the federal government and the United Church of Canada were held vicariously liable as employers of the perpetrator in a residential school.

29 See Baudouin & Deslauriers, *supra* note 2 at 426 ff.

30 Unless the defendant chooses not to plead the limitation period as a defence, and agrees to let the lawsuit proceed.

31 Generally, two years for battery or six years for breach of fiduciary duty. In Quebec, the basic limitation period for extra-contractual responsibility is three years (art. 2925 C.C.Q.). In Ontario, there is no statutory limitation period applicable to actions for breach of fiduciary duty.

32 *M.(K.)* v. *M.(H.)*, *supra* note 8, especially at 35. This decision draws a distinction between the recollection of an event and an awareness or understanding of that event and its impact on one's life (*A.* v. *B*, [1998] R.J.Q. 3117 (C.S.)).

33 At least one case suggests that it can apply to physical abuse: *K.L.B.* v. *British Columbia*, [1998] B.C.J. No. 470 (B.C.S.C.), online: QL. The issue was raised in *T.B.* v. *New Brunswick Protestant Boys' Home*, [1998] N.B.J. No. 109 (N.B.Q.B.), online: QL, but the case settled out of court.

34 Art. 2904 C.C.Q. Also, where the damage manifests itself gradually, the period runs from the day it first appears, art. 2926 C.C.Q. For a discussion of delayed prescription with respect to sexual assault, see N. Des Rosiers & L. Langevin, *L'indemnisation des victimes de violence sexuelle et conjugale* (Cowansville, Qc.: Yvon Blais, 1998) at 57-67.

35 For a more detailed analysis of this issue, see Des Rosiers & Langevin, *ibid.* at 41ff.

36 [1998] 2 S.C.R. 3. See L. Langevin, "*Gauthier* c. *Beaumont:* la reconnaissance de l'impossibilité psychologique d'agir " (1998) 58 R. du B. 167.

37 "To be a cause of impossibility to act, the fear must be of an objectively serious harm, must exist throughout the period when it was impossible to act and must subjectively be determinative of this impossibility to act..." (*Gauthier* v. *Beaumont, ibid.* at 51). In a case of child abuse, a psychological impossibility to act would have to be proved through an expert witness. The basis would probably be a psychiatric assessment of post-traumatic stress disorder. One difficulty with such an assessment is that a psychiatrist is only brought in to provide such an assessment years after the traumatic events and, paradoxically, only after the survivor has chosen to act (by instituting a civil claim, or at least consulting a lawyer). Important though this precedent is, it was not a unanimous decision. The dissent of Lamer, C.J.C. and McLachlin J. suggests a number of points that could be used in the defendants' case.

38 *A. c. B.*, *supra* note 32 (a case of incest, where the limitation period was extended); *G.B. v. A.B.*, [1998] Q.J. No. 1588 (Sup. Ct.), online: QL. Another incest case cites *M.(K.) v. M.(H.)*, *supra* note 8, but without applying it: *Gauthier v. Lapointe*, [1999] Q.J. No. 385 (Sup. Ct.), online: QL.

39 British Columbia, *Limitation Act*, R.S.B.C. 1996, c. 266, s. 3 (4)(k)(i)-(ii), 3(l); Newfoundland, *An Act to Revise the Law Respecting Limitations*, S.N. 1995, c. L-16.1, s. 8 (2); and Saskatchewan, *The Limitation of Actions Act*, R.S.S. 1978, c. L-15, s. 3.1(a).

40 The common law does not apply where a limitations statute speaks expressly to discoverability. See *Rarie v. Maxwell* (1999), 168 D.L.R. (4th) 579 (Man. C.A.).

41 Case management is a tool that many courts now employ to ensure that actions proceed at a reasonable pace. Case management is run by judges, whose concern (among others) is to avoid undue delay in getting an action to trial. This may be very helpful to a plaintiff faced with a defendant who is stalling the action. It may also be awkward if a plaintiff is not quite ready to proceed. For a discussion of case management, see K. Roach, "Fundamental Reforms to Civil Litigation" in *Rethinking Civil Justice: Research Studies for the Civil Justice Review*, vol. 2 (Toronto: Ontario Law Reform Commission, 1996) 383 at 429 [hereinafter *Rethinking Civil Justice*].

42 Some provinces will provide legal aid assistance for a civil action for sexual abuse on a discretionary basis depending on the applicant's financial situation and the merits of the case. See the following Internet sites: <http://www.canlaw.com/legalaid/aidoffice.htm> and <http://www.gov.bc.ca> (date accessed: 16 November 1999).

43 This is because courts have tended to recognise that breach of fiduciary duty often warrants full indemnification, particularly where the breach is intentional. The higher award is known as solicitor and client costs, as opposed to the more common award of party and party costs. Also, where one party to litigation makes an offer to settle which the opposing party refuses and a court awards an amount to the offering party which meets or exceeds its offer, then the party that refused the offer will generally be required to pay to the offering party a higher portion of their legal costs (either on a solicitor-client scale, or, in some cases, all of that party's legal costs). For example, Ontario, *Rules of Civil Procedure*, R.R.O. 1990, Reg. 194, r. 49 as am. Note that this type of rule also provides a financial incentive for defendants to settle claims.

44 Settlements are discussed more fully under "Settlements and Alternative Dispute Resolution" in section h.

45 See art. 1611 C.C.Q., and Linden, *supra* note 2 at 100 ff.

46 These may include expenses for therapy, medication, transportation, expert advice, travel, telephone, and legal costs incurred during a criminal trial, where applicable, as well as loss of income for attending a criminal trial. They also include future losses, such as loss of future income, future expenses for therapy, drug rehabilitation, tuition fees for retraining, *etc.* A plaintiff may also claim the cost of expert witnesses and the costs of an action (*e.g.* court fees to file a claim, costs of service, *etc.*).

47 The cost of expert witnesses such as therapists and actuaries can be in the order of $7,500-$15,000, with fees in the range of $1,000 per day. "The Civil Action", *supra* note 21 at 221, n. 68.

48 While this distinction is clear in theory, in practice it is less so. The usual heads of damages are: total temporary incapacity; permanent partial incapacity; loss of earning power; cost of equipment and future care; expenses; pain and suffering; and loss of enjoyment of life. The quantification of these categories can be difficult. For example, should permanent partial incapacity be treated as pecuniary or non-pecuniary damages? If non-pecuniary, they are subject to the ceiling set by the Supreme Court of Canada in its 1978 trilogy (*infra*, note 105)– the ceiling is now valued at $260,000. Another difficulty, particularly when dealing with a fault (like childhood sexual abuse) committed years ago, is how to establish the percentage of incapacity that is actually due to that fault, and not to other causes such as the vicissitudes of life in the intervening years.

49 In a recent case, a jury awarded $1 million in punitive damages against an insurer that denied a claim under a fire insurance policy despite overwhelming evidence that the fire was accidental. Although the Ontario Court of Appeal reduced this unusual punitive damage award to $100,000, the risk of punitive damages can have a chilling effect on defendants (*Whiten* v. *Pilot Insurance Co.*, [1999] 42 O.R. (3d) 641 (C.A.)). See also art. 1621 C.C.Q., and the Quebec *Charter of Human Rights and Freedoms*, *supra* note 3, art. 49.

50 For a recent review of punitive damage law in this and other contexts, see B. Feldthusen, "Punitive Damages: Hard Choices and High Stakes" [1998] N.Z.L.R. 741.

51 Art. 1621 C.C.Q. As the Quebec *Charter of Rights and Freedoms*, *supra* note 3, provides for punitive damages, a plaintiff must prove that he or she suffered an intentional, illicit breach of a Charter right in order to recover such damages (*ibid.*, art. 49 (2)). Some courts seem to be imposing a third condition as well – that the defendant not have been convicted of a criminal offence for the same misconduct in respect of which punitive damages are being sought. See *Papadatos* v. *Sutherland*, [1987] R.J.Q. 1020 (C.A.) and discussion in Des Rosiers & Langevin, *supra* note 34 at para. 315 ff.

52 Normally, recovery depends on the direct victim having died. In Ontario, under the *Family Law Act*, R.S.O. 1990, c. F.3, s. 61 indirect victims may recover damages for their own losses even in cases where the direct victim has not died. See *Vaiman* v. *Yates* (1987) 60 O.R. (2d) 696 (H.C.).

53 Ideally, the plaintiff can invest a lump sum award in order to provide investment earnings for the future. In some cases, however, plaintiffs may spend the money in a short period of time. See J. Tibbetts, "Native Woes Pile Up with Lawsuit Money" *The Ottawa Citizen* (26 December 1998) A4.

54 Art. 1615 C.C.Q. does, however, provide that where the plaintiff's condition has not stabilised by the time of the judgment, he or she has the right to apply for additional damages within a three-year period.

55 Courts in common law provinces have no inherent power to order periodic payments (see *Watkins* v. *Olafson*, [1989] 2 S.C.R. 750). In Quebec, art. 1616 C.C.Q. permits courts to order periodic payments against the wishes of the parties only in the case of physical injuries to minors.

56 See *Court of Queen's Bench Act*, R.S.M. 1987, c. C-280, ss. 88.1, 88.2, 88.3, 88.4 (am. by S.M. 1993, c. 19, s. 6); *Courts of Justice Act*, R.S.O. 1990, c. C-43, s. 116 (am. by S.O. 1996, c. 25, s. 1(20)).

57 It is not just individuals who may be insolvent. As a result of claims filed by survivors of the Mount Cashel orphanage, the Christian Brothers of Ireland in Canada decided to wind up their charitable organization and to apply for liquidation. This was granted in October 1996 and since that time a liquidator has been in place. Survivors were invited to file claims by February 14, 1997. See *Eighth Report of the Provisional Liquidator* (July 22, 1999) and the resulting order of the Ontario Court of Justice (file 98-CL-002670) (July 27, 1999).

58 See "The Civil Action", *supra* note 21. See generally B. Feldthusen, O. Hankivsky & L. Greaves, "Therapeutic Consequences of Civil Actions for Damages and Compensation Claims by Victims of Sexual Abuse" (2000) 2:1 C.J.W.L. [forthcoming in 2000]. The authors interviewed civil sexual assault plaintiffs, claimants for compensation for sexual abuse under the Ontario Criminal Injuries Compensation scheme, and claimants under the *Grandview Settlement Agreement*, The Grandview Survivors Support Group and the Government of Ontario, 1994 [hereinafter *Grandview Agreement*].

59 See O.M. Fiss, *The Civil Rights Injunction* (Bloomington, Ind.: Indiana University Press, 1979); R.E. Easton, "The Dual Role of the Structural Injunction" (1990) 99 Yale L.J. 1983; N. Gillespie, "Charter Remedies: The Structural Injunction" (1990) 11 Advocates' Q. 190.

[60] To take an example from another context, the plaintiffs in the *Eldridge* case used a Charter remedy to have the Supreme Court of Canada mandate the provision of sign language services for Deaf patients in hospitals (*Eldridge* v. *British Columbia (A.G.)*, [1997] 3 S.C.R. 624 [hereinafter *Eldridge*]).

[61] See, for a discussion of the role of settlements, J. Esser, "Evaluation of Dispute Processing: We Do Not Know What We Think and We Do Not Think What We Know" (1999) 66 Den. U. L. Rev. 499.

[62] Many of the children sterilised had mental or physical disabilities. All were sterilised under the terms of the *Sexual Sterilization Act*, R.S.A. 1955, c. 311, which was repealed in 1972. See Government of Alberta, News Release 99-033, "Stratton Agreement concludes sterilisation negotiations" (2 November 1999).

[63] Ontario, *Rules of Civil Procedure*, R.R.O. 1990, Reg. 194, r. 49 and in particular, r. 49.07(6); Quebec, art. 2633 C.C.Q.

[64] Structured settlements are similar to periodic payments, but usually involve the purchase of an annuity or investment of a lump sum in a trust fund, to generate an income for the plaintiff. There are tax advantages available for structured settlements through which the parties determine the criteria to quantify the periodic payments, and the defendant purchases the appropriate annuity necessary to meet the obligations. The tax and other advantages vary from case to case.

[65] O.M. Fiss, "Against Settlement" (1984) 93 Yale L.J. 1073.

[66] See M. Galanter & M. Cahill, " 'Most Cases Settle': Judicial Promotion and Regulations of Settlements" (1994) 46 Stan. L. Rev. 1339.

[67] See the collection of essays on access to civil justice: A.C. Hutchinson, ed., *Access to Civil Justice* (Toronto: Carswell, 1990), in particular W.A. Bogart & N. Vidmar, "Problems and Experience with the Ontario Civil Justice System: An empirical Assessment" in *ibid.* 1; and C. Belleau & V. Bergeron, "L'accessibilité à la Justice Civile et Administrative au Québec" in *ibid.* 77.

[68] See Alberta Law Reform Institute, *Civil Litigation: Judicial Mini Trial* (Discussion Paper No. 1) (Edmonton: Alberta Law Reform Institute, August 1993).

[69] See Ontario Law Reform Commission, *Prospects for Civil Justice* (Study Paper) by R.A. Macdonald (Toronto: Ontario Law Reform Commission, 1995) [hereinafter *Prospects for Civil Justice*].

[70] See A. Stitt, F. Hardy & P. Simm, "Alternative Dispute Resolution and the Ontario Civil Justice System" in *Rethinking Civil Justice*, *supra* note 41, vol. 1, 449.

[71] For an example of an attempt to negotiate a relatively comprehensive alternative dispute resolution process in a situation of institutional child abuse, see the *Guiding Principles for Working Together to Build Restoration and Reconciliation* developed in connection with the "exploratory dialogues" held among representatives of the government of Canada, church groups, Aboriginal leaders and healers and survivors of residential schools (September 14, 1999).

[72] As noted, defendants may require disclosure of medical records, income tax statements, employment records, even personal diaries.

[73] Feldthusen, Hankivsky & Greaves, *supra* note 58, quoting litigants who emphasised the need for supportive therapy during the litigation.

[74] *Ibid.*, reporting an extremely high degree of client satisfaction with their own lawyers.

[75] "Lawyers Swoop to Cash in on Native Claims" *The Globe and Mail* (10 July 1999) A1.

[76] He also expressed concern over the manner in which potential plaintiffs were being asked to write about their experiences, as well as over the terms of the contingency agreements they were being asked to sign.

[77] R. 1602.1 states, in part: "No member shall initiate contact with a prospective client who is in a weakened state." According to an amendment passed on June 10, 1999, "weakened state" is defined as "a physical, emotional or mental condition which may render a prospective client unduly vulnerable to persuasion or importuning by a lawyer and shall, ... be deemed to include the state of any prospective client who is an alleged victim of physical and/or sexual abuse."

[78] Nine civil litigants reported spending an average of $20,000 on their court cases ranging from $1,500 (pro bono service) to $50,000. These were actions against individual defendants, not institutions and some were undefended. See Feldthusen, Hankivsky & Greaves, *supra* note 58.

[79] Contingency fees are expressly permitted in Alberta, British Columbia, Saskatchewan, Manitoba, the Yukon, New Brunswick, Nova Scotia, Prince Edward Island and Newfoundland. See Alberta, *Judicature Act*, R.S.A. 1980, c. J-1, s. 46; British Columbia, *Legal Profession Act*, S.B.C. 1998, c. 9, s. 94, repealing R.S.B.C. 1996 (Supp.), c. 255; Saskatchewan, *Legal Profession Act*, S.S. 1990, c. L-10.1, s. 64; Manitoba, *Law Society Act*, R.S.M. 1987, c. L-100, s. 58; Yukon, *An Act to Amend the Legal Profession Act*, S.Y. 1987, c. 27, s. 2, repealing R.S.Y. 1986, c. 100; New Brunswick, An Act Respecting the Law Society of New Brunswick, S.N.B. 1996, c. 89, s. 115, repealing *Judicature Act*, R.S.N.B. 1973, c. J-2, s. 72.1; Nova Scotia, *Civil Procedure Rules*, r. 63.17; Prince Edward Island,

Rules of Court Supreme Court of P.E.I, r. 57; Newfoundland, *Rules of Supreme Court*, s. 55.16 (Sch. D of *The Judicature Act*, R.S.N. 1986, c. 42). Ontario specifically prohibits contingency fees except in the case of class actions: see *Solicitors Act*, R.S.O. 1990, c. S-15, s. 28; *Class Proceedings Act*, S.O. 1992, c. 6, s. 33.

80 In provinces where formal contingency arrangements are not permitted, lawyers may defer billing to assist the client. Even then, the client may have to fund the disbursements incurred in preparation, including the cost of obtaining expensive medical and other reports and hiring expert witnesses. Plaintiffs may be entitled to make a claim for compensation to provincial criminal injuries compensation boards, and use the compensation so obtained to help finance the lawsuit. As noted earlier, class actions and combined actions may reduce the plaintiff's costs.

81 According to a survey conducted by *Sondagem* November 25 to December 2, 1998 of 1,039 individuals, 65% of the respondents believed that plaintiffs lose control of their problems before the courts. See P. Noreau, "Accès à la justice: réfléchir autrement les rapports entre la société et l'institution judiciaire" (La déjudiciarisation: une affaire de justice et de société, 20 January 1999) [unpublished].

82 T. Tyler, "The Role of Perceived Injustice in Defendant's Evaluations of their Courtroom Experience" (1984) 18 Law & Society Review 51.

83 See Feldthusen, Hankivsky & Greaves, *supra* note 58, reporting that litigants found cross-examination highly stressful.

84 See Feldthusen, Hankivsky & Greaves, *ibid*. Most litigants reported that they were well treated by judges.

85 For example, the fact that a particular defendant had abused persons other than the plaintiff at another institution would likely be excluded on these grounds. However, given the more relaxed standard of proof in civil cases, this type of similar fact evidence may be more readily accepted in civil actions than in criminal cases.

86 This problem was raised in the "Enfants de Duplessis" class action (see *Kelly*, *supra* note 17). See the report of the Quebec Public Protector, recommending government compensation in Quebec, Discussion and Consultation Paper, "Les 'enfants de Duplessis' à l'heure de la solidarité" (Quebec: National Assembly, 22 January 1994).

87 According to the *Sondagem* survey (P. Noreau, *supra* note 81) 86% of respondents believed that people are not comfortable in court.

[88] For an example, see L. Cipriani, "La justice matrimoniale à l'heure du féminisme: analyse critique de la jurisprudence québécoise sur la prestation compensatoire, 1983–1991" (1995) 36 C. de D. 209.

[89] *A.M.* v. *Ryan*, [1997] 1 S.C.R. 157, 143 D.L.R. (4th) 1.

[90] See discussion of the credibility of sexual abuse victims in Des Rosiers & Langevin, *supra* note 34 at 279-82.

[91] See R. Ross, *Dancing With A Ghost: Exploring Indian Reality* (Markham, Ont.: Octopus, 1992) at 3-4.

[92] See *Naraine* v. *Ford Motor Co.* of Canada (No. 4) (1996), 27 C.H.R.R. D/230 at D/234.

[93] See, for example, the Supreme Court of Canada in *Curatrice publique (Québec)* v. *Syndicat des employés de l'Hôpital Saint-Ferdinand*, [1997] 3 S.C.R. 211.

[94] See Feldthusen, Hankivsky & Greaves, *supra* note 58. Interviews with former residents of Grandview training school demonstrate the importance of having the government and other institutions assume responsibility for institutional abuse quite independent of fault finding. In the study, many survivors expressed anger that they had not yet secured the promised apology form the Government of Ontario. A letter of apology over the signature of the Attorney General and Minister Responsible for Native Affairs was issued in May, 1999.

[95] Anglican Church of Canada, Press Release, "Church Leader Says Court Rulings Could Jeopardise Church Work – Liability Issues Will Force Churches to 'Reassess' Risk of Certain Programs" (17 June 1999), online: <http://www.anglican.ca/news/ans> (date accessed: 16 November 1999); United Church of Canada, Press Release, "Supreme Court Decision Has Serious Implications for United Church Groups and Programs" (17 June 1999), online:<http://www.uccan.org/newsreleases> (date accessed: 16 November 1999); "Churches Fear Financial Ruin from Lawsuits" *The Ottawa Citizen* (1 April 1999) A1. See also *Report of the Provisional Liquidator, supra* note 57.

[96] See *e.g. Wood* v. *Kennedy* (1998), 165 D.L.R. (4th) 542 (Ont. Ct. Gen. Div.).

[97] See D. Shuman, "When Time Does not Heal: Understanding the Importance of Avoiding Unnecessary Delay in the Resolution of Tort Cases" [forthcoming]. Delay was one of the most frequently cited complaints reported in Feldthusen, Hankivsky & Greaves, *supra* note 58.

[98] See L. Lévesque, "Les tribunaux restent mal perçus" *Le Devoir [Montréal]* (22 January 1999) A2, citing a *Sondagem* survey on the public perception of the courts. According to the survey, 72% of respondents who have been to court have a negative perception of the courts. See P. Noreau, *supra* note 81.

[99] See S.E. Merry, "Sorting Out Popular Justice" in S.E. Merry & N. Milner, eds., *The Possibility of Popular Justice: A Case Study of Community Mediation in the United States* (Ann Arbor, Mich.: University of Michigan Press, 1995).

[100] A recent high-profile example arose from the refusal of the Canadian Red Cross to apologise to recipients of tainted blood even when given an opportunity to do so by Krever J. during his Commission inquiry. The relevant portions of the transcript are quoted in the *Vancouver Sun* (25 March 1997) A13. The Red Cross and the Federal government did eventually apologise. See D. McDougall, "Krever Recommends No-Fault Compensation in Blood Scandal, Ottawa Apologises" *Canadian Press Newswire* (26 November 1997). See A. Fayant, "Love Means Never Having to Say You're Sorry: the Federal Government Expresses Its Profound Regret to Aboriginal People" 27 *Briarpatch* (22 March 1998) 2 at 2-3. For the apologies extended by Canadian churches, see *e.g.* L. Slobodian, "United Church Apologises for Residential Schools" *Catholic New Times* (22 September 1998) 8; "Presbyterian Church Confesses to Natives" *Canadian Press Newswire* (27 November 1995).

[101] With respect to the beneficial effects of a judgement, see *Leroux* v. *Montréal (Communauté urbaine de Montréal)*, [1997] A.Q. No. 2262 (Sup. Ct.), online: QL. The judge recognised the responsibility of the police for unjustly arresting and accusing the plaintiff, and the therapeutic effect of the judgement: "The court hopes that this judgement will, in addition to compensation for the damages and losses sustained, provide the plaintiff with the peace of mind required to resume her career." (*ibid.* at para. 318 [unofficial translation]).

[102] See "The Civil Action", *supra* note 21; E. Sheehy, "Compensation for Women Who have been Raped" in J.V. Roberts & R.M. Mohr, eds., *Confronting Sexual Assault: A Decade of Legal and Social Change* (Toronto: University of Toronto Press, 1994) 205; N. West, "Rape in the Criminal Law and the Victim's Tort Alternative: A Feminist Analysis " (1992) 50 U. of T. Fac. of L. Rev. 96. In the American film *A Civil Action*, starring John Travolta, parents who have lost a child to leukemia, potentially as the result of contaminated water in their town, sue the two polluting companies. During a meeting with their lawyer, the parents' representative emphasises that they are not looking for monetary compensation by suing, but rather a conviction of the guilty parties and a public apology. The trial ends with a settlement with one of the companies. The parents feel ambivalent, because they are entitled to neither an apology nor acknowledgement from the companies. The film is a good fictional account of the therapeutic effect of a trial.

103 The respondents in the study conducted by Feldthusen, Hankivsky & Greaves, *supra* note 58, reported recovery as follows: the average civil plaintiff received in excess of $200,000; the Grandview survivors received up to $60,000 each, as well as direct payment benefits such as one-on-one and private residential therapy costs, tuition and books, laser scar and tattoo removal, medical and dental funds, the costs for independent legal advice and a contingency fund of up to $3,000; most CICB claimants received in the $5,000–$10,000 range.

104 See Des Rosiers & Langevin, *supra* note 34 at 162ff.

105 See *Andrews* v. *Grand and Toy* Alberta Ltd., [1978] 2 S.C.R. 229; *Thornton* v. *Board of School Trustees (Prince George)*, [1978] 2 S.C.R. 267; *Teno* v. *Arnold*, [1978] 2 S.C.R. 287.

106 Note that the Supreme Court itself has departed from the damage ceiling in a defamation case (*Hill* v. *Church of Scientology*, [1995] 2 S.C.R. 1130) where it felt that the circumstances differed significantly from the physical injury cases in which the ceiling was set. Arguably, child abuse cases (and sexual abuse cases generally) are also in a different category and should therefore not be subject to the cap. See discussion in Des Rosiers & Langevin, *supra* note 34 at 164-70, para. 308; L. Langevin, "Childhood Sexual Assault: Will There Ever Be a Civil Remedy" (1992) 10 C.C.L.T. 86; and *Y.(S.)* v. *C.(F.G.)* (1996), 26 B.C.L.R. (3d) 155 (C.A.).

107 See Feldthusen, Hankivsky & Greaves, *supra* note 58. See also the *Grandview Agreement, supra* note 58.

108 The sample sizes are too small in the study conducted by Feldthusen, Hankivsky & Greaves, *ibid.* Moreover, the responses indicate a large degree of individual variation.

109 Feldthusen, Hankivsky & Greaves, *ibid.*

110 See *Family Law Act*, R.S.O. 1990, c. F-3, s. 61. as am. by S.O. 1992, c. 32, S.O. 1997, c. 20, S.O. 1998, c. 26.

111 See, for an analogous situation, *Elliott* v. *Canadian Broadcasting Corp.* (1995), 25 O.R. (3d) 302 (Ont. C.A.) dismissing an action for group defamation.

112 This possibility is discussed by D.G. Réaume & P. Macklem, "Education for Subordination, Redressing the Adverse Effects of Residential Schooling", a research paper submitted to the Royal Commission on Aboriginal Peoples (Canada) in *For Seven Generations, Pour sept générations* (Ottawa: Libraxus Inc., CD-ROM, 25 April 1996).

113 *Supra* note 24.

D. Criminal Injuries Compensation Programs

1. Introduction

Criminal injuries compensation programs are designed to provide financial compensation to victims of violent or personal crimes. They offer partial restitution for losses arising from injuries caused by such crimes. Generally, they are structured to discourage the representation of applicants by lawyers or paralegals. The application process is intended to be simple, effective, inexpensive and quick. It has been observed that

> [t]he most likely rationale for a Canadian compensation scheme is that it is seen as a form of social welfare based at least in part on the moral duty to aid innocent sufferers of an egregious event that might befall any of us.[1]

2. Description

Criminal injuries compensation programs are created by provincial statute and administered according to the specific rules and standards established by each province. This means that there are differences in allowable benefits, eligibility criteria and application processes among the nine provincial programs in Canada.[2] Nonetheless, these programs have much in common, both in their design and their practical operations. Their general characteristics, which are also their most common features, relate to:

a. Underlying principles

b. Eligibility criteria

c. The application process

d. Benefits available

e. Delays for making an application, or limitation periods

a.   Underlying principles

Many statutes governing compensation programs include a list of principles announcing how victims of criminal acts should be treated by the criminal justice system generally, and by the criminal injuries compensation process in particular.[3] These principles refer to the need to treat victims with "courtesy and compassion" and with "respect for their dignity, privacy and convenience". More specifically, they include the notion that victims should receive prompt and fair financial redress for the harm that they have suffered. Whether explicit in the statute or not, this is the key idea that underlies all criminal injuries compensation programs.

b.   Eligibility criteria

Each criminal injuries compensation statute is intended to provide compensation only for personal injury or death resulting from a crime committed within the province. Most incorporate a schedule specifically listing those *Criminal Code* offences whose commission entitles the victim to apply for compensation. These offences include murder, manslaughter, sexual assault and robbery. Typically, the following categories of persons are eligible to apply for benefits:

- the victim;

- if the victim has died, his or her dependents or immediate family (*i.e.* for the loss of the victim's financial support); and

- the person responsible for the maintenance or support of the victim.[4]

In some provinces, a claimant must report the offence to the proper authorities in order to be eligible to receive compensation.[5] In other provinces, failure to report the offence may be a significant factor in diminishing the size of the award. Some provinces specify an additional duty upon claimants to reasonably cooperate with the authorities investigating the offence.[6] Failure to do so may result in the award being decreased or refused.

c. Application process

In most provinces, a person seeking compensation for a criminal injury submits a written application along with any documentation that supports the claim.[7] In some, it may also be possible to have an in-person hearing.[8] The application is usually submitted to a government official charged with this function,[9] or to an administrative tribunal. In British Columbia, for example, applications are handled by the Workers' Compensation Board, while in Ontario, applicants appear before a specialised body designated as the Criminal Injuries Compensation Board.

It is not always necessary for criminal charges to have been laid or a conviction registered in order for a compensation claim to proceed.[10] In some provinces, compensation may be awarded even where a court has acquitted a person accused of having committed the crime. The basis for compensation is whether the board or government official is satisfied that the applicant has been the victim of a criminal offence. The acquittal of any particular person accused of the offence is not a determining factor.

The decision to grant compensation, and the amount of the award, are administrative determinations left to the discretion of the commission or board. These decisions may be reconsidered where there is new evidence. In some provinces, they may also be externally reviewed, usually by an administrative appeal board.[11] Only questions of law (and not questions of fact) may be raised where appeals to a court are permitted.[12]

d. Benefits available

The compensation provided by criminal injuries compensation programs is primarily for pecuniary loss, that is, specific out-of-pocket expenses incurred as a direct result of the criminal injury. Each province establishes a maximum amount of compensation that is available to applicants. This ranges from the $5,000 maximum in New Brunswick to Alberta's $110,000 maximum.[13] In the other provincial programs, maximums are between $20,000 and $50,000. Awards may be made in the form of lump sum or periodic payments,[14] or a combination of the two.

Most commonly, awards are granted for the following types of loss:

- expenses actually and reasonably incurred resulting from the victim's injury or death;

- emergency expenses resulting from a personal injury or death, such as medical or funeral expenses;

- loss of wages as a consequence of total or partial disability affecting the victim's capacity to work;

- financial loss to dependents of a deceased victim;

- counselling or therapy expenses;[15] and

- maintenance of a child born as a result of a sexual assault.

Some provinces also provide compensation for non-pecuniary losses such as pain and suffering and loss of enjoyment of life.[16]

Most provinces make provision for interim payments if needed. These normally are payments that cover immediate medical or other urgent expenses incurred before the board or adjudicator has determined the final amount of the award to be paid. As a rule, interim payments are granted only when a board is reasonably certain that it will award compensation to a victim. Nonetheless, should the board make a final determination not to award the victim any compensation, any interim payments received will not have to be repaid.[17]

Applying for financial compensation through a criminal injuries compensation program does not deprive a victim of the right to sue for damages in a civil court. Where compensation has been paid, however, the province is subrogated to the victim's right to collect from the perpetrator. This means that the province will take over the victim's right to sue for damages. Damages awarded by the court, or agreed to in a settlement, are first paid to the province to cover its legal costs and the amount of compensation paid. The victim then receives whatever sums are recovered over and above these amounts.[18] Similarly, any money that victims receive under some other provincial or federal statute that compensates them for their injury, or from their employer (if the injury disabled them) would be deducted from the amount of compensation to be paid under a criminal injuries compensation program.[19]

e.   Limitation periods

All provincial statutes in Canada provide that an application for compensation normally must be made within one year after the date of injury or death. Provinces such as Nova Scotia[20] and New Brunswick[21] make an exception for victims of sexual abuse. Alberta, Manitoba and Saskatchewan incorporate what is known as the "delayed discoverability" test into their limitation periods. In other words, the limitation period for bringing an application does not begin until the victim fully recognises the connection between the criminal act and the injury suffered. The limitation period in the Quebec statute has also been interpreted favourably toward survivors of childhood sexual abuse.[22] Most provinces make provision for the Minister or the board responsible for the program to extend the time for bringing an application if it is considered to be warranted in the circumstances. For this reason, claimants will only rarely be denied compensation solely on the grounds that the limitation period ran out, so long as they have a reasonable excuse for failing to file on time.

3.   Assessment

Overview

While survivors of institutional child abuse are not engaged in the design of the criminal injuries compensation process, its sole purpose is to provide claimants with compensation. Consequently, it is a process that can be expected to be respectful of them. Criminal injuries compensation boards have only a very narrow fact-finding capacity. They are restricted to verifying that the claimant has been the victim of a criminal act and has suffered injuries as a result. Accountability is not part of any board's mandate. The making of an award does not depend on establishing the liability or guilt of a specific individual.

A criminal injuries compensation process is fair, in that claimants are compensated only in accordance with a set of pre-determined administrative rules and guidelines. If the State sets out to reclaim, from the perpetrator, the amount it has paid to the victim, then the rules of the civil justice system apply to ensure the perpetrator is treated fairly. Moreover, while the State has a first claim on damages recovered from the perpetrator up to the amount it has paid, the victim will receive any additional money that is collected.

Criminal injuries compensation programs may be seen as an acknowledgement by the State of its failure to protect citizens from harm and its responsibility to make up for that failure. The process does not involve apology or any specific attempt at reconciliation between perpetrator and victim. In addition, because these programs offer no benefits other than financial compensation, they are not effective in meeting any of the other needs of survivors of institutional child abuse.

The category of beneficiaries is restricted to victims themselves or to those who have incurred expenses as a result of a victim's injuries. Families, communities and peoples are not eligible to recover for any harms that they may have suffered in their own right. Finally, the restricted mandate of criminal injuries compensation programs means that they cannot be an effective vehicle for promoting public education about institutional child abuse or for encouraging measures intended to prevent it.

a.   Respect, engagement and informed choice

The process of seeking compensation from a criminal injuries compensation program seems to satisfy, at least to some degree, the principles of respect and engagement. Because these are non-adversarial administrative programs that expressly compensate victims of crime and deal only with people who have suffered as a result of crime, they can be expected to treat claimants respectfully.

The fact that it is the injured person who initiates the process enhances that person's control over the options available to him or her. In the nine provinces where they exist, these programs offer victims a viable option for obtaining compensation in addition to, or even in lieu of, civil actions. However, this may not add to the informed choice of survivors unless they are made aware of this option and the consequences of their choice. For example, it is not clear that all those who go through the criminal justice system, or simply report a crime, are informed that a criminal injuries compensation program exists in their province.[23]

This process does not engage survivors in its design. However it does provide a forum in which they can describe in their own words the criminal act they experienced, as well as the nature and impact of the injuries they suffered as a result. While applicants must produce substantiating documents if they wish to establish the validity of their claim, they are not required to undergo cross-examination. In many provinces, they are able to successfully bring an application without having to rely on a lawyer or paralegal to represent them.

b.   Fact-finding

The criminal injuries compensation process is not primarily intended to determine all the facts surrounding a criminal act, such as who committed the crime and why. It is certainly not designed to determine systemic causes of particular crimes, such as institutional child abuse. The process is meant only to determine whether the applicant was the victim of a crime, and if so, to assess the amount of compensation to which that person may be entitled under the statute.

Where there has been no criminal prosecution or civil action in respect of the event for which a claim is made, the compensation process may serve as a forum for bringing the significant facts of a crime to light. The evidentiary basis for the decision, however, comes mainly from the uncontested information provided by the applicant. While the board may also assess the facts based on information contained in the relevant police and medical reports, it has no authority to conduct an investigation.

c.   Accountability

Under criminal injuries compensation programs, decision-makers are not given the authority to identify or hold accountable those who are responsible for crimes. Their statutory role is limited to deciding whether an applicant is a victim of a designated criminal offence. This does not involve any determination of who was responsible for the offence, either directly or indirectly.

d. Fairness

There are only two parties involved in the criminal injuries compensation process – the applicant and the State. The State is bound by the legal rules of procedural fairness in conducting the application and decision-making process. Applicants are allowed to describe their own injuries and substantiate them as well as they can. The decision-maker then assesses the evidence provided, determines whether to make an award, and decides how much compensation to grant. Review or appeal procedures are limited, as are the amounts at stake. Generally, there is a mechanism for the reconsideration of awards where new evidence is provided. Most programs also provide for appeals to courts on a question of law.

The party normally absent from this process is the perpetrator (or the alleged perpetrator).[24] Does fairness require that he or she be heard? Given that the compensation flows only from the State, and is not dependent upon the victim identifying the person who caused the injury, there is no unfairness in excluding the perpetrator (or alleged perpetrator) from the hearing process. That is, as long as the perpetrator (or alleged perpetrator) is not publicly identified by the applicant or the board, no damage to his or her reputation ought to result. If the State later seeks to recover the compensation it has paid to a victim from the perpetrator of the injury, it must pursue a civil action. At this point, the procedural safeguards of the ordinary civil process will come into play to ensure fairness to all parties, including the alleged perpetrator.

e. Acknowledgement, apology and reconciliation

The person who committed the crime is usually absent from the criminal injuries compensation process. Consequently, the process does not provide a forum for acknowledgement, apology and reconciliation between the wrongdoer and the victim. At best, it is a tangible form of State recognition that the applicant has suffered harm due to a criminal act, through no fault of his or her own, and is therefore entitled to compensation.[25] Where there has been no criminal conviction this process even permits acknowledgement that a criminal harm has been caused. The board may award compensation regardless of whether a criminal charge has been laid or what verdict has been entered. The criminal injuries compensation process may therefore be seen as an additional opportunity for acknowledgement of the harm the survivor has suffered, even if it does not hold any particular individual responsible. To the extent that the rationale for these compensation programs is the State's failure to protect its citizens from criminal acts, they reflect an acknowledgement and implicit apology by the State for that failure.

f.   Compensation, counselling and education

Criminal injuries compensation programs, as their title suggests, are largely restricted to providing financial compensation for the harm resulting from the commission of a crime. They do little to address the other needs of survivors of institutional child abuse. Moreover, the compensation is aimed at specific monetary losses (such as lost wages) and expenses directly related to the treatment of the injuries suffered. Five provinces do, however, also offer compensation for pain and suffering.[26] But given the fairly low ceilings on total awards, the amount available to compensate for pain and suffering – once actual losses and expenses are accounted for – is not likely to be high. One author has observed that

> [t]here is no acceptable rationale for refusing compensation under those heads of non-pecuniary damage which society has, through its courts, been willing for centuries to compensate. The continued refusal to permit such awards in some of the schemes highlights the point that they may not be comprehensive compensation schemes at all![27]

g.   Needs of families, communities and peoples

Families of victims are only able to claim compensation either on behalf of victims who died as a result of their injuries or for the expenses they incur to maintain a victim. These programs do not address the needs of family members for the difficulties or harm they themselves may suffer as a result of the victim's injuries. For example, any claim for injuries caused because a survivor of child abuse is abusive to a spouse and children is beyond the reach of these statutory programs. Communities, peoples or other groups who may have been harmed as a result of institutional child abuse are also unable to benefit from such programs, as they are not included in the list of eligible applicants in any of the provincial statutes.

h.   Prevention and public education

Criminal injuries compensation programs have no prevention component; nor is public education an explicit part of their mandate. Some provinces do provide for surcharges or fines for criminal and quasi-criminal offences as a means of partially funding the schemes.[28] But the deterrent effect of these is quite low, and in any event, the surcharge or fine arises in the criminal process, not the criminal injuries compensation process. Since criminal injuries compensation programs are widely publicised, one could say that they add to the message that the State abhors crime – particularly crimes against the person – and that it seeks to protect citizens from the harms caused by crime. This message does not, however, serve any educational function about institutional child abuse in particular.

4.   Conclusion

Although criminal injuries compensation programs reflect a concern for most of the evaluation criteria, they do so at a rudimentary level. Survivors are not engaged in the design of the process, even if its non-adversarial character shows respect for them. The process is voluntary and does not require survivors to give up the right to pursue other options. It permits many facts to be revealed. But the limited scope of inquiry offers little chance to understand systemic problems and the organisational context of abuse. There is a general acknowledgement of wrongdoing but there is little opportunity for achieving accountability, and almost none for apology and reconciliation.

The process is fair to all parties. However, the needs of survivors for counselling and educatiion are not addressed, and the level of compensation itself is quite low. Criminal injuries compensation programs are not designed to meet the needs of families, communities and peoples and have no direct preventive or educational component.

Recommendations

CRIMINAL INJURIES COMPENSATION programs should explicitly provide for extended limitation periods in cases of sexual or physical abuse committed while the claimant was a child.

Considerations:

Incorporation of the "delayed discoverability" rule or a statutory extension of the limitation period would be consistent with the treatment of child abuse claims in civil actions for damages.

SURVIVORS OF INSTITUTIONAL CHILD ABUSE should not be refused compensation solely because they do not report the abuse to the police or automatically cooperate in an investigation.

Considerations:

Adjudicators should take into account that a claimant's failure to cooperate with the police may result from a distrust of authority originating in the very abuse for which compensation is being sought.

CRIMINAL INJURIES COMPENSATION BOARDS should publish the framework or analytical screen used to determine their awards, as well as their decisions, withholding the names of the claimants.

Considerations:

Publication of awards would promote consistency, especially among provinces with similar ceilings for claims.

This would enable policymakers to assess the adequacy of the program and determine where adjustments should be made.

---

[1] P. T. Burns, *Criminal Injuries Compensation*, 2d ed. (Toronto: Butterworths, 1992) at 95.

2   Alberta, *Victims of Crime Act*, R.S.A. 1996, c. V-3.3; British Columbia, *Criminal Injury Compensation Act*, R.S.B.C. 1996, c. 85; Manitoba, *Victims' Rights and Consequential Amendments Act*, R.S.M. 1998, c. 44; New Brunswick, *Victims' Services Act*, R.S.N.B. 1988, c. V-2.1; Nova Scotia, *Victims' Rights and Services Act*, R.S.N.S. 1989, c.14; Ontario, *Compensation for Victims of Crime Act*, R.S.O. 1990, c. C-24; Prince Edward Island, *Victims of Crime Act*, R.S.P.E.I. 1988, c. V-3.1 (amendments being introduced in the coming session of the Legislature); Quebec, *Act Respecting Assistance for Victims of Crime*, R.S.Q. c. A-13.2 and *Act Respecting Compensation for the Victims of Crime*, R.S.Q. c. I-6; Saskatchewan, *The Victims of Crime Act*, 1995, R.S.S. 1995, c. V-6.011. Newfoundland, the Northwest Territories, Nunavut and the Yukon did not have criminal injuries compensation programs as of the completion of the Commission's research (October 1999).

3   Alberta, *Victims of Crime Act*, *supra* note 2, s. 2; Manitoba, *Victims' Rights and Consequential Amendment Act*, *supra* note 2, s. 3; Quebec, *Act Respecting Assistance for Victims of Crime*, *supra* note 2, s. 3; Nova Scotia, *Victims' Rights and Services Act*, *supra* note 2, s. 3; New Brunswick, *Victims' Services Act*, *supra* note 2, ss. 2-6; Prince Edward Island, *Victims of Crime Act*, *supra* note 2, s. 2.

4   In addition, some provinces provide compensation to any other person who incurred certain expenses on behalf of the deceased victim. See, for example, New Brunswick, *Victims' Services Act*, *supra* note 2, s. 3(1)(c); Nova Scotia, *Victims' Rights and Services Act*, *supra* note 2, s. 11A(1)(h); and Prince Edward Island, *Victims of Crime Act*, *supra* note 2, s. 16(1)(d)(I).

5   See, for example, New Brunswick, *Compensation for Victims of Crime Regulation – Victims' Services Act*, N.B. Reg. 96-81, s. 4(1)(b); and Alberta, *Victims of Crime Act*, *supra* note 2, s. 12(2)(b).

6   See, for example, Nova Scotia, *Victims' Rights and Services Act*, *supra* note 2, s. 11D(3); and Manitoba, *Victims' Rights and Consequential Amendments Act*, *supra* note 2, s. 31.

7   The province of Saskatchewan, for example, has a printed application for criminal injuries benefits that sets out a series of questions and indicates what supporting material is required.

8   For example in Prince Edward Island, an applicant may request a hearing, but otherwise, the final decision is taken simply upon a review of the documents submitted. It appears that a hearing has been held only once in the last ten years. In British Columbia, an applicant may appeal the first decision, based strictly on a written application, and request an oral hearing.

9   Such as the Director of Victim Services in Nova Scotia.

10 British Columbia, *Criminal Injury Compensation Act, supra* note 2, s. 8; Ontario, *Compensation For Victims of Crime Act, supra* note 2, s. 16; Prince Edward Island, *Victims of Crime Act, supra* note 2, s. 22 (4).

11 In Quebec, for example, victims are entitled to an administrative revision of the admissibility decision, and, if required, an appeal to the *Tribunal Administratif du Québec* (*Act Respecting Assistance for Victims of Crime, supra* note 2).

12 For example, in Ontario, Alberta, Nova Scotia and Prince Edward Island.

13 *Victims' Benefits Regulation*, Alta. Reg. 201/97, s. 5(2); and New Brunswick, *Compensation for Victims of Crime Regulation – Victims' Services Act, supra* note 5, s. 6(1).

14 The Quebec model offers periodic payments which include compensation for temporary or permanent incapacity and therapeutic help. See N. Des Rosiers & L. Langevin, *L'indemnisation des victimes de violence sexuelle et conjugale* (Cowansville, Québec: Yvon Blais, 1998) at 199, para. 360.

15 Very few provinces offer to pay for counselling, and those that do offer very low amounts. For example, Saskatchewan offers a maximum of $1,000 (*The Victims of Crime Act, supra* note 2, s. 8(3)).

16 For example, British Columbia, *Criminal Injury Compensation Act, supra* note 2, s. 2(4)(f); Ontario, *Compensation for Victims' of Crime Act, supra* note 2, s. 7(1)(d); New Brunswick, *Compensation for Victims of Crime Regulation – Victims Services Act, supra* note 5, s. 6. Alberta compensates for shock or "nervous shock," which it defines fairly broadly: *Victims' Benefits Regulation, supra* note 12, Sch. 2, n. 4. In New Brunswick, the maximum amount of an award for pain and suffering is $1,000, see *Compensation for Victims of Crime Regulation – Victims' Services Act, supra* note 5, s. 6(2). In British Columbia, the maximum award, including compensation for non-pecuniary losses, is $50,000 for cases involving the most serious injuries: see pamphlet entitled "Compensation for Victims of Crime" (Vancouver: Workers' Compensation Board of British Columbia, 1996).

17 For example, Ontario, *Compensation for Victims of Crime Act, supra* note 2, s.14 or Nova Scotia, *Victims' Rights and Services Act, supra* note 2, s. 11I.

18 For example, Manitoba, *Victims' Rights and Consequential Amendments Act, supra* note 2, s. 35(1).

19 For example, Manitoba, *ibid.*, s. 33; New Brunswick, *Compensation for Victims of Crime Regulation – Victims Services Act, supra* note 5, s. 7(b), (c).

20 A claim can be made "at any time", if the perpetrator was in a position of trust with respect to, or had charge of the victim, or the victim was dependent on that person. For example, *Victims' Rights and Services Act, supra* note 2, s. 11B(2).

21 The period is one year from disclosure to the police. For example, *Victims Services Act, supra* note 2, s. 3(2).

22 See among others: *Sauveteurs et victimes d'actes criminels – 9*, [1990] C.A.S. 46; *Sauveteurs et victimes d'actes criminels – 1*, [1996] C.A.S. 1.

23 The Victim/Witness Assistance Programs in Nova Scotia and Prince Edward Island do, however, provide assistance with criminal injuries compensation claims.

24 Some provinces do inform the perpetrator or alleged offender of an upcoming hearing. See for example Ontario, *Compensation for Victims of Crime Act, supra* note 2, s. 9. In Ontario the Criminal Injuries Compensation Board has also adopted guidelines that require the Board to notify alleged offenders (but only "those who have not been convicted of a crime of violence": see *Criminal Injuries Compensation Board: Guidelines for the Public* (Toronto: Criminal Injuries Compensation Board, July 1999) at 9).

25 As noted above under "Eligibility", most statutes specify that applicants may be excluded from recovery of compensation or have it reduced if they failed to co-operate with the police or contributed by their own unlawful conduct to their injuries. If the circumstances of child abuse in an institution are properly understood, a failure to have reported the incident at the time should not be a bar to recovery of an award. The obligation to notify or cooperate with the police is perhaps better understood as arising once the victim has made a complaint to the police or has come forward to make a claim to a criminal injuries compensation program.

26 British Columbia, *Criminal Injury Compensation Act, supra* note 2, s. 2(4)(f); Alberta, *Victim's Benefits Regulation – Victims of Crime Act*, Reg. 201/97, Sch.2; Ontario, *Compensation for Victims of Crime Act*, supra note 2, s. 7(1)(d); New Brunswick, *Compensation for Victims of Crime Regulation – Victims' Services Act, supra* note 5, Sch. 2, Band 1, 8, 11; Prince Edward Island, *Victims of Crime Act, supra* note 2, s. 19(1) (f).

27 Burns, *supra*, note 1 at 156.

28 For example, Alberta, *Victims of Crime Act, supra* note 2, s. 9(2); Manitoba, *Victims' Rights and Consequential Amendments, supra* note 2, s. 17(2).

E. *Ex gratia* Payments

1. Introduction

The State has the power or "prerogative" to make voluntary payments to compensate people for losses or injuries that they have suffered.[1] Where governments have no clear legal obligation to pay compensation – or where that obligation has not yet been judicially established – but it is in the public interest to do so, the mechanism for providing compensation is known as an *ex gratia* payment. If potential *ex gratia* payments will be significant, the decision to make an award or to establish a framework of payments is made at the Cabinet level. The authorisation for the payment is provided by an Order-in-Council.[2]

There are no limits on the types of situations for which *ex gratia* payments may be made. For example, they have often been used to compensate individual public employees whose personal property has been damaged or stolen in the course of their employment.[3] In addition, the federal government has established general compensation programs for groups of people who have suffered extraordinary losses. Examples include compensation to Canadians of Japanese ancestry who were interned during the Second World War;[4] persons given "depatterning" or massive electroshock treatments at Montreal's Allan Memorial Institute;[5] persons who received HIV-infected blood, and persons who suffered physical deformities because their mothers were given thalidomide during pregnancy.[6] Recently, compensation was given to Canada's Second World War veterans who survived Japanese prisoner of war camps in Hong Kong.[7]

Although survivors of institutional child abuse might receive compensation by way of a particular *ex gratia* payment made to them as individuals, *ex gratia* payment programs intended to compensate groups of beneficiaries are a more likely type of response to providing compensation for institutional child abuse.

2.   Description

The Treasury Board of Canada's *Policy on Claims and Ex Gratia Payments* defines an *ex gratia* payment as

> ... a benevolent payment made by the Crown under the authority of the Governor in Council ... to anyone in the public interest for loss or expenditure incurred for which there is no legal liability on the part of the Crown. An *ex gratia* payment is an exceptional vehicle used only when there is no statutory, regulatory or policy vehicle to make the payment.[8]

Decisions on whether or not to establish a program of *ex gratia* payments, how to define eligible recipients, and what conditions to attach to the compensation paid are discretionary and can be tailor-made according to circumstance.[9]

Two preconditions must be met before an *ex gratia* payment will be made. First, the Crown must have no legal liability to make a payment for the loss suffered or the expenditure incurred. Second, it must be in the public interest for the Crown to provide financial compensation to the claimant or claimants.

There are no formal guidelines as to what constitutes the public interest. Nonetheless, the cases of *ex gratia* payment programs mentioned earlier provide some benchmarks for the types of situations that may warrant large-scale compensation. In every case, the victims were blameless for the losses they experienced. The federal government was not legally liable for their losses, but there was a nexus between some policy, action or inaction by a public body or publicly supported authority and the harm being compensated. The injured parties suffered significant physical, psychological or emotional hardship. The combination of circumstances in each case led the government to conclude that establishing an *ex gratia* payments program was in the public interest for moral, humanitarian and social justice reasons.

Whether the State is legally obliged to pay for losses incurred is often difficult to establish. In many cases, the absence of liability was clearly decided before *ex gratia* compensation was sought. For example, following the Second World War, individual Canadians of Japanese ancestry were not successful in suing the federal government for their wartime losses.[10] Subsequently, the Japanese-Canadian community successfully conducted a campaign to obtain redress through political and administrative processes, rather than judicial processes.[11]

In other cases, such as the federal government's Extraordinary Assistance Program of *ex gratia* payments to people who had contracted HIV through blood or blood products, compensation was offered before the question of legal liability was decided by the courts.[12] This suggests that if legal liability is uncertain, and the process to determine the issue would be long or costly, governments may also establish an *ex gratia* payment program. However, persons who receive compensation under such a program normally must first sign a waiver of their rights to institute new or pursue existing civil actions against the government.[13] They therefore give up the opportunity to obtain a judicial determination and assessment of legal liability in exchange for receiving immediate payment.

The existence of alternative sources of compensation also affects whether an *ex gratia* payment program will be established or a payment made.[14] Governments typically will not authorise an *ex gratia* payment if, for example, a third party is legally liable or if an insurance fund will cover the loss.

An *ex gratia* payment may therefore be a viable option for those seeking financial compensation if the government is not legally liable to pay (or has not yet been determined to be legally liable for losses suffered by an individual or group), there is no alternative source of compensation available, and payment from the government would be in the public interest.

Many of those affected by institutional child abuse would qualify. People who resided in institutions and suffered losses or injuries that the law does not recognise as compensable (such as the loss of language or culture) could be eligible to receive an *ex gratia* payment. People who were not personally exposed to abuse in residential institutions, but who suffered secondary trauma or side-effects (such as those who were witnesses to serious abuse, or the adult partners, children or members of the home communities of survivors) might also be able to make a case for an *ex gratia* payment. Again, *ex gratia* payments may be made to people who find themselves denied compensation due to the expiry of a limitation period or a program deadline.

3. Assessment

Overview

Ex gratia payments are a compensation mechanism. The fact that payments are made may itself reflect sensitivity to the experiences of survivors of institutional child abuse. But real respect and engagement are best demonstrated when governments consult with potential beneficiaries and negotiate the terms and conditions of the payments with them. An *ex gratia* payment program is not a fact-finding process, although it may require certain information from applicants. The decision to make an *ex gratia* payment or to establish a general compensation program may be based on the results of a separate, fact-finding process.

Unless the government directly caused the harm for which it is providing compensation, accountability of wrongdoers will not be a component of an *ex gratia* payment program. The administration of the program will be subject to the legal rules of procedural fairness. Once launched, *ex gratia* payment programs tend to be expeditious. Given the age and life expectancy of many survivors of institutional child abuse, administrative efficiency can be seen as an important component of fairness to them. Nonetheless, the actual payments made are not usually fine-tuned to the particular losses or harms suffered by a particular individual.

As compensation mechanisms, *ex gratia* payment programs are not meant to address other needs of survivors – for example, counselling and education. They can, however, be delivered with official words or acts of acknowledgement and apology, and thereby promote reconciliation. Whether families, communities or peoples are included as beneficiaries of an *ex gratia* program will depend on the scope and design of the specific program. Prevention and public education are not primary objectives of *ex gratia* payment programs, although well-publicised compensation programs may indirectly promote both.

a. Respect, engagement and informed choice

The process of applying for, being found eligible to receive, and then accepting an *ex gratia* payment is an administrative exercise. As such, it will usually not be a process that engages or empowers survivors of child abuse. But people seeking *ex gratia* compensation, or the organisations representing them, have often been actively involved with governments in negotiating the criteria of eligibility, the amounts of compensation, and other terms of payment.[15] Furthermore, the negotiations leading up to the creation of an *ex gratia* payment program are normally accompanied by public awareness and education campaigns launched by representatives of the individuals or groups asking for compensation.[16] These campaigns are designed to win popular support and to convince elected officials that an *ex gratia* payment program would be in the public interest. A successful public awareness and education effort can draw the persons seeking compensation and their supporters closer together.[17]

The negotiation, public awareness and education processes leading up to an Order-in-Council for *ex gratia* payments have the potential to actively engage those seeking this form of redress, as well as the public at large. Whether people offered compensation feel that they have made a well-informed decision depends in part on how they view the terms of the offer. An offer that is seen as unreasonably small or is accompanied by very short time limits or other conditions can leave the intended recipient feeling that the opportunity to make a well-informed choice has not been afforded.[18]

b. Fact-finding

The offer of an *ex gratia* payment is often the outcome of separate fact-finding exercise such as a public inquiry or an Ombudsman's report.[19] Fact-finding to establish an archival record is however rarely a part of the payment process itself. While the public justification for a particular program may allude to certain facts as background, these tend not to be detailed and do not address specific cases.

Survivors may focus their energies on helping others who have been similarly victimized, on educational, legal, or political efforts to prevent others from being victimized in the future, or on attempts to bring offenders to justice. Common to all these efforts is a dedication to raising public awareness. Survivors understand full well that the natural human response to horrible events is to put them out of mind. They may have done this themselves in the past. Survivors also understand that those who forget the past are condemned to repeat it. It is for this reason, that public truth-telling is the common denominator of all social action.

– *"Trauma & Recovery" by J. Lewis Herman, at p. 208*

Those who apply for an *ex gratia* payment need to provide sufficient factual information to establish that they suffered a loss compensable under the program. The information required from applicants is usually defined by the terms of the Order-in-Council establishing the program and set out in the application forms developed for the compensation program in question.[20] Obviously, a documentary application process has a limited fact-finding capacity.

c.   Accountability

An *ex gratia* payment program normally only requires claimants to file an application and provide supporting documents. The process is not designed to hold wrongdoers to account. No one need be formally called upon to explain or justify his or her actions. Furthermore, since receipt of an *ex gratia* payment usually requires the beneficiary to agree not to pursue any other legal recourse, many effective avenues for seeking personal accountability of wrongdoers are, in fact, foreclosed to those who opt into a standard *ex gratia* payment program.

d.   Fairness

The application and decision processes that lead to a determination of entitlement are guided by the legal rules of procedural fairness governing all administrative determinations. The applicant is entitled to an opportunity to make her or his case before an impartial decision-maker.[21] Since the process involves no attribution or admission of wrongdoing, fairness to alleged perpetrators is not an issue. Once a government decides to establish an *ex gratia* payment program, claimants will usually receive compensation sooner than if they had brought a civil action.[22] The ability to fast-track payments may offer a significant advantage to many aging survivors of institutional child abuse.[23] For these survivors, timely and efficient redress can be a feature of fairness.

The compensation awarded through an *ex gratia* payment order may not reflect the full extent of a claimant's losses. Often each eligible applicant will receive the same amount. For example, $21,000 was given to each applicant under the Japanese-Canadian redress program and $24,000 to each Hong Kong veteran under their compensation program. In these situations, the payments received are a generic recognition of the harm done rather than an attempt at individual accounting for losses and injuries. Given the disparity in the nature and severity of abuse that may have been suffered, uniform awards could be seen by some as unfair.

e. Acknowledgement, apology and reconciliation

When governments provide compensation by means of *ex gratia* payments, there need not be any accompanying acknowledgement of legal responsibility. Yet the fact of the payment may serve as an implicit acknowledgement to survivors that the government accepts a moral responsibility for harm they have suffered. Sometimes an *ex gratia* payment may be combined with other non-monetary benefits, such as an official acknowledgement or an apology. For example, Canadians of Japanese ancestry received an official acknowledgement of the injustices inflicted on them during World War II, along with their *ex gratia* payment.[24] When official gestures of acknowledgement and apology are made in combination with the financial compensation offered, reconciliation is facilitated.

f. Compensation, counselling and education

A carefully designed *ex gratia* compensation process has the potential to be straightforward, sensitive, and less intimidating and bewildering for applicants than traditional judicial and administrative processes. It remains, however, a process designed to financially compensate survivors, but not to meet any of their other identified needs: therapy, counselling, education or training. Additional components would have to be built into an *ex gratia* payment program in order for it to do so.

g. Needs of families, communities and peoples

Unless an *ex gratia* payment program specifically includes families, communities and peoples, they will not receive any benefits. Should it do so, however, children, spouses, and whole communities could be made eligible. Financial compensation may even be granted for injuries and losses not recognised by the civil justice system. The positive impact of the *ex gratia* payment program upon the Japanese-Canadian community suggests that the process can be designed to meet many non-monetary needs of communities. Maryka Omatsu described the impact as follows:

> The last consequence of the settlements – and the most difficult for me to evaluate – is the effects of the outcome on my community and my family. Some effects are straightforward. When my mother received her $21,000 payment, I asked her what she intended to do with it. She replied, "I think I'll put it into a five-year Guaranteed Investment Certificate."
>
> Now when I travel across the country I notice that the nisei are more willing to speak to me about their past. Often it is with great difficulty, shame, and anger that the pent-up sorrows come spilling out, but at least now they are able to give voice to those feelings. The NAJC helped to educate the community about the true facts of the 1940s, thus ending years of speculation and rumour. Psychologically, for some who preferred to believe that the Canadian government had acted paternalistically, the act of facing the mounting evidence of their government's cold-hearted racism was difficult to bear. As Joy Kogawa has expressed it, finally we could feel comfortable in our skin.[25]

h.   Prevention and public education

Ex gratia payment programs do not necessarily educate the public about harms that have occurred. In some cases, such as those of the Hong Kong veterans and Canadians of Japanese ancestry, an extensive public awareness and education process was necessary to generate the political support necessary for the program to be established. It is difficult to know whether making *ex gratia* payments has a preventive effect by inducing governments who are responsible for the well-being and protection of children to be more diligent in performing their responsibilities. At the very least, however, large-scale payments made to redress historical wrongs are a reminder to future governments of their obligations to prevent their recurrence.[26] Only if an *ex gratia* payment process were combined with other components would it directly address specific prevention and education objectives.[27]

4. Conclusion

Ex gratia payments are a mechanism for the State to pay for certain damages – not because it has a legal obligation to offer compensation, but because it believes it to be in the public interest to do so. Their comparative advantages are that they do not require issues of legal liability to be resolved, and that they permit compensation to be delivered relatively quickly to individuals and communities. Their primary disadvantage for survivors is that the amount of compensation provided will usually be much less than what could be obtained through a court-ordered award of damages. In addition, because the primary object of an *ex gratia* payment program is compensation, many of the other needs of survivors, their families and their communities may not directly be addressed. However, where an *ex gratia* payment program is made part of a larger redress process, it can be structured to meet a broader range of needs of those offered compensation.

Recommendations

GOVERNMENTS SHOULD REVISE POLICIES on providing compensation by way of *ex gratia* payments to include classes of persons who suffered harm, directly or indirectly, as a result of policy decisions later found to have been inappropriate, even when others are potentially liable in a civil action.

Considerations:

Normally governments are not civilly liable for damages flowing from policy, planning or executive decisions. Where a misguided policy opens the door to, or facilitates the commission of a civil wrong by others, *ex gratia* payments should not be excluded as a means to acknowledge the wrongful policy.

EX GRATIA **PAYMENTS** should be offered in cases where an otherwise meritorious and provable claim cannot be pursued because it falls outside a limitation period, or where liability is uncertain and it is not in the public interest to defer compensation until litigation has concluded.

EX GRATIA **PAYMENT OFFERS** to individuals should include reimbursement for the costs of seeking professional advice in order to make an informed decision about whether to accept the offer.

GOVERNMENTS SHOULD REVISE POLICIES on paying compensation so as to provide a mechanism for expedited, interim and "without prejudice" *ex gratia* payments.

---

[1] P. Lordon, *Crown Law* (Toronto: Butterworths, 1991) at 432: "The Crown has the power, generally characterised as prerogative in nature, to make gifts in the form of *ex gratia* payments."

2   For example, the *Japanese Canadians Redress Report* (Canada, Department of Canadian Heritage, Final Report on the Implementation of the Japanese Canadians Redress Agreement (Ottawa: Department of Canadian Heritage, 1997) [hereinafter *Japanese Canadians Redress Report*]), Annexes 'D' and 'E' indicate that close to $377 million was paid to Japanese Canadians and payments of $24,000 each to Canada's approximately 350 Hong Kong veterans could come to $8.4 million – see "Justice for Veterans" *Toronto Star* (15 December 1999) A16.

3   Lordon, *supra* note 1 at 433. See also, for 1993–94, 1994–95, 1996–97, 1997–98, Canada, *Public Accounts of Canada*, Vol. II, Part II, Section 10 (Ottawa: Receiver General for Canada), where examples of *ex gratia* payments include compensation for damage to clothing, theft of briefcase, damage to eye glasses, *etc.*

4   *Japanese Canadians Ex Gratia Payments Order Authorising the Making of an Ex Gratia Payment to Certain Eligible Persons of Japanese Ancestry as Redress for Injustice suffered during and after World War II*, P.C. 1988-2552 (5 November 1988).

5   *Order Respecting Ex Gratia Payments to Persons Depatterned at the Allan Memorial Institute Between 1950 and 1965*, P.C. 1992-2302 (16 November 1992) [hereinafter the *AMI – Depatterned Persons Assistance Order*], reproduced in *Schrier* v. *Canada (A.G.)*, [1996] F.C.J. No. 246 at para. 4 (T.D.), online: QL [hereinafter *Schrier*].

6   *HIV Infected Persons and Thalidomide Victims' Association Orders which Provide for the Making of Ex-Gratia Payments to Individulas who Received HIV – Infected Blood Products and to Individuals whose Mothers Administered Kevadon or Falimol (Thalidomide) and Consequently Suffered Physical Deformitie*s, P.C. 1990–4/872 (10 May 1990), as am. by P.C. 1991–7/2543 (16 December 1991) [hereinafter *HIV-Infected Persons and Thalidomide Victims Assistance Order*].

7   "Justice for Veterans", *supra* note 2.

8   Canada Treasury Board of Canada Secretariat, *Policy on Claims and Ex gratia Payments* (Ottawa: Treasury Board Secretariat, 1998) at para. 3, online: <http://www.tbs-sct.gc.ca/pubs_pol/dcgpubs/RiskManagement/claiexgratpaym_e.html> (date accessed: 16 November 1999) [hereinafter *Policy on Claims and Ex gratia Payments*]. Provincial governments also have the power to make *ex gratia* payments. The scope and application of *ex gratia* payments may vary slightly in the provinces. The discussion of *ex gratia* payments in this section is based on the federal policy for *ex gratia* payments.

9   "The key to *ex gratia* payments is that there is no legal obligation on the Crown to pay. The Crown only makes such payments when it feels morally obliged to do so or wishes to do so for policy reasons. Thus, an *ex gratia* payment is totally discretionary, and a claimant does not have a legal right thereto."

(Lordon, *supra* note 1 at 434). The *AMI – Depatterned Persons Assistance Order*, *supra* note 5, provided *ex gratia* payments to any "depatterned person", as defined in the order, and so did not include an applicant who was a fetus (*in utero*) at the time that his mother was a depatterned person. See the *Schrier* case for details (*supra* note 5). On the other hand, the Nova Scotia government's compensation to persons infected by HIV through the blood supply included special compensation for the spouses and children of those who were infected (*e.g.*, funds to cover post-secondary education expenses for dependent children and a death benefit for spouses and children). See Canada, Commission of Inquiry on the Blood System in Canada, *Final Report*, vol. 3 (Ottawa: Minister of Public Works & Government Services Canada, 1997) (Commissioner: H. Krever) at 1031-32 [hereinafter *Krever Report*].

10 *Nakashima* v. *Canada*, [1947] Ex. Ct. 486 and *R.* v. *Iwasaki*, [1970] S.C.R. 437.

11 This campaign is described in M. Omatsu, *Bittersweet Passage – Redress and the Japanese Canadian Experience* (Toronto: Between the Lines, 1992) and in R. Miki & C. Kobayashi, *Justice in Our Time – The Japanese Canadian Redress Settlement* (Vancouver: Talonbooks, 1991).

12 *Krever Report*, *supra* note 9 at 1031-32.

13 For example see the *AMI – Depatterned Persons Assistance Order*, *supra* note 5, and the *HIV-Infected Persons and Thalidomide Victims Assistance Order*, *supra* note 6.

14 *Policy on Claims and Ex gratia Payments*, *supra* note 8 at para. 7.3.4.

15 The National Association of Japanese Canadians and its members were very involved in shaping the redress package for Japanese Canadians which ulti-mately resulted in *ex gratia* payments of $21,000 to each eligible applicant. See Omatsu, *supra* note 11 at 100-101 for details. Janet Connors, President of the Nova Scotia Hemophilia Society, and her husband Randy Connors negotiated with the Nova Scotia Health Minister the principles to be included in the agree-ment reached to compensate persons infected by HIV through the blood supply. Nova Scotia Department of Health, News Release, "Health – Hemophilia Agreement" (27 May 1993).

16 The five-year long redress campaign waged by the National Association of Japanese Canadians included, for example: publication of the community's spe-cific redress demands in a 1984 document called *Democracy Betrayed* (quoted in Miki & Kobayashi, *supra* note 11 at 11), release of a 1986 report commissioned from Price Waterhouse entitled *Economic Losses to Japanese Canadians After 1941* (quoted in Miki & Kobayashi, *ibid.* at 108, 109), and the formation in 1987 of a nation-wide coalition of broad-based support, the National Coalition for

Japanese Canadian Redress, that held a rally on Parliament Hill involving some 15,000 supporters, in April 1988 (see Miki & Kobayashi, *ibid.* at 123). See *Japanese Canadians Redress Report, supra* note 2 at 13.

[17] See Miki & Kobayashi, *supra* note 11 at 12: "Redress was a complex issue that reverberated in every nook and cranny of my community, and it was a volatile issue that, at times, threatened to divide us. In the process, though, it was a liberating issue that brought us together in our desire to reach a meaningful settlement." See also Omatsu, *supra* note 11 at 171: "[B]y bringing a shameful past into the open and, more importantly, by demanding and fighting for its rights, the community became engaged in an important healing process."

[18] These inferences are based on observations from the Commission of Inquiry on the Blood System in Canada, *Krever Report, supra* note 9 at 1032: "Most infected individuals and their families accepted the assistance packages out of an immediate need for financial assistance.... Many witnesses who testified at the hearings criticized the 'arbitrary' deadline for application because it did not give them adequate time to consider pursuing legal action, under which they might have been able to secure greater compensation." Some survivors of institutional child abuse expressed serious concerns to the Law Commission of Canada about feeling pressured by governments to accept offers of financial compensation. See for example, L. Hill, "Enough is Enough – Report on a Facilitated Discussion Group Involving the Deaf Community Responding to the Minister's Reference on Institutional Child Abuse" (March 1999) [unpublished research report archived at the Law Commission of Canada] at 36: "At JIC [the compensation program for former students at Jericho Hill Provincial School for the Deaf and Blind], people are being pressured into signing applications in a hurry and submit to deadlines".

[19] For example, the *B.C. Ombudsman's Report* on the collapse of the Principal Group of Companies resulted in *ex gratia* payments to compensate investors for the government's administrative negligence (Ombudsman of British Columbia, *Public Report No. 19: The Regulation of AIC Ltd. and FIC Ltd. by the B.C. Superintendent of Brokers (The Principal Group Investigation)* (Victoria: B.C. Ombudsman, 1989) [hereinafter *B.C. Ombudsman's Report*].

[20] See, for example, the applications provided to Japanese Canadians or persons who suffered physical deformities from thalidomide: *Japanese Canadians Redress Report, supra* note 2 at 6 and see *Mercier-Néron* v. *Canada (Minister of National Health and Welfare)*, [1995] F.C.J. No. 1024 at paras. 3-6 (T.D.) [hereinafter *Mercier-Néron*], online: QL.

21 See *Mercier-Néron, ibid.* at para. 14: "The duty to act fairly must be complied with even when the government, responsible as here for implementing a program of ex gratia payments established by order in council, derives its enabling power from the royal prerogative. The performance of this function may also be reviewed by the courts." See also Lordon, *supra* note 1 at 434: "If the Crown delegates to one of its agents the duty to determine whether such a payment should be made, the exercise of that function by the delegate may be subject to judicial review."

22 For example, over a period of six years, 17,984 payments were issued to Japanese Canadians. See *Japanese Canadians Redress Report, supra* note 2 at 13-14.

23 In British Columbia a large number of the depositors of the Principal Group Ltd., for example, were over 50 years of age. See *B.C. Ombudsman's Report, supra* note 19 at 4-5.

24 *Japanese Canadians Redress Report, supra* note 2 at 5.

25 Omatsu, *supra* note 11 at 170-71.

26 See the remarks of Alan Borovoy, General Counsel of the Canadian Civil Liberties Association concerning the campaign of Canadians of Japanese origin to obtain redress: "By your campaign of seeking compensation, you are not living in the past, you are working for the future. You are helping to create a precedent from which future governments would find it very hard to retreat. You're serving notice to whoever is going to be in government, that from now to the end of time, to whatever extent they are tempted to depart so radically from the norms of civilized behaviour, at the very least there will be a price to pay." (quoted in Miki & Kobayashi, *supra* note 11 at 127).

27 The redress package for wartime internees included $12 million for the Japanese Canadian community to promote the educational, social and cultural well-being of the community and $24 million to create an organization to foster cross-cultural understanding and help eliminate racism. See *Japanese Canadians Redress Report, supra* note 2 at 5.

F. Ombudsman Offices

1. Introduction

The Ombudsman is an independent and impartial institution of government that is meant to provide an efficient procedure for investigating complaints, bureaucratic errors and abuses of power. The Ombudsman also has authority to recommend corrective action. The International Bar Association has defined the Ombudsman as:

> ... an Office established by constitution or statute, headed by an independent, high level, public official, who is responsible to the Legislature or Parliament, who receives complaints from aggrieved persons against government agencies, officials and employers, or who acts on his own motion, and has the power to investigate and recommend corrective action and issue reports.[1]

Ombudsman offices exist in eight Canadian provinces.[2] Despite numerous recommendations to establish a federal Ombudsman, the Parliament of Canada has not done so to date.[3]

The role of the Ombudsman is not to affix blame or assess a penalty, but rather to resolve a complaint against government in a manner that is fair, just, and practical.[4] In so doing, the Ombudsman can serve to give voice to those who might otherwise not be heard.[5] Complaints about both contemporary and historical occurrences may be investigated. In addition to this investigatory function, an Ombudsman may take on a "watch dog" role over the implementation of recommendations made by public inquiries.[6]

2. Description

The essential characteristics of an effective Ombudsman's office are independence, flexibility, accessibility and credibility.[7] In several provinces, the enabling statute specifically provides that the Ombudsman is an "officer of the Legislature",[8] independent of the executive branch of government. Appointment and removal processes are designed to reinforce the Ombudsman's independence and impartiality. In every case, appointment is for a set term.[9] Usually, an

Ombudsman can be removed only for cause or incapacity, on the recommendation of the provincial legislature.[10]

a.   Triggering an Ombudsman investigation

An investigation by the Ombudsman may be triggered by an individual complaint, or may be undertaken on the Ombudsman's own initiative. In some provinces, an Ombudsman investigation may also be launched by a reference from a legislative committee, the Lieutenant-Governor in Council or the Attorney General. As a rule, an Ombudsman is authorised to investigate any complaint that a decision, recommendation, act or omission by an official is:

- contrary to the law;

- unreasonable;

- unjust;

- oppressive;

- improperly discriminatory;

- wrong;

- based on a mistake of fact or law; or

- the result of negligence or misconduct.[11]

Therefore, there are broad grounds upon which an Ombudsman may investigate, and conclude, that the government acted improperly.

All provincial statutes allow for public complaints to an Ombudsman. However, some provide that only those who are directly affected, and not third persons, may do so. There are statutory procedural safeguards to protect the confidentiality of complaints by prisoners in provincially-run correctional facilities or patients in provincial mental health institutions.[12] Generally, complaints from individuals must be made within a reasonable period of time and in writing.[13]

Ombudsman offices can also refuse to investigate a complaint. They can decline if:

- the complaint is made more than one year after the complainant knew of the decision, recommendation, act or omission in question;

- the complaint is judged to be frivolous, vexatious, or not made in good faith; or

- there are other appropriate remedies available to the person complaining.[14]

b. Jurisdiction and authority to investigate

The powers of an Ombudsman are restricted to the investigation of government action in the implementation of government policy. This encompasses the actions of provincial Ministries, Crown Agencies, municipal boards and agencies, and school and hospital boards among others. The actions of the legislature and the courts are, however, excluded from review by the Ombudsman.[15] An Ombudsman may only investigate the conduct of the government of the province or territory under whose jurisdiction he or she was appointed.[16]

The jurisdiction of the Ombudsman is also limited to investigating certain kinds of decisions. Most provincial statutes prohibit the Ombudsman from probing any decision, recommendation, act or omission where there exists a right of appeal, objection, or a right to apply for a review by a court or a tribunal. Most also prevent the Ombudsman from investigating the actions of the Cabinet, provincially appointed arbitrators, Crown Counsel and Crown solicitors. In some provinces, the prohibition extends to ministerial staff, and the Deputy, Associate Deputy or Assistant Deputy Ministers who report directly to the Minister. These restrictions typically apply regardless of whether the investigation results from a citizen's complaint or from the Ombudsman's own initiative.

c.   Investigatory powers

Ombudsman offices have wide powers to investigate, which they can use according to their own discretion and judgement. Investigations are private and confidential unless the Ombudsman decides that they should be open to the public. The Ombudsman has the ability to compel a person either to appear personally or to produce documentation and information relating to the investigation. Individuals may be examined under oath. In most provincial acts, witnesses are protected against the use of their evidence in subsequent judicial proceedings. The Ombudsman has the authority to inspect the premises of an agency or department that is under investigation simply by giving notice to the head of the department or agency prior to the inspection.

The Ombudsman is usually required to keep a complainant informed of the progress of the investigation. If the Ombudsman's report or recommendations are likely to adversely affect them, both the person complaining and the government department or official being investigated have the right to be heard, either personally or through a lawyer. The Ombudsman must furnish the results of the investigation to the complainant within a reasonable time. Any proceedings taken by an Ombudsman are not subject to review by courts unless there is an excess of legislative authority. Moreover, unless an Ombudsman acts in bad faith, he or she cannot be sued for anything done, reported or said in the course of exercising his or her functions.

d.   Power to report and recommend action

Generally, upon completing an investigation, an Ombudsman is required to report findings to the Minister or head of the public body concerned. The Ombudsman's report may contain a wide variety of recommendations, including recommendations that:

- the grievance be referred back to the administrative agency or its officer allegedly causing that grievance;

- an omission be rectified;

- a decision be cancelled or rectified;

- a practice be altered; and/or

- a law causing the grievance be reconsidered.

The Ombudsman's recommendations often contain criticisms not only of individuals but also of general policies and procedures. While an Ombudsman may make a variety of recommendations, there is no direct power to implement or enforce them. Nor can an Ombudsman report on unimplemented recommendations. However, at the time of making recommendations, an Ombudsman has the power to insist that the ministry or municipality concerned provides information about compliance with the recommendations within specified time limits. If the ministry or municipality fails to act within the given time period, the Ombudsman has the authority to submit a formal report to the Lieutenant Governor-in-Council or Premier, and the Legislative Assembly. Submission to the Legislative Assembly makes the report a matter of public record.

The reports and recommendations of an Ombudsman usually carry considerable weight with politicians, government officials, and the public. While an Ombudsman has no statutory power to enforce recommendations, the moral authority behind the office can sometimes be sufficient to ensure that responsible officials will carry them out.

3. Assessment

Overview

The Ombudsman process is flexible and informal, allowing for the engagement of survivors of institutional child abuse in a respectful manner. An Ombudsman has the discretion not to require a person's participation in an investigation, leaving that choice up to the complainant or any other affected person. An Ombudsman has the powers necessary to conduct a thorough fact-finding exercise, but only in connection with governmental action. While an Ombudsman can point out where unlawful conduct has occurred, he or she has no authority to make a final determination on legal liability. An Ombudsman's report is, consequently, better suited to pointing out systemic flaws than to holding individuals to account.

There is no formal process that an Ombudsman's investigation must follow, although general legal rules of procedural fairness will apply. The perceived fairness of a particular investigation will depend to a large extent on how it is conducted. Adverse findings must be reported to government, and those individuals or agencies affected will have the opportunity to respond before a report is made. An Ombudsman's report can promote public acknowledgement of a wrong committed by government. This may, in turn, facilitate apology and reconciliation.

An Ombudsman can recommend that any form of compensation or other redress be provided. Therefore, simply by making it public, an Ombudsman's report may begin to meet other needs of survivors. If an investigation addresses the full impact of institutional child abuse, it may also help to respond to the needs of families, communities and peoples. An Ombudsman's report may lead to systemic changes that help to prevent further abuse. If the report is well-publicised, it can also serve a role in public education.

a.   Respect, engagement and informed choice

An Ombudsman has control over the conduct and procedure of any investigation. As a result, he or she may follow a flexible and informal process that allows survivors to tell their story in the manner they desire. For example, the investigation may be designed to permit survivors to keep the details of the abuse they suffered confidential, or to avoid cross-examination.[17] While an Ombudsman has the power to compel testimony, he or she also has the discretion not to do so, and to involve survivors only to the extent that they wish.

An individual or group of survivors may initiate an investigation by filing a written complaint. For example, the British Columbia Ombudsman investigated a complaint filed by the Sons of Freedom Doukhobor Children that they were physically and psychologically harmed while confined in the New Denver institution.[18] In Quebec, the Comité des orphelins et orphelines institutionnalisés de Duplessis and thirty individuals filed complaints with the Quebec Ombudsman that they suffered harm during childhood because they were unjustly classified and treated as psychiatric patients.[19] In both cases, the Ombudsman recommended that the government consult with the complainants collectively to determine the means by which they would be heard. In both, the Ombudsman also recommended that all parties, including victims' representatives, take part in the negotiations to set up and implement a proposed no-fault compensation program.

b.   Fact-finding

The wide investigatory powers given to an Ombudsman – together with the statutory function to act as an overseer of administrative bodies and decisions – make the office well-suited to fact-finding. Although limited to investigating acts of public officials within its own province or territory, the Ombudsman will generally have unrestricted access to government documents, offices and institutions. As well, an Ombudsman has the power to subpoena witnesses and to compel testimony, and is not constrained by the rules of evidence that apply to courts. The examination may, consequently, be wide-ranging. An Ombudsman does not have the power to hold persons criminally liable. Therefore, when allegations in a complaint point to criminal conduct, it is critical that the Ombudsman coordinate fact-finding with police. If this is not done, there is a risk that the Ombudsman's investigation could taint evidence, so that it can no longer be relied on in a criminal trial.

The Ombudsman determines the extent of the investigation, and can choose whether or not to hear from those who allegedly committed the abuse. Hearing complainants in a confidential setting can also help an Ombudsman gain a better insight into the personal consequences of abuse and better situate those facts being made part of the public record. In contrast to the judicial fact-finding process, an Ombudsman's investigation can also be forward-looking. This can help establish an independent and permanent record of the abuses that took place and the failure of those in positions of responsibility to protect children in their care.[20]

c. Accountability

An Ombudsman has the jurisdiction to investigate the acts, omissions and policy decisions of public officials that may have been insulated from direct public scrutiny in the past. This jurisdiction includes the power to require individuals, officials and organisations to explain their role, or their complicity, in institutional child abuse. It extends to naming names.[21] Nonetheless, the Ombudsman process is not designed to establish the accountability of individual perpetrators by formally assigning legal responsibility.

The Ombudsman process is well-suited to holding accountable the institutions that are linked to government. Ombudsman reports can publicly criticise the institution and the responsible government agency for not having implemented safeguards to prevent abuse. Public criticism generated by an investigation, findings and recommendations of the Ombudsman is itself a form of institutional accountability.

d. Fairness

The Ombudsman's role is to investigate and make recommendations. The process does not generate legally enforceable findings, and is not adversarial. Whether the investigation is fair to all parties will depend on the manner in which it is conducted. Interviews are confidential and witnesses are not subject to cross-examination. For this reason, it may seem that the Ombudsman process is not fair to those suspected of abuse or concealment of abuse. This concern can lead an Ombudsman to refrain from making findings that directly point to wrongdoing by specified individuals.

When an Ombudsman decides to investigate a complaint, he or she must first inform the Minister and/or the ministry affected. In addition, any adverse finding must be presented to the government agency, or individual affected, before being made public. The agency and any affected persons may then make oral or written representations and respond to preliminary findings. These procedures ensure that the investigation will be conducted thoroughly and impartially, and will respect the requirements of procedural fairness to all parties.

e.   Acknowledgement, apology and reconciliation

The Ombudsman's wide scope for investigation allows for social and psychological studies and inquiries into the management processes of an institution. These can enable the Ombudsman to uncover possible explanations as to why abuse occurred. As well, the Ombudsman's report can implicitly contain an acknowledgement of wrongdoing and a plea for apology. For example, a report may recommend that the government or institution responsible provide an official acknowledgement of the wrongs that occurred, and a full and adequate explanation for why certain policy decisions were taken. A report might even recommend that the government offer a public apology to those who were harmed.

The authority to make recommendations is especially powerful in cases where the Ombudsman concludes that the allegedly culpable parties refused to accept responsibility – blaming either other parties or the prevailing values at the time the abuse occurred. After concluding that the courts could not respond to survivors' needs for procedural reasons, one Ombudsman's report suggested that an out-of-court settlement, including an acknowledgement of the harm suffered, be negotiated.[22] The report also concluded that apologies on the part of the government, the medical establishment and the religious orders involved would undoubtedly be a good place to begin to acknowledge the harm done.[23]

f.   Compensation, counselling and education

The flexibility and scope of the Ombudsman process permits many of the other needs of survivors to be met. While an Ombudsman cannot order payment of financial compensation, he or she can make such a recommendation. Moreover, an Ombudsman can recommend that more comprehensive redress programs be established. As well, an Ombudsman can suggest how to design and negotiate redress programs in a manner that promotes healing. Recommendations can deal with potential features of redress programs – including the opportunity for survivors to receive therapy, counselling, education, and training services.

g. Needs of families, communities and peoples

An Ombudsman has authority to conduct an investigation that includes families, communities, and peoples affected by institutional child abuse. Family members and representatives of communities can be given the opportunity to state the personal effects of abuse. Recommendations can be made about establishing community initiatives to redress the social and economic effects of child abuse. However, the private nature of many investigations may not satisfy the needs of families, communities and peoples for a public catharsis. Because the Ombudsman has no power to make a binding determination of accountability or to order acknowledgement or an apology, their needs for reconciliation and healing may not be fully met.

h. Prevention and public education

An Ombudsman can investigate and document the past; make recommendations to deal with present needs of survivors; and offer recommendations to try to ensure that the abuse does not recur. An Ombudsman's report can encourage institutions to make systemic changes to enhance prevention. It can facilitate a change in perceptions, attitudes and behaviour in an institution. It can also assist in promoting public engagement with strategies for prevention.

The report of an Ombudsman is an excellent tool for public education. In outlining the causes and effects of institutional abuse, it may generate an understanding of the needs of survivors and sympathy for those who suffered the most. The report may also help overcome public attitudes that prevent a more general reconciliation with groups whose members have been disproportionately affected by institutional child abuse.[24]

4. Conclusion

Because it results only in recommendations, the Ombudsman process can provide only a partial solution for survivors. An Ombudsman cannot command an apology or order financial compensation. Through the informal authority of moral suasion, however, an Ombudsman's report has the power to change the way people think. The process is well-suited to respecting survivors' needs for acknowledgement while preserving their dignity and privacy. Twice in recent years, the process has proven that it can make an important contribution toward uncovering and understanding historical child abuse.

Ombudsman offices currently operate in only eight provinces. For other jurisdictions, including the federal government, this option is not available to survivors of institutional child abuse. Given the potential of the Ombudsman process to uncover past cases of child abuse and its authority to propose systemic remedies, an argument can be made that Ombudsman-like processes should be created and deployed to oversee the administration of services for children in these jurisdictions.

Recommendations

JURISDICTIONS THAT DO NOT now have an Ombudsman's office or similar institution should consider enacting legislation to establish one.

Considerations:

> Where specialised Ombudsman's offices exist in a jurisdiction, but they do not have authority to examine questions of institutional child abuse, either a general Ombudsman office or another specialised Ombudsman (such as, in the case of the federal government, an Aboriginal Ombudsman with authority to investigate abuse in residential schools) should be created.

OMBUDSMAN STATUTES should be amended (where necessary) to require that governments table a response to an Ombudsman report in the legislature within a specified delay.

---

1 K. D. Anderson, "The Ombudsman as an Administrative Remedy" (Occasional Paper #41) (Edmonton: The International Ombudsman Institute, 1987) at 1.

2 Alberta, *Ombudsman Act*, R.S.A 1980, c. O-7; British Columbia, *Ombudsman Act*, R.S.B.C. 1996, c. 340; Manitoba, *Ombudsman Act*, R.S.M. 1987, c. O-45; New Brunswick, *Ombudsman Act*, R.S.N.B. 1973, c. O-5; Nova Scotia, *Ombudsman Act*, R.S.N.S. 1989, c. 327; Ontario, *Ombudsman Act*, R.S.O. 1989, c. O-6; Saskatchewan, *Ombudsman and Children's Advocate Act*, R.S.S. 1978, c. O-4. In Quebec, the Ombudsman is known officially as the Public Protector, *Public ProtectorAct*, R.S.Q. c. P-32. Unofficially, the Public Protector's office uses the term Ombudsman.

3 Canadian Ombudsman Association, *A Federal Ombudsman for Canada* (Discussion Paper) (June 1999) at 10, online: <http//ftp.ombudsman.on.ca> (date accessed: 16 November 1999) [hereinafter A Federal Ombudsman for Canada]; Canadian Bar Association, *Resolution at the 1990 National Convention*, Vancouver, B.C.; *Report of the Committee on the Concept of the Ombudsman* (Ottawa, July 1977). The Canadian Ombudsman Association has also called for the establishment by legislation of a Parliamentary Commission of

Aboriginal Affairs in 1998 (Canadian Ombudsman Association, News Release, "Canadian Ombudsman Association Formed" (24 June 1998)). The federal Parliament has, however, created specialised Ombudsman offices with limited jurisdiction: for example, the Commissioner of Official Languages, the Privacy Commissioner and the Information Commissioner.

4   *A Federal Ombudsman for Canada, ibid.* at 4.

5   This was the case, for example, with the former students of Jericho Hill, the "children of Duplessis" and the Doukhobor children who were interned at New Denver.

6   For example, in British Columbia, the Gove Inquiry into Child Protection recommended that the Province report to the B.C. Ombudsman on its plans for implementation of the recommendations contained in its report. British Columbia, *Report of the Gove Inquiry into Child Protection in British Columbia – A Commission of Inquiry into the Adequacy of the Service, Policies and Practices of the Ministry of Social Services as They Relate to the Apparent Neglect, Abuse and Death of Matthew John Vaudreuil* by Judge T. Gove (Victoria: Ministry of Social Services, 1995) at Recommendation 118. See also Ombudsman of British Columbia, *Public Report No. 36: Getting There: A Review of the implementation of the Report of the Gove Inquiry into Child Protection* (Victoria: B.C. Ombudsman,1998).

7   *A Federal Ombudsman for Canada, supra* note 3 at 2.

8   Alberta, *Ombudsman Act, supra* note 2, s. 2(1); New Brunswick, *Ombudsman Act, supra* note 2, s. 5; Ontario, *Ombudsman Act, supra* note 2, s. 2.

9   The term of office varies by province. The term is five years in the provinces of Alberta, Nova Scotia, Saskatchewan and Quebec. In Manitoba and British Columbia, the term is six years. In Ontario and New Brunswick, the term is ten years. The legislation for the provinces of Alberta, British Columbia, New Brunswick, Nova Scotia and Ontario provides that the appointment of the Ombudsman can be renewed but no limit is put on the number of renewals. By contrast, in Manitoba and Saskatchewan, the legislation only permits one term renewal. In Quebec, the Public Protector remains in office even after his or her five-year term lapses until he or she is replaced.

10   This is the case in British Columbia, Alberta, Saskatchewan, Ontario, Nova Scotia and New Brunswick.

11   See for example Nova Scotia, *Ombudsman Act, supra* note 2, s. 20(1); Saskatchewan, *Ombudsman and Children's Advocate Act, supra* note 2, s. 24(1); and Quebec, *Public Protector Act, supra* note 2, s. 26.1.

12 Alberta, *Ombudsman Act, supra* note 2, s. 13(2)(a),(b); British Columbia, *Ombudsman Act, supra* note 2, s. 12(3); New Brunswick, *Ombudsman Act, supra* note 2, s. 13(4); Nova Scotia, *Ombudsman Act, supra* note 2, s. 12(4); Ontario, *Ombudsman Act, supra* note 2, s. 16(2)(a),(b),(c); Quebec, *Public Protector Act, supra* note 2, s. 22; Saskatchewan, *Ombudsman and Children's Advocate Act, supra* note 2, s. 17.

13 Often, the Ombudsman office will assist complainants in the process of filing a written statement of their grievances.

14 See for example Alberta, *Ombudsman Act, supra* note 2, s. 14; New Brunswick, *Ombudsman Act, supra* note 2, s. 15; Nova Scotia, *Ombudsman Act, supra* note 2, s. 14(1)(a); Saskatchewan, *Ombudsman and Children's Advocate Act, supra* note 2, s. 18(1)(ff); and Quebec, *Public Protector Act, supra* note 2, s. 18(1). Quebec even requires the termination of an Ombudsman investigation where judicial proceedings are launched.

15 *British Columbia Development Corp.* v. *British Columbia (Ombudsman)*, [1984] 2 S.C.R. 447.

16 So, for example, a provincial Ombudsman could not investigate abuse in a federal institution, or in a private or religious institution. Given that there are only three federal specialised Ombudsman offices, the Ombudsman process is not currently an option for the investigation of wrongdoing at residential schools for Aboriginal children.

17 The British Columbia Ombudsman did not document specific examples of abusive conduct at Jericho Hill School because: "We believe that those who state they have been abused should be believed and that recounting the details is unnecessary, disrespectful and undignified. So far as specific incidents are concerned, the students who were abused are entitled to their privacy, unless they choose otherwise." (Ombudsman of British Columbia, *Public Report No.32: Abuse of Deaf Students at Jericho Hill School* (Victoria: B.C. Ombudsman, November 1993) at para. 12 of cover letter [hereinafter *Jericho Hill Report*]).

18 Ombudsman of British Columbia, *Public Report No. 38: Righting the Wrong – The Confinement of the Sons of Freedom Doukhobor Children* (Victoria: B.C. Ombudsman, April 1998) [hereinafter *Righting the Wrong*].

19 Quebec Public Protector, *The 'Children of Duplessis': A Time for Solidarity* (Discussion and Consultation Paper for Decision-Making Purposes) (Quebec: Public Protector, 22 January 1997) [hereinafter *A Time for Solidarity*].

20 For example, in *Righting the Wrong*, *supra* note 18, the British Columbia Ombudsman made the finding that the actions, decisions and omissions of the government caused irreplaceable loss to the children of New Denver by removing the children from their parents, alienating them from family and community life and forcing them to live in an institutional setting.

21 This power is not necessarily always exercised, however. For example, the British Columbia Ombudsman notes at the start of her report on the Doukhobor children at New Denver: "Since the public officials who were involved have not been contacted directly by my office, they too are entitled to their privacy. It is inappropriate to lay blame for the wrongs done at the feet of specific people." (*Righting the Wrong*, *ibid.* at para. 3 of cover letter).

22 *A Time for Solidarity*, *supra* note 19 at section 8.3.1.

23 *Ibid.*

24 For example, the British Columbia Ombudsman's report on the provincial government's handling of the complaints of sexual abuse involving Deaf children at the Jericho Hill Provincial School for the Deaf brought to light the various difficulties posed to the Deaf community in general. See *Jericho Hill Report*, *supra* note 17.

G. Children's Advocates and Commissions

1. Introduction

In Canada, public bodies created to advance and protect the rights and interests of children date from the late 1970s and early 1980s.[1] Today they may be found in six provinces, under many different names. In Alberta, Saskatchewan and Manitoba,[2] the term is Children's Advocate. In Ontario, the term is Office of Child and Family Service Advocacy.[3] British Columbia has a Child, Youth and Family Advocate, as well as a Children's Commission, [4] In Quebec, the Commission des droits de la personne et droits de la jeunesse plays this role.[5]

The specific roles and functions of these offices vary from province to province. Some, like Alberta's Children's Advocate Office, are designed to give children a voice and support in dealing only with the child welfare system.[6] Others, such as British Columbia's Children's Commissioner and Quebec's Commission des droits de la personne et droits de la jeunesse have been given broader powers to advance and protect the rights of children and youth receiving government services. A key role of the British Columbia Children's Commission is to resolve complaints concerning decisions about the provision of services to children and youth. It also monitors the government's internal process for handling complaints.[7] The Commission des droits de la personne et droits de la jeunesse is responsible for protecting the interests and rights of youth recognised under Quebec's *Youth Protection Act*.[8]

2. Description

In spite of their varying names, mandates and powers, all child advocacy offices perform four similar functions. They:

a. Inform young people about their rights and assist them in advocating for their own interests

b. Help resolve concerns about government services provided for children and youth and, when necessary, formally investigate complaints

c. Report findings and make recommendations and

d. Conduct research and public education

These four areas of responsibility involve both preventative and educational activities.

a. Informing and advocating

The primary objectives of these bodies are to make children and youth, including children in care, aware that they are entitled to receive services that respect their best interests and rights – and to promote these interests and rights.[9] In some cases, the rights and interests to be publicised and advanced are specifically set out in a statute. For example, Quebec's *Youth Protection Act* recognises a number of rights, including a child's entitlement to receive adequate health, social and educational services.[10] The British Columbia *Child, Family and Community Services Act* lists the rights of children in care. These rights include the right to reasonable privacy and to have one's own belongings; the right to not be punished physically, or in any other abusive way; and the right to receive medical and dental care.[11]

Information is provided to children and youth through various means – from toll-free phone lines to websites, brochures and other publications. As well, since knowledge varies widely,[12] outreach programs are common. Often these programs actively involve youth themselves.[13]

In addition to informing youth in care and children of their rights, these bodies act as advocates. This means they are meant to assist children in making their voices heard and, if necessary, speaking for them. In some jurisdictions, their roles may include taking steps to obtain judicial or administrative remedies.[14]

b. Helping to resolve problems and investigating complaints

Advocacy offices have the authority to investigate concerns about government services provided to a child or groups of children. Investigations may focus either on an individual's personal situation or systemic problems. For example, claims that staff at one detention centre in Ontario used excessive force in physically restraining youth and discriminated against youth from visible minority groups, prompted an investigation by the Office of Child and Family Service Advocacy. The investigation led to a review of the policies, practices and systems that were in place, but did not seek to assign individual culpability.[15]

In order to carry out effective investigations, all of these bodies are given basic fact-finding powers. They may compel disclosure of information held by officials and may enter institutions to conduct interviews or obtain records.[16] In some jurisdictions, those who obstruct or interfere with investigations may be charged.

c.   Making recommendations

Flowing from the authority to investigate problems and report findings is the power to make recommendations respecting the provision of services to an individual or group of young people.[17] The extent of an advocate's power to enforce recommendations varies. In most provinces, the advocate has no authority to direct child welfare officials to act in a certain way. Again, in the case of systemic problems, an advocate may make recommendations for organisational changes – such as changes to policies or procedures – but most have no power to order compliance with their recommendations.

Some bodies may be able to achieve compliance by referring an unresolved matter to a tribunal. This power is granted, for example, where recommendations to remedy the infringement of a child's or children's rights are not complied with, or where attempts fail to settle a complaint about the breach of the rights of a child in care.

d.   Conducting research and public education

In addition to their investigation and problem-solving functions, children's advocates engage in research and public education activities. Some have conducted reviews of provincial child welfare systems. One such review suggested, for example, that since the child protection system and residential foster providers occupy positions of trust, they should be held to a higher standard of care than the children's biological families.[18] Others have attempted to provide a forum where youth in the system can convey their stories and observations in their own words.[19] Still others have sponsored research about legal issues such as how to reconcile the duty of professional confidentiality with the duty to report abuse.[20]

Research documents, investigation reports that are not confidential, and annual reports are useful tools of public education. For example, the British Columbia *Children's Commission 1998 Annual Report* provides a breakdown of complaints related to rights violations. It indicates that slightly more than one-quarter of the total complaints were about infringements of a child's right to receive guidance and encouragement to maintain his or her cultural heritage; and slightly less than one-quarter of the complaints related to the right to be fed, clothed and nurtured.[21]

3.   Assessment

To what degree can children's advocates and commissions meet any of the needs of adult survivors of institutional child abuse? Given that these bodies are designed to look after the interests of young people (usually up to the age of 18) now in care, they obviously cannot meet survivors' needs to expose historical facts, hold wrongdoers accountable, and obtain acknowledgements, apologies and compensation for what happened to them in the past. But they do play a key role in preventing institutional child abuse today, and in educating the public about the rights and well-being of young people in care – one of the enduring needs expressed by survivors.

a.   Informing and advocating

Pure advocacy is largely about empowering young people to speak for themselves, as well as engaging other persons concerned about their well-being to be a voice for children who need one.[22] Since these bodies empower and enlist others to become advocates, they have an ideal opportunity to collaborate with adult survivors. Some adult survivors want to play an active role in preventing child abuse. Enlisting their help not only meets survivors' needs; it adds a strong voice to the cause of children's rights.

b. Helping to resolve problems and investigating complaints

Normally young people use internal channels to seek a resolution of any concerns about services provided. Only when internal mechanisms fail to produce a satisfactory result, will a children's advocate be called upon.[23] Because children's advocates investigate complaints at arm's length from the service provider, abuse is not as easy to cover up or cloak in indifference. The assurance that young people today will have someone safe to turn to for help responds to survivors' concerns that allegations of physical and sexual abuse will be taken seriously.

c. Making recommendations

Children's advocates and commissions have the authority to recommend actions both to resolve individual problems and to produce wider-reaching, systemic changes to an organisation. System improvements are among the ways survivors express a need to see prevention made a priority. Soliciting the insights and advice of survivors when investigations or systemic reviews are conducted, would enrich the perspective of children's advocates. It can also assist survivors in their personal healing by engaging them in preventive activities.[24]

d. Conducting research and public education

Survivors can make a significant contribution to framing the scope of and approach taken to research on institutional child abuse. The researchers for the Ontario *Voices from Within* project met with youth advisory groups (comprising youth in care who had not been part of the focus groups interviewed) to receive their views on the presentation of themes and quotations in the report.[25] The Law Commission benefited greatly from the participation of survivors on the study panels established for this reference. Survivors can also meet their desire to educate the public about institutional abuse by sharing the lessons of their own experiences in campaigns launched by children's advocates.

4.   Conclusion

Children's advocates and commissions play a very limited role in meeting the needs of survivors and their families. Their advocacy, investigative, advisory and research functions can help to ensure that young people in out-of-home care do not suffer the harms that survivors experienced in the past, or if they do, that an independent advocate will be there to assist them. These bodies have an opportunity to engage survivors in prevention and public awareness activities that could satisfy part of their need to feel that society has learned from past mistakes.

Recommendations

JURISDICTIONS THAT DO NOT now have independent bodies to act as children's advocates should consider enacting legislation to establish them.

THE MANDATES OF CHILDREN'S advocates and commissioners should be broad enough to assist children and youth living in residential institutions and other types of out-of-home care settings, as well as those living at home.

CHILDREN'S ADVOCATES AND COMMISSIONS should establish and consult regularly with advisory committees made up of people who are or have been in care, including adult survivors of institutional child abuse.

Considerations:

These committees could advise them generally on how they carry out their advocacy roles and specifically on matters related to education, research and systems reviews.

---

1   Quebec created the Youth Protection Commission in 1977: *Youth Protection Act*, R.S.Q. 1977, c. P-34. In Ontario the Advocacy Office has been in operation since 1978: Office of Child and Family Service Advocacy, *Voices From Within – Youth Speak Out: Youth in Care in Ontario* by K. Snow (Toronto: Queen's Printer, April 1998) (Chief Advocate: J. Finlay) at 1 [hereinafter *Voices From Within – Youth Speak Out*].

2   *Child Welfare Act*, S.A. 1984, c. C-8.1, s. 2.1 [hereinafter *Child Welfare Act* (Alberta)], *The Ombudsman and Children's Advocate Act*, S.S. 1994, c. O-4, s. 12.6 [hereinafter *Ombudsman and Children's Advocate Act* (Saskatchewan)]; *The Child and Family Services Act*, S.M. 1985-86, c. C-80, s. 8.1-8.14 [hereinafter *Child and Family Services Act* (Manitoba)].

3   *Child and Family Services Act*, R.S.O. 1990, c. C-11, s. 102 [hereinafter *Child and Family Services Act* (Ontario)].

4 *Child, Youth and Family Advocacy Act*, R.S.B.C. 1996, c. 47 [hereinafter *Child, Youth and Family Advocacy Act* (B.C.)]; *Children's Commission Act*, S.B.C. 1997, c. 11 [hereinafter *Children's Commission Act* (B.C.)].

5 *Charter of Human Rights and Freedoms*, R.S.Q. c. C-12, s. 57.

6 *Child Welfare Act* (Alberta), *supra* note 2, s. 2.1(3) and S. Osinchuk, *Children's Advocate Services in Canada 1998* (Edmonton: Children's Advocate Office (Alberta), 7 May 1998) at 4.

7 *Children's Commission Act* (B.C.), *supra* note 4, s. 4; British Columbia, Children's Commission, *The Children's Commission 1998 Annual Report* (Victoria: The Children's Commission, April 1999) (Commissioner: C. Morton) at 11 [hereinafter *Children's Commission 1998 Annual Report*].

8 *Youth Protection Act*, R.S.Q., c. P-34.1, s. 2 [hereinafter *Youth Protection Act* (Quebec)]. In 1995, the Youth Protection Commission merged with the Commission des droits de la personne to become the Commission des droits de la personne et des droits de la jeunesse under the *Charter of Human Rights and Freedoms*, *supra* note 5, ss. 57, 58.1.

9 For example, Ontario's Office of Child and Family Service Advocacy is required to "co-ordinate and administer a system of advocacy ... on behalf of children and families who receive or seek approved services," while Alberta's Children's Advocate must "represent the rights, interests and viewpoints of children who receive services under this Act." *Child and Family Services Act* (Ontario), *supra* note 3, s. 102(a); *Child Welfare Act* (Alberta), *supra* note 2, s. 2.1(3)(c).

10 *Youth Proctection Act* (Quebec), *supra* note 8, s. 8.

11 *Child, Family and Community Services Act*, R.S.B.C. 1996, c. 46, s. 70.

12 *Voices From Within – Youth Speak Out*, *supra* note 1 at 11. See also British Columbia, Ministry for Children and Families, "Know Your Rights under the Child, Family and Community Service Act – A Guide for Young People in Care", online: British Columbia Ministry for Children and Families website <http://www.mcf.gov.bc.ca> (date accessed: 14 June 1999).

13 H. Sylvester, N. Harvy, L. Sam & D. Tom, *The Youth Report – A Report About Youth by Youth* (Victoria: The Children's Commission, April 1999).

14 For example, in Quebec, the Commission is required "to take the legal means it considers necessary to remedy any situation where the rights of a child are being encroached upon." *Youth Proctection Act* (Quebec), *supra* note 8, s. 23 (c).

15 J. Finlay, *Report by the Office of Child and Family Service Advocacy – Care of Youth at Thistletown Regional Centre, Syl Apps Campus* (Toronto: Office of Child and Family Service Advocacy, October 1992) at 1 [hereinafter *Report on Thistletown Regional Centre*].

16 See for example: *Children's Commission Act* (BC), *supra* note 4, s. 5; *Child, Youth and Family Advocacy Act* (B.C.), *supra* note 4, ss. 7, 10; *Child and Family Services Act* (Manitoba), *supra* note 2, ss. 8.3(c), (d), 8.5, 8.6; *Youth Protection Act* (Quebec), *supra* note 8, s. 26.

17 See for example: Child, *Youth and Family Advocacy Act* (B.C.), *supra* note 4, s. 4(1)(e); *Ombudsman and Children's Advocate Act* (Saskatchewan), *supra* note 2, s. 12.6(1)(d); *Child Welfare Act* (Alberta), *supra* note 2, s. 2.1(4)(c); *Child and Family Services Act* (Manitoba), *supra* note 2, s. 8.3(a).

18 Alberta, Children's Advocate, *In Need of Protection – Children and Youth in Alberta* (Edmonton: Children's Advocate & Child Welfare Review Office, July 1993) (Children's Advocate: Bernd Walter).

19 *Voices From Within – Youth Speak Out, supra* note 1.

20 C. Bernard, *L'Obligation de signalement pour les intervenants liés par le secret professionnel* (Quebec: Commission des droits de la personne et des droits de la jeunesse, October 1996).

21 *Children's Commission 1998 Annual Report, supra* note 7 at 34, 44.

22 Osinchuk, *supra* note 6 at 10.

23 For example, the British Columbia Children's Commission cannot accept a complaint before it has been reviewed internally by the Ministry for Children and Families, online: <http://www.childservices.gov.bc.ca/work/complaints.html> (date accessed: 12 October 1999).

24 For example, in Ontario the advocate who investigated the Thistletown Centre also interviewed youth who had been discharged from the Centre. *Report on Thistletown Regional Centre, supra* note 15 at 5.

25 *Voices From Within – Youth Speak Out, supra* note 1 at 51.

H. Public Inquiries

1. Introduction

A public inquiry is an official, independent public investigation ordered by a federal or provincial cabinet.[1] Public inquiries are of two main types. Some, like the Royal Commission on Aboriginal Peoples and the Mackenzie Valley Pipeline inquiry, are established to investigate and make recommendations concerning a broad area of public policy. In other cases, such as the Marshall inquiry and the Morin inquiry,[2] the mandate of the inquiry is to investigate specific events, to make findings about them, and usually to make recommendations about how future occurrences may be prevented.

The activities and reports of public inquiries are often the focus of media attention. But inquiries have no power to impose formal sanctions on individuals or organisations or to implement any of their recommendations.[3]

> One of the primary functions of public inquiries is fact-finding. They are often convened, in the wake of public shock, horror, disillusionment, or scepticism, in order to uncover 'the truth'. Inquiries are, like the judiciary, independent; unlike the judiciary, they are often endowed with wide-ranging investigative powers. In following their mandates, commissions of inquiry are, ideally, free from partisan loyalties and better able than Parliament or the legislatures to take a long-term view of the problem presented.[4]

Provincial governments have already appointed several inquiries to examine complaints of child abuse – and the way these complaints were handled – at specific institutions.[5] In addition, the Royal Commission on Aboriginal Peoples recommended that the federal government appoint a public inquiry to investigate and document the origins and effects of residential schools on all Aboriginal peoples.[6] In Australia, the Human Rights and Equal Opportunity Commission conducted an inquiry into the separation of indigenous children from their families and communities.[7] Also in Australia, a commission of inquiry examined whether there has been any abuse, mistreatment or neglect of children in Queensland's institutions.[8]

2.   Description

Public inquiries play an important role in Canadian public life.[9] They have been praised for facilitating broad public participation, contributing to public awareness and education, and laying the basis for the development of effective public policy. They have also been criticised as being a symbolic or expensive means of delaying action on social issues and for being unnecessarily legalistic and adversarial.[10] The procedures of a number of recent inquiries have been challenged on constitutional grounds.[11] Over the years, several law reform commissions have recommended significant changes to the way public inquiries are conducted.[12]

a.   Mandate

The terms of reference of a public inquiry are set out in the Order-in-Council by which it is created.[13] The terms of reference establish the purpose, scope and limits of the inquiry, and often require it to report within a specified time.[14] Inquiries typically are given a wide mandate to investigate past events, and to determine the knowledge and responses of officials to these events. They may be empowered, for example,

- to study comparable and related events;

- to recommend remedial action in response to past events; and

- to make recommendations concerning how similar events might be prevented, monitored or remedied in the future.

A public inquiry appears to have no guaranteed legal status ensuring it the time and resources necessary to investigate all matters within its mandate.[15] Nevertheless, the independence of inquiries to conduct their own research and investigations, to reach conclusions free of executive interference and to publish their reports has been described as "their most important and distinctive attribute as an instrument of government".[16] This independence, which is frequently thought to be signalled by appointing judges as commissioners, increases their credibility and distinguishes them from any investigation undertaken by the government or by public service officials.

b. Procedures

Within the terms of the Order-in-Council by which they are established, inquiries determine their own procedures. They may retain researchers to conduct studies on any matter within the mandate of the inquiry.[17] Public hearings are common, and a broad range of people may be invited to participate, often in innovative ways. Some public inquiries adopt court-style hearings in which individuals and organisations are represented by lawyers who present evidence and cross-examine witnesses. Such hearings usually focus on investigating specific allegations of wrongdoing, and any systemic problems connected to that wrongdoing. Individuals and groups are often invited to call evidence and make submissions when inquiries are primarily focussed on the systemic causes and effects of wrongdoing, the means to remedy harm done, and to prevent its reoccurrence.[18]

While inquiries do not make final determinations of liability for wrongdoing, their findings can adversely affect reputations. For this reason, those being investigated by an inquiry are entitled to reasonable notice if they are likely to be identified as having engaged in misconduct. They must be given a full disclosure of evidence, an opportunity to be heard in person or through a lawyer,[19] and the right to examine witnesses.[20] Inquiries have the power to compel individuals to provide evidence and produce documents, although such evidence may be inadmissible in subsequent legal proceedings.[21] Unlike the courts, inquiries are free to express their conclusions in any manner they deem appropriate. Inquiries have the authority to frame the issue under investigation in novel ways, and assess the value of the evidence received as they see fit.[22]

3. Assessment

Overview

A public inquiry may, in principle, set its own rules of procedure. This gives it the flexibility necessary to satisfy the principles of respect, engagement and informed choice. As a fact-finding process, inquiries have the capacity to conduct research and consider a broad range of evidence. They are well-suited to situating individual wrongdoing in its wider context and identifying the systemic weaknesses that may have contributed to this wrongdoing.

Public inquiries cannot pronounce on the guilt or legal liability of those involved in their processes. They can, however, be effective at publicising facts connected with the subject of the inquiry – for example, the context of child abuse at one or several institutions. In this way, they can provide a form of public accountability. Inquiries are bound by legal rules of procedural fairness and must give individuals and organisations an opportunity to respond to allegations of misconduct against them. As a result of their wide-ranging approach to evidence and procedure, public inquiries may be in a good position to promote acknowledgement and apology.

Public inquiries cannot directly offer benefits, services or other compensation to respond to other needs of survivors of institutional child abuse. However, they can make recommendations that may carry sufficient moral force to ensure that at least some benefits, services or other compensation are implemented.[23] There is no restriction on who can participate in a public inquiry. Inquiries may invite family members as well as representatives of communities and groups to take an active role in the proceedings. Recommendations can take into account their needs as well as the needs of individual survivors. Finally, inquiries can play an important role in raising public awareness of an issue such as institutional child abuse, and in recommending measures of prevention.

a.   Respect, engagement and informed choice

How well inquiries meet the goals of respect, engagement and informed choice for survivors depends largely on the way they are conducted. Normally, inquiries have the power to compel anyone with information relevant to the inquiry to testify and to produce documents. Sometimes, concerns about privacy and respect lead commissioners to conclude that a public investigation of witnesses

> … would be a mistake, that it would be preferable to conduct an informal investigation to avoid requiring victims to relive in public the trauma of abuse and to avoid the risk of compromising the reputations of innocent persons.[24]

In other words, an inquiry that controls its own procedures could elect to hear only from survivors who want to testify and have the appropriate support available. The inquiry could receive testimony in a confidential setting. Such closed hearings promote respect and informed choice for survivors of child abuse, but may diminish public engagement with the inquiry's work, limiting its educational role. In addition, if survivors who testify are to be insulated from cross-examination, or in some cases even protected from testifying against their wishes, then the inquiry process cannot be used to "name names" and assign individual blame. How well an inquiry engages survivors may also depend on its composition. The choice of inquiry commissioners can be tailored for expertise, public reputation or demographics. Commissioners could, for example, include survivors of institutional child abuse or other former residents of a children's institution.[25]

b.   Fact-finding

Public inquiries have a great potential to uncover facts. But since an inquiry is not a court, any factual conclusions it reaches are not binding on a court that later may be required to hear a case relating to the same matter. An inquiry may have to decide whether to concentrate on issues of individual wrongdoing or to explore systemic issues. An emphasis on systemic issues is less likely to provoke legal challenges to the inquiry. In addition, investigation of the broader systemic issues may accomplish a good deal of what could reasonably be expected from an inquiry that focusses on individual wrongdoing.[26]

Because inquiries are entitled to conduct their own research and consider broad contextual evidence, they can contribute to a better understanding of the reasons why wrongdoing may have occurred and its effects on individuals and communities. Experts who collect data for an inquiry can be invited to testify about their findings, even though much of this type of evidence is not admissible or relevant in a civil or criminal proceeding.[27] Inquiries can examine an act of abuse not only as the act of "an identifiable author", but also as "the product of the activity of an organisation or the product of a complex process".[28] They can investigate social and organisational responses to abuse in a manner that focusses on both "the structure of decision-making"[29] and the reasons why abuse of children was either tolerated or ignored by society.

c. Accountability

Can public inquiries promote accountability when they have no authority to impose sanctions on individuals? They do – if accountability is seen as simply establishing public awareness of the wrongdoer and the extent of the wrong. Public inquiries have the power to call individuals and organisations to account and to require them to explain their roles in perpetuating and condoning abuse. Unlike a court, a public inquiry is permitted to compel a wrongdoer to testify and to produce relevant evidence.[30] Public inquiries are well-suited to holding organisations and society accountable for institutional child abuse. Most organisations depend on a good public reputation. Inquiries can engage in direct and innovative fact-finding into the organisational knowledge and culture of an institution. They frequently make recommendations about what administrative and educational changes will best prevent the reoccurrence of the events they examine.

Inquiries can also promote social and governmental accountability for both historical and contemporary wrongdoing by contributing

> … to a process of attitudinal change in which the interested public begins to demand answers about officially recognised problems.… The immediate sanction is not a legal one but rather the anxiety and embarrassment caused by public criticism. Social accountability is related to non-carceral forms of social control that rely on perceptions of being under surveillance rather than the imposition of coercive legal sanctions.[31]

Exploring systemic failings and wrongdoings that flow from the actions of individuals, organisations and even social attitudes is an important role of public inquiries. It can ensure accountability towards those who have been wronged, even in the absence of an attribution of individual blameworthiness.[32]

d. Fairness

From time to time, there has been controversy over the fairness of public inquiries. Even if the emphasis of the inquiry is on examining systemic and policy issues, it will still be necessary to establish an evidentiary basis of the events that triggered the wrongs in the system. This unavoidably leads to an examination of the conduct of individuals (even if they are not named) at specific times, dates and places, as well as the roles of supervisors and administrators. Many have criticised the power of inquiries to compel testimony of suspected wrongdoers. Nevertheless, the Supreme Court has recently endorsed the fairness of the inquiry process by emphasising that those compelled to testify will, in most cases, enjoy immunity from the subsequent use of compelled testimony and documents in criminal proceedings. The Court recognised that adverse findings by an inquiry may have severe effects on the reputation of individuals and organisations. But it noted that inquiries ensure procedural fairness by requiring that those facing allegations of misconduct receive notice of the allegations, disclosure of evidence, and the opportunity to cross-examine witnesses and present their own evidence.[33]

The fairness of an inquiry to survivors of institutional child abuse will depend on how it is conducted. For example, survivors can be forced to testify about their experiences in a public, perhaps highly publicised or even televised forum.[34] But an inquiry may decide to conduct some proceedings in private with appropriate support people. It would then have to provide alleged wrongdoers with the opportunity to cross-examine adverse witnesses and call evidence in their own defence. It might be possible for survivors to testify without being cross-examined if the inquiry concluded in advance that it would not consider allegations of misconduct by named individuals or make such adverse findings. These restrictions may not, however, satisfy the need of survivors to name those who abused them in the past.

e.   Acknowledgement, apology and reconciliation

Public inquiries have the potential to provide a public acknowledgement of wrongdoing, even if they have no power to compel such an admission from wrongdoers. An important function of a well-publicised inquiry is its effect on "perceptions, attitudes and behaviour".[35] This process of "social accountability" has motivated governments, agencies, institutions and individuals to recognise their role in past wrongdoing and take steps to achieve reconciliation.[36] The flexibility of the inquiry process allows them to acknowledge the past in a way that respects the experiences and needs of survivors.

Whether a public inquiry can also provide a vehicle for apology by wrongdoers depends on its context. Suspected wrongdoers may be reluctant to acknowledge or apologise for their behaviour for fear of public embarrassment or the negative implications it may have on criminal, civil or administrative proceedings. Because an inquiry may situate wrongdoing in its broader, systemic context, it may also serve as a setting and the occasion for the confession, contrition and apology that is a first step to healing and reconciliation.

f. Compensation, counselling and education

Public inquiries allow survivors to reveal their stories of abuse and its effects in a non-adversarial environment. But because they lack the power to make findings of criminal or civil liability or to impose punishment or award damages or compensation, inquiries cannot meet all needs expressed by survivors. However, they can make a wide range of recommendations about the need to establish compensation programs, provide counselling services and offer education and training. These recommendations can be cast so as to respond directly to the particular needs of those who have appeared before the inquiry.

g. Needs of families, communities and peoples

For the same reasons that public inquiries can be responsive to a broad range of individual needs, they also have the potential to respond to the needs of families, communities and peoples affected by institutional child abuse. Unlike a criminal or civil trial, for example, there are no pre-existing restrictions on who can participate in a public inquiry. Nor are there any restrictions on granting an active role in the process to organisations representing families, communities or peoples. Inquiries may offer funding to facilitate testimony and research by these groups. Some have even given such groups carriage of a portion of the inquiry's hearings.[37]

Since the inquiry into the Mackenzie Valley Pipeline, inquiries have not been reluctant to hold community hearings in otherwise neglected locations, including remote communities and prisons. Doing so allows family members, and representatives of communities and peoples, to speak about the effects of abuse without having to launch a lawsuit to establish their entitlement to compensation. In this sense, an inquiry can be an excellent vehicle to make findings about the secondary harms that institutional child abuse has caused to families, communities and peoples. The findings would sustain wide-ranging recommendations to meet the diversity of both the financial and non-financial needs expressed.

h. Prevention and public education

Among the most important functions of an inquiry is its capacity to increase public awareness of a pressing social issue and its causes, and potential preventive measures. Inquiries can achieve these goals through innovative hearings, the commissioning of research and well-written reports. They bring "new ideas into the public consciousness. They have expanded the vocabulary of politics, education and social science".[38] In other words, the decision to initiate a major inquiry "is a decision not only to release an investigative technique but a form of social influence as well".[39]

Public inquiries can clearly contribute to educating the public about institutional child abuse, although their ability to actually prevent such abuse in the future is less certain. An inquiry report, unlike a judicial or administrative decision, will be focussed on explaining institutional child abuse and its causes. This educational function, combined with an inquiry's authority to make recommendations about the design of institutions and the implementation of procedures to ensure that abuse is prevented in the future, may nonetheless contribute to prevention by putting pressure on governments and organisations to react.

4. Conclusion

As recognised by the Royal Commission on Aboriginal Peoples and others, public inquiries have significant potential as a means of investigating the incidence, causes, and effects of institutional child abuse. They can examine the past without the restrictions placed on courts. They can commission their own research and listen to survivors in a non-adversarial setting. They can be concerned not only with survivors, but with the effects that the abuse had on families and communities. They can be an effective vehicle for public education.

Public inquiries can be both expensive and time-consuming. These are potential drawbacks to consider when choosing this process to redress historical cases of child abuse. Survivors may feel the money directed to an inquiry would be better spent directly on helping them to heal. They may also be sceptical of a process that could delay the opportunity for individuals to access immediate and more tangible forms of redress. In addition, the inquiry process can be unfair to alleged abusers if care is not taken to protect their rights. Public inquiries are most likely to make their distinctive contributions by holding organisations and governments (not individuals) accountable for abuse, and by raising public awareness about abuse and its prevention.[40]

 Recommendations

GOVERNMENTS SHOULD WEIGH the following factors when determining whether to launch a public inquiry into allegations of institutional child abuse:

1. Whether individuals have made allegations of multiple abuse affecting several children and authorities have not responded;

2. Whether a primary goal of the inquiry would be to identify systemic weaknesses and failures;

3. Whether a criminal investigation is ongoing or charges have been laid;

4. Whether an Ombudsman or a children's commissioner has authority to investigate; and

5. Whether any other fact-finding process more attuned to meeting the needs of survivors exists.

Considerations:

Even in a jurisdiction with an Ombudsman or a children's commissioner or advocate, a public inquiry may still be appropriate because: (1) the issue involves a private institution; (2) there is need for special resources or expertise; (3) the investigation must be concluded in a short period; and (4) the investigatory powers of a children's commissioner or a children's advocate may be limited to current abuse.

IF A PUBLIC INQUIRY into institutional child abuse is established, the order-in-council should clearly set out its objectives and the key questions to be addressed (*e.g.*, whether the focus will be on determining wrongdoing, or on systemic and organisational aspects of abuse, or both).

Considerations:

The mandate should be communicated to all potential participants; in particular, former residents and employees of the institution(s) being investigated.

The commission should be accorded resources that are sufficient to accomplish its mandate in the time allotted to it.

When a commission of inquiry is established, procedural matters for its consideration should include:

Whether to hold the hearing in public and how to protect the confidentiality of former residents of an institution.

If former residents of an institution are dispersed geographically, how to ensure they are able to attend the inquiry.

How to ensure counselling and peer support is available to former residents during the course of the inquiry.

How to ensure that both the process and the commission's report meet the communication requirements of former residents, including for example, the need for interpreters and the need to publish documents in alternate formats.

IF A PUBLIC INQUIRY into institutional child abuse is established, respect for survivors should be reflected in its membership.

Considerations:

Where an inquiry has several members, the inquiry should reflect expertise not only in law, but also in disciplines experienced in dealing with the impact of institutional child abuse (such as therapists and social workers). The inquiry should demonstrate sensitivity to the specific socio-demographic makeup of survivors.

---

[1] For a recent assessment of public inquiries, see the collection of papers produced for the conference "Commissions of Inquiry: Praise or Re-appraise" (Faculty of Law, Queen's University, 12-14 February 1999) [hereafter "Inquiries Conference"].

[2] These were inquiries into the wrongful convictions of Donald Marshall Jr. and Guy Paul Morin.

[3] For a complete discussion of the powers of an inquiry see: *Canada (A.G.) v. Canada (Commission of Inquiry on the Blood System)*, [1997] 3 S.C.R. 440 [hereinafter *Inquiry on the Blood System*].

4   *Phillips* v. *Nova Scotia (Commission of Inquiry into the Westray Mine tragedy)*, [1995] 2 S.C.R. 97 [hereinafter *Phillips*] at para. 62, per Cory, J.

5   See Appendix B, Section 3. See also R. Bessner, *Institutional Child Abuse in Canada* (Ottawa: Law Commission of Canada, October 1998) at 152-65. Available in hard copy from the Law Commission of Canada and online: <http://www.lcc.gc.ca>.

6   Canada, *Report of the Royal Commission on Aboriginal People: Looking Forward, Looking Back*, vol. 1 (Ottawa: Canada Communication Group, 1996) at 385, CD ROM: *For Seven Generations, Pour sept générations* (Ottawa: Libraxus Inc., CD-ROM, 1997) at records 1940–1953. The Royal Commission recommended that the majority of commissioners be Aboriginal people. It envisioned public hearings held across the country "to enable the testimony of affected people to be heard"; and research commissioned to examine the effects of residential schools, to identify the abuse that occurred and to recommend remedial actions by governments and churches including, as appropriate, apologies, compensation and funding for treatment.

7   Australia, Human Rights and Equal Opportunity Commission, *Bringing Them Home: Report of the National Inquiry into the Separation of Aboriginal and Torres Strait Islander Children from Their Families* (Canberra: Sterling Press Pty. Ltd., 1997). It considered public and confidential evidence from 535 Indigenous people; detailed many stories of childhood abuse and its devastating effects and made 54 recommendations calling for reparation to all victims including apologies, compensation, rehabilitation, social and cultural development and a national commemorative day. The inquiry and its reports raised public awareness of the abuses. Some of its recommendations have been implemented, but most have not. A further report reviewing the government's response and entitled *Bringing them home: Implementation Progress Report* was pepared by Dr. David Kinley in September 1998. See also M. Gannage, *An International Perspective: A Review and Analysis of Approaches to Addressing Past Institutional or Systemic Abuse in Selected Countries* (Ottawa: Law Commission of Canada, 1998) at 132-45. Available in hard copy from the Law Commission of Canada and online: <http://www.lcc.gc.ca>.

8   Queensland, Australia, *Report of the Commission of Inquiry into Abuse of Children in Queensland Institutions* (Brisbane: Commission of Inquiry into Abuse of Children in Queensland Institutions, May 1999) (Chair: L. Forde). The Commission's inquiry encompassed the period from 1911 to the present day and more than 150 orphanages and detention centres. It found that unsafe, improper and unlawful care or treatment of children had occurred in the past while children were under the care, detention or protection of Queensland's

institutions. In contemporary institutions, it found far fewer incidents of abuse and breaches of regulations but identified deficiencies in current systems and programs of residential care facilities that place children at risk of harm. The Commission gathered information from over 300 people and made 42 recommendations, including suggestions for legislative and administrative reforms, social changes, and specific actions to offer redress to survivors of past institutional abuse. See the government's response: Queensland, Australia, *Queensland Government Response to Recommendations of The Commission of Inquiry into Abuse of Children in Queensland Institutions* (Brisbane: Queensland Government, August 1999).

9   The Law Reform Commission of Canada [a predecessor to the Law Commission of Canada] noted that over 400 federal inquiries had been conducted between 1867 and 1977. Law Reform Commission of Canada, *Administrative Law: Commissions of Inquiry* (Working Paper 17) (Ottawa: Law Reform Commission of Canada, 1977) at 10. Almost 190 inquiries were held in Ontario between Confederation and 1984. Ontario Law Reform Commission, *Report on Public Inquiries* (Toronto: Ontario Law Reform Commission, 1992) at 7.

10   M. Trebilcock & L. Austin, "The Limits of the Full Court Press: Of Blood and Mergers" (1998) 48 U.T.L.J. 1.

11   See for example: *Starr* v. *Houlden*, [1990] 1 S.C.R. 1366, 68 D.L.R. (4th) 641; *Phillips*, *supra* note 4; *Inquiry on the Blood System*, *supra* note 3.

12   *Report on Public Inquiries*, *supra* note 9; Alberta Law Reform Institute, *Proposals for the Reform of the Public Inquiries Act* (Edmonton: Alberta Law Reform Institute, 1992); *Administrative Law: Commissions of Inquiry*, *supra* note 9.

13   *Inquiries Act*, R.S.C. 1985, c. I-11, s. 2.

14   R. Centa & P. Macklem, "Securing Accountability Through Commissions of Inquiry: A Role for the Law Commission of Canada" in "Inquiries Conference", *supra* note 1 at 24. Frequently, public inquiries request and receive extensions of time.

15   *Dixon* v. *Canada (Commission of Inquiry into the Deployment of Canadian Forces to Somalia)* (1997), 149 D.L.R. (4th) 269 (Fed. C.A.). See P. Desbarats, "The Independence of Public Inquiries: *Dixon* v. *Canada*" (1997) 36 Alta. L. Rev. 252.

16   *Report on Public Inquiries*, *supra* note 9 at 205.

17   *Inquiries Act*, *supra* note 13, s. 11.

18   L. Salter, "The Two Contradictions in Public Inquiries" in P. Pross, I. Christie & J. Yogis, eds., *Commissions of Inquiry* (Toronto: Carswell, 1990) 173 at 186.

[19] *Inquiries Act, supra* note 13, s.13.

[20] *Canada (A.G.)* v. *Canada (Commission of Inquiry on Blood Systems), supra* note 3.

[21] *Inquiries Act, supra* note 13, ss. 4,5. See also *British Columbia Securities Commission* v. *Branch*, [1995] 2 S.C.R. 3. For a view that it may be more difficult to conduct successful criminal prosecutions and perhaps civil actions after an inquiry see K. Roach, "Public Inquiries, Prosecutions or Both" (1994) 43 U.N.B.L.J. 415.

[22] R. A. Macdonald, "Commissions of Inquiry in the Perspective of Administrative Law" (1980) 18 Alta. L. Rev. 366; M. R. Damaska, *The Faces of Justice and State Authority* (New Haven: Yale University Press, 1986) at 123.

[23] The record of inquiries in having recommendations implemented is mixed. To take one example, the Hughes Inquiry into the Mount Cashel orphanage (submitted in May 1991 and published in April 1992) recommended the establishment of a compensation fund and an arbitration process for handling claims (Recommendations 33 and 34). See *Report of the Royal Commission of Inquiry into the Response of the Newfoundland Criminal Justice System to Complaints* (St. John's: Queen's Printer, 1991), vol. 1 at 515. At the end of 1999 no such fund or process had yet been put in place.

[24] T. Berger, "Commissions of Inquiry Keynote Address" in "Inquiries Conference", *supra* note 1 at 21.

[25] Presumably former residents of a particular institution should not be sitting on an inquiry into that institution. The Royal Commission on Aboriginal Peoples recommended that any inquiry investigating residential schools have a majority of Aboriginal commissioners (*Report of the Royal Commission on Aboriginal People, supra* note 6 at 385, rec. 1.10.2).

[26] It is possible to inquire into circumstances involving potential civil or even criminal liability, however, without impairing the ability of the inquiry to proceed, to reach conclusions, and to make recommendations, and without stating any conclusions with respect to liability. See Ontario, *Report of the Royal Commission of Inquiry into Certain Deaths at the Hospital for Sick Children* (Ontario: Ministry of the Attorney General, 1984) (Grange Commission). See also *Phillips, supra* note 4. In the *Phillips* case Sopinka J., for the majority, ruled the stay of the Westray inquiry should be lifted because the respondents' criminal trial was proceeding without a jury, before a judge alone.

[27] See for example, *W.R.B.* v. *Plint*, [1998] B.C.J. No. 2294 (B.C.S.C.), online: QL, where the evidence of an historian was not allowed in a claim for sexual and physical abuse in a residential school.

28 P. Robardet, "Should We Abandon the Adversarial Model in Favour of an Inquisitorial Model in Commissions of Inquiry?" in Pross, Christie & Yogis, *supra* note 18, 111 at 125.

29 Salter, *supra* note 18 at 174-5.

30 In exceptional circumstances, a prohibition on testifying may be the only way to protect the right against self-incrimination, but in most cases that right will be adequately protected so long as the testimony and documents produced at an inquiry are not used in subsequent proceedings unless independently obtained.

31 K. Roach, "Canada Public Inquiries and Accountability" in P. Stenning ed., *Accountability For Criminal Justice* (Toronto: University of Toronto Press, 1995) 268 at 274.

32 This view is reflected in the report of the Inquiry into Certain Events at The Prison for Women in Kingston:

> During the entire process of this inquiry, and in particular in the writing of this report, I have concluded that it would not be fair for me to embark upon a personal attribution of responsibility, for many reasons. Many persons were not called to testify and had therefore no opportunity to address allegations that might have been made against them. The witnesses who were called were not meant to be singled out as blameworthy, but were called for the sake of expediency, as the ones who had the most to contribute to the unfolding of the narrative. Many individuals who, by their own account, made errors, or whose actions I found did not meet a legal or policy standard or expectation, are otherwise greatly committed to correctional ideals for women prisoners. They were part of a prison culture which did not value individual rights. Attribution of personal blame would suggest personal, rather than systemic shortcomings and justifiably demoralize the staff, while offering neither redress nor hope for a better system in the future. (Canada, *Report of the Commission of Inquiry into Certain Events at the Prison For Women* (Ottawa: Canada Communication Group, 1996) (Chair: L. Arbour) at xiii).

33 *Phillips, supra* note 4; *Inquiry on the Blood System, supra* note 3. Some judges have also stated that a witness could be exempted from testifying before a public inquiry under s. 7 of the *Canadian Charter of Rights and Freedoms* (Part I of the *Constitution Act, 1982*, being Schedule B to the *Canada Act* 1982 (U.K.), 1982, c. 11 [hereinafter *Charter*]) if the inquiry was conducted primarily for the purpose of obtaining evidence for the prosecution of a witness and that inquiries

can order publication bans and delay their reports when necessary to protect the fair trial rights of individuals. See *Phillips, supra* note 4 *at* 129, per Cory J. (Iacobucci and Major JJ. concurring).

34 The inquiry into institutional child abuse at Mount Cashel was televised throughout Newfoundland.

35 G. Le Dain, "The Role of the Public Inquiry in our Constitutional System" in J. Ziegel, ed., *Law and Social Change* (Toronto: Osgoode Hall Law School, York University, 1973) 79 at 85.

36 For example, the Commission on Donald Marshall's wrongful conviction inspired Dalhousie Law School to take steps to acknowledge racism and seek reconciliation with minority communities. See Roach, *supra* note 31 at 284.

37 This was done in the recent inquiry into the wrongful conviction of Guy Paul Morin, where counsel for the Jessops and for several parties granted standing on systemic issues were funded, although from different sources. Ontario, *Report of the Commission on Proceedings Involving Guy Paul Morin*, vol. 1 (Toronto: Queen's Printer, 1998) at 18, online: <http://www.attorneygeneral.jus.gov.on.ca/morin/morin.htm> (date accesssed: 16 November 1999). In addition, the parties granted standing on the systemic issues called much of the evidence during Phase VI of the Inquiry (the systemic phase), sometimes in shared panel presentations. (*Ibid.* at 17).

38 T.R. Berger, "The Mackenzie Valley Pipeline Inquiry" (1976) 83 Queen's Quarterly 1 at 2.

39 Le Dain, *supra* note 35 at 85.

40 In November 1999 the government of Nova Scotia announced the appointment of the Honorable Fred Kaufman to conduct an inquiry into processes for responding to allegations of institutional child abuse. See Nova Scotia, Department of Justice, Press Release "Retired Judge to Conduct Independent Review" (30 November 1999), online: <http://www.gov.ns.ca/news/details.asp?id=19991201002> (date accessed: 17 January 2000).

I. Truth Commissions and Similar Processes to Address Systemic Human Rights Abuses

1. Introduction

It is a principle of international law that successor governments are responsible for the actions of their predecessors. This principle means, among other things, that a state has a duty to compensate victims of human rights violations regardless of the government in power at the time of the violation.[1] Many nations have faced, or will face, the challenge of correcting past systemic or institutional human rights abuses. This challenge confronts nations converting (sometimes abruptly) from autocratic to democratic rule. In South Africa and many Eastern European countries, this transition involved the denunciation of an entire prior regime. In other cases, the challenge arises out of social change where values and assumptions are rethought and found wanting. The history of the black struggle in the United States is one example. Another is Australia's attempt to come to terms with the forcible separation of indigenous children from their families, over a period of 60 years. The recognition by Canadians of the abuse of trust and authority and the unacceptable racial attitudes that sustained policy in relation to Aboriginal peoples and their children is also an example.

Over the past 20 years, a number of governments have responded to the challenge of dealing with an unsavoury past by creating bodies popularly know as truth commissions. These commissions have sometimes been established as a result of a negotiated transition to democracy. The South African Truth and Reconciliation Commission (SATRC) is an example. Governments in other countries have unilaterally set up analogous processes under a policy of "lustration", which means "to clarify by bringing things to light".[2] Truth commissions have different forms, depending on the extent of negotiations leading up to their creation, the nature of the human rights violations, the needs of survivors, and the social and political makeup of the successor state.

2. Description

A truth commission process reflects a conscious renunciation of, and a complete break from, a past when those in authority tolerated, encouraged and even committed massive human rights violations. Its fundamental purpose is to discover the truth and to assemble an accurate and verifiable record of it. Recognising and validating the pain and suffering of survivors and their families becomes a vehicle to promote a collective understanding of past abuse. Together this validation and understanding are seen as the starting point for reconciliation.

A truth commission is premised on the belief that recognition and explicit denunciation of the past can be a powerful guarantee against repetition. The report of the Argentinean Truth Commission is entitled *Nunca Mas*, or "never again". Likewise, the report of the South African Truth and Reconciliation Commission refers to George Santayana's words etched above the entrance to Dachau: "Those who forget the past are doomed to repeat it." A truth commission attempts to record history in a manner that cannot be denied or contradicted by subsequent generations.

a. The establishment of truth commissions

Successor governments in some countries making the transition to democracy compromise with predecessor regimes in exchange for a peaceful transfer of power.[3] Truth commissions created as part of such a compromise differ from international criminal prosecutions like the Nuremberg Trials following World War II, and domestic criminal and civil processes that expose past wrongdoing.

Truth commissions may be established with competing and conflicting goals: the need for justice and to discover the truth, and the need for peace and harmony through which perpetrators can be reconciled with survivors. Yet justice without at least some retribution is unlikely, as is reconciliation without at least some compensation. In addressing these competing goals, a truth commission may prefer one over the other, or may even try to blend them. To date, a range of approaches – from the blanket amnesty of the Chilean National Commission on

Truth and Reconciliation,[4] to the limited amnesty of the South African Truth and Reconciliation Commission – have been adopted.

The SATRC functions in tandem with the existing legal system and provides a forum to which perpetrators of "gross violations of human rights" may apply for amnesty.[5] Amnesty is granted only when the Commission is convinced that:

- the applicant has made full disclosure of all relevant facts;

- the act or omission to which the application relates was associated with political objectives and committed in the course of apartheid conflicts; and

- the acts were not perpetrated out of personal malice or for personal gain.[6]

The "lustration" processes in some former communist countries of Eastern Europe are not negotiated; nor do they involve the possibilities of prosecution or amnesty. Rather, they employ informal sanctions through public exposure of human rights abuses. Government and secret police files are opened to reveal the names of collaborators. As a result, many countries initiated mass purging of government officials.[7]

A truth commission may be formally constituted in different ways. South Africa's Truth and Reconciliation Commission was entrenched in its Interim Constitution. Its mechanism was provided for by the *Promotion of National Unity and Reconciliation Act*, enacted by Parliament in 1995.[8] By contrast, the Sabato Commission in Argentina was established by an executive order of a successor government, and directly appointed by the President.

b.   Mandate and powers of truth commissions

The mandate, power and jurisdiction of truth commissions can vary widely. Argentina's Sabato Commission was appointed to collect evidence of human rights violations committed by the state's security agents and to prepare a report on its findings. The Commission had no jurisdiction to determine responsibility for these crimes or to try offenders; nor did it have the power to subpoena witnesses or compel testimony. It relied upon voluntary testimony, the cooperation of human rights organisations and its own investigations and inspections.[9]

South Africa's Truth and Reconciliation Commission has the broadest mandate and widest powers of any truth commission. Its objective is to "promote national unity and reconciliation in a spirit of understanding that transcends the conflicts and divisions of the past [by] establishing as complete a picture as possible of the causes, nature and extent of the gross violations of human rights" committed during the apartheid era.[10] The SATRC is required by the Interim Constitution to facilitate "… the granting of amnesty to persons who make full disclosure of all the relevant facts relating to acts associated with apartheid." It has a duty to establish and to make known "the fate or whereabouts of victims [and to] restore the human and civil dignity of such victims"[11] affording them an opportunity to relate their own accounts of the violations. It is authorised to recommend reparation for violations. Finally, it must compile a comprehensive report, including the recommendation of measures to prevent the future violation of human rights in South Africa.[12]

c.   Structure and process of truth commissions

The uniqueness of each country and the types of injustices investigated mean that truth commissions also show a variety of structures and procedures. However, some features are common. All are required to complete their work within a fixed deadline. All are authorised to investigate government records, collect data from non-governmental and international organisations, interview witnesses and victims, demand the delivery of documents, and search and seize with a warrant. Both oral and written evidence is collected. Public and private hearings are held. Most are required to prepare a public report about the human rights abuses committed over a specified period of time. Many truth commission processes are designed so that witnesses do not require legal assistance when appearing. Some, such as the SATRC, also provide emotional and logistical support to victims who appear as witnesses.

Commissioners are usually prominent citizens with a reputation for integrity and impartiality. In Argentina, the chair of the commission was Ernesto Sabato, a distinguished author. In South Africa, Nobel Peace Prize winner Archbishop Desmond Tutu, was appointed to chair the SATRC. The structure of a commission also depends on the nature and scope of its mandate. For example, the SATRC established three committees to deal with three aspects of its mandate: the application for and granting of amnesty; an investigation into apartheid's legacy of abuse (which provided a forum for people to make allegations of abuse); and the making of recommendations for interim measures, compensation, *ex gratia* payments, restitution or rehabilitation.

Truth commissions are typically autonomous, legislated bodies; but they are not courts with the power to determine criminal or civil liability. They do, however, have the authority to grant amnesty to those who may otherwise face criminal prosecution. Perpetrators may apply for amnesty in exchange for telling the truth. But they are not obligated to participate in the amnesty application process. It is usually an offence to impede the work of a truth commission.

3.   Assessment

Overview

Truth commissions seek to engage both survivors and perpetrators in their processes on a voluntary basis. While these processes are respectful of survivors as a whole, achieving their goal of collective reconciliation may result in a loss of respect for the experiences of individual survivors. Fact-finding is a central objective of a truth commission. How effectively a truth commission accomplishes this task depends on the extent of the power it is granted, the resources at its disposal and the cooperation it receives from those involved with the system under which abuses were committed.

Public accountability is an outcome of the investigatory process of truth commissions. However, commissions may not always require wrongdoers to make reparations for the harm they caused. Truth commissions provide a measure of procedural fairness, as all parties have an opportunity to be heard. Survivors may feel that the process is not fair because perpetrators are able to admit to wrongdoing without being held liable. Truth commissions are a good forum for acknowledgement and may also provide a forum for public apologies, on an official or non-official level.

In general, truth commissions may recommend, but cannot order, financial compensation for victims. They may also recommend the provision of services such as vocational, therapeutic or educational services to survivors. For families, communities and peoples, truth commissions may fulfil a need by providing information and painting a complete picture of the systemic causes of the abuse.

Finally, truth commissions can serve as a means of educating the public, not only locally but also nationally and even internationally.

a.   Respect, engagement and informed choice

A truth commission provides a forum for the public recognition of victims' and survivors' stories, and in some instances for those of the perpetrators of abuse. This public recognition of the harms suffered or committed is a first expression of respect for victims and survivors. There is a danger, however, that the process may sacrifice or diminish respect for individual survivors in order to achieve the benefit of a collective reconciliation. Respect for individual survivors requires their active and voluntary engagement in the commission's work.

Although truth commissions universally attempt to engage survivors in the process, the manner in which they do so varies. South Africa's Truth and Reconciliation Commission employed a separate committee whose purpose was to listen to and record survivors' individual stories. By contrast, in Argentina and Chile much of the information gathered for the commissions' reports came through human rights and non-governmental organisations or from the examination of public records. Although numerous victims were interviewed, the focus of the commissions' work was on establishing a broad historical understanding of the abuse rather than on locating and involving specific individuals in the process.

Truth commissions do not force victims to participate or act as witnesses. There is usually an option to proceed publicly, privately, or by simply forwarding written submissions. Some survivors nonetheless feel that they are not engaged in the process and that their needs and rights are not respected. This occurs, for example, when truth commissions permit perpetrators to escape a criminal prosecution despite the contrary wishes of their victims. Some victims feel that substituting a truth commission for the criminal justice process sends a message that the wrongs committed against them are less significant than those for which criminal punishments are handed out.[13]

b.   Fact-finding

The search for truth is a paramount objective of truth commissions. Finding facts and creating an historical record of wrongs are the foundations for reconciliation and healing. Truth commissions typically employ a wide variety of fact-finding techniques. These include opening previously confidential files and reports; questioning officials, non-governmental organisations, churches and international human rights agencies; and receiving oral and written submissions from survivors and their families. Time and money are the principal constraints on the capacity of truth commissions to establish a complete picture of abuses and the reasons they occurred.

The success of a truth commission in uncovering facts will also depend on the powers that it has been granted. For example the Sabato Commission did not have the authority to subpoena witnesses or compel production of testimony. It was unable to overcome any perpetrator's refusal to cooperate. Some commissions offer amnesty in exchange for telling the truth, thus rewarding disclosure. Even though these statements are not subjected to cross-examination (as in a criminal trial), the facts are often verified through the sheer number of people who report witnessing or experiencing the same things, or through organisational records that clearly delineate patterns of abuse.[14]

c.   Accountability

The formal record of truth commissions identifies individual and institutional perpetrators of human rights abuses, describes the offences committed, exposes their motives and attitudes, and clearly denounces their conduct. It publicly declares that perpetrators, and the regimes that allowed them to commit abuses, are responsible for their actions, and also holds them accountable. Individual criminal or civil accountability is exchanged for this collective assignment of responsibility. Of course, complete accountability occurs only when offenders take personal responsibility for their actions and attempt some form of restitution or reparation.

Truth commissions can occasionally sever the link between responsibility and the obligation to repair harm done. In South Africa, once a perpetrator has convinced the Amnesty Committee of the SATRC that he or she has provided a complete and accurate confession, neither an apology nor any form of restitution has to be offered. In Argentina, under pressure from the military, a law was passed to create an irrefutable presumption of innocence for soldiers and officers who had acted in obedience to their superiors, thus effecting a complete denial of accountability from the Sabato Commission.

The primary purpose of truth commissions is to recognise the harms caused by a particular regime against a large group of people. Although perpetrators are named – as a group and in many cases, individually – this accountability may be less than satisfactory for survivors if there is no corresponding obligation to effect reparation.

d.   Fairness

Truth commissions are not judicial bodies. They do not seek to balance competing accounts of the facts and arrive at a just solution. They focus on providing a forum to acknowledge suffering and creating a foundation for collective healing. All survivors and their families are invited, but not compelled, to tell their individual stories. Wrongdoers are usually also provided a forum to describe their wrongdoing and to admit their responsibility. Truth commissions generally make a concerted effort to ensure that all possible participants are informed of the process and that the process is accessible to individuals from all affected areas of the country. In this way, they can be seen as respecting the requirements of procedural fairness for all parties.

Yet many victims and survivors do not feel that truth commissions produce fair outcomes. They believe that their right to obtain justice has been sacrificed in exchange for the truth. They express the unfairness of watching perpetrators participate in the truth commission process and then return to their lives of relative affluence while their victims continue to suffer. Many survivors feel that the process is unfair to them unless a significant sanction and the obligation to provide reparation is imposed on perpetrators.

e.   Acknowledgement, apology and reconciliation

Truth commissions acknowledge abuses in order to establish a basis for reconciliation. But there is usually little hope for reconciliation between survivors and wrongdoers without a full and public apology for the harms inflicted. Some truth commissions offer a forum for apology, such as that provided by the SATRC during amnesty applications. In other cases, such as in Chile and Argentina, the truth commission process simply does not seek an apology nor expect one. In those countries, it was understood that officials of the predecessor regime had not experienced a moral shift and were unlikely to offer apologies or admit their wrongdoing.[15]

Apologies are not necessarily a goal of a truth commission. After all, a forced or mandated apology has little meaning. Where there is no legal requirement for an apology as a condition of amnesty, the individual apologies that have been given are generally well-received and seen as sincere.[16] Acknowledgement and apology can also occur through truth commissions on a non-official level. For example, the SATRC created a Register of Reconciliation web page. It provides a forum for people who did not commit gross violations of human rights, but wish to indicate their regret for their failure to do more to prevent such violations. Truth commissions can serve the process of reconciliation by acknowledging the extent of suffering and the extent of the wrongs committed, as well as providing a forum for apology.

f.   Compensation, counselling and education

Truth commissions are not designed to provide financial compensation to survivors of abuse or their families. Some have authority to, and do in fact, recommend financial reparations. For reasons ranging from political unwillingness, to budgetary restraints, to the number of victims and logistical difficulties, these recommended payments are often not fully made. In Argentina and Chile, reparation payments were not part of the mandate of the truth commissions, even though some efforts at financial compensation did follow the commissions' reports.[17]

The SATRC has employed a separate committee to deal with issues of reparation and rehabilitation. This committee can make recommendations regarding all forms of reparation, including financial compensation. However, an application must be made within a specified time limit, must arise from a "gross violation" of human rights and the applicant must not have been an active combatant against the previous regime. The committee has made a number of recommendations regarding interim reparations for victims, but none of these can be enforced in the civil courts.

The truth commission process involves confronting old wounds and perhaps long-buried pain. This process itself may be therapeutic. Having a perpetrator finally admit what had been denied by authorities can validate years of suffering. To assist victims to come to terms with these acknowledgements, truth commissions often employ counsellors and psychologists.

In many cases, victims suffer significant social, emotional and health problems as a result of the abuse. Many are under-educated, under-employed and poor. Truth commissions often have the power to make recommendations regarding the provision of therapeutic, educational and vocational services. South Africa's Reparation and Rehabilitation Committee is now doing so.

g.   Needs of families, communities and peoples

For the families of victims and survivors, knowledge of what occurred is a first step towards healing. Many families of "disappeared" loved ones in South Africa, Chile and Argentina have stated that learning the truth is more important than any form of justice or compensation. To finally know that a beloved son or daughter did not merely disappear or die of natural causes helps put closure on the loss, allowing the process of grieving to be resolved. Culturally sensitive support and counselling is likely necessary throughout a truth commission process.

In many cases, human rights abuses have affected entire peoples. Truth commissions provide a forum for them to express their voices. If a case is examined merely on an individual basis, or even in terms of its effect on a given community, the picture will be incomplete. Receiving submissions, support, input, testimony, records and feedback from representative organisations, and directly consulting with the peoples affected, is a precondition to making recommendations about compensation, healing and rehabilitation that are appropriate and desired.

Truth commissions can also examine policies, legislation and public attitudes that fostered or permitted human rights abuses to occur. They offer a forum for non-victims to acknowledge and come to terms with the human rights abuses that occurred under institutions that they supported. In South Africa, sectoral hearings under the SATRC examined the role of various sectors of civil society such as churches, courts, news media, and social services in apartheid.[18] In the words of the SATRC Chairperson, "Our whole nation needs healing.... Perpetrators are, in their own way, victims of the apartheid system and they too need healing."[19]

h.   Prevention and public education

Truth commissions generate a permanent, undeniable, public acknowledgement of human rights abuses, and the policies, legislation and ideologies that allowed them to occur. They attempt to make a clear break with past practices, expose those practices and unequivocally label them as wrong. They compel the recognition that biases and prejudice are not simply historical, but a present danger.

Truth commissions can also serve as instruments of education. They re-examine history, in a less comfortable but more inclusive way. Individual stories move the abstract idea of abuse to the personal. This allows citizens to regard each other, perhaps for the first time, as fellow human beings. In South Africa, black guerrilla activists learned that they did not kill "whites"; they killed fathers and wives and sons. White security forces learned that they did not kill "kaffirs" but destroyed families, communities and homes. Truth commissions often make recommendations about specific plans for public education in schools, by television and other media, the Internet, and a wide distribution of reports and documents. Because most truth commission reports attract international publicity, they ensure that past human rights abuses become part of international consciousness.

4. Conclusion

Truth commissions are designed to be more than mere fact-finding bodies. They are non-adversarial forums for ascertaining the extent of, and the reasons for, human rights violations. They are also vehicles of social reconciliation and healing. As such, they are usually adopted as responses to situations where significant social upheaval and harm has occurred. A truth commission process might possibly be adapted for dealing with past institutional child abuse, in situations where the abuse caused not only individual children and their families to suffer but also caused significant damage – even intergenerational damage – to whole communities or peoples.

The greatest strengths of a truth commission process are its ability to provide a forum for the truth to be told, and for serious human rights abuses to be publicly acknowledged and officially denounced. Democratic governments, replacing authoritarian regimes as a means to build or restore social harmony, have used truth commissions the most. However, a truth commission can also be used, following a period of changes in social attitudes and practices, to acknowledge past abuses and to officially document and denounce what happened. It is for this purpose that a truth commission process might have offered some redress for Canadians of Japanese ancestry who were displaced during World War II, and might today be a possible redress process for survivors of child abuse in institutions.

A TRUTH COMMISSION HAS the potential to be an appropriate forum for providing redress where large numbers of people spread over a wide geographic area have suffered abuses over several generations, and the goals of fact-finding and healing cannot be achieved without a generalised amnesty for wrongdoers.

Considerations:

The decision whether to establish a truth commission or some other truth-finding procedure is a matter to be determined by governments in cooperation with the affected communities and peoples. If it were agreed to establish a truth commission, then certain issues related to the operation of the commission would need to be considered, including the following:

- A truth commission should have the power to compel production of government and institutional evidence. It must be capable of exploring the evidence left by the institutions in question, and relevant internal records.

- The information-gathering process should be more respectful of survivors and more therapeutic than it is in criminal or civil actions. The process should not force survivors to tell their stories. Those who do participate should be able to testify, publicly or privately, in a safe and supportive environment.

- A truth commission should encourage the presentation of official, public apologies that are meaningful. In addition, the process could create a forum similar to South Africa's "Register of Reconciliation" web page, where individuals can make informal or personal apologies.

---

1   D.F. Orentlicher, "Settling Accounts: The Duty to Prosecute Human Rights Violations of a Prior Regime" (1991) 100 Yale L. J. 2544; B. Walsh, "Resolving the Human Rights Violations of a Previous Regime" (1996) 158:3 World Affairs 111. A report from a seminar conducted by the Human Rights Group of the

University of Limburg in Maastricht, The Netherlands, stated: "as a matter of principle every State has the responsibility to redress human rights violations and to enable the victims to exercise their right to reparation. States must faithfully apply international, regional and national norms of human rights". See T. Van Boven *et al.*, eds., *Seminar on the Right to Restitution, Compensation and Rehabilitation for the Victims of Gross Violations of Human Rights and Fundamental Freedoms* (Utrecht, Netherlands: Studie – En. Informatiecentrum Mensenrechten, Netherlands Institute of Human Rights, 1992) at 4 and 16.

[2] M.S. Ellis, "Purging the Past: The Current State of Lustration Laws in the Former Communist Bloc" (1996) 59:4 Law & Contemp. Probs. 181.

[3] Examples include: Chile (1978), Argentina (1986-1990), Guatemala (1986), El Salvador (1987), Uruguay (1986), and South Africa (1994); see M. Gannage, *An International Perspective: A Review and Analysis of Approaches to Addressing Past Institutional or Systemic Abuse in Selected Countries* (Ottawa: Law Commission of Canada, 1998) at 64. Available in hard copy from the Law Commission of Canada and online: <http://www.lcc.gc.ca>. See also M. Scharf, "The Case for a Permanent International Truth Commission" (1997) 7 Duke J. of Comp. & Int'l L. 375 at 379.

[4] Chile, Comision Nacional de Verdady Reconciliation, *Report of the Chilean National Commission on Truth and Reconciliation*, trans. P.E. Berryman (Notre Dame, Ind.: University of Notre Dame Press, 1993).

[5] Committee Reports: Amnesty Committee Report, *Truth Talk: The Official Newsletter of the Truth and Reconciliation Commission* (April 1998).

[6] *Promotion of National Unity and Reconciliation Second Amendment Act*, 1997 (Statutes of South Africa, Act No. 34 of 1995) s. 20(3) [hereinafter *Promotion of National Unity and Reconciliation Act*].

[7] For example, in Romania an estimated 90% of government administrators were removed from their jobs. See D. Bronkhorst, *Truth and Reconciliation: Obstacles and Opportunities for Human Rights* (Amsterdam: Amnesty International, Dutch Section, 1995) at 81.

[8] *Supra* note 6.

[9] The Sabato Commission was widely criticized for this lack of power. Many felt that the Commission's work was greatly impeded, effectively granting perpetrators total immunity. See Americas Watch, *Truth and Partial Justice in Argentina* (New York/Washington D.C.: Americas Watch, 1987) at 16.

[10] *Promotion of National Unity and Reconciliation Act*, *supra* note 6 at s. 3.

[11] *Ibid.* at s. 6.

12 *Ibid.* at s. 3(5).

13 *Azanian Peoples Organization (AZAPO)* v. *The President of the Republic of South Africa*, 1996 (4) S.A.L.R. 671 (CC). This lawsuit, launched by the family and supporters of murdered activist Steve Biko, challenged the constitutional validity of the SATRC. Although the lawsuit failed, many supported it, demonstrating that there are some South African victims of apartheid who do not feel respected by or engaged in the SATRC process.

14 There is also evidence that in the SATRC process, perpetrators on both sides of the apartheid conflict were motivated to tell the truth by a sincere desire for reconciliation, not just to escape criminal sanctions. In the words of Commissioner Mary Burton, these are the true "miracles of reconciliation" that make the fact-finding role of the SATRC so critical for the nation's healing. T. Winslow, "Reconciliation: The Road to Healing?: Collective Good, Individual Harm?" (1997) 6:3&4 Track Two 112.

15 Even in South Africa, there have been cases where perpetrators have disclosed their abuses publicly and continued to justify the goals of apartheid, thus rendering reconciliation impossible. "South Africa. A pardon too far" *The Economist* (16 August 1997) 35.

16 In some cases apologies have been met with applause, tears and even thanks. See F. Ross, "Blood Feuds and Childbirth: The TRC as Ritual" (1997) 6:3&4 Track Two 7.

17 Argentina Law 23.466, 30 October 1986. These efforts were largely unsuccessful. For example, in Argentina, a pension plan was implemented for the next of kin of the "disappeared" but evidentiary difficulties and the refusal of the military to cooperate have created obstacles to accessing this source of compensation.

18 D. Dyzenhaus, *Judging the Judges, Judging Ourselves, Truth, Reconciliation and the Apartheid Legal Order* (Oxford: Hart Publishing, 1998)

19 "The Chronicle Interview: Archbishop Emeritus Desmond Tutu" (Spring 1996) 33:4 The UN Chronicle 46 at 48.

J.   Community Initiatives

1.   Introduction

Responses to the abuse perpetrated against children in institutions need not come exclusively from the State or from the organisation that administered the institution where the abuse took place. As survivors and their communities recognise the serious and lasting effects of abuse, they are beginning to craft their own paths to healing. These alternative community-based processes complement those offered by the official justice system.

Most grassroots community initiatives are conceived and undertaken independently of government. They usually receive some financial assistance from governments, churches, community and social service organisations, and others committed to helping. The majority of these initiatives share four key features: they are dedicated to healing the harmful effects of abuse; they are carried out in survivors' communities; they are tailored to the particular needs of individual communities; and survivors play a central role in shaping them.

2.   Description

Since every community initiative is unique, it is not possible to present a generic description of their characteristics. Instead, this section highlights different types of initiatives now in operation to show their range and scope. First to be described are helping and healing projects based in non-Aboriginal communities: the community of youth in care; a church congregation; and the community of British Columbia residential school survivors. Second, attention will be given to programs set up within Aboriginal communities. Third, this section examines initiatives of churches and governments to fund and to foster the development of community-based healing initiatives for survivors of institutional child abuse.

All of these projects result from the determination of people to confront their problems, to heal themselves, to help heal their neighbours, and to repair both individual and community relationships that have been badly damaged. By canvassing the types of projects that have been set up outside the framework of official systems of redress, the Commission hopes to present a rich portrait of alternative ways in which survivors' needs can be met. It also means to highlight its belief that non-governmental initiatives and programs intended to strengthen communities are a key response to redressing past harm and a central component of prevention.

a.   Initiatives based in non-Aboriginal communities

i.   *National Youth in Care Network projects*

The National Youth in Care Network (NYICN) is a non-profit organisation directed by and for young people, aged 14 to 24, who are or have been in the care of child welfare authorities across Canada. The NYICN supports the development of local and provincial networks for youth in care. It is founded on a belief in "youth helping youth" and recognition that this approach empowers them. A major objective of NYICN is to facilitate healing and provide a voice and support system to youth in care, many of whom have grown up experiencing serious neglect and abuse.[1]

The NYICN has undertaken various projects to gather first-hand information on the violence and abuse experienced by these young people and to examine ways to help them deal with the effects. It published a book, *Pain ... Lots of Pain*, about family violence and abuse suffered by youth in care. A young man who spent his childhood as a permanent ward of the Crown wrote the book.[2] It attempts to answer questions such as "Are the unique and special needs of abuse victims in care met by the 'system' which is not their 'home'? And what do youth in care who receive 'treatment' think about these services?"[3]

A few years after publication of this book, the NYICN undertook a project to give young people the opportunity to express their feelings, thoughts, and opinions about their pre-care and in-care experiences and to identify what they need to heal from the violence and abuse that they suffered. The NYICN held 19 focus groups, involving 85 youth in care, and produced a report entitled: *Into the Hands of Youth: Youth in and from Care Identify Healing Needs.*[4] The report summarised the participants' personal experiences of violence and abuse and identified peer support groups as being crucial to their healing process. The Family Violence Prevention Division of Health Canada funded both of these NYICN projects.

ii. The Community Services Council (CSC) of Newfoundland and Labrador, community-based research on abuse

The Community Services Council (CSC) of Newfoundland and Labrador is an independent, non-profit organisation dedicated to improving social development through social policy and planning activities. The Council's Working Group on Child Sexual Abuse initiated a research project to explore how communities can take a more active role in the prevention of child sexual abuse. The first phase of this project involved interviewing survivors of child sexual abuse and offenders, in order to identify family and community attitudes that make children vulnerable to such abuse. Findings were reported in a discussion paper issued in 1996.[5]

Next, focus group discussions and interviews in selected communities were held to gather locally-based information on why the needs of victims of sexual abuse and offenders were not being met effectively and how communities' responses could be improved.[6] Discussions revealed that some members of the community, including survivors, social workers and community activists, are valuable sources of knowledge. The working group concluded that the general population was poorly informed about child sexual abuse. To remove the shroud of secrecy, fear, denial and victim-blaming, it recommended that concerted efforts at public education be made.

iii. Formal apology of St. Andrew's United Church congregation

In 1996, the congregation of St. Andrew's United Church in Port Alberni, British Columbia, set up a church discussion group to learn more about church-run residential schools for Aboriginal students and about the experiences of children at these schools. The desire of church members to gain a better understanding was sparked by their shock as the crimes of Arthur Henry Plint unfolded in court and were reported by the media.[7] In particular, they wondered what effect the Alberni Residential School, run by the United Church, had on their Aboriginal neighbours.

After holding several monthly meetings and discussions, which included guest speakers from the United Church of Canada and former students of the Alberni Residential School, members of the congregation decided they wanted to do something more than just listen and learn. In consultation with members of local First Nations communities, they conceived the idea of preparing and delivering a formal apology. The outcome was an apology ceremony and dinner, presented by the congregation of St. Andrew's United Church in May 1997, for all the Nuu-Chah-Nulth people whose lives were affected by the Alberni Residential School.[8]

b.   Initiatives based in Aboriginal communities

i.   *Alkali Lake community-based inquiry and healing initiatives*
During the early 1970s, the Shuswap community of Alkali Lake, British Columbia, suffered from a very high level of alcoholism. In 1972, two community members decided to become sober and to encourage other members of the community to do so as well. Without any government subsidies or assistance, the community implemented a program of intervention and support for those who wished to overcome their alcoholism. This voluntary program was only one step on the road to healing. Since community members had attended St. Joseph's Residential School near Williams Lake, survivors also began to deal with the abuse they had experienced there. The community decided to establish its own commission of inquiry into the experiences of some of its members.[9] The inquiry was presided over by a community Elder, a Band Council member and a survivor. In June 1997, they heard from nine former students of St. Joseph's Residential School. The inquiry provided the opportunity for these students to tell their stories of abuse and to participate in a group counselling session.[10]

ii.   *The Provincial Residential School Project*
The Provincial Residential School Project is a First Nations organisation that reports to the First Nations Summit of British Columbia chiefs. It was created in 1995 to support individuals in British Columbia's Aboriginal communities who wished to make complaints to the Royal

Canadian Mounted Police of physical and sexual abuse in residential schools. The project provides former residential school students with information about healing and about pursuing justice through the criminal or civil courts. Staff, including trained crisis counsellors, is available to listen to those who wish to talk of their experiences. Survivors are also referred to providers of longer-term care – such as traditional Aboriginal healers, counsellors experienced in dealing with residential school survivors and therapists. An important feature of the project is the workshops offered to community workers to inform them about the history of residential schools and their impact on individuals and families, suicide prevention, sexual abuse response, and the civil and criminal justice systems.

iii. Turtle Island Native Network website

The Turtle Island Native Network (http://www.turtleisland.org) is a multi-purpose website that provides information about all aspects of Aboriginal people's lives. Pages are dedicated to education, culture, healing and wellness, communities, and business. It serves needs and interests much wider than those of survivors of residential schools. But through its Healing and Wellness and Discussion pages, survivors can access a "virtual library", as well as enter into discussions with their online community.

From the Healing and Wellness page, survivors can click on Turtle Island's Residential Schools Resources Page and link to other websites that contain information related to residential schools. The Discussion page also has links to different types of discussion forums, including a moderated chat group for former students of residential schools.

c. Funds and programs committed to helping survivors of abuse

i. Anglican Church of Canada's healing fund

In 1991, the Anglican Church of Canada formed the Residential Schools Advisory Group. It also initiated a fund to provide financial assistance for projects to help Aboriginal people overcome their residential school experiences. By December 1998, the fund had distributed more than

$350,000 to Aboriginal groups organising healing initiatives.[11] The Residential Schools Advisory Group administers the healing fund, reviews applications and makes grants. Applications may be made by Aboriginal communities and organisations, as well as by former staff and other affected persons.[12]

A variety of projects have received funding. They include a residential school conference organised by the Nishnawbe-Aski Nation for Aboriginal and non-Aboriginal participants from northern Ontario; and a seminar organised by Equay-Wuk (Women's Group) of Sioux Lookout, Ontario, to address issues of family violence, sexual abuse, and the residential school experience. The fund also contributed to the Pelican Lake Healing Gathering. The gathering brought together former students of the Pelican Lake Residential School to participate in workshops, talking circles, and a healing ceremony.[13] The gathering took place on the site of the old school, near Sioux Lookout.

ii.   United Church of Canada's Healing Fund

In 1994, the General Council of the United Church of Canada set up a fund, financed through voluntary contributions, that the church used to provide support for healing initiatives in Aboriginal communities. "The Healing Fund was established as one important way for the church to live out its 1986 Apology to First Nations."[14]

The Healing Fund Council, composed of the All Native Circle Conference and the British Columbia Division of Native Ministries, developed criteria for funding community healing initiatives. It aslo makes decisions on funding applications. In October 1998, it approved 20 out of 35 proposals for funding. Some examples of the proposals that were approved include the following:[15]

> Anishinabek Survivors of Residential Schools, Armstrong, Ontario: A series of workshops to be presented to ten First Nations communities across northern Ontario, their purpose being to raise awareness of the history of residential schools and to encourage survivors to begin their personal recovery.

Guy Hill Residential Schools Gathering, Winnipeg, Manitoba: A gathering of former residential school students, to focus on spiritual healing, cultural renewal, and working towards developing healthy families and communities.

Tsawwassen First Nation, Delta, British Columbia: A project aimed at restoring the language of the Tsawwassen First Nation.

Cooperative Cross Cultural Alcoholic After Care Counselling, North Bay, Ontario: To organise an ongoing after care service to help participants through the healing process by teaching them to live without drugs or alcohol and to draw support from traditional Aboriginal teachings, healing circles, and purification lodges.

iii. *Canadian Conference of Catholic Bishops' healing fund*

In 1998, to fulfil commitments it had made to the Royal Commission on Aboriginal Peoples, the Canadian Conference of Catholic Bishops (CCCB) established the Council for Reconciliation, Solidarity and Communion. The CCCB also established a fund to be administered by the Council, meant to support community-oriented projects initiated by Aboriginal Peoples.[16] The fund finances projects designed to increase awareness of Aboriginal issues or to provide training and professional development for those who are already involved in community healing processes. It also supports pastoral gatherings, healing circles, and other forums for listening and sharing whether within a community or cross-culturally.[17]

The fund is sustained through voluntary contributions from Catholic dioceses and other Catholic organisations. In January 1999, the council administering this fund, composed of Aboriginal Catholic leaders and representatives from the Canadian Conference of Catholic Bishops, approved 20 projects for a total value of $109,350.[18] Among the projects selected were: frontline worker training and professional development for the Laichwiltach Family Life Society in British Columbia; a community healing and wellness conference coordinated by Peetabeck Health Services of Fort Albany, Ontario; a winter healing initiative for Mohawks in Oka and Kanesatake, Quebec; and Cree language revitalisation projects at the Marcelin/Kihiw School in Saskatchewan.[19]

How did I get to residential school was by Indian Agents. I remember them pulling me away from my mother. I was six years old. And how they got me on that bus and said I would see my sister. And I never did see her. The first day all I can remember, I just cried and cried and cried. They couldn't stop me from crying, I wouldn't. I just kept crying for my mommy 'cause they just pulled me away from her. They told my mum if I didn't go, she could get into trouble. She said I had to go.

Quote from a former residential school student in Breaking the Silence by the Assembly of First Nations, at pp.38-39 iv.   Gathering Strength and the Aboriginal Healing Foundation

On January 7, 1998, the Government of Canada responded to the report of the Royal Commission on Aboriginal Peoples by announcing an action plan, called Gathering Strength. The Minister of Indian Affairs and Northern Development delivered an official Statement of Reconciliation on behalf of the Government. Included in this statement was an acknowledgement of the role of the Government of Canada in the development and administration of the residential school system; recognition of the harmful effects this system produced in communities; and an apology to those who suffered physical and sexual abuse: "To those of you who suffered this tragedy at residential schools, we are deeply sorry."[20]

A cornerstone of Gathering Strength was the government's contribution of "$350 million for community-based healing as a first step to deal with the legacy of physical and sexual abuse at residential schools."[21] In April 1998, the Aboriginal Healing Foundation was created as an arm's-length, Aboriginal-run, not-for-profit corporation, to develop and carry out a plan to administer the healing fund.[22]

The Foundation developed four themes under which proposals for project funding can be submitted:

- Healing

- Restoring Balance

- Developing and Enhancing Aboriginal Capacities

- Honour and History.[23]

In June 1999, the Foundation announced more than $2 million in funding for the first 35 projects it had selected under the healing and development themes. The types of projects supported by this first round of funding included: education about the history and legacy of residential schools, curriculum development, training of community members, counselling and trauma work, traditional healing approaches, sex offender programs, and support for direct therapeutic approaches.[24]

> ### v. *Comité des orphelins et orphelines institutionnalisés de Duplessis*

The Comité des orphelins et orphelines institutionnalisés de Duplessis (COOID) was set up as a non-profit organisation in 1992 by a group of "Duplessis orphans" who became members of its board of directors. For the last three years, the Quebec Ministry of Health and Social Services has funded it.[25] COOID offers a number of services to provide moral, psychological and concrete support to "orphans". For example, the office is a resource and drop-in centre for anyone who wants information about the "Duplessis orphans" and for "orphans" needing someone to listen to their concerns. The office also makes referrals to other sources of assistance. Since a number of the "orphans" have low literacy skills, COOID assists individuals with their written communications – writing letters, filling out forms, and learning to read. Finally, the COOID organises social events where the "orphans" can meet with their peers to discuss issues of common interest.[26]

> ### vi. *Deaf, Hard of Hearing and Deaf-Blind Well-Being Program*

In 1987, when many former students from Jericho Hill School came forward to disclose that they had been sexually abused, the Greater Vancouver Mental Health Services Society (GVMHSS) began providing counselling services to them and their families. They continued to receive counselling on an *ad hoc* basis until 1992 when the GVMSS took steps to establish, in consultation with the community, the Deaf, Hard of Hearing and Deaf-Blind Well-Being Program.

The program, operated through funding from four ministries of the Government of British Columbia[27] offers therapeutic and other well-being services. Therapies are adapted to its clientele's communication needs. For example, American Sign Language (ASL) interpretation services are available for survivors' therapy sessions. While initially conceived only for survivors of sexual abuse at Jericho Hill School, the program gradually began to provide therapeutic and other services to Deaf, Hard of Hearing and Deaf-Blind persons in various British Columbia communities.

3. Assessment

Overview

The initiatives of no two communities are exactly alike. Yet they all incorporate some critical features for ensuring effective redress for survivors of institutional child abuse. Community initiatives are inherently respectful of survivors, as they are usually managed by survivors. Even where an outside organisation runs a community initiative, the engagement of survivors will be a necessary component if the initiative is to succeed. Fact-finding, on the other hand, is not an essential function of a community initiative. A program may involve a recounting of experiences by survivors and others affected by abuse, but this will normally not involve a formal testing of the reliability of these stories.

Community initiatives do not have the power to hold people and organisations to account for their conduct. Fairness to all parties is not a goal of community initiatives, although they may be helpful to perpetrators as well as survivors. As processes that seek to foster healing and well-being, community initiatives can create a climate favourable to acknowledgement and even apology. Conversely, acts of acknowledgement and apology may lead to the creation of community initiatives.

The extent to which community initiatives respond to the other needs of survivors depends on the scope and purpose of individual programs. Community initiatives also provide an opportunity to engage survivors' families, communities and peoples, allowing them to play an active role in healing. The linkage serves to raise public awareness about child abuse, especially where funding is externally provided.

a. Respect, engagement and informed choice

Community initiatives are well-suited to ensuring respect, engagement and informed choice by survivors. Since they are invariably conceived and carried out by, or in the interests of, survivors, and their communities, they are necessarily attuned to their sensitivities and capacities.

Similarly, a community initiative does not have to adapt or reinvent itself (as some other approaches might) in order to engage survivors. Community-based initiatives place survivors at the heart of their processes. Survivors can lead their own healing initiatives – contributing to survivor-run support groups, resource centres for survivors, or survivor-led inquiries. Alternatively, where the responsibility for a community initiative comes from an outside organisation, such as a government-funded health service, the input of survivors is central to their effective design and implementation.

Participation in a community initiative will not normally prevent an individual from pursuing any other avenues of redress. Community initiatives foster choice by survivors because participation is entirely voluntary.

b. Fact-finding

Some community initiatives may involve exploring what happened to survivors, while others may not engage in any type of information gathering. Even when survivors and others recount and record their experiences, community initiatives are not intended to offer the type of fact-finding process followed by courts. If they do involve gathering facts, they do not force anyone to disclose information and they do not make official pronouncements on the reliability of the facts presented. They simply allow survivors and others affected by abuse to tell their stories, to have a forum where they will be listened to and their experiences will be noted, sometimes recorded for posterity – but not officially judged. In identifying Honour and History as one of its project funding themes, the Aboriginal Healing Foundation recognised the value of the type of fact-finding about the residential school experience that can be carried out within a community initiative.[28]

c. Accountability

Community initiatives have no power to hold people and organisations legally accountable for their conduct. This is a prerogative of formal legal processes. Ascertaining who is responsible and who should be held morally accountable can, however, be an important part of the healing process. Community initiatives focus on healing individuals and their communities, on preventing further harm through awareness and education, on restoring balance and harmony to families and communities, and on developing the capacity of the community to take care of itself.

d.   Fairness

Fairness to all parties is neither a goal nor a preoccupation of community initiatives. They are undertaken to help survivors, their families and communities as a whole. If they also manage to assist those who directly or indirectly were responsible for abusing children, this is simply a by-product of their role in healing survivors and their communities. Taking into account the interests and needs of abusers – simply to be fair to everyone involved – is almost never a goal of a community initiative.

e.   Acknowledgement, apology and reconciliation

A community initiative will not necessarily lead to an acknowledgement that harm was done, much less an apology or an attempt to reconcile abusers with the people they hurt. However, as non-adversarial processes intending to foster healing and well-being, community initiatives operate in a climate that is favourable to producing an acknowledgement and even an apology for the harm done. The initiative of the St. Andrew's congregation, which began as an information-gathering process and turned into a formal apology ceremony, is an example of the beneficial results that this climate can produce.

Acknowledgements and apologies do not only arise as a consequence of community initiatives; sometimes they precede, and may even stimulate the creation of new community initiatives. The Anglican and United Churches of Canada established healing funds after they acknowledged their roles in the residential school system and apologised for the harm done. The Government of Canada established the Aboriginal Healing Fund at the same time that it delivered its Statement of Reconciliation. In these examples, the acknowledgements and apologies led to further funding for programs to promote community-based healing.

f. Compensation, counselling and education

Among all the redress options, community initiatives are probably best suited to address one compelling need of all survivors – the need to have direct input into how they want to approach their healing. Community initiatives are not meant to provide direct financial compensation to survivors. But launching community-based inquiries, offering counselling and therapy, providing drug and alcohol rehabilitation programs, and facilitating opportunities to learn (to parent well, to break the cycle of abuse, to speak the language of one's ancestors, to read, to form healthy long-term relationships) are ways of addressing survivors' other needs. In addition, as the National Youth in Care Network's study and consultations with Grandview survivors have confirmed, individual survivors of abuse need peer support to heal. This kind of support is always possible through community initiatives.

g. Needs of families, communities and peoples

Families, communities and peoples also need to heal in concrete ways. By placing survivors' families and communities at their heart, community initiatives give them an opportunity to be a central part of the therapeutic process. This is especially important for communities and peoples that have traditionally been deprived of opportunities to control their own future.

h. Prevention and public education

Prevention, raising public awareness and educating the public about the nature, causes and harmful effects of child abuse are often key goals of community initiatives. They are the primary objectives of websites about abuse, workshops on improving parenting skills, and materials published on the history of residential schools. Sharing this history contributes to prevention as it helps Aboriginal children break the cycle of abuse when they become adults. Community initiatives can also serve an important educational and preventative function as Canadians come to a better appreciation of the legacy of child abuse in residential institutions.

4. Conclusion

Assessing community initiatives against the same framework as conventional legal processes reveals that they respond very effectively to the needs of survivors and their communities. The great strengths, collectively, of community initiatives are their capacities to satisfy many of the needs of survivors and their communities by fostering individual and communal healing. They can also play an essential role in engaging survivors and their families in other formal processes for providing redress, and in rebuilding communities damaged by institutional child abuse.

Recommendations

SURVIVORS AND THEIR COMMUNITIES should be encouraged to experiment with different projects and programs organised and administered at the community level.

Considerations:

A first step is to make available information about other initiatives so that the full range of possible initiatives can be considered.

Existing healing and reconciliation funds, whether established by government or others, should be active in providing seed money for innovative programs.

COMMUNITY-BASED PROGRAMS should be assisted in sharing their experiences so that new programs could be modelled on successful initiatives.

Considerations:

This might involve sponsoring publications, videos and websites or even paying the transportation costs to enable those who are managing successful programs to visit communities that wish to set up their own program.

ORGANISATIONS THAT SPONSORED RESIDENTIAL facilities and governments should continue to make resources available to support local initiatives through which social services are delivered to survivors of physical and sexual abuse.

---

1   Information about the National Youth in Care Network can be found on-line: <http://www.youthincare.ca> (date accessed: 8 November 1999).

2   B. Raychaba, *"Pain ... Lots of Pain" Family Violence and Abuse in the Lives of Young People in Care* (Ottawa: National Youth in Care Network, 1993).

3   *Ibid.* at back cover.

[4] National Youth in Care Network, *Into the Hands of Youth: Youth in and from Care Identify Healing Needs* (Ottawa: National Youth in Care Network, April 1996).

[5] Working Group on Child Sexual Abuse, *It's Hard to Tell Discussion Paper – A report or interviews with survivors and offenders of child sexual abuse with a focus on family and community attitudes* (St. John's: Community Services Council of Newfoundland and Labrador, 1996).

[6] Community Services Council of Newfoundland and Labrador, *Shifting the Focus: Community Discussions on Child Sexual Abuse – Report on Findings* (St. John's: Community Services Council of Newfoundland and Labrador, 1997).

[7] Plint pleaded guilty to sixteen counts of indecent assault, which he committed against boys under his supervision at the Alberni Residential School, between the years 1948 to 1953. He was sentenced to serve a total of 11 years in prison. *R. v. Plint*, [1995] B.C.J. No. 3060, online: QL.

[8] This initiative is an example of a grassroots effort to come to terms with a dark past and to help two communities begin to reconcile. For more information on the apology of the St. Andrew's church congregation and meaningful apologies in general, see Law Commission of Canada, *Apologising for Serious Wrongdoing: Social, Psychological and Legal Considerations* by S. Alter (Ottawa: Law Commission of Canada, 1999). Available in hard copy from the Law Commission of Canada and online: <http://www.lcc.gc.ca>.

[9] Commissioners of the Alkali Residential School Inquiry, *Alkali Residential School Inquiry Report* (British Columbia: Musqueam Nation Hall, 26 June 1997).

[10] Based on information provided to the Law Commission at meetings held in the community, 6-7 October 1998, and additional information provided by Charlene Belleau.

[11] L. Larmondin, "Church commits increased funding to Aboriginal healing" (10 December 1998), online: Anglican Church of Canada <http://www.anglican.ca> (date accessed: 16 April 1999) [hereinafter Larmondin].

[12] "Granting Criteria for Education, Healing and Reconciliation Programs / Events Related to Residential Schools Issues" (last update 29 June 1999), online: Anglican Church of Canada <http://www.anglican.ca> (date accessed: 14 September 1999).

[13] Larmondin, *supra* note 11; and Anglican Church of Canada, "Aboriginal Healing and Reconciliation Grants 1993–1998, Diocese of Keewatin," (Toronto: Anglican Church of Canada, undated but obtained 12 July 1999).

[14] United Church of Canada, "The Healing Fund Connection" (9 March 1999), online: United Church of Canada: <http://www.uccan.org/Healing.htm> (accessed: 14 September 1999).

[15] United Church of Canada, "Report of the Healing Fund Council Executive" (Winnipeg: October 1998) online: United Church of Canada <http://uccan.org/HFCEreport.htm> (date accessed: 18 September 1998).

[16] Council for Reconciliation, Solidarity and Communion, *Charting a New Course – Reconciliation, Solidarity and Communion Initiative in the Spirit of the Great Jubilee* (Pamphlet) (Ottawa: Canadian Conference of Catholic Bishops, 1998) [hereinafter *Charting* pamphlet]; Canadian Conference of Catholic Bishops, Press Release, "Charting a New Course – Reconciliation, Solidarity and Communion Initiative in the Spirit of the Great Jubilee" (15 September 1998); Canadian Conference of Catholic Bishops, "Background Information – Initiative for Reconciliation, Solidarity and Communion" (17 June 1998). All of the above is online: Canadian Conference of Catholic Bishops <http://www.cccb.ca> (date accessed: 15 September 1999).

[17] See *Charting* pamphlet, *ibid*.

[18] Canadian Conference of Catholic Bishops, Media Release, "Background Information – Initiative for Reconciliation, Solidarity and Communion" (17 June 1998), online: Canadian Conference of Catholic Bishops <http://www.cccb.ca> (date accessed: 15 April 1999).

[19] Canadian Conference of Catholic Bishops, Media Release, "Fund for Reconciliation, Solidarity and Communion Contributes More Than $100,000 for Aboriginal Community-based Initiatives" (21 January 1999), online: Canadian Conference of Catholic Bishops <http://www.cccb.ca> (date accessed: 15 April 1999).

[20] Minister of Indian Affairs and Northern Development "Notes for an Address by The Honourable Jane Stewart Minister of Indian Affairs and Northern Development" (Ottawa, 7 January 1998) at 3, online: Indian and Northern Affairs Canada <http://www.inac.gc.ca/info/speeches/jan98/action.html> (date accessed: 15 September 1999).

[21] *Ibid*. at 4.

[22] The Aboriginal Healing Foundation, "Backgrounder," (undated) at 1, online: Aboriginal Healing Foundation <http://www.ahf.ca/backgrounder.htm> (date accessed: 10 June 1999).

23 The Aboriginal Healing Foundation, *Aboriginal Healing Foundation Program Handbook 1999* (Ottawa: The Aboriginal Healing Foundation, 1998) at 10, [hereinafter *Handbook 1999*], online (2nd edition): <http://www.ahf.ca/english/handbook.html> (date accessed: 21 December 1999).

24 Aboriginal Healing Foundation, Press Release, "Healing Residential School Survivors, their Families & Descendants: AHF funds first 35 community projects" (23 June 1999), online: http://www.ahf.ca/englis/re10699.html> (date accessed: 21 December 1999).

25 Based on information provided by a COOID employee, 15 September 1999.

26 Comité des orphelins et orphelines institutionnalisés de Duplessis, *Rapport d'activités du 1er avril 1998 au 31 mars 1999* (Montreal: COOID, adopted at the general meeting 18 June 1999).

27 Based on information provided by the coordinator of the Well-Being Program.

28 Survivors have told the Foundation that public communication on the residential school experience will also be healing for them. *Handbook 1999, supra* note 23 at 18.

K. Redress Programs

1. Introduction

Former residents of institutions for children currently have a number of options when considering how to obtain redress for the harms they have suffered. Each of the approaches already reviewed has the capacity to respond to one or more of the identified needs of survivors. Some are better-suited to meeting specific needs than others. Some may address a wider range of needs than others. Some are more attuned to the needs of families and communities than others. All, however, confront survivors with the necessity of making trade-offs between their needs. For this reason, genuine responsiveness to the needs of individual survivors requires that they be given full information about the characteristics of each approach to redress.

It should not be assumed that the features of existing approaches are forever fixed. Improvements to all of them could reduce the need for trade-offs and make each more responsive to survivors' needs. Various recommendations to achieve this objective have already been made. However, the Minister's fundamental question to the Law Commission remains: is there some other approach (or approaches) that would better "address wrongdoing, while affording appropriate remedies, and promoting reconciliation, fairness and healing"?

The desire for another type of process to resolve past cases of institutional child abuse has already led to the creation of innovative "redress programs".[1] This is the term the Commission has chosen to describe any programs designed specifically to provide financial compensation and complementary non-monetary benefits to survivors and others harmed by institutional child abuse. Governments often sponsor these programs in whole or in part; but the programs do not involve proceedings before the courts or any existing administrative agency.

In some cases, these programs emerged as an alternative dispute resolution response to civil actions filed by survivors. In others, they were established before a lawsuit had been commenced. Redress programs have certain affinities with truth commissions in that they seek to develop and provide forms of redress that promote healing and reconciliation. But they are also intended to deliver financial compensation to survivors – usually by means of an *ex gratia* payment. They also have affinities with community initiatives that respond directly to the specific needs of survivors, their families and their communities. But they have this difference: they are not voluntary grassroots processes, but are official responses to the threat of civil liability. They typically find their legal foundation in a governmental policy decision and need not be formally established by legislation.[2] Consequently, these redress programs can be as expansive and innovative as the imagination and resources of their creators allow.

There is no single model or legislative template for the design or administration of redress programs – not even a general statute like one that frames public inquiries.[3] Nevertheless, they all share an overriding goal: to respond to the needs of survivors of institutional child abuse in a way that is more comprehensive, more flexible and less formal than existing legal processes. Every time such a program is contemplated, it is necessary to consider the following basic questions:

Input:	Who will design the program, and how?
Beneficiaries:	Whom will the program serve?
Harms:	For what harms will the program provide redress?
Redress:	What compensation and benefits will be offered?
Validation:	How will claims be validated?
Outreach:	How will the program be made known to potential claimants?
Duration:	How long will it last?
Administration:	Who will administer the program?

The answers to these questions will determine the credibility, effectiveness and success of any given redress program. More than this, the processes by which these questions are developed and negotiated can make or break a redress program. The description that follows draws on a number of existing and contemplated redress programs for dealing with institutional child abuse from across Canada:[4]

- the Helpline Agreement (St. John's and St. Joseph's Training Schools);

- the Grandview agreement;

- the New Brunswick compensation agreement in respect of the Youth Training School at Kingsclear, the former Dr. William F. Roberts Hospital School and the former Boys' Industrial Home;

- the Reconciliation Agreement between the Primary Victims of George Epoch and the Jesuit Fathers of Upper Canada;

- the Nova Scotia compensation program in respect of Shelburne Youth Centre, the Nova Scotia School for Girls and the Nova Scotia Youth Training School;

- the Jericho Hill Individual Compensation Program;

- the Alternative Dispute Resolution project in respect of former students of the Sir James Whitney School;

- the settlement reached by Maple Leaf Gardens;

- the offer made by the Government of Quebec to the Duplessis Orphans; and

- the ongoing negotiations between the federal government and various Aboriginal communities relating to abuse committed in residential schools.

Each of these programs is referred to only as an example. The list should not be considered as comprehensive or as setting out an exhaustive inventory of the possible models for redress programs.

2. Description

Redress programs are always undertaken in the shadow of the formal justice system. This applies whether the disclosure of abuse that prompts the redress program comes about unofficially (for example, through media reports from individual survivors[5]) or officially (such as through the findings of a public inquiry[6] or an investigation by an

Ombudsman.)[7] Once there has been public exposure of past child abuse in an institution, those employed at, or who are responsible for that institution live under the very real threat of civil litigation and, sometimes, criminal prosecution. Whether any lawsuits have actually been filed is, for the purpose of deciding the scale and scope of a redress program, not relevant.

A well-designed redress program can be an attractive option both for those seeking redress and for governments and organisations attempting to respond to the harm caused. Those offering the program can avoid the costs of having to defend numerous civil actions (participants in a redress program are usually required to give up their right to sue as a condition of their participation). These organisations are also better able, at least in theory, to manage and control the costs of the compensation and benefits to be awarded. They are usually aware of the number of potential claimants and the aggregate cost of paying these claims. In addition, by seeking a comprehensive settlement, the organisations are in a position to marshall non-financial benefits such as counsellors, therapists and education or training programs more efficiently. Finally, they might genuinely feel that to be proactive in trying to meet the claims of survivors and facilitate healing is simply the right thing to do. Acknowledgement and apology can be as important to those who are wrongdoers (or who employed wrongdoers) as to those who are wronged.

Survivors may also find a redress program to be a desirable option. They may prefer a less adversarial, more rapid process that offers a wider range of benefits, meeting more of their needs. They may wish to avoid both the risk of being disbelieved in a civil action for damages because they are not "good witnesses", and the pain of a second victimisation. In return, they may be willing to give up the potential for a higher monetary award from the court. They may also wish to embark on a program that engages them in its design, that is inclusive and respectful, that provides an acknowledgement and an apology, and that has a public education and prevention component.

At the beginning of Part II, eight criteria were listed by which approaches to redress could be assessed. In many cases, this assessment is a relatively straightforward exercise, since the essential elements of most official processes are fixed in advance. The character of the criminal justice process, civil actions, criminal injuries compensation programs, Ombudsman processes, investigations by children's advocates and commissions, and public inquiries are not really open to negotiation. All features of a redress program, by contrast, are negotiable. For this reason, a truly responsive redress program can emerge only from a negotiating process that reflects the basic principles of respect, engagement, choice and fairness.

a.   Input

A key factor in the success of a redress program is the degree to which it responds to the needs of its intended beneficiaries. The most direct way is to involve intended beneficiaries (either directly if their numbers permit, or through their own chosen representatives, especially if the beneficiaries are numerous or widely dispersed) in negotiating the terms of the program. This was done in the case of the Grandview Agreement and the agreement relating to the St. John's and St. Joseph's Training Schools, among others. The terms of these programs were established through negotiations among former students, the Ontario government and, in the case of St. John's and St. Joseph's, the Catholic Church and the lay order that ran the schools. The Alternative Dispute Resolution Project for former students of the Sir James Whitney School for the Deaf was also the result of a lengthy negotiation process between staff from the Ontario Ministry of Education and Training, the Ontario Ministry of the Attorney General and former students. So too were the Guiding Principles for Working Together to Build Restoration and Reconciliation that resulted from the exploratory dialogues conducted among Aboriginal survivors of residential schools, the Aboriginal leadership, churches and the federal government.

Some redress programs are not the result of full-blown negotiations. Those wishing to offer redress may choose to do no more than consult with survivors – or those who work with or represent survivors – before determining how to structure a redress program and what types of benefits to offer. The resulting program is then presented on a take-it-or-leave-it basis. Such a procedure does not, obviously, engage survivors as fully as comprehensive negotiations.

Providing survivors with the opportunity to participate in negotiations does not guarantee their effective participation. There may be cases where survivors wish a lawyer or other dispute settlement professional to be part of the team that negotiates an agreement with the party or parties offering redress. Such assistance may be essential for survivors to feel that they are negotiating on a more or less "level playing field". Given the disparity of resources between those offering redress and survivors, it may be necessary to ensure that the cost of obtaining such professional assistance is reimbursed as part of any settlement.

Another issue relates to representation, in those cases where all survivors do not collectively meet with those proposing a redress program. Whether negotiators should be elected and whether the agreement reached should be subject to ratification by a vote of eligible survivors are questions of design that can only be answered on a case-by-case basis. It is important to ensure that representatives keep the interests of survivors paramount.

This is a particular concern where a redress program also contemplates the payment of benefits to communities or groups. In some cases, the direct participation of the community in the negotiations is essential to achieving an inclusive process. Finding an appropriate balance in the entitlements of all those harmed by institutional child abuse, and developing a compensation package that respects this balance, requires the opportunity for ongoing input from all survivors. This is true even in cases where the negotiations are being conducted by organisations that represent survivors.

b.   Beneficiaries

Redress programs are, above all, aimed at former residents of an institution for children or youth who suffered abuse while living at the institution. Depending on the range of harm that will be compensated, benefits may be limited to those who directly suffered physical or sexual abuse. They may also be made available more broadly – for example, to those who witnessed the abuse, or even to all former residents of an institution. Where psychological or cultural abuse is seen to have been pervasive at a particular period at an institution, all former residents from that period might be considered eligible for some basic level of compensation and access to therapy.

Beyond the former residents themselves, others may be seen as having needs deserving of redress. Where a survivor of abuse has become violent or sexually abusive, wholly or in part as a result of his or her experiences, the survivor's own victims are appropriate beneficiaries to consider for inclusion under a redress program. Spouses, partners, siblings, children and parents of the survivor are those most likely to have suffered directly from the survivor's aggressive or destructive behaviour. To the extent a redress program aims at inclusivity, these family members have a good claim to be compensated for the harms they endured. The Helpline Agreement is an example of a program that provided for counselling for family members.[8] Survivors may feel that some benefits offered to them, in particular educational benefits, could be more fully enjoyed by their children. Redress agreements should provide for at least some benefits to be transferable within a family.

Communities have also been harmed by institutional child abuse. Establishing community-based programs to combat alcoholism, drug dependency and family violence might well fall within the terms of a redress agreement. By casting the range of beneficiaries and the kinds of benefits that may be transferred as broadly as possible within a survivor's family and community, redress programs can help to break the cycle of abuse passed on from one generation to the next. Similarly, support for community-based education about the culture and language of an Aboriginal survivor may be an important part of an inclusive redress program.

c.   Harms

Children living in institutions were potentially subject to various types of harms. They include physical and sexual abuse, psychological and emotional abuse, neglect, the failure to provide needed medication or treatment, the deprivation of an adequate education and the suppression of one's language, religion or culture. While physical and sexual abuse are recognised in law as giving the person harmed a right to sue for damages, many of the other kinds of abuse just noted are not so clearly viewed as legally compensable, and some are not considered compensable at all.

The scope of a redress program need not be restricted to providing compensation and benefits only for those harms that are currently recognised by the civil law. Indeed, one of the advantages of a redress program is that it can be designed to address a wider variety of harms than those covered by the judicial process. A redress program can also be tailored to meet the needs of anyone who was seriously harmed, in any manner, while residing at an institution.

Conversely, a redress program might be designed to provide compensation only for harms not recognised by the courts or a criminal injuries compensation program. Or, it may offer compensation for a narrower range of harms than those recognised by the courts. For example, the Jericho Individual Compensation Program provides compensation for those who suffered sexual abuse but not for those who were subjected to physical abuse.[9] In such cases, survivors are obliged to seek redress for these other harms through one of the more traditional processes such as a civil action or a criminal injuries compensation program.

In general, redress programs take an expansive view of the harms for which compensation will be offered. Taking a holistic approach can be an especially important consideration where the purpose of, or the practices within an institution constituted what is now understood to be cultural abuse.

d.   Redress

   i.   *Range of benefits*
The range of benefits that may be provided through a redress program is much broader than those obtainable through the courts. Benefits are not constrained, as are judicial orders, by considerations of compulsory enforcement. They may be as varied as the needs of survivors, their families and their communities. In general, courts can only offer financial compensation to survivors. This section reviews the types of financial and non-financial benefits that have been included in various redress programs. It should be noted that no one program has necessarily offered all of them.

The cornerstone of most redress programs is an amount of money, paid either in a lump sum or on a periodic basis. Usually the award is intended to compensate for the pain and suffering of the claimant as a result of the abuse she or he experienced. Like a court award of damages, it can also be extended to cover loss of income and loss of enjoyment of life flowing from the abuse. Usually a program will set a scale of payments that is meant to correspond to the duration and severity of the abuse suffered. The manner in which these scales operate will be discussed in more detail in sub-section *ii*: *Level of benefits*.

Redress programs usually specify the type of abuse for which financial compensation is being provided. Even though non-financial benefits are usually offered for a broad range of harms, eligibility for a monetary award has almost always been limited to those who suffered physical or sexual abuse, or both – as in the Helpline Agreement and the Grandview Agreement. There is, of course, no necessary reason why this should continue to be the case, especially since courts themselves are beginning to recognise emotional and psychological harm as compensable.

Some redress programs also offer financial counselling. The need to provide potential beneficiaries with information about the financial advantages and disadvantages of seeking redress through the compensation program – as compared to bringing a civil action – has already been noted. It is a key element of providing survivors with the information necessary to make a meaningful choice. In addition, financial counselling is usually intended to provide survivors with a broad range of services and may include: assistance in determining, where such a choice is possible, whether to take a lump-sum or a periodic payment; advice about how best to manage or invest the money received; and general assistance with establishing a budget.

Other benefits tend to address more specific needs of claimants. Therapy is often identified as a primary need. It can be both lengthy and costly. Programs may allocate a specific amount for such services to the claimant, or they may undertake to pay a therapist directly. Some programs allow survivors to choose the therapist and the form of therapy they prefer. Others designate those therapists whose services will be paid for. Often there is a ceiling either on the amount allocated to therapy, or on the period for which funding will be provided.

Failure to provide a proper education was part of the harm that many former residents of institutions feel they suffered. They also believe it had an effect on their job opportunities later in life. In recognition of this, some programs offer to pay for educational counselling, the costs of educational upgrading, or vocational training. Payments might include, for example, registration fees, tuition, books, and a living allowance. The Grandview Agreement included vocational or educational training as part of the benefits offered. Some survivors may use an educational benefit for personal development or to learn about their culture. Former residents of schools for Aboriginal students might, for example, apply this benefit to learn or re-learn their native language or to take courses on Aboriginal history or spirituality. Others might wish to transfer the benefit to their children.

Finally, some benefits within a redress program cannot be measured in dollars. Primary among them is the offering of an apology – an acknowledgement of the harm done and the fact that it was not the fault of the survivor; an expression of regret; and an undertaking to make all possible efforts to prevent such abuse from recurring. This kind of statement, addressed privately to the survivor or publicly to a particular group of survivors (or both), can be a central part of a redress program. Apologies have, in fact, been made a feature of several of them, including the following:

- The Helpline Agreement offered a personal, written apology, expressed in terms set out by the survivor, to every survivor who wanted one. As well, the Archbishop of Ottawa and the Archbishop of Toronto published a joint pastoral letter which became the basis for a homily delivered by Archbishop Marcel Gervais in Ottawa and by Auxiliary Bishop Terence Prendergast, S.J. in Toronto.[10]

- The Grandview Agreement stated that each beneficiary was entitled to receive an individual acknowledgement from the Ontario Government in a form to be agreed upon by the individual, the Grandview Survivors' Support Group and the government, after the conclusion of criminal proceedings relating to the abuse.[11] The Attorney General also undertook to read out a general acknowledgement in the legislature.[12]

- Under the Jericho Individual Compensation Program, the Attorney General sent a personal apology to all survivors who requested one.[13]

In addition to apologies directed to survivors, it is also possible to imagine separate apologies directed to families of survivors and communities.

Another intangible but very real benefit sought by many survivors is the recording of their experiences. A recorder is selected, and given the task of interviewing survivors about their experiences at an institution and the subsequent course of their lives. The report is then published and distributed to all the survivors, and more broadly, if desired. A recorder's report has been prepared in the case of the primary victims of George Epoch and the Cape Croker Reserve[14] and in respect of abuse at the St. John's and St. Joseph's Training Schools.[15] A video and booklet was produced as a result of the Grandview Agreement.[16] The experiences at Jericho Hill were the subject of a documentary broadcast on the CBC television program *Witness*.[17] Other forms of recording experiences include 1-800 numbers with answering machines, and mail-in registers for audiotapes. Collecting and archiving survivors' experiences – and making them available to other survivors, to researchers and to the general public under conditions agreed to by survivors – is a significant non-monetary benefit that can be incorporated into any redress program.

Redress programs can also provide for memorials.[18] Memorials serve many functions. They can provoke reflection among the general public. They can symbolise a commitment to prevent harm from recurring. They can acknowledge the harm done to those who are no longer alive. Some survivors would prefer a memorial to be a physical structure; for others, it should be a place of remembrance, like a museum, that can serve an active educational role. Some survivors want a memorial that focusses on a particular institution; others, a memorial that is devoted to a particular group of survivors. Many survivors feel it is important to create a memorial that draws attention to and denounces a particular policy that caused harm. Whether a memorial is established, its type, and the conditions for its ongoing maintenance can only be negotiated on a case-by-case basis in each particular redress program.

ii.   Level of benefits

An accurate estimate of the number of potential claimants and the level of benefits to be paid out is an essential element in the design of a redress program. If the estimate is too low, a fiscal crisis for the funding organisation can result. If the number is too high, negotiators may be inappropriately discounting their calculations in individual cases, based on an inaccurate assessment of the total impact of a settlement. Estimating the number of claimants is not an easy process. The Nova Scotia redress program was based on an initial estimate of 350 claimants. In fact, 1,450 claimants eventually filed applications.

Deciding how much money to allocate to each type of benefit offered, and to each type of harm suffered, will be influenced by several pragmatic considerations such as:

- How much money is available for the redress program as a whole?

- What types of benefits are the priorities?

- How many claimants are anticipated?

These and related factors must be considered when designing benefit levels in a redress program. Moreover, financial benefits under a redress program are always calculated against the backdrop of awards likely to be made in a judicial proceeding. The level of benefits must be attractive enough to claimants so that they will opt for the program, rather than launch a civil action. But the level of benefits may reasonably be expected to reflect the lower cost and greater certainty of recovery for claimants under a redress program, when compared to civil actions.

In view of the large number of claims likely to be forthcoming in a short period of time, and the desire to deal with these claims both quickly and with a minimum of administrative costs, finding appropriate mechanisms to ensure consistency and fairness among claimants has been a preoccupation. The tendency in redress programs has been to establish a sliding scale of awards according to a negotiated grid. Among the considerations factored into these grids have been: the types of harm to be compensated; the degree of severity of the harm suffered; and the duration of the harm. Each category on the grid is then attributed a corresponding range of monetary compensation. The grids applied in the Grandview and the Jericho Hill programs are examples of this approach.

Jericho Individual Compensation Program Compensation Chart[19]

	Abuse	Compensation Amount
Tier 1	Sexual abuse	$3,000
Tier 2	Serious Sexual Abuse	Up to $25,000
Tier 3	Sexual Abuse – Serious and Prolonged	Up to $60,000

Grandview Matrix[20]

Acts Alleged	Harm/Injury	Evidence/ Proof	Award Range
Repeated serious sexual abuse (sexual intercourse anal or oral) & physical beating and threats.	Continuing harm resulting in serious dysfunction. Adjudicator applies standards set out in Agreement.	Possible: Medical, psychological, therapist, police reports, direct evidence of victim if credible, witnesses, documentary, conviction of perpetrator.	$40,000 - $60,000
Physical abuse involving hospitalisation with broken bones or serious internal injuries.	Harm sufficient to justify award must be demonstrated. Adjudicator applies standards set out in the Agreement.	Same as above.	$20,000 - $40,000 "mid range"
Isolated act of sexual intercourse, oral or anal sex or masturbation with threats or abuse of position of trust.	Harm sufficient to justify award must be demonstrated. Adjudicator applies standards set out in the Agreement.	Same as above.	$20,000 - $40,000 "mid range"
No physical interference – forms of "mistreatment" i.e., cruel conduct that was prolonged and persistent. Confinement in segregation alone will not attract an award. Segregation may be justified in accordance with administrative authority. Abusive segregation cannot be.	Long term detrimental impact – conduct must not have been lawful or condoned. The nature of the harm will determine once proof of the acts are accepted whether a minimal recovery or a higher award.	Same as above.	$3,000 on proof of acts of abuse or mistreatment. $10,000 - $20,000 where serious harm found by the adjudicator.

A grid permits those funding a redress program to estimate and to control its total cost. The ranges within each category allow some discretion to adjudicators to tailor their awards to the circumstances of each individual claimant. The premise is that within the established ranges some differentiation of claims to recognise the unique situation of each claimant is possible, but that the cost and time required to establish anew the amount of every claim would not be justifiable given the desire to make compensation available in a timely and efficient manner. While these grids have mainly been used for physical, sexual and psychological abuse, they could also be extended to cover other types of abuse, such as emotional, educational and cultural abuse, as well as neglect.

e.   Validation

i.   How?

The procedure for determining which claimants are entitled to the compensation and benefits offered is a difficult element to design in a redress program. In order to receive the support of survivors, funders and, ultimately, the public (particularly when compensation is paid partly or wholly by the State), a redress program will have to be founded on a process to validate claims that strikes a delicate balance. The process must be sufficiently rigorous that it has credibility with program funders, survivors and the public by minimising the potential for exploitation of the program through fraudulent claims. But it must not put applicants through a procedure that simply duplicates the adversarial and formal legal process of a criminal or civil trial.

Striking this balance is an art, not a science. It must be acknowledged that no validation process (including those of the civil and criminal justice systems) is, or can be, perfect. This acknowledgement is especially important since there are those who believe that the judicial process is the gold standard and that its procedures for testing the validity of claims should always be used.

How elaborate and demanding the validation procedure should be may depend on the number of claimants involved; the physical, emotional and psychological capacity of claimants to sustain the procedure; the nature and level of compensation and benefits being offered; the existence of other, independent procedures for confirming the claims; and the amount of time and resources available to devote to the process.

Those offering redress must be careful to design a validation process that is proportionate to the compensation and benefits being offered. For example, if the benefit replicates services available through other government programs, the process may not need to be as rigorous as in cases where significant monetary awards are being made. It is also important that they allocate their resources in accordance with a realistic estimate of the anticipated demand. Finally, it is essential that the validation process be sufficiently credible that workers at institutions do not have their reputations unfairly impugned. This may even require that they be provided with an opportunity to clear their names should a claimant identify them, even confidentially, as an abuser or a passive but knowing bystander.[21]

A validation process can take many forms. It may be founded exclusively on a documentary record: adjudicators will rely on a written application accompanied by the submission of any supporting documents and other material. This would be similar to the procedure adopted in a number of provinces by criminal injuries compensation boards. In documentary hearings, the application should be verified independently by persons with access to any records or files that may substantiate the claim. They can include medical records, school report cards and attendance records, police reports, personnel records and institutional correspondence.[22]

The more serious and detailed the allegations, the more substantiation may be required. Conversely, where a claim does not rely on a specific allegation, only minimal documentation should be required. This could be the case, for example, where a redress program recognises and is intended to compensate for loss of culture and language at a residential school for Aboriginal children, or for lost wages at any institution where children missed out on schooling because they were made to work without pay. In these types of cases, validation need require nothing more than simply establishing that a claimant attended a particular institution, and for what period of time.

The degree of validation required may also depend on the nature of the benefit being sought. Given that therapy for those in need of healing is a general social good, regardless of the reason that the therapy is needed, a validation process for persons only seeking therapy should not be excessive. British Columbia's Residential Historical Abuse Program is a case in point. It provides intensive counselling and therapy to individuals who claim they were sexually abused in a provincially-operated institution or a provincially-supervised form of care, based on a simple application and verification of the person's residency at the time of the disclosed abuse.[23]

A validation process may involve an oral hearing, in which the applicant presents his or her claim to an individual adjudicator or to an adjudication panel. Such a hearing provides an opportunity for claimants to describe directly and in their own words the abuse they suffered and the impact it has had on their life. For adjudicators, it provides an opportunity to directly assess the claimant's current circumstances and his or her credibility. At an oral hearing, experienced adjudicators are often able to validate claims with a minimum of intrusive questioning.

Redress programs do not generally provide for an appeal from a decision to reject a claim. Establishing a formal appeal process would blur the distinction between a redress program and a formal court proceeding. It would, to some extent, also defeat the goal of resolving claims more rapidly than courts are able to do. Nevertheless, some validation processes provide for a rehearing where new evidence has come to light, or a summary reconsideration of the first decision by a panel of other first-instance decision-makers.

Ordinarily, those funding a redress program should have no particular reason to seek a review of any compensation granted, since the validation process is one they themselves created or agreed to in negotiations. Moreover, since the objective of the program is to provide redress (by contrast, say, with a criminal process where the outcome may be the conviction of a defendant), it is more consistent with that objective to err occasionally on the side of over- rather than under-compensating. However, an appeal procedure should not be designed to let claimants simply choose the forum or the adjudicator they wish.

Naturally, it is not possible to precisely predict all contingencies that may arise once survivors come forward with claims. Allowances must be made and flexibility must be built into the program. Nonetheless, where a process is poorly designed or administered, or where completely unforseeable events unfold, funders may be forced to revise the validation or appeal process in midstream. This is unfortunate because it undermines the goodwill that the program may have fostered in survivors. More dangerously, it can harm survivors by casting doubt on the legitimacy of the claims of all those who have already received an award under the flawed program. Once again, the case for carefully designing a validation process is tied to protecting the interests of both those funding the program and its intended beneficiaries.

ii.   By whom?

To evaluate the validity of a claim for redress, those designing such programs have generally sought adjudicators whose skills are suited to some aspect of these claims. Adjudicators are often chosen from among those with legal training. So, for example, the Grandview claims were heard and determined by lawyers or law professors appointed by the Ontario government. Therapists may also have an important role to play on adjudication panels, given their understanding of the effects of child abuse on adult survivors.[24] Those experienced in personal injury claims adjudication can also be good choices as decision-makers in a redress program.[25] Sometimes, adjudication is simply carried out by employees of the government that funds the program,[26] although this may lead to a perception of a conflict of interest.

Because the claims process is non-adversarial and because adjudicators will not normally have the benefit of argument from lawyers to assist them in sifting facts, two- or three-person panels should be preferred over adjudicators sitting alone. In putting together multi-member panels to hear claims under a redress program, it is important to select adjudicators with complementary backgrounds. For example, those who have experience in recognising and identifying the effects of institutional abuse could be coupled with adjudicators whose main experience is in assigning fault. Beyond ensuring professional expertise, some programs have tried to ensure that the personal characteristics of adjudicators are likely to ease the stress of the process for applicants. So, for example, in recognition of the fact that all Grandview claimants were women, all Grandview adjudicators were women, and one was an Aboriginal woman. Care must be taken, however, to choose adjudicators who also have credibility with program funders and the public, and to design the process by which they are assigned to individual cases in a manner that is fair and impartial.

f.   Outreach

Participation of key parties is just one factor in the successful design of a redress program. The program must provide for effective outreach to former residents of targetted institutions. Comprehensive outreach is needed so as to ensure, as far as possible, that all potential claimants are made aware, in a timely way, of the program being offered, and provided the information necessary to make an informed decision about whether to participate.

How to contact former students or residents is a troublesome issue. Attendance records are usually in the hands of the authorities who were in charge of the institution, and the authorities may be somewhat less zealous than survivor groups about seeking out the greatest number of former residents possible. For example, in the Alternative Dispute Resolution Project of the Sir James Whitney School for the Deaf, the representatives of former students split off from the joint government-former student board. They launched their own outreach effort because they felt that the Ontario government was not doing all it should to inform former students of the existence of this redress program.

There is a further difficulty. Even if accurate attendance records can be obtained, they will give no indication of the present whereabouts of former residents. Some net-casting process must be developed.

This raises a third concern. How can an outreach process be designed so that it is least likely to cause harm to potential claimants? For example, a letter sent to the home of a former resident risks being opened by a spouse or partner who may then learn, for the first time, about a hidden aspect of a survivor's past. A telephone call, a personal visit or similar first contact can be troubling for a survivor who may have sought for a number of years to suppress memories of childhood abuse. The use of popular media – radio and television programs, newspaper and magazine stories – is one way of heightening public awareness of a redress program without directly intruding on the lives of survivors. Publicising redress programs in general circulation mailings such as electricity and telephone bills, broadly advertising telephone help-line numbers, and posting information in post offices, community centres or physicians' offices are other ways to facilitate inquiries by potential claimants in a fashion that is responsive to survivors' needs.

g. Duration

Simply providing information is not sufficient to ensure that potential claimants come forward. Former residents must have adequate time to consider the offer of a redress program and to decide whether they wish to participate. The duration of the period for filing a claim must be realistic given the sensitive nature of the abuse and the importance of this decision.

Any deadline for submitting a claim forces survivors to face painful issues from their past according to a schedule not of their choosing. Not all survivors may be ready to deal with these issues immediately. The period for filing claims must also take into account the difficulty of contacting former students who may be scattered across the country and even abroad. Tracing the current whereabouts of former residents is a daunting task, due to the passage of years and even decades since they attended these institutions. It is particularly difficult to trace women, who may have married and changed their names, possibly more than once, in the intervening years.

Program deadlines must be administered flexibly. In the case of the St. John's and St. Joseph's program, for example, a group of claimants applied in the initial claims period. That period was then extended, which allowed a second group to apply. Claimants still came forward even after this second period had expired. In view of the particular emotional and other challenges facing adult survivors of institutional child abuse, the time period within which to apply for benefits under a redress should be relatively lengthy. Out-of-time applicants should not

> I just couldn't put down on paper the details of the sexual abuse I suffered.
>
> *Quoted in The Vision to Reconcile: Process Report on the Helpline Reconciliation Model Agreement by Doug Roche and Ben Hoffman, at p.22*

> I've been keeping silent for 44 years. I joined Helpline to stop the abuse of children. I have confidence in you. I have no confidence in the Church.
>
> *Quoted in The Vision to Reconcile: Process Report on the Helpline Reconciliation Model Agreement by Doug Roche and Ben Hoffman, at p.22*

have their claims automatically dismissed without at least a summary inquiry into the reasons for the delay.

Another important factor to consider in setting the claim period is that survivors may wish to consider their other options before deciding whether to participate in a redress program that closes off some of those options. Not all possible options will necessarily be clear when a program is first offered. Courts are continually developing the law as it relates both to the types of harm that are compensable, and the responsibility of organisations that may have sponsored institutions for abuse committed by employees of the institution. In addition, it may take a certain time before a number of procedural questions relating to a potential lawsuit are sorted out. This has been an issue for former residents of the Jericho Hill School, for example, where the period to apply for benefits under the Jericho Individual Compensation Program expired before the viability of a contemplated class action was determined.[27]

h.   Administration

Who administers a redress program is another central design component that must be determined at the outset. It is often the case that the funding body also takes primary responsibility for administering a program. One difficulty with this arrangement is the perception of a potential conflict of interest that it generates. Another is that it requires the survivors, once again, to place their trust for an important aspect of their lives in the hands of the same body that they assert betrayed that trust at one time. These difficulties can be resolved or minimised in a number of ways.

Where the redress program has been established through extensive negotiations, a level of trust can be built between the survivors and those acting on behalf of the government, church or other body offering redress. Furthermore, if those involved in the negotiations remain involved in the administration of the program, the problem of trust may be largely overcome. In the Grandview case, for example, the Ontario government formed a small team to work with survivors during the negotiations and beyond. Continuity is therefore an important part of effective administration, both from a practical and from a human point of view.

Another option is to set up an independent body at arm's length from the funder to administer the program. Although this does not seem to have been tried yet with any redress program, the idea is not entirely novel. Arm's-length bodies do administer certain social services for survivors or their communities. For example, the government of British Columbia provides funding for the Deaf, Hard of Hearing and Deaf-Blind Well-Being Program, which delivers mental health services through the Greater Vancouver Mental Health Service Society. Again, funding for community initiatives related to healing in Aboriginal communities is provided by the federal government but administered by the arm's-length Aboriginal Healing Foundation.

Where a survivors' group maintains a link with those administering the program, it can serve as a conduit for information to survivors. This may alleviate some of the problems in administration, and strengthen the credibility of those charged with administering the program. Generally, though, survivors' groups have quite limited resources. To be most useful, both to survivors and to those managing a redress program, they require ongoing support for their work, whether through direct funding or through infrastructure assistance, or both.

3.   Assessment

Overview

Redress programs offer all the latitude required to engage survivors and to treat them with respect. These programs are set up specifically to respond to the needs of survivors, and both their design and delivery will normally reflect that fact. So will the negotiation process through which they are established.

Fact-finding in the legal sense is usually not an essential component or primary goal of a redress program. While the validation process does serve to verify the abuse for which former residents are seeking redress, the process will frequently be private and confidential. Similarly, while the claims process may reveal that certain people perpetrated abuse, no public accounting will take place. The establishment of a redress program, funded by those who were responsible for the institution, is in itself a form of institutional accountability and acknowledgement, although the program itself will not point the finger at individual abusers.

One goal of a redress program may be to establish an historical record by receiving and collecting the experiences of survivors. Another may be to determine how certain policies and practices came to be tolerated. This type of fact-finding may be a feature of redress programs.

The fairness of a given redress program will depend largely on the validation process. A redress program should be considered fair to survivors where its validation process is based on objective, consistent and relevant criteria. As long as adjudicators are carefully selected and the validation is agreed upon in advance, the process is also fair to those who fund the program. Employees and former employees of institutions may, however, feel that the private nature of the process and their exclusion from it means that the process is not fair to them.

Redress programs generally include acknowledgement and apologies – public and collective, private and individual, or both. If a redress program is designed to combine material and spiritual benefits, and is administered in a manner sensitive to the needs of survivors, it can be an effective vehicle for promoting reconciliation. These programs have the flexibility and scope necessary to provide for a wide range of survivors' needs, including money, therapeutic services, education and medical benefits. They can also be designed to address a variety of needs felt by families, communities and even peoples.

The capacity of a redress program to serve the goals of public education and prevention also depends on its design. If its processes are not public, the experiences related by survivors cannot serve to educate others about the scope and scale of abuse suffered. Nonetheless, the very existence of a redress program is a public recognition that harms were done to children in institutions, and that in itself may serve to promote prevention efforts.

a. Respect, engagement and informed choice

Redress programs are the most open-ended option for survivors, having no predetermined rules or limits as to what they can offer. They are created expressly to resolve the claims of those who suffered harm as children in institutions. Respect for former residents should be a cornerstone of all redress programs. How can such respect be measured? An awareness of the needs and the particular sensibilities of survivors should be demonstrably reflected in the design of the process and the manner in which it is delivered.

From a procedural perspective, respect in the design of a redress program can be gauged by answering questions such as:

- To what extent were former residents involved in the design of the program?

- Was there a concerted effort made to inform former residents of the existence of a program, and to explain its key points?

- Were resources provided so that survivors could form their own support group to provide input into the development of the program and support each other through the redress process?[28]

- Were the survivors able to consult with those who have been involved in other redress programs, to get an idea of what elements of the program proved successful, and which proved problematic?

From a substantive perspective, the crucial determinants of how well the process respects survivors are:

- Do the benefits offered relate closely to the needs expressed?

- Is the compensation offered proportionate to the harm done?

- Are those conducting the validation process familiar with the particular circumstances of child abuse survivors?

- How are survivors treated throughout the application and validation processes, and in the delivery of benefits?

The extent to which survivors are involved in, or at least aware of, the development of a redress program will affect their ability to make an informed decision as to whether they wish to participate in the program or not. This is important because usually, participation in a redress program is conditional on the claimant agreeing, in a legally binding way, not to sue those responsible for the institution where they claim they were abused. Informed choice depends on a person's ability to assess the risks and benefits of one option over another. The more involved former residents have been in the design of a program as it is being developed, the better chance they have of making a truly informed decision. It is worth noting that even where survivors are engaged in the establishment of a redress program and have their own legal representatives, they may still feel disempowered. Study panel members and others indicated to the Law Commission that even those who seek to help survivors may be convinced that they know best about what choices survivors should make. Whatever good intentions may lie behind it, this attitude is the last thing survivors need. It is certainly not a reflection of true respect.

b.   Fact-finding

A redress program is meant to be a clear alternative to proceedings before courts. It is intended to focus on helping survivors, without making this help dependent on the complex process of assigning legal fault. Consequently, fact-finding about individual cases is not a primary goal of a redress program, at least not in the precise way that goal is pursued in a civil or criminal action.

Some fact-finding is, however, essential to the validation of a claim for redress. To be credible, a redress program must be able to substantiate the accuracy of the claims submitted. There are diverse ways to achieve this goal. For example, in the process designed for former students of the Sir James Whitney School for the Deaf, a research consultant investigated all sources of information available to validate the claim.

This type of fact-finding has a very specific and, in a sense, private purpose. Its aim is to verify the legitimacy of the claim of an individual survivor. Once that is done, or once a claim has been accepted, the factual basis on which it has been accepted does not become a matter of public record. Details of individual claims and awards are kept confidential. This is necessary because redress programs are designed to be non-adversarial. This means that the alleged perpetrators of abuse do not have an opportunity to counter the allegations, because the basis for compensation is the evidence of harm done, not the identification of the wrongdoer.

While fact-finding occurs, it does not necessarily serve to expand the public understanding of what occurred in a particular institution, why it occurred or who was responsible for it. A final report, in the nature of those written at the end of public inquiries, containing conclusions and recommendations, is not necessarily a part of a redress program. But, where it is, the process can provide as complete a picture as an Ombudsman investigation or a public inquiry.

Some redress programs do provide for the publication of a recorder's report. The preparation of a recorder's report cannot strictly be considered a fact-finding exercise. It is simply a gathering and recording of experiences. The purpose is not to verify the factual accuracy of the memories recounted, but to accept them as offered and to preserve them. Also, these reports are intended primarily for the former residents of the particular institution to which they relate. The reports are not widely published and distributed, so they do not really serve to advance public awareness or understanding of what took place. On their own, they cannot serve as historically accurate accounts of the events at an institution, even if they were more generally available.

c.   Accountability

With respect to fact-finding, redress programs are not designed to name names and hold specific individuals to account for specific instances of abuse. In fact, redress programs may be seen as a way to set aside the difficult issues involved in assigning individual accountability in favour of providing compensation on a collective basis. In such cases, a redress program reflects a choice by the organisation that administered or funded an institution for children to compensate survivors of abuse at that institution without admitting legal liability or requiring proof of the legal liability of specific perpetrators. Therefore, while the redress program does not assign accountability to individuals as part of its process, its very existence represents a form of institutional accountability.

It is possible to design a redress program that provides an opportunity for perpetrators, co-workers who knew of the abuse, or even administrators and supervisors of institutions to come forward publicly to acknowledge their responsibility. In this sense, the program would have characteristics similar to those of a truth commission, without the feature of amnesty. While voluntary acknowledgements may not be common in the absence of immunity from prosecution, it might prove to be therapeutic if an abuser has already decided to plead guilty to a criminal charge. They can also be meaningful in the case of co-workers and supervisors who failed to denounce abuse of which they were aware.

d.   Fairness

A redress program awards compensation and benefits to those whose claims have been validated. Invariably, this validation process is not adversarial. In other words, claimants do not have to personally confront those whom they allege abused them.

The absence of alleged perpetrators from redress programs has caused a concern about the fairness of these programs. Persons associated with the institutions where abuse is alleged to have occurred have protested, in some cases, that their reputations are being undermined through a process which allows them no opportunity to counter the allegations that have been made. To put it simply, they do not have an opportunity to tell their side of the story. How damaging is this to the legitimacy of redress programs?

Redress programs do not balance the interests of all parties in the way that civil and criminal processes do because they do not have the same purpose as those processes. No individual will be convicted of a crime or ordered to pay damages as a result of a redress program. It is true that redress is based on a claim of wrongdoing, and where that claim alleges physical or sexual abuse, it must be based on an allegation against an individual wrongdoer. That alleged wrongdoer does not then have an opportunity to respond to the allegation.

There is a trade-off, however. The redress process is confidential. The alleged perpetrator does not have an opportunity to reply, but neither is he or she called to account or made legally liable for the wrongs he or she is alleged to have committed. [29]

One may argue that the reputation of those who were employees at these institutions is tarnished by the fact of a redress program. There are two aspects of this concern. First, totally innocent employees may have no way of publicly clearing their names. Second, employees collectively have no way of refuting general allegations. To a large extent, however, this is unavoidable. The reputations of an institution and its former employees are tarnished once widespread allegations of abuse emerge, whether or not there have been criminal convictions or judgements in civil actions. The public judges much more rapidly and harshly than the courts, and does so regardless of the existence of a redress program. Recovering from allegations that may never be proven (or disproven) is a big hurdle for institutions as well as individuals.

The fairness that operates in a redress program is a kind of collective fairness. It says, "harms were done to innocent children – we will provide redress for those harms", without further burdening victims with the rigours of a civil action. In turn, they will accept lesser compensation than that to which they may be entitled under the law. Redress programs should be considered fair when they incorporate a validation process that is based on objective, consistent and relevant criteria. Fairness in our society does not begin and end with the adversarial processes of civil courts.

e.   Acknowledgement, apology and reconciliation

The offer of financial compensation or benefits through a redress program is a concrete acknowledgement of moral, if not legal, responsibility for harms done to children and youth in institutional care. Many survivors want acknowledgement in more than a material form, however. While the awarding of compensation and benefits is clearly important to survivors, compensation without an explicit acknowledgement of the wrongs that were done and a specific apology will not be seen as satisfactory by most.

Redress programs to date have generally involved the offer of an apology. There are many different types of apologies. They may be given to survivors, their families and whole communities. They may be addressed to individual survivors or to an entire group of survivors. Private apologies, addressed to individuals or their families, may be in a standard format or may recognise specific acts committed by particular individuals.[30] The specific language of public apologies, addressed to groups of survivors, groups of families, communities and peoples is usually, although not always, negotiated.

Redress programs are well-suited to eliciting apologies. How well they are suited to promoting reconciliation will depend upon a number of factors, both tangible and intangible. The desire for reconciliation must be sincere, and it must be mutual. In order to be able to promote reconciliation, those offering redress must overcome the distrust and often the cynicism of former residents of these institutions. A redress program that responds to key survivor needs may pave the path to reconciliation.

The path can be smooth or rocky. For example, did survivors have to fight long and hard to get recognition and compensation, or was the group in charge of their institution amenable to the idea of compensation from the outset? Was it the initiative of the institution, or those responsible for it, to offer compensation? Did the compensation and benefits offered, and the process for obtaining them, demonstrate sensitivity to the key issues and needs of survivors? A program that scores well on these and similar questions has a better chance of promoting reconciliation than one which, though possibly well-intentioned, puts the interests of the organisation over those of the survivors.

f.   Compensation, counselling and education

The particular content of redress programs is usually negotiated between survivors and those responsible for an institution. They are open-ended and can provide any form of benefits or compensation. The only constraints on them are the creative and financial resources of those funding the program and their moral and political will. Redress programs clearly can meet survivors' needs for financial compensation for pain and suffering and for other monetary benefits. But they are also suited to providing for other needs of survivors. As a number of redress programs have demonstrated, a variety of services may be offered: different types of therapy, various forms of counselling (financial, educational), training (vocational, life skills), benefits transferable to family members, medical and dental benefits (such as scar reduction surgery), and support for survivor groups.

Almost all survivors share some of these needs. Others may relate more directly to the needs of particular groups of survivors. For example, former residents of Grandview wanted the costs of tattoo removal to be covered. Aboriginal survivors may want counselling from traditional Aboriginal healers, or instruction in an Aboriginal language. Deaf survivors may want more therapists to be trained in American Sign Language or Langue des signes québécoise, so that they can receive counselling without the need for an interpreter. Redress programs have the flexibility and scope necessary to respond to these needs, subject only to financial constraints and the priorities or objectives of the program.

g.   Needs of families, communities and peoples

A redress program can be designed to address the needs of families, for the same reasons and within the same constraints as set out above. This can occur in two ways. The claims process may be broad enough to permit claims by family members directly for specific harms they have suffered. If these claims are validated, family members can receive awards in their own right. Another approach is to allow survivors to transfer certain of their own non-monetary benefits to members of their family, if they so choose. Therapy, training and educational benefits are those most likely to be transferred.

Where an affected community can be defined with some precision, a redress program could offer services to the community as a whole. For example, it could provide the funding for a community wellness program, offering a variety of counselling services, and be accessible to all members of the community, not just survivors. Such an approach makes sense in a community where many people, across generations, directly or indirectly, have suffered as a result of abuse in institutions for children. Examples of programs like this can be found in the list of programs that received funding in 1999 from the Aboriginal Healing Foundation, or in others undertaken following the uncovering of abuse in an institution.

How well are redress programs able to address the needs of Aboriginal peoples with respect to issues arising out of abuse at residential schools? Again, nothing prohibits a program from being designed to address needs on a collective rather than an individual scale. However, it is difficult to assess and to address the needs of Aboriginal peoples in their collective capacity. Acknowledgement and apologies can be given collectively. A redress program may also involve a commitment to record and analyse the residential school experience. But other needs may be best met on a community-by-community basis.

Part of the difficulty is that redress programs are usually tied to particular institutions, and therefore aim at rectifying the harms done at those institutions. Only a program designed to redress the harms of residential schools generally can hope to meet the needs of all Aboriginal peoples. This is, in fact, the rationale underlying the creation of the Aboriginal Healing Foundation. Rather than selecting the form of redress itself, the federal government has left it up to an arm's-length Aboriginal organisation to decide what community programs to fund.

h. Prevention and public education

Redress programs are generally not well-publicised outside the community of former residents for whom they are designed. The validation processes, unlike in criminal and civil trials, are not public events. The individual awards themselves remain confidential, with only the ranges being made public.

As an exercise in public education, redress programs may have only a limited value. The fact that such a program is established sends a message to the public. It means that the funding organisation has recognised that harms were committed against innocent children and that there is a duty to help them heal, even decades after the abuse occurred.

Redress programs to date have generally not dealt with prevention explicitly. One could say that the mere fact of having a government or other body make the public gesture of acknowledging the harm that was done in an institution for which it was responsible may well lead to measures being taken to prevent a recurrence of such events. Unlike Ombudsman investigations, children's advocates offices, public inquiries, and truth commissions, redress programs usually do not have a research and recommendation component. Recommendations on how to avoid a recurrence of abuse emerge, if at all, from the efforts of those who are funded under a community-based benefit included as part of a redress program.

4.   Conclusion

The Commission views redress programs as only one of several options available to survivors of institutional child abuse. They are not a perfect solution. But given the wide diversity of circumstances and needs of survivors, negotiated redress programs offer the best opportunity to meet these needs while respecting the other goals that any approach to providing redress must pay attention. This said, the situation of different groups of survivors are simply too diverse to be satisfied by any single template for redress programs.

One of the main attractions of redress programs, for all parties, is that they are meant to be more expeditious, less costly (both for claimant and for compensator) and less emotionally difficult for survivors than established legal procedures. Because they can be designed and administered on a case-by-case basis, they have the capacity to respond to a greater range of needs and a wider category of victims than do the civil and criminal justice processes.

To be successful, redress programs must be carefully planned to respond to the particular needs of the survivors they are intended to serve.[31] Equally, they must be fiscally responsible and realistic, particularly where they are funded through the public purse. With the experiences of past redress programs as guides, institutions, governments and survivors should now be in a position to fashion responsive and responsible redress programs that can be supported by all affected parties and by the public.

Recommendations

A REDRESS PROGRAM should be designed with input from the group it is intended to benefit.

Considerations:

The most credible form of input is negotiation directly with former residents or their representatives.

The circumstances of negotiations should ensure, to the extent possible, that the former residents are on an equal footing with those offering redress. It may also involve funding a survivors' group so that information is disseminated to as many former residents as possible, and they are aware of the progress of negotiations. This should involve ensuring that this group has the means to hire the professional help they require, if they choose, to assist in the negotiations. This may include lawyers, interpreters or others such as survivors from other institutions who former residents feel they need.

Disseminating this information would enable survivors to provide their views to those negotiating on their behalf.

A REDRESS PROGRAM should offer compensation and benefits that respond to the full range of survivors' needs.

Considerations:

In institutions where physical or sexual abuse was pervasive, residents may have suffered psychological and emotional damage as a result, even if they themselves were not victims of such abuse.

In institutions where the culture of the resident population was consistently undermined (*e.g.* in certain residential schools for Aboriginal children or certain schools for Deaf children), residents may have suffered long-term harms as a result.

Deprivation of an adequate education should also be considered as a basis for redress.

REDRESS PROGRAMS should offer a wider range of benefits than those available through the courts or administrative tribunals.

Considerations:

Survivors may require support in the form of services as much as they require financial compensation.

The categories of benefits or services which may be offered through a redress program should not be considered closed. Survivors should have the opportunity of receiving those benefits which are best suited to their needs.

Redress programs should be flexible about how they distribute benefits. The program itself need not provide the benefits directly, but may simply be willing to fund a variety of services in the community so long as they are directly related to survivors' needs.

FAMILY MEMBERS should be entitled to certain benefits of a redress program.

Considerations:

Where a family member has suffered harm as a result of the abuse of a relative in an institution, he or she should be entitled to receive reasonable compensation or to participate in certain of the benefits offered to survivors, in particular, therapy or counselling.

Survivors should also have the option of transferring benefits such as education benefits to a family member.

BEST EFFORTS should be made to contact as many former residents as possible to inform them of the redress program in a timely fashion, while respecting their privacy.

Considerations:

Outreach efforts should protect the privacy of former residents by avoiding direct approaches, for example, through the mail.

General outreach (*i.e.* notices and advertisements) can target settings where survivors are likely to see them, for example, wherever mental health services are provided, Aboriginal friendship centres, community groups, continuing education institutions.

Former residents serving time in prison should be given an equal opportunity to participate in redress programs – outreach to the prison population should therefore be undertaken, and accommodation made to enable prisoners to present their claims. The information provided in outreach letters or advertisements should be in clear and accessible language.

Verbal outreach (*e.g.* via radio or a toll-free 1-800 number) is as important as written communication.

Outreach should commence well in advance of the program itself, to allow former residents the time needed to consider their options and to maximise the number of claimants who apply within the set period.

THE CLAIMS PERIOD should be designed to ensure that the maximum number of claimants has an opportunity to apply.

Considerations:

A claims period should be set for a realistic duration, and should not be terminated prematurely.

Termination of a claims period should only occur with reasonable notice.

A REDRESS PROGRAM must be based on a clear and credible validation process.

Considerations:

The focus of the validation process should be on establishing what harms were suffered at the institution, the effects of those harms, and the appropriate level of compensation.

The standard of proof required should be commensurate with the benefits offered.

Those determining the validity of claims should be impartial decision makers. Members of adjudication panels should have the appropriate professional background, training or life experience to recognise the harms of institutional child abuse. They should have experience with a compensation process, rather than only a fault-finding process.

The onus should be on those organising the redress program to corroborate, to the extent possible, the experiences recounted by those claiming compensation. All possible sources of corroboration should be canvassed, including institutional archives, school performance and attendance records, contemporaneous medical, social service or police reports, and the verdicts of criminal proceedings, if any.

THE ADMINISTRATION OF A REDRESS PROGRAM should have the confidence of both funders and beneficiaries.

Considerations:

Where possible, those administering a program should be independent of those funding it.

An attempt should be made to assure continuity in the administration of the program, both for the sake of efficiency and to facilitate the development of a relationship of trust with survivors.

Adjudication panels should have some members whose backgrounds reflect the backgrounds of the claimants.

BEST PRACTICES IN REDRESS PROGRAMS should be assembled by an independent body, such as a university department or research institute, for the benefits of society as a whole, as well as survivors.

Considerations:

Programs to train survivors or their representatives in the negotiation of redress programs should be established.

Those who negotiate on behalf of governments or churches should also receive training or have knowledge about the circumstances and effects of institutional child abuse.

THERE SHOULD BE A PLACE (OR PLACES) where those who lived in institutions can record their experiences and where historical materials concerning these institutions can be gathered.

Considerations:

The recording of experiences could be done in a variety of formats – tape-recorded conversations, interviews, monologues, original artwork, photographs, written remembrances, videotapes, *etc.* Contributions need not be limited to experiences of abuse, but could include all recollections of life in an institution.

Contributions could come from individuals, groups, and/or communities.

Procedures should be in place to ensure that no allegations or accusations are made against named or identifiable individuals. Where such allegations or accusations are made, they should be deleted or expunged.

---

1   In the Discussion Paper that preceded this report, the Law Commission referred to the potential of approaches that it labelled "restorative programs". See Law Commission of Canada, *Minister's Reference on Institutional Child Abuse* (Discussion Paper) (Ottawa: Law Commission of Canada, December 1998) at 38-40. Available in hard copy from the Law Commission of Canada and online: <http://www.lcc.gc.ca>. Upon further consideration, the Commission is of the view that the term "redress program" more accurately describes the approach to redress discussed in this section.

2   They may however be affected by the requirements of legislation. For example, claimants who are on social assistance and receive a financial compensation award may have their social assistance benefits reduced by a corresponding amount, unless such awards are specifically excluded in the social assistance legislation.

3   See, for example, *Inquiries Act*, R.S.C. 1985, c. I-4. As experience is gained with redress programs in various situations, it may be opportune to contemplate general framework legislation of this kind.

4   Note that no redress program was ever implemented in respect of the survivors of the first, ground-breaking large case of child abuse in an institution – the case of Mount Cashel. The Hughes Inquiry did recommend the establishment

of such a program, but the recommendations were not followed. See Newfoundland, *Report on the Royal Commission of Inquiry into the Response of the Newfoundland Criminal Justice System to Complaints* (St. John's: Queen's Printer, 1991) (Commissioner: The Hon. S.H.S. Hughes) at 33-4.

5 As was the case with Martin Kruze and his experiences at Maple Leaf Gardens.

6 Such as, New Brunswick, *Report of the Commission of Inquiry Established by Order-in-Council 92-1022* (New Brunswick: Attorney General, 17 February, 1995) (Chair: The Hon. Richard L. Miller); Nova Scotia, *Report of an Independent Investigation in Respect of Incidents and Allegations of Sexual and Other Physical Abuse at Five Nova Scotia Residential Institutions* (Halifax: Ministry of Justice, 1995) (President: The Hon. Stuart G. Stratton); and T. Berger, *Report of the Special Counsel regarding claims Arising out of Sexual Abuse at Jericho Hill School* (Victoria: B.C. Ombudsman, 1995).

7 Ombudsman of British Columbia, *Abuse of Deaf Students at Jericho Hill School: Report No. 32* (Victoria: B.C. Ombudsman, 1993).

8 The Family Service Centre of Ottawa-Carleton is responsible for providing counselling services under the *Helpline Reconciliation Model Agreement*, Between Helpline, The Ottawa Brothers, The Toronto Brothers, The St. John's Training School of Boys, The Archdiocese of Toronto, The Archdiocese of Ottawa and the Government of Ontario (unpublished, 1992) [hereinafter Helpline Agreement]. The Centre reports having counselled 91 families or family members (Communication from the Family Service Centre of Ottawa-Carleton (25 June 1999)).

9 Berger, *supra* note 6.

10 The text of the "Pastoral Letter" of April 21, 1996 is contained in Appendix B to *Reconciliation: An Ongoing Process, RPIC Chairman's Personal Report* by D. Roche (Ontario: Reconciliation Process Implementation Committee, 30 June 1996).

11 *Grandview Settlement Agreement*, The Grandview Survivors Support Group and The Government of Ontario, 1994 [hereinafter *Grandview Agreement*] at para. 4. 5. 0.

12 *Ibid.* at para. 2. 3. 0.

13 British Columbia, *Jericho Individual Compensation Program: Terms of Reference* (Victoria: Ministry of the Attorney General, 15 November 1996) at 8 para 16.

14 M.L. Mussell, *In The Spirit of Healing – Recorder's Report Written for the Survivors*, a report prepared for the Reconciliation Implementation Committee – Reconciliation Agreement between: The Primary Victims of Epoch and the Jesuit Fathers of Upper Canada (place of publication unknown: October 1995).

[15] B.C. Hoffman, *The Search for Healing, Reconciliation and the Promise of Prevention – The Recorder's Report Concerning Physical and Sexual Abuse at St. Joseph's and St. John's Training Schools for Boys*, a report prepared for the Reconciliation Process Implementation Committee, Ontario (place of publication unknown: Concorde Inc., 30 September 1995) [hereinafter *Hoffman*].

[16] *Until Someone Listens: Recovery from Institutional Abuse*, produced for the Grandview Survivors Support Group (Toronto: Laura Sky and Skyworks Charitable Foundation, 1999) 120 mins; L. Sky & V. Sparks, *Until Someone Listens* (Work Book) (Toronto: Skyworks Charitable Foundation, 1999).

[17] *Jericho Walls of Silence* (Vancouver: Glynis Whiting and Agnes Wilson – Jericho Productions Inc., 1999). This independent production was first aired on CBC's *Witness* (18 February 1999). The documentary was not part of the B.C. government's redress program in respect of Jericho Hill, but is mentioned here as another example of how the experiences of survivors may be preserved.

[18] Examples of memorials are described above in Part I.D.a. "Establishing a historical record; remembrance".

[19] British Columbia, *Jericho Individual Compensation Program: Terms of Reference* (Victoria: Ministry of the Attorney General, 15 November 1996) at 7.

[20] *Supra*, note 11 at para. 4.2.6.

[21] For example, some former employees of the Nova Scotia School for Boys who said the allegations concerning them were false, took polygraph tests and lobbied the Nova Scotia Government to have input into a review of the Government's compensation program. See "Letters clear some accused of abuse" *Canadian Press Wire Service* (25 June 1998), online: QL (CPN) and "Jail employees call for investigation" *Canadian Press Wire Service* (20 September 1998), online: QL (CPN). See also discussion under "Fairness" in the Assessment Section, *infra*.

[22] Occasionally the validation process is not even negotiated. In the *Eighth Report of the Provisional Liquidator* of the affairs of the Christian Brothers of Ireland in Canada, (May 31, 1991), the liquidator recommended the establishing of a claims procedure in which the standard of proof would lie between a *prima facie* case and a civil balance of probabilities (para. 25) and in which a psychologist would review the Statutory Declarations of each claimant and conduct personal interviews (para. 38).

[23] British Columbia, *Residential Historical Abuse Program* (pamphlet) (Victoria: Ministry of Health, revised October 1996).

24 The Jericho Individual Compensation Program Compensation Panel is composed of two lawyers and one therapist. See Law Commission of Canada, *Redress Programs Relating to Institutional Child Abuse in Canada* by G. Shea (Ottawa: Law Commission of Canada, 1999) at 11. Available in hard copy from the Law Commission of Canada and online: <http://www.lcc.gc.ca>.

25 Awards made to Groups 1 and 2 under the St. John's and St. Joseph's Helpline Agreement were adjudicated by persons seconded from Ontario's Criminal Injuries Compensation Board. See *Helpline Agreement*, *supra* note 8 at para. 4.0 and Shea, *ibid*. at 37.

26 In New Brunswick this was done by lawyers of the provincial Department of Justice. See Shea, *supra* note 24 at Section 5.

27 The deadline for applications was September 30,1998. Some former students preserved their options by filing applications before the deadline was set to expire but did not sign releases to renounce their right of action and to receive compensation. Many others opted to receive compensation and renounce their right of action, even though the certification of the class action had not yet been determined. See L. Hill, "Enough is Enough – Report on a Facilitated Discussion Group Involving the Deaf Community Responding to the Minister's Reference on Institutional Child Abuse" (March 1999). [unpublished research report archived at Law Commission of Canada].

28 Their input need not be determinative – the party or parties offering compensation have their own constraints to consider: financial, legal, perhaps even political. After all, the broader the support for a redress program and the more affordable it is, the more durable the program.

29 See *supra* note 21.

30 For example, the *Helpline Agreement*, *supra* note 8, allowed former students of St. John's and St. Joseph's to state what they wanted their personal apology to contain.

31 Sometimes it will even be necessary to undertake an extensive negotiation process simply to set a framework within which individual redress programs might then be negotiated. For an example see *Guiding Principles for Working Together to Build Restoration and Reconciliation* (September 14, 1999), a document resulting from a series of eight exploratory dialogues held between September 1998 and May 1999 among survivors of residential schools attended by Aboriginal children, Aboriginal leaders and healers, counsel, and senior officials within government and church organisations.

L. Maintaining a Diversity of Approaches to Providing Redress

The Law Commission believes that the values and principles set out in the first section of this Part must be respected in the design and operation of processes for providing redress to survivors of institutional child abuse. This applies to any new approaches that are created or any existing processes that are chosen by survivors. Above all else, approaches to redress are the instruments through which a society puts into practice its ideals and aspirations.

The various sections of this Part have evaluated the strengths and weaknesses of processes available for redressing the harms caused by institutional child abuse. To guide its analysis, the Law Commission developed eight criteria of assessment (as discussed in Section A: Criteria of Assessment, Approaches to Redress, and Guiding Principles) – reflecting its best judgement of the most relevant standards for determining the appropriateness or adequacy of any given process. These criteria address the substantive needs of survivors; procedural considerations relating to fairness for all parties; the interests of families, communities and peoples; and societal needs for reconciliation, education and prevention.

None of the existing approaches evaluated by the Commission fully met all of these standards. But every process had something positive to offer in one or more respects. In view of these differing strengths, and the diversity of the individual needs and preferences of survivors, the Commission does not recommend the adoption of a single, obligatory approach to redress. While new approaches should be found or created, it is also important to maintain, strengthen, and support existing recourses available to adult survivors of child abuse. This is why the Commission has made several recommendations about how existing legal processes might be improved so as to respond more effectively to the needs of adult survivors of institutional child abuse, while still preserving fundamental principles of procedural fairness for alleged wrongdoers.

But there are limits to how much procedural adjustment can be undertaken with a view to making existing judicial and administrative processes more responsive to the needs of survivors. Often an existing process reveals its limitations not so much in its detail, but in its assumptions and its goals. No amount of tinkering can turn an adversarial process into one that is driven by therapeutic considerations or the goal of reconciliation. No amount of tinkering can turn an investigatory and recommendatory process into one that provides enforceable remedies. No amount of tinkering can turn a process intended to declare a witness and a loser into one that accommodates several competing interests. And no amount of tinkering can turn a process meant simply to resolve a conflict between individuals into one that focusses primarily on building or rebuilding communities.

These realizations lie behind contemporary efforts to develop other approaches to redress such as children's advocates and commissions and truth and reconciliation processes. The former seek to meet the needs of children today; of the several needs identified by survivors, they address only prevention and public education. The latter puts the therapeutic needs of communities into the spot-light, even at the risk of not meeting other, non-therapeutic needs of survivors and their families. Depending on the nature, extent, duration and location of the abuse and the period of time when it took place, each can be an appropriate approach to redressing at least some of the harm suffered. But like current judicial and administrative approaches, neither has the capacity to meet a broad range of survivors' needs.

Two approaches to redress do, however, have this potential: community initiatives and redress programs. They reflect two complementary ways to nurture institutions that are grounded in, and reflect, community involvement. Both stress diversity and pluralism.

The engine of the former is the local community. Community-generated initiatives are an essential component of social life in any liberal democratic society. The Law Commission believes that governments should not attempt to monopolise approaches to redress. Grassroots programs that recognise and respond to the harms caused by institutional child abuse should be encouraged, promoted and funded.

Redress programs, by contrast, are official responses to survivors' needs negotiated with groups and communities. They are the official response that can be most effectively designed to meet the complete range of goals that have been identified. Negotiating a series of focussed redress programs should be a preferred approach. The Law Commission believes that redress programs would be an effective complement to existing legal approaches.

The Law Commission does not, however, favour adopting a single or an exclusive official approach. It supports various efforts to better accommodate the needs of survivors within traditional legal processes. But it also supports community initiatives and redress programs that move beyond traditional responses. In particular, it believes that establishing comprehensive and credible redress programs is the best investment of time and energy for those who seek to respond to the individual and collective needs of survivors and their communities.

Part III – Commitments

A. Prevention

The Commission's assessment of various possible responses to institutional child abuse has revealed that, with the exception of children's advocates and commissions and (if designed with this goal in mind) community initiatives and redress programs, they have a limited capacity to satisfy survivors' and society's needs for ongoing prevention. Processes to redress a harm are by nature reactive; they respond to wrongs that have already been committed. Effective prevention strategies must be proactive as well as reactive; they must be able to produce systemic changes.

The Commission recognises both the importance that survivors attach to prevention and the high social costs engendered by inadequate safeguards against institutional child abuse. It believes that the abuse of children in out-of-home care settings continues to this day. As a result, it interprets the Minister's letter as having invited it to also examine the information and knowledge, social values, objectives, strategies and measures that underpin frameworks to prevent child abuse.

Two questions structure the Commission's inquiry. First, do Canadians have enough information and knowledge about the abuse of children and youth in today's institutions to enable them to develop suitable prevention mechanisms? Second, how can the existing frameworks and strategies designed to protect children and youth from abuse be improved in order to provide better protection against all of the types of abuse that can arise in out-of-home care settings? While the following discussion begins by assessing the existing information base, the Commission acknowledges, indeed insists, that stopping child abuse is not so much a question of knowledge as it is a question of will.

1. The Information Base

As Canadians became more aware of child abuse in the 1960s and '70s, both the public and policy-makers began to ask: "Is this new? Is it getting worse? Or is it just that we are finally recognising it?"[1] Similarly, in the 1980s and '90s, as more and more adults came forward with stories of abuse they had suffered years or decades ago in institutions, the public and policy-makers also began to wonder: Is this type of abuse still happening today? Is the abuse different than in the past? Is it more, or less widespread? Asking these questions, in a manner directed to understanding the scope and scale of abuse, is an important part of the process of deciding how to deal with or prevent it. Unfortunately, Canadians do not have a very complete picture of who the children living in today's institutions are, much less the nature and kinds of actual and potential abuse that they face.

Children and youth placed in out-of-home care today live mainly in foster and group homes. Others reside in young offender facilities, facilities for children with disabilities, mental health centres, private boarding schools, orphanages and hospitals.[2] In Ontario, it was recently estimated that 16,000 children and youth are in some form of out-of-home care at any one time.[3] No one knows all the types of out-of-home placements for Canadian children, or how many children reside in them.[4]

Furthermore, there is no Canada-wide bank of information that provides data on the abuse of children and youth in out-of-home care settings. There is also no networking system between provincial infor-mation banks in place. Each province and territory determines how to collect its data on child abuse and neglect. Because these data are extracted from systems developed to meet the particular priorities and needs of each jurisdiction, they are not generally comparable.[5]

Since the criminal law enforcement system is invoked only in serious cases of physical and sexual abuse, it is mainly the provincial and territorial child welfare systems that monitor and intervene in cases of child abuse and neglect. These child welfare systems were originally designed to protect children and youth from abuse in the home and to remove them from their homes, if necessary, to ensure their safety.

Although child protection laws have been extended over the years, their primary focus remains on abuse arising in the home and family environment, not institutional settings.[6] In a few jurisdictions, provincial child protection laws only encompass cases of neglect and abuse by parents or guardians.[7]

The focus of provincial and territorial child welfare systems reflects society's understanding of child abuse. The physical abuse of children was recognised as a social problem in the 1960s. Measures to provide greater protection to children against physical abuse, for example through the introduction of mandatory reporting laws in the mid- to late-'60s, were followed in the 1970s and '80s by the growing recognition of child sexual abuse as another harm facing children and youth.[8]

Awareness of child abuse was partly a by-product of the efforts of feminists to obtain recognition of abuse as stemming from the vulnerability and lack of power of dependent women and children. Child abuse came to be seen as part of a category of pathologies referred to as "family violence" or "domestic violence".[9]

Because child abuse entered public consciousness as a problem that exists in families, efforts to understand and deal with it have centred on the family environment. This manner of framing the problem has had a negative impact on the empirical data being collected about child abuse in institutions. This information is often peripheral to, or just a by-product of, information being gathered about domestic abuse.[10]

Statistics Canada's annual statistical profile of family violence in Canada illustrates this effect. Since 1998, as part of the federal government's family violence initiative, the Canadian Centre for Justice Statistics has produced an annual report that contains data, based on child welfare and police reports, on incidents of physical and sexual assaults on children. The data include figures for assaults by "non-family" as well as "family" members, but disclose no information about institutional child abuse. They do not reveal whether any of the assaults occurred in institutional care settings.[11] Instances of institutional abuse might be embedded in the data of the family violence profile, but they are not clearly indicated and, therefore, remain invisible.

The same situation holds true for the resources that are available through Health Canada's National Clearing House on Family Violence.

On its website,[12] the Clearing House provides much useful information about child abuse within the family, but offers little data on the abuse of children in other settings. Ironically, one document in the Clearing House's collection is critical of the lack of this type of empirical data:

> Many thousands of children are sexually abused each year within family settings (intra-familial abuse). The British Columbia study suggests that annually across Canada there are thousands of children who are sexually abused outside family settings (extra-familial abuse) and within the context of multiple victim child sexual abuse occurrences discussed in this report. The British Columbia findings underscore the need to document Canadian experiences with these abuses and the prevalence and annual incidence of all forms of child sexual abuse. This critical data would provide the empirical foundation needed to understand the scope of the problem, to enlist the resources necessary to aid communities across Canada in responding effectively to such abuses, and to implement comprehensive strategies to prevent future abuse.[13]

In 1990, Rix Rogers, at that time a special adviser to the Minister of National Health and Welfare, highlighted the need to have an information centre that contains data on all aspects of child abuse. He drew attention to certain populations of children, including those with disabilities and those living in institutions, because they are even more vulnerable than the rest,[14] and recommended the establishment of a national resource centre on child abuse.[15] The federal government responded with a commitment to "strengthen" the services provided by the National Clearing House on Family Violence.[16]

The Law Commission believes that a child-centred approach to gathering information and conducting research related to child abuse and neglect would eliminate the tendency to focus almost exclusively on family settings. It is important to examine and to understand *what* is happening to children and youth, rather than just *where* it is happening. In addition, the Commission believes that a comprehensive and long-term picture of child abuse needs to be created in order to better inform both policy-makers and the public.

> It has become more and more important to be able to look at child abuse and neglect across jurisdictions and over time to try to understand what

demands are made on our response systems, how well these demands are met and what impact our efforts are having.[17]

Tabulating figures on child abuse for the entire country requires significant collaboration and cooperation. The same holds true for the sharing and building of an information base. The Commission sees the Canadian Incidence Study of Reported Child Abuse and Neglect as a commendable model for this type of initiative. Academic researchers from across Canada are working on the study, in collaboration with child welfare agencies in every province and territory, including Aboriginal child welfare agencies. The study addresses four principal types of abuse: physical, sexual, and emotional abuse, as well as neglect. Among other things, its goals are to provide countrywide estimates of the incidence of child abuse and neglect, to improve our understanding of the forms and severity of the abuse, and to collect information that will help to develop programs and policies for at-risk children and youth.[18]

All governments must play a leadership role in the prevention of child abuse by sharing data and building a more child-centred, as opposed to family-centred, knowledge base. Today, much of the research available on the subject of institutional child abuse comes from foreign sources. This research suggests a number of conclusions about the scope and effect of child abuse outside the family setting.[19] The findings include the following:

- The main kinds of abuse arising in institutional settings are emotional and psychological abuse, sexual abuse, physical abuse, neglect (or the failure to meet the basic needs of children), and systems abuse (or the abuse that occurs when the institution itself or the overarching child care systems within which it operates do not function in a child-centred way that respects the dignity, rights and developmental needs of the children).[20]

- The abuse and maltreatment of children in out-of-home care cannot be viewed simply as the acts of aberrant individuals who work with children. Rather it must also be understood as resulting from a number of interrelated program and system factors.[21]

- Young people who have been abused while in care have in common a lack of power or influence, limited knowledge of how the organisation works, little awareness of their rights and how to assert them, and uncertainty about or a reluctance to make complaints regarding those on whom they depend for the basic elements of living.[22]

Children who live in institutions or other out-of-home settings are not a random sample of the general child population. They tend to be in such care either due to prior abuse or neglect at home or because they have certain emotional, behavioural, cognitive or physical difficulties. They all have complex needs and, at the same time, they are the types of children that society seems to devalue the most and care about the least.[23]

These observations suggest that prevention requires addressing a wide range of actions perpetrated by individuals and systems, as well as dealing with issues of education and empowerment, and responding appropriately to children with complex needs. The next section canvasses some of the frameworks and strategies for preventing institutional child abuse.

2. Frameworks and Strategies for Preventing Institutional Child Abuse

Frameworks and strategies for preventing institutional child abuse are either proactive or reactive; both are necessary. Proactive responses consist of a range of measures that aim to prevent, or reduce the risks of abuse. For example, parents and educators may teach children about "good touching" and "bad touching", institutions may carefully screen potential employees, and legislatures may enact laws obliging everyone to report any suspicions of abuse or neglect involving an institutionalised child.

Reactive strategies recognise that appropriate mechanisms must be put in place to deal with abuse when it does arise. For example, independent bodies with power to inquire into any suspicions expressed about abusive practices can be established. These bodies can collaborate with others who share a responsibility for the well-being of children and youth in care.

To establish effective approaches for handling institutional child abuse, however, it is necessary to lay a foundation of clearly stated values and principles that affirm and support children's rights and developmental needs.[24] This suggests that frameworks and strategies for preventing institutional child abuse must have two components: a suitable foundation of values and principles to support these frameworks, and a comprehensive network of proactive measures.

a.   Values and principles

The programs, policies and practices of institutions that care for children are shaped by certain values and principles, whether formally stated in writing or informally communicated by the attitudes and actions of those in control. If they do not reflect the belief that the needs and rights of children are paramount, the best interests of children and youth will always be sacrificed in the interest of others in the system who have more power and influence. For example, in an institution where the administration puts the well-being of children first, a report of suspected child abuse will be acted upon swiftly. Conversely, in the institution where child-centred policies and practices are weak, the administration might decide to put its good reputation or its desire to avoid a public scandal ahead of the well-being of its young charges.

Values and principles must serve as the foundation for effective prevention strategies that affirm the rights and respect the developmental needs and well-being of the children in institutional settings.[25] The United Nations *Convention on the Rights of the Child* is a powerful affirmation of this perspective.[26] Canada ratified the Convention in 1991, and federal, provincial and territorial governments share responsibility for its implementation.[27] Articles 3, 6,19, 25 and 27 are particularly significant for children in care. They declare:

Article 3

1. In all actions concerning children, whether undertaken by public or private social welfare institutions, courts of law, administrative authorities or legislative bodies, the best interests of the child shall be a primary consideration.

2. States Parties undertake to ensure the child such protection and care as is necessary for his or her well-being, ... and, to this end, shall take all appropriate legislative and administrative measures.

3. States Parties shall ensure that the institutions, services and facilities responsible for the care or protection of children shall conform with the standards established by competent authorities, particularly in the areas of safety, health, in the number and suitability of their staff, as well as competent supervision.

Article 6

1. States Parties recognise that every child has the inherent right to life.

2. States Parties shall ensure to the maximum extent possible the survival and development of the child.

Article 19

1. States Parties shall take all appropriate legislative, administrative, social and educational measures to protect the child from all forms of physical or mental violence, injury or abuse, neglect or negligent treatment, maltreatment or exploitation, including sexual abuse, while in the care of parent(s), legal guardian(s) or any other person who has the care of the child.

2. Such protective measures should, as appropriate, include effective procedures for the establishment of social programmes to provide necessary support for the child and for those who have the care of the child, as well as for other forms of prevention and for identification, reporting, referral, investigation, treatment and follow-up of instances of child maltreatment described heretofore, and, as appropriate, for judicial involvement.

Article 25

1. States Parties recognise the right of a child who has been placed by the competent authorities for the purposes of care, protection or treatment of his or her physical or mental health, to a periodic review of the treatment provided to the child and all other circumstances relevant to his or her placement.

Article 27

1. States Parties recognise the right of every child to a standard of living adequate for the child's physical, mental, spiritual, moral and social development.[28]

One way in which governments can honour the values and principles set out in the Convention is to ensure that their laws, programs, policies and actions comply with it. Recent reforms made by the Province of British Columbia to its child welfare system in the wake of the Gove Inquiry are examples of fundamental systemic changes that are consistent with the principles and values espoused by the Convention.

In 1994, following the suffocation of five-year-old Matthew Vaudreuil by his mother, Judge Thomas Gove headed an inquiry into child protection in British Columbia.[29] Matthew was well-known to the child welfare system. During his life, people concerned about his safety and well-being had made at least 60 calls on his behalf. Judge Gove concluded that: "British Columbia's entire child welfare system must be reformed if the province is to institute more responsive child protection",[30] and called for a system of co-ordinated, multi-disciplinary services, which would be child-centred and would give children a stronger voice.[31] The British Columbia government responded by establishing a new ministry dedicated entirely to children (the Ministry for Children and Families). It also appointed an independent commission (the Children's Commission) to promote greater openness and accountability in the delivery of services to children in care.[32] An important function of the new Children's Commission is to review and resolve complaints made by children, or people representing them, about breaches of their rights in care.[33]

Other examples of child- or youth-centred reforms to service delivery systems can be found in initiatives as diverse as the Canadian Hockey League's Players First policy;[34] in the guiding principles of Choices for Youth,[35] the organisation that took over the care of youth from Mount Cashel; and in the Meadow Lake Tribal Council's child care training program.[36] In each case, respect for children and youth and a focus on their well-being are paramount values.

If governments, organisations and communities that deliver services to children and youth put young people's interests first, a climate will be created that is conducive to their healthy development, and inhospitable to abuse and neglect.[37] Once a child-centred approach is fully embraced, more resources can be channelled into meeting children's developmental needs, since less money will be required to repair the damage inflicted by abuse.[38]

b.   Proactive responses

Obviously, values and principles are the foundation upon which to build effective child prevention strategies. But they are only the beginning. Concrete measures, such as public education programs, employee training and operational audit programs need to be developed as well, to complete the protective scheme. This section presents a framework that embraces a range of "best practices" or "promising practices" that could be implemented to make children safer in out-of-home care.[39]

This framework is not exhaustive. Moreover, it does not prescribe how to go about implementing the strategies listed. This framework is, in short, just a first step towards developing and maintaining accessible inventories of proactive prevention practices that have been created, evaluated and shown to reduce the risks exposing children and youth to abuse in out-of-home care. It comprises twelve elements:

    i.   Building Public Awareness

    ii.   Educating Children and Youth About Sex and Personal Safety

    iii.   Educating Everyone About Children's Rights

    iv.   Opening Up Institutions

    v.   Adopting Preventive Practices in Recruitment

    vi.   Ensuring Appropriate Training and Professional Development

    vii.   Establishing Clear and Formal Rules of Operation

    viii.   Actively Supervising People Who Work with Children

    ix.   Conducting Safety and Quality of Care Audits

x. Establishing Reporting and Investigation Protocols

xi. Creating an Independent Process to Resolve Children's Complaints

xii. Providing Adequate Institutional Resources

i. Building public awareness

Canadians are familiar with many stories of children who survived institutional child abuse, such as the boys of Newfoundland's Mount Cashel, the girls at Grandview, and Aboriginal children who attended residential schools. They also know that many infamous institutions have been closed. This might lead many to believe that institutional child abuse is largely a problem of the past. Because they lack information about, and a clear understanding of, the enduring and potentially cyclical effects of past abuse, Canadians are often unaware of the nature and scope of child abuse and maltreatment in today's institutions.

While media coverage of historical child abuse often presents the many sides of a story, including the devastating impact of the abuse on survivors, news reports seldom focus on prevention. An awareness of child abuse needs to be raised, in much the same way that it has been for the issues of domestic violence and drunk driving. Improving public awareness and education is everyone's responsibility, from journalists and broadcasters, to governments, private corporations and non-profit organisations.[40] Even individual citizens can find ways to participate in this public awareness and education process.[41]

ii. Educating children and youth about sex and personal safety

All children and youth, but especially those who are at greater risk because they are in out-of-home care,[42] must be taught what is an appropriate inter-personal interaction, and what is not.[43] The information they are given must be age and ability appropriate.[44] The purpose of teaching children about sex and safety is not to have them assume the responsibility for their own protection. It is, rather, to give them the confidence that comes with knowing the difference between right and wrong.[45]

iii. Educating everyone about children's rights

Canada is committed to implementing the *Convention on the Rights of the Child*, and to enacting laws that set out the rights of children, in general, and of those in care, in particular. This is, however, only a first step. Young people are not well informed about their rights or how to ensure that these rights are not violated.[46] Furthermore, children, youth and adults alike need to learn about the rights of young people in care, why these rights are important, and how to assert them.

iv. Opening up institutions

All children and youth in out-of-home care are removed from their families and familiar environments. Sometimes they are physically isolated, depending on how far away from their home communities they are taken. In all cases they are emotionally isolated, because they lose the constant, direct contact they have had with family members and friends. Institutions and other facilities must make concerted efforts to minimise the isolation of their residents from positive family influences. Children in out-of-home care who reside at some distance from their home communities must be given the opportunity to maintain strong bonds with their families and communities; otherwise, they will quickly become outsiders.

Total institutions and other private facilities must also take steps to minimise their own isolation from society. They must become less "total" by welcoming interaction with, and the involvement of, community members. For example, they can encourage local volunteers to participate in the activities of the institutions. Structurally, it is important that all institutions:

> operate on the notion of the 'inverted triangle'. The most important people are the children and the least important is the director. Such organisations are open, and supportive of employees and children, ...[not] closed hierarchical organisations where staff are disempowered, uninformed, and unsupported by management.[47]

v. Adopting preventive practices in recruitment

Before any organisation that provides services to children hires a staff member or enlists a volunteer, that person's qualifications and character must be carefully scrutinised. Preventive recruiting practices include, for example, thoroughly checking employment and character references by means of an established, comprehensive list of probing inquiries, performing criminal record checks and consulting child abuse registers. Although verifying the credentials of new employees and volunteers is important, careful screening is only one of a variety of risk management practices that organisations should adopt.[48] An individual's clean record is not an ironclad guarantee for the future.

vi.   Ensuring appropriate training and professional development

Everyone who works with children, including volunteers, must be trained to recognise the signs of every type of abuse (not only physical and sexual) and neglect that can occur in care.[49] All workers need to participate in training programs to instruct them on what to do if they suspect that a child in care is being abused, neglected or otherwise maltreated.[50] "The rights of children and young people in treatment must be acknowledged and articulated in all training approaches."[51]

vii.   Establishing clear and formal rules of operation

All agencies that provide out-of-home care for children need to ensure that their operations are guided by clear, written information about the organisation's goals and operations. This information may include mission statements, codes of conduct, policies, procedures and other operating guidelines, all of which help to clarify the standard of care expected in the facility.[52]

viii.   Actively supervising people who work with children

Proactive, supportive and steady supervision helps prevent child abuse.[53] In addition, managers and administrators need to monitor the general work environment for signs of poor working conditions such as high levels of stress, staff burn-out, low morale, and under-resourced services.[54] Poor working conditions affect the quality of care being provided and put the children in care at higher risk of physical and emotional maltreatment or abuse from staff.[55]

ix.   Conducting safety and quality of care audits

Periodic audits must be conducted to evaluate the quality of care that children receive in residential settings. A quality assurance and safety audit can examine whether the physical set-up and operational practices of the residence present risks to the children. The process

Three months ago, I drove up to St. John's and watched the lads coming and going for several hours. You could see by their faces that it's not the same today as when we were there. These kids are happy, they're friendly, they're what kids should look like. So changes are being made since our time.

Quoted in The Vision to Reconcile: Process Report on the Helpline Reconciliation
Model Agreement by Doug Roche and Ben Hoffman, , at p. 21

should engage and involve both residents and members of staff in the information-gathering and evaluation process. Auditors must be independent from the institution being examined.[56]

x.   Establishing reporting and investigation protocols

All institutions and service-providers that offer care to children and youth outside the home must have protocols in place to govern their responses to disclosures or suspicions of abuse. Protocols are written guidelines on the reporting and investigation of abuse, neglect or maltreatment.[57] Because they are living documents, they need to be constantly reviewed and improved.[58]

xi.   Creating an independent process to resolve children's complaints

When children and youth in out-of-home care have concerns or complaints about the quality of the care that they receive, they should have access to both formal and informal, internal and external complaint resolution processes.[59] For serious complaints, such as allegations of sexual abuse, physical injury or emotional trauma, they must have recourse to an independent complaint response and resolution system such as the children's advocates and children's commissions.

xii.   Providing adequate institutional resources

A residential care facility that does not have sufficient financial or human resources to operate effectively cannot create a safe and positive living and learning environment for its young people.

> By starving group care and other social welfare programs of the resources they need to operate effectively, our society not only prevents them from meeting their objectives, but also sets up their clients for abuse at the hands of direct care workers who are too stretched and frustrated to respond effectively.[60]

* * * * *

Institutions that adopt a framework of proactive prevention strategies such as those just outlined should be better able to recognise, control and manage the risks of abuse facing children and youth living in out-of-home care settings. Risk management is now a legal obligation for every organisation engaged in the care of children. As the Supreme Court of Canada recently noted:

> If the scourge of sexual predation is to be stamped out, or at least controlled, there must be powerful motivation acting upon those who control institutions engaged in the care, protection and nurturing of children. That motivation will not in my view be sufficiently supplied by the likelihood of liability in negligence.... Beyond the narrow band of employer conduct that attracts direct liability in negligence lies a vast area where imaginative and efficient administration and supervision can reduce the risk .... Holding the employer vicariously liable for the wrongs of its employee may encourage the employer to take such steps, and hence, reduce the risk of future harm.[61]

The obligation to institute appropriate safeguards should not, however, be viewed as simply an attempt to protect organisations from the threat of liability for the wrongful acts of employees. Rather, it stems from a duty to provide care that is animated by concern for the best interests and developmental well-being of young people. Institutions must, of course, respect the legal rights of children. But they must do more. They must respect all the interests and needs of children in their care. Therefore, in developing frameworks and protocols to recognise, control, reduce and manage risk, and to minimise lawsuits, it is important to stay abreast of all developments in the field of prevention.

Finally, the obligation of institutions to adopt preventative strategies does not lead to the conclusion that only they have such a duty. Prevention and risk reduction will be most successful when society at large conscientiously embraces this role and its responsibilities.

c. Reactive responses

No matter how child-centred and proficient society becomes at risk management, and regardless of how solid the design of its proactive prevention strategies and frameworks, abuse will still occur in institutional settings. For this reason, well-coordinated and effective reactive measures – the steps that are taken to contain the abuse after it happens – must also be put into place. These measures include imposing statutory duties on persons to report cases of abuse, conducting independent investigations, counselling primary and secondary victims, counselling violent or abusive caregivers, treating sexual offenders, and so on.

In institutional settings, effective reporting and investigation systems are critical to ensuring appropriate and timely responses. To date, most child abuse reporting and investigation practices have been designed to address domestic abuse. It is important to recognise the special problems associated with the reporting and investigation of abuse in institutions, and to adjust these practices so they are well-suited to institutional settings.

i. Reporting suspicions or disclosures

Despite the existence of laws that require professionals and other persons to report cases of known or suspected abuse, not all child abuse is, in fact, reported. The true extent of this "under-reporting" is unknown. A 1990 survey in Ontario observed that estimates of child physical and sexual abuse and neglect derived from reports to child protection agencies do not accurately portray the extent of child maltreatment in the community.[62] "[I]t has been estimated that as many as 90% of cases are not reported to child welfare agencies."[63]

There are a number of reasons for this low reporting rate. Most jurisdictions do not explicitly impose a duty to report upon all employees of an institution. Quebec is an exception. Its *Youth Protection Act* imposes upon "any employee of an institution" the obligation to report when "the security or development of a child may be in danger".[64] Where the obligation to report institutional abuse is not clearly stated, employees could be unsure about their duty to report, and be reluctant to do so for fear of the consequences.[65]

One might reasonably conclude that legislative amendments are needed to create or clarify this duty. However, domestic child abuse is significantly under-reported even where the duty to report these cases is clear and well known.[66] Therefore, greater legislative certainty in mandatory reporting provisions alone is unlikely to have much impact. To get to the root of under-reporting, all of the reasons for not reporting abuse in institutional settings need to be identified and weighed.[67]

Fears about the adverse consequences of reporting institutional abuse can create a powerful barrier.[68] Professionals who are required by law to report child abuse, such as physicians and teachers, have expressed worry that reporting may damage the relationship and trust built up between them and the child, especially if the child is not ready to disclose.[69] In addition, children or their family members may not disclose institutional abuse out of fear that they will be harassed by certain staff members or deprived of needed services.[70] As well, persons required by legislation to report abuse will face a dilemma when it comes to deciding whether they should report a serious situation that is located in a powerful institution. They may be aware of the problems that previous whistleblowers have encountered[71] and the low level of protection to which they will be entitled by law.[72] They may also be conscious of the unequal power between themselves and the institution they would be exposing.[73]

The reporting process itself can be another deterrent to disclosure. Legislation usually requires that incidents be reported to the child protection authority that placed the child in the institutional setting where the alleged abuse occurred. Unless an alternate reporting avenue is available, such as to an independent child advocate, victims will be disinclined to report.

> Many children indicated that if their rights were violated by a residential care facility, they would be reluctant to raise concerns with the same worker who arranged for the placement.... The nature of any child welfare system is such that an external means to ensure accountability will always be necessary.[74]

An Ohio test of alternative reporting processes found that the willingness to report increased where there was an outside, independent advocate mandated to receive reports.[75]

Uncertainties, and especially misconceptions, about what constitutes abuse and neglect in institutional settings are a further obstacle to reporting. The very professionals who are mandated by legislation to report abuse are often ill prepared to recognise it, especially in "grey zone" cases such as emotional neglect. One report notes that "Physicians lack knowledge of and training in forms of abuse that do not have clearly identifiable physical indicators ...."[76] Another concludes that teachers often do not know what signs to look for and feel they have not been sufficiently trained to detect sexual, physical, or emotional abuse.[77] One expert has even observed that many front-line workers seem to be poorly informed:

> When talking to residential workers about child abuse it is often staggering to see how little they understand about the nature of abuse and the many and varied forms which abuse can take.[78]

Children and youth who experience institutional abuse may not disclose it, even indirectly, because of the number of physical or psychological barriers they may encounter. Children with disabilities, for example, may believe that only severe physical harm constitutes abuse.[79] They may have been conditioned to discount the non-physical forms of abuse:

> Interviewers for the research considered it probable that some people with disabilities may have become so accustomed to forms of violence most other citizens would consider serious that they see only the most egregious acts against them as worthy of special attention and possible disclosure.... As a result they may be more likely to talk about the sexual assault and less likely to talk about the other forms of violence.[80]

Again, children in institutions may be physically isolated from persons to whom they would be able to disclose, or they may lack the means, because of their special communications needs, to talk with them:

> Lack of physical contact with persons who can receive complaints is an obstacle to disclosure encountered particularly by individuals with mobility impairments.... Lack of access to technical devices [and interpreters] that can serve as a bridge between survivors and others in a position to help was identified as a further problem that can hamper disclosure.[81]

Finally, limitations inherent in child protection laws may also undermine the reporting of institutional child abuse. Laws that were primarily designed to protect children who are physically or sexually abused by their parents, have been adapted and extended to institutional settings. Their framework and definitions are not always well-suited to protecting children from the kinds of maltreatment to which they may be exposed in institutions, such as inappropriate lock-up or medication practices, or other systems abuses.

Legislation needs to recognise the difference between familial, foster and institutional abuse. Without this recognition, ... States must 'stretch' their intrafamilial-oriented statutes to incorporate institutional abuse. Such legislative omission can have far-reaching effects, for example conducting investigations of institutional abuse within the less-appropriate intrafamilial or foster care framework.[82]

The above list of reasons for failing to report or disclose institutional child abuse demonstrates that under-reporting cannot be overcome simply by legislative action. Social action, such as education and training, is also required. More importantly, the length of this list suggests a pressing need to fully review and assess the concept and practices of mandatory reporting. Is reporting the most effective strategy for responding to abuse? If so, is mandatory reporting the best way to achieve this goal? What additional strategies can be put in place to achieve the reporting objectives that the system is not currently meeting? The Roeher Institute observes:

Depending on the legal framework, mandatory reporting can trigger a chain of investigations and other events that survivors may perceive as invasive and against their own best interests and preferences. Although mandatory reporting may have merit, it is not clear that mandatory intervention by police, social workers and departmental ministers is an unqualified benefit. Instead, interventions should be guided by the survivor's express wishes. Survivors should have the option of pursuing administrative rather than judicial processes to address violent or abusive incidents, if they wish.[83]

ii.   Investigating suspicions or disclosures

The investigation of institutional child abuse, like the reporting of it, often raises complex issues. Complications can arise from factors such as: the number of children in the out-of-home setting who may have been affected; the possible behavioural problems and developmental limitations of the residents; the number of parties responsible for these children (including various government agencies and parents); and the fact that one or more staff members may be placed under investigation. Several human dimensions can arise, especially in institutional settings, which can further compound the complexity of the issues. For example, some victims of institutional abuse may also have suffered from abuse in their homes; others may have disabilities and special needs that make communication difficult; parents who have entrusted their children to institutional care may suffer vicarious trauma or distress when they learn their children have been abused in care; and staff may react negatively to investigations undertaken in their workplaces.[84]

The objectives of most investigations of institutional child abuse incidents are usually broad. One goal is to protect the child from further harm, assess the impact of the incident on the child, and ensure his or her therapeutic and medical needs are met. Typically, investigations also seek to determine whether standards of care, policies, procedures, regulations or other administrative safeguards have been violated, in order to help determine necessary corrective actions.[85] Some argue that special knowledge and skills are needed to investigate abuse in institutional settings:

> The skills necessary for the successful completion of an investigation, assessment and corrective action are beyond the scope of child protective services personnel with experience in familial maltreatment. Workers report little knowledge of proper and approved restraint techniques, crisis de-escalation in institutional settings, and psychological, medical, and pharmacological treatment of psychological or psychiatric disorders.... The decision-making process in maltreatment in out-of-home care is further complicated because it rests on three questions that are not appropriate to familial abuse: (1) Did the reported incident occur independent of mitigating circumstances, intent or severity? (2) Are the child care worker, supervisor, and the administrator culpable and in what manner? (3) Is the problem administratively redressable? Within this framework for decision-making the need for specialized units or personnel to perform independent investigations and to make and monitor corrective recommendations is obvious.[86]

A fundamental concern is how to ensure the impartiality and independence of investigations of institutional child abuse. If the alleged abuse entails criminal conduct, the police will become involved in the investigation. In many cases however, the same child welfare authority that is responsible for having placed the child at risk will carry out the investigation. This raises the possibility of a conflict of interest. The conclusions of the Forde Inquiry on this issue are apt:

The independence of the investigation is crucial. When an institution has failed to protect a child to the extent that abuse may have occurred, that institution should not be relied upon to investigate the incident. Indeed, even the supervising authority or department is not well placed to investigate abuse because of their role in child placement, monitoring and supervision. To ensure that investigations are rigorous and objective, the response must be 'as structurally and functionally independent as political and economic constraints will allow.'[87]

In the six provinces where children's advocate offices exist there is such an independent, external mechanism in place to receive and investigate allegations of institutional abuse. These offices operate at arm's length to the service delivery systems they investigate. However, unless they also have the authority to report their findings and recommendations directly and publicly to the legislature, they may not be perceived as truly independent, and their credibility may be compromised.

Problems that may arise in investigating allegations of institutional child abuse can largely be remedied by coordinating both legislative and non-legislative responses. Providing more targeted training about the conduct of investigations of institutional abuse, establishing interdisciplinary and arm's length investigation teams, and ensuring that the requisite investigation and reporting powers are supported by legislation are some steps towards improving investigation processes. When reports of abuse in institutional settings are not substantiated because aspects of the investigation system are inefficient or ineffective, young people are re-victimised. For them, this weakness in the investigation process compounds the original abuse. The child's trust in "the system" is destroyed because, first, it let the abuse happen and then, even when the abuse was reported, it could not stop it.

* * * * *

Canadians need to improve their knowledge and understanding of the nature and scope of child abuse occurring in out-of-home care. Collaborative efforts across all sectors of society are required to use this new knowledge and understanding to devise more effective prevention strategies in their communities. Of course, whatever the frameworks and strategies developed to enhance prevention of child abuse, they must place young people first.

Recommendations

THE VALUES AND PRINCIPLES set out in the *Convention on the Rights of the Child*, should be the foundation upon which all programs and services for children and youth in out-of-home care are built.

Considerations:

Governmental and non-governmental organisations that deliver programs and services to children outside the home to assist in their personal growth or well-being should review, and if necessary revise, their guiding instruments (such as laws, by-laws, missions statements, policies and standards) to ensure that they clearly and formally articulate and reflect the rights and best interests of the children in their care and are consistent with the values and principles set out in the *Convention on the Rights of the Child*.

GOVERNMENTS, RESEARCH INSTITUTIONS and non-governmental organisations should coordinate their efforts to compile and disseminate an inventory of promising and proven measures to prevent the abuse of children in out-of-home care.

Considerations:

A number of published and unpublished studies and reports have already been produced which relate to the vulnerability and experiences of children and youth in residential and out-of-home care. As a first step, Health Canada could create an inventory of these reports (which have been prepared by provincial Ombudsman offices, children's advocates and children's commissioners, by independent researchers under contract to governments, by non-governmental organisations and by others). The inventory, along with links to electronic copies or information on how to obtain copies of these materials, could be made available online through an electronic resource centre such as the National Clearing House on Family Violence.

The objective in compiling and coordinating information is to raise awareness and provide resources for education. Governments should not control or horde information and a plurality of non-governmental research bodies should be supported.

RESEARCH AGENCIES, non-governmental organisations and governments should compile a comprehensive, inter-disciplinary, and public review of child abuse reporting laws and practices.

Considerations:

This review should explore the reasons mandatory reporting provisions are not working and suggest alternative approaches and frameworks that could lead to more voluntary disclosures, encourage reporting of all types of abuse affecting all children and youth, and produce interventions that are responsive to the young people's needs and serve their best interests.

This review should also examine whether current laws adequately identify the out-of-home care facilities to which they apply, whether they envision licensing and mandatory, independent inspections, and whether they require comprehensive investigations of systemic features of a facility where abuse is reported.

RESEARCH AGENCIES, non-governmental organisations and governments should sponsor research into the most appropriate strategies for healing the harms of institutional child abuse.

Considerations:

The need to understand how to help survivors overcome the negative effects of institutional child abuse is pressing. Traditional legal redress processes have shown their limited capacity to meet the needs of survivors. Newer, more comprehensive redress programs are being established without any clear understanding of the kinds of individual and collective therapeutic needs of survivors and their communities.

Collaborative research funding programs could be an effective means of promoting the necessary research.

---

[1]   A. Wachtel, *The "State of the Art" in Child Abuse Prevention, 1997*, a research report prepared for the Family Violence Prevention Unit, Health Canada (Ottawa: Public Works and Government Services Canada, 1999) at 15, online: Health Canada: <http://www.hc-sc.gc.ca/hppb/familyviolence> (date accessed: 16 November 1999).

2   Based on "Population in collective dwellings, 1996 Census" from the 1996 Census Nation tables, online: Statistics Canada <http://www.statcan.ca/english/Pgdb/People/Families/famil62a.htm> (date accessed: 20 October 1999); Ontario, Office of Child and Family Service Advocacy, *Voices From Within – Youth Speak Out: Youth in Care in Ontario* (Toronto: Queen's Printer, April 1998) (Chief Advocate: J. Finlay) at 53 [hereinafter *Voices From Within – Youth Speak Out*].

3   *Voices From Within – Youth Speak Out, ibid.*

4   To assemble this type of information on a Canada-wide basis requires drawing on various sources of data. For example, information collected through the 1996 census provides data on populations of children and youth under 15 living in collective dwellings such as general, psychiatric and physically handicapped hospitals, children's group homes and orphanages, correctional and penal institutions and work camps. See CD-ROM: *Nation Series Complete Edition – 96 Census*, 4th ed. (Ottawa: Statistics Canada, September 1998) at "Population in Collective Dwellings." Information on children and youth in the care of child protection services in various jurisdictions is available through statistical reports of the Working Group on Child and Family Services Information. See Federal-Provincial Working Group on Child and Family Services Information, *Child and Family Services Statistical Reports 1994–95 to 1996–97*, online: Health Canada, National Clearing House on Family Violence <http://www.hcsc.gc.ca/hppb/familyviolence/child.htm> (date accessed: 29 September 1999) [hereinafter *Child and Family Services Statistical Report*].

5   See for example, *Child Family Services Statistical Report, ibid.* at 1.

6   Wachtel, *supra* note 1 at 13:

> The concentration on family as the prime locus of child abuse and neglect reflected not only the apparent facts but also the particular focus of the lead institutions involved in the response. The mandate of child protection was to assure the home was a safe haven for children, that parents were able and willing to protect their children and, if not, that alternate care was provided. Maltreatment of children outside the home was not the child welfare system's particular concern.

7   *Child Welfare Act*, S.A. 1984, c. C-8.1, s. 1(2); *Child and Family Services Act*, S.S. 1989-90, c. C-7.2, s. 11.

8   Wachtel, *supra* note 1 at 9-15, "Part 1. Discovery and Evolution".

9   C. Bagley & R. Thomlison, eds., *Child Sexual Abuse: Critical Perspectives on Prevention, Intervention, and Treatment* (Toronto: Wall & Emerson, Inc., 1991) at 2; D. Finkelhor, *Child Sexual Abuse: New Theory and Research* (New York: Macmillan, Inc., 1984) at 3-4.

10 Queensland, Australia, *Report of the Commission of Inquiry into Abuse of Children in Queensland Institutions* (Brisbane: Commission of Inquiry into Abuse of Children in Queensland Institutions, May 1999) (Chairperson: L. Forde) at 14 [hereinafter *Forde Inquiry Report*]. The report noted that the empirical base explaining the causes of child abuse is strongest in the family setting because of a predominance of research into familial abuse.

11 Statistics Canada, *Family Violence in Canada: A Statistical Profile 1998* by V. Pottie Bunge & A. Levett (Ottawa: Statistics Canada, May 1998) Table 4 at 22 and Statistics Canada, *Family Violence in Canada: A Statistical Profile 1999* by R. Fitzgerald (Ottawa: Statistics Canada, June 1999) Table 4.4 at 30 [hereinafter *Family Violence Profile 1999*].

12 <http://www.hc-sc.gc.ca/hpp6/familyviolence/index.html>. (date accessed: 17 January 2000).

13 Health Canada, *Multiple Victim Child Sexual Abuse: The Impact on Communities and Implications for Intervention Planning* by Child and Youth Mental Health Services, British Columbia Ministry of Health (Ottawa: Ministers of Health and Supply and Services, 1994) at 13.

14 National Health and Welfare, *The Summary Report of the Special Advisor to the Minister of National Health and Welfare on Child Sexual Abuse in Canada – Reaching for Solutions* by R. Rogers (Ottawa: Canada Communication Group, 1990) at 18.

15 National Health and Welfare, *The Report of the Special Advisor to the Minister of National Health and Welfare on Child Sexual Abuse in Canada – Reaching for Solutions* by R. Rogers (Ottawa: Canada Communication Group, 1990) at 30.

16 Government of Canada, *Federal Response to Reaching for Solutions – Report of the Special Advisor on Child Sexual Abuse* (Ottawa: Canada Communication Group, 1992) at 6.

17 Wachtel, *supra* note 1 at 15, "Revisiting the Numbers".

18 Health Canada, "The Canadian Incidence Study of Reported Child Abuse and Neglect – Information from the Child Maltreatment Division" in *Information* (Ottawa: Health Canada, January 1998) and N. Trocmé, "Project Update" *CIS Newsletter* (1 October 1998) at 1-2. Since the study focuses on cases of child abuse and neglect which have been identified by or reported to child welfare agencies it will only capture incidents of abuse and neglect of children in out-of-home care that normally are dealt with through the child welfare system. Therefore, abuse occurring in foster care could be documented by this study, but abuse occurring in a youth detention facility or hospital setting would not be captured unless it was reported to a child welfare agency. Clearly, the primary focus of the study will be child abuse and neglect arising in the home.

[19] J. Levine Powers *et al.*, "Institutional Abuse: A Review of the Literature" (1990) 4:6 Journal of Child and Youth Care 81; Department of Justice Canada, *Technical Report: Violence in Institutional Facilities Against Persons with Disabilities – A Literature Review* by The Roeher Institute (Ottawa: Research, Statistics and Evaluation Directorate, Civil Law and Corporate Management Sector, Department of Justice Canada, 1995); Institute for Human Resource Development, Review of *"The Needs of Victims of Institutional Child Abuse"* (Ottawa: Law Commission of Canada, 1998) at "Appendix II – Literature Review" [hereinafter IHRD Report]. Available in hard copy from the Law Commission of Canada and online: <http://www.lcc.gc.ca>.

[20] *Forde Inquiry Report*, *supra* note 10 at 11-12; *IHRD Report*, *supra* note 19 "Appendix II" at 5.

[21] Levine Powers, *supra* note 19 at 89.

[22] *Forde Inquiry Report*, *supra* note 10 at 18. For a discussion of the types of policies, procedures and practices that contribute to systems abuse and general principles to prevent or minimise it see New South Wales, Australia, Minister for Community Services, *Systems Abuse: Problems and Solutions* by J. Cashmore, R. Dolby & D. Brennan (New South Wales Child Protection Council, 1994).

[23] Levine Powers, *supra* note 19 at 88; *Forde Inquiry Report*, *supra* note 10 at 16 and 28-9.

[24] G. Thomas, "The Responsibility of Residential Placements for Children's Rights to Development" in R. Hanson, ed., *The Institutional Abuse of Children & Youth* (New York: Haworth Press, 1982) 23 at 23-24. In this article George Thomas described the process whereby he came to such a realisation. He set out to produce an inventory of "best practices" for preventing the abuse of children in institutions. But his approach proved impractical because such practices were in short supply and the practices that did exist did not necessarily reflect a child-centred, child-affirming philosophy. He concluded, "[I]t became apparent that enforceable and effective standards cannot be written unless one first identifies the specific rights of children which these standards are intended to implement."

[25] The vision set out in the *National Children's Agenda* discussion paper also recognizes the paramount importance of children's developmental needs and well-being. See Canada, Federal-Provincial-Territorial Council of Ministers on Social Policy Renewal, *A National Children's Agenda – developing a shared vision* (Canada: Federal-Provincial-Territorial Council of Ministers on Social Policy Renewal, May 1999) at 6.

26 *Convention on the Rights of the Child*, 20 November 1989, 28 I.L.M. 1456. The full text of the Convention is online <http://www.pch.gc.ca/ddp-hrd/english/rotc/croc.htm> (date accessed: 16 November 1999).

27 Department of Canadian Heritage, *Convention on the Rights of the Child – First Report of Canada* (Ottawa: Human Rights Directorate, Department of Canadian Heritage, May 1994) at 1.

28 Other Articles of special importance to children in care include Articles 20, 23, 29, 30, 31, 32, 34, 37 and 39.

29 British Columbia, *Report of the Gove Inquiry into Child Protection in British Columbia – A Commission of Inquiry into the adequacy of the service, policies and practices of the Ministry of Social Services as they relate to the apparent neglect, abuse and death of Matthew John Vaudreuil* by Judge T. Gove (Victoria: Ministry of Social Services, 1995).

30 *Ibid.* at 243.

31 Child Welfare League of Canada and Ontario Association of Children's Aid Societies, *Canada's Children ... Canada's Future – Final Conference Report for the Second National Policy Conference on Children* (November 1996) (Ottawa: Child Welfare League of Canada and Ontario Association of Children's Aid Societies, 1997) at 22.

32 British Columbia, The Children's Commission, *The Children's Commission 1998 Annual Report* (Victoria: The Children's Commission, April 1999) (Commissioner: C. Morton) at 1.

33 *Children's Commission Act*, S.B.C. 1997, c. 11, ss. 4(1)(f) and 10.

34 Canadian Hockey League, *Players First: A Report Prepared for the Canadian Hockey League* by G. I. Kirke, Q.C. (Toronto: Canadian Hockey League, 7 August 1997) at 23.

35 B. Lynch *et al.*, "Unfinished Business: The Mount Cashel Experience" (1991) 6:1 Journal of Child and Youth Care 55 at 65.

36 In 1989, the Meadow Lake Tribal Council of Saskatchewan invited the University of Victoria's School of Child and Youth Care to join it in a partnership to create an accredited, community-based, post-secondary education program to train child care workers. The nature and characteristics of the program were built upon a foundation of seven guiding principles, including the recognition of children's well-being as central to the well-being of families and communities. See A. Pence & M. McCallum, "Developing Cross-Cultural Partnerships: Implications for Child Care Quality Research and Practice" in P. Moss & A. Pence, eds., *Valuing Quality in Early Childhood Services: New*

Approaches to Defining Quality (London and New York: Paul Chapman Publishing and Teachers College Press, co-publishers, 1994) at 114. See also, J. Ball & A. Pence, "Beyond Developmentally Appropriate Practice: Developing Community and Culturally Appropriate Practice" in *Young Children International* (Victoria: School of Child and Youth Care, University of Victoria, March 1999) 46 at 50.

37 This view is supported by observations in the *Forde Inquiry Report, supra* note 10 at 23-24:

> The philosophy and orientation of departments responsible for children in institutional care will influence the quality of, and approach to, service delivery. A common complaint about institutions and bureaucracies is that the processes reflect the needs of the system rather than those of the clients they are supposed to serve. A child-oriented focus can reduce the level of risk of institutional abuse. This orientation is based on a set of clear principles and guidelines that start, as the paramount consideration, with the features of caregiving or services that are likely to promote children's security and wellbeing.

38 Some research has been done which indicates that long-term savings can be achieved through prevention work. J. Meston, *Child Abuse and Neglect Prevention Programs* (Ottawa: Vanier Institute of the Family, June 1993) at 23: "Québec researcher C. Bouchard makes the point that one dollar invested in prevention could result in a savings of three to seven dollars later."

39 Some other frameworks of preventive strategies are compiled in the following: Office of the Child and Family Service Advocacy, *Voices from Within – Youth Speak Out, supra* note 2; Institute for the Prevention of Child Abuse, *Preferred Practices for Investigating Allegations of Child Abuse in Residential Settings* (Toronto: The Institute for the Prevention of Child Abuse, 1992) at 40-43; and S. Rogow & J. Hass, *The Person Within: Preventing Abuse of Children & Young People with Disabilities – A Handbook* (Vancouver: BC Institute Against Family Violence, 1999) at 20-32 [hereinafter *The Person Within*] and accompanying video *The Person Within* produced for B.C. Institute Against Family Violence (Vancouver: Creative Media Productions, 1999) 28:20 min.

40 The Roeher Institute, *Harm's Way – The Many Faces of Violence and Abuse Against Persons with Disabilities* (Toronto: The Roeher Institute, 1995) at 194 [hereinafter *Harm's Way*].

41 For example, an individual in Oshawa, Donna McAllister, created a web site to present information about the "Duplessis orphans." See E. Thompson, "Orphans get website" *The Montreal Gazette* (19 August 1999) A11.

[42] Children who are in out-of-home care because they were removed from abusive homes need especially to be educated about healthy interpersonal interaction. They need to un-learn behaviour they were taught by bad example at home. See T. Cavanagh Johnson, *Sexual, Physical and Emotional Abuse in Out-of-Home Care* (New York: Haworth Maltreatment and Trauma Press, 1997) at 3:

> Among the issues that need to be addressed with children in out-of-home facilities are their rights and responsibilities related to their bodies. When children have been sexually, physically, and/or emotionally abused or neglected, they often do not have good self-protection skills. We make assumptions that all children know when someone is violating them. If they have not been taught or cannot model their behaviour on people who raised them, they often do not know.

[43] See The Roeher Institute, *No More Victims – A manual to guide the legal community in addressing the sexual abuse of people with a mental handicap* (Toronto: The Roeher Institute, 1992) at 55: "[A]ny prevention strategy must include ongoing sex education and personal safety education for children [that is age and ability appropriate]. The acquisition of knowledge and skills can be empowering, and can often help protect a person from abuse or further abuse."

[44] J. Renvoize, *Innocence destroyed – A study of child sexual abuse* (New York: Routledge, 1993) at 91:

> People often dislike the idea of teaching 'innocent' children, with or without disabilities, about sex. But, as we have seen, because of their acceptance of adult direction children with learning difficulties are particularly open to abuse, and it is essential that within the bounds of their own understanding they are taught about good and bad sexuality, learning sufficient self-assertiveness to be able to say 'no!' to potential abusers. They also must learn about their rights over their own bodies, ...in doing so they will learn how to distinguish between appropriate and inappropriate touching by others.

[45] S. Swanson, *Taking Care – A Child Abuse Prevention Manual for Canadian Early Childhood Educators* (Vancouver: Early Childhood Educators of British Columbia, April 1997) at 48.

[46] H. Sylvester, N. Harry, D. Tom & L. Sam, *The Youth Report – A Report About Youth by Youth* (Victoria: The Children's Commission, April 1999) at 26 [hereinafter *The Youth Report*]. See also *Voices From Within – Youth Speak Out, supra* note 2 at 11-12.

[47] P. Suche *et al.*, *Independent Review of Reporting Procedures in Children's Residential Care Facilities* (Prepared for the Minister of Family Services, Manitoba, 1992) at 93 [hereinafter *Independent Review of Reporting Procedures*].

[48] For a thorough review of preventive hiring practices see British Columbia, Ministry of the Attorney General, *Help Stop the Abuse: A Handbook for Employers and Volunteer Coordinators*, 3d ed. (Victoria: Ministry of the Attorney General, March 99) at 9-41 [hereinafter *Help Stop Child Abuse*]. See also C. Senn, *Vulnerable: sexual abuse and people with an intellectual handicap* (Toronto: The G. Allan Roeher Institute, 1988) at 46 [hereinafter *Vulnerable*]; R. Bloom, "Institutional Child Sexual Abuse: Prevention and Risk Management" (1994) 12:2 Residential Treatment for Children and Youth 3 at 4-6; and A. Davison, *Residential Care – The provision of quality care in residential and educational group care settings* (England: Arena Ashgate Publishing, 1995) at 272.

[49] For an example of a training program designed for the child care community see B. Prager & P. Rimer, *Making a Difference: The Child Care Community Response to Child Abuse – Resource Manual* (Toronto: The Metropolitan Toronto Special Committee on Child Abuse, 1996).

[50] *Help Stop Child Abuse*, *supra* note 48 at 46.

[51] *The Person Within*, *supra* note 39 at 23.

[52] *Help Stop Child Abuse*, *supra* note 48 at 45. Some governments and agencies have introduced practice standards to establish a minimum standard of care that is expected in the delivery of services to children in out-of-home care. See, for example, the standards for foster homes and children's residential services developed by the Government of British Columbia: Ministry for Children and Families, *Standards for Staffed Children's Residential Services Provided under the Child, Family and Community Service Act* 1998 (Victoria: Ministry for Children and Families, December 1998); Ministry for Children and Families, *Standards for Foster Homes Approved under the Child, Family and Community Service Act 1998* (Victoria: Ministry for Children and Families, September 1998).

[53] *Help Stop Child Abuse*, *supra* note 48 at 47.

[54] Bloom, *supra* note 48 at 11.

[55] D. Nevin, "Staff Training Needs Around Sex Abuse in Residential Treatment" (1993) 11:1 Residential Treatment for Children and Youth 63 at 65.

[56] For example see the quality assurance process applied to assess the Jericho Residential Program described in *Inside Quality Assurance Report Jericho Residential Program* prepared by B. Smith (Vancouver: Jericho Residential Program, Ministry of Social Services, August 1996).

[57] For general information on reporting abuse see *Help Stop Child Abuse*, *supra* note 48 at 63-74. For an example of a reporting and investigation protocol developed by the Roman Catholic Church see *Archdiocese of Toronto Procedure for Cases of*

Alleged Misconduct (Effective November 1991). For examples of investigation protocols developed collaboratively by police and child protection services see *Child Sexual Abuse Protocol – Guidelines and Procedures for a Coordinated Response to Child Sexual Abuse in Metropolitan Toronto*, 3d ed. (Toronto: Metropolitan Toronto Special Committee on Child Abuse, March 1995). Anecdotal evidence suggests that very clear protocols are needed everywhere, which take people through the step-by-step process of what to do when abuse is suspected or disclosed. Then, when a situation arises they will have a protocol to turn to for clear guidance. See *Harm's Way, supra* note 40 at 101:

> [T]he research uncovered a peculiar situation in the absence of clear policy and procedures in community service-providing agencies. Several social workers attached to a large care facility were interviewed and reported that they were in the anomalous position of fielding an alarming number of calls from community-based group homes and other service providing agencies…. As one of the respondents described the situation, "The number of service providers who call us to ask what they are supposed to do or to ask whether or not something constitutes abuse is alarming…. It is disturbing that the community agencies seeking help were in fact operating under reasonably clear provincial policy, which outlines what should be done when abuse or violence occurs in ministry-funded or -licensed settings. Constructive policy measures are no guarantee that those charged with responsibility for understanding and implementing policy actually do so."

[58] See M. Wells, "Fair and Effective Procedures for Institutional Response to Sexual Abuse Complaints" in *Civil Liability for Sexual Assault in an Institutional Setting* (Toronto: Canadian Institute Publications, 1995) at 2-4.

[59] For example, in British Columbia, a youth in care receiving services from the Ministry for Children and Families has the right to complain about the services or perceived violations of his or her rights. Internal avenues of complaint include talking with a youth worker or supervisor or contacting the Ministry's Complaint Resolution Manager. External avenues of complaint include contacting the Children's Commission, the Ombudsman, or the Office of the Child, Youth and Family Advocate. This complaint process is outlined online: Children's Commission <http://www.childservices.gov.bc.ca/youngpeople/guide/> (date accessed: 16 November 1999).

[60] J. Beker, "Institutional Abuse: The Tip of the Iceberg?" *Child & Youth Care Forum* 20:6 (December 1991) 377 at 378.

[61] *Bazley* v. *Curry*, [1999] S.C.J. No. 35 (S.C.C.) per McLachlin J. at para. 32-33, online: QL.

62 H. MacMillan *et al.*, "Prevalence of Child Physical and Sexual Abuse in the Community – Results from the Ontario Health Supplement" *Journal of The American Medical Association* 278:2 (9 July 1997) 131.

63 *Family Violence Profile 1999*, *supra* note 11 at 27.

64 *Youth Protection Act*, R.S.Q. c. P-34.1, s. 39.

65 Indeed, in some jurisdictions, a liberal or resourceful interpretation may be required to find a statutory duty to report abuse in out-of-home care settings. See *e.g. R. v. Kates*, [1987] O.J. No. 2032, (Dist. Ct.), online: QL. The court ruled that Ontario's *Child and Family Services Act* was not intended solely to protect children from abuse by parents, and that the words "having charge of a child" were broad enough to include a staff person at a day care centre.

66 See *e.g.* S. Loo *et al.*, *Child Abuse: Reporting and Classification in Health Care Settings* (Ottawa: Health Canada, August 1998) at 19, online <http://www.hc-sc.gc.ca/hppb/familyviolence/child.htm> (date accessed: 16 November 1999) "A recent survey of psychologists in British Columbia indicated that the respondents possessed a high level of knowledge of the reporting law, but this did not by itself increase their propensity to report."

67 For an example of this type of review, on a smaller scale, see Manitoba Family Services, *Independent Review of Reporting Procedures* by P.C. Suche, J. Rogers & P. Vincent (Winnipeg: Manitoba Family Services, February 1992).

68 Loo, *supra* note 66 at 20, notes: "[C]oncerns about a perceived breach of confidentiality cause anxiety among professionals about reporting suspected abuse."

69 R. Tite, "Detecting The Symptoms of Child Abuse: Classroom Complications" (1994) 19:1 Canadian Journal of Education 1 at 9.

70 *The Person Within*, *supra* note 39 at 15. *Harm's Way*, *supra* note 40 at 85.

71 See for example M. Farr, "Would *you* blow the whistle on sex abuse?" *Chatelaine* (March 1999) at 72-80.

72 Legislation creating a duty to report in Canada offers immunity from civil action to those who report in good faith, but only a few statutes protect informants from other types of reprisals. See for example: *Youth Protection Act*, R.S.Q. c. P-34.1, s.134 and *The Child and Family Services Act*, S.M. 1985-86, c. C-80, s. 18.1(3). These basic protections are meagre in contrast to the protection offered by more comprehensive statutory safety-nets such as the *Whistleblower Protection Act* 1994, of Queensland Australia, which entitles whistleblowers to compensation in tort for reprisals, gives public service whistleblowers the right to appeal to be relocated and makes those who engage in retribution against the whistleblower criminally liable. See *Whistleblowers Protection Act* 1994, (Queensland) Report

No.2A, as in force 28 July 1999 (includes am. up to Act No. 33 of 1999), online: Office of the Queensland Parliamentary Counsel <http://www.legislation.qld.gov.au> (date accessed: 20 October 1999), ss. 42 to 46.

[73] B.C. Hoffman, *The Search for Healing, Reconciliation, and the Promise of Prevention – The Recorder's Report concerning Physical and Sexual Abuse at St. Joseph's and St. John's Training Schools for Boys*, a report prepared for the Reconciliation Process Implementation Committee, Ontario (place of publication unknown: Concorde Inc., 30 September 1995) at 276:

> The [legacy of the survivors of St. John's and St. Joseph's Training Schools for Boys] presents us with a tragic opportunity to observe the structural dimensions of child physical and sexual abuse in institutional settings. Because of the scale of the abuse and the fact that it was perpetrated by Christian Brothers – that is, because two of the most powerful and significant institutions in society, the government and the Catholic Church, are key actors – we are able to see more clearly the role of power and the price of its abuse. We are able to understand ... the need, in even the best of settings, for the whistleblower, the need for empowerment of individuals to raise questions of conscience and to question conduct without fear of recrimination.

[74] *Independent Review of Reporting Procedures, supra* note 67 at 135.

[75] N. Rindfleisch, "Political Obstacles to Reporting in Residential Care Settings" in A. Maney & S. Wells, eds., *Professional Responsibilities in Protecting Children – A Public Health Approach to Child Sexual Abuse* (New York: Praeger, 1988) at 60.

[76] Loo, *supra* note 66 at 46.

[77] Tite, *supra* note 69.

[78] Davison, *supra* note 48 at 288.

[79] *The Person Within, supra* note 39 at 15.

[80] *Harm's Way, supra* note 40 at 77.

[81] *Ibid.* at 81-82.

[82] *Forde Inquiry Report, supra* note 10 at 27.

[83] *Harm's Way, supra* note 40 at 193-194.

[84] Institute for the Prevention of Child Abuse, *supra* note 39 at 1-2 and 16.

[85] *Forde Inquiry Report, supra* note 10 at 25.

86 M. Nunno & J. Motz, "The Development of an Effective Response to the Abuse of Children in Out-of-Home Care" (1988) 12 Child Abuse & Neglect 521 at 525.

87 *Forde Inquiry Report, supra* note 10 at 26. See also *Independent Review of Reporting Procedures, supra* note 67 at 90: "It is recommended that: A central team be established to conduct investigations of allegations of abuse in children's residential care facilities. The team be assigned to the office of The Children's Advocate."

B.   Reflections

1.   The Recommended Approaches

To conclude this Report, it is appropriate to return to the letter that launched the Reference. In that letter, the Minister of Justice asked the Law Commission to prepare "a report addressing processes for dealing with institutional child physical and sexual abuse". She charged the Commission with evaluating various approaches to providing redress for adult survivors. The Minister's inquiry was premised on an explicit acknowledgement that "lengthy civil and criminal trials are not ideal processes in this context".

The Law Commission has attempted to respond to the Minister's letter by addressing four main questions:

- **Needs:** What are the needs of adult survivors of institutional child abuse? What are the needs of their families, communities and peoples?

- **Existing Remedies:** What remedies can the formal, established processes for redress actually deliver? How well do these remedies respond to the needs identified?

- **Improvements:** Are there steps that can be taken to improve each of these processes for survivors?

- **New Approaches:** Might there be better ways of meeting the full range of their needs in a manner that promotes reconciliation, fairness and healing?

Part I describes the circumstances that often, and may still, characterise the experience of children who are placed in residential institutions. It sets the context for the Law Commission's review of redress processes and explains how the Commission came to develop its understanding of the current needs of those who have been harmed by institutional child abuse. Its aim is to develop an understanding of the issues raised by institutional child abuse: in particular, the needs of survivors, as expressed by the survivors themselves. The scale and scope of the needs identified reveal the deep and long-lasting impact of childhood abuse – on survivors, their families and their communities, and the wide range of responses that must be implemented in order to provide appropriate redress today.

Throughout, Part I reflects the Commission's view that institutional child abuse is not just a pathology arising from the actions of individuals. Our assumptions as a society about children and about the role of residential instutions in providing for their care are also at issue. Yet Canadian law remains based on an understanding of wrongdoing and harm that emphasises individuals and individual reparations. This understanding, in turn, shapes how survivors state and rank the responses they feel would best address their needs.

Part II examines various processes for redressing the harms caused by such abuse. In its inventory of these processes, the Commission has tried to be as inclusive as possible. It begins with existing legal approaches involving courts, administrative tribunals and *ad hoc* executive processes. It then investigates and evaluates several other approaches that it believes could offer some measure of redress for survivors. They include approaches tried in Canada, as well as those put into place in other countries; responses initiated by governments and those developed by non-governmental organisations such as churches, community groups and local social service agencies; and processes intended to provide redress to individual survivors, as well as those designed to offer a remedy for groups of survivors and their communities.

The Commission acknowledges and appreciates that most of the existing processes under review are general purpose legal and policy instruments. However suitable and effective they might be for responding to harms caused by institutional child abuse, they were not developed with this goal specifically in mind. In assessing these processes and suggesting possible improvements to them, the Commission is mindful of the procedural and structural constraints imposed by the overall objectives of these processes and by general principles of Canadian law.

Any new approaches, of course, need not be established as redress mechanisms available to remedy all wrongdoing or as permanent features of the legal landscape. Their design and operation may be more closely linked to addressing specific situations, such as providing recourse for those who are survivors of physical and sexual abuse. In such approaches, the range of remedies offered to those who have been harmed, the character of the sanctions imposed on those who may be wrongdoers or who supervised or employed wrongdoers, and the manner in which these goals are achieved will often depart significantly from the more familiar models of judicial and administrative processes. Remedies, sanctions and procedures can be purposely created to achieve a precise objective. For example, some – which the Law Commission has called community initiatives – seek to respond directly to the needs of survivors through "from the ground up" healing and compensation programs. Others, such as truth and reconciliation commissions, are aimed both at healing and at reconciling parties in a collective manner, but may not be oriented towards either punishment of wrongdoers or compensation of survivors.

In developing its comparative analysis and assessment of possible approaches to redress, the Law Commission concluded that it would be instructive to evaluate them all on the basis of a set of common standards. Eight different criteria of assessment were developed:

- Does the process promote respect, engagement and informed choice by survivors?

- How effective is it as a fact-finding mechanism?

- Does it lead to accountability?

- Is it fair to all parties involved?

- Does it promote acknowledgement, apology and reconciliation?

- Does it address other needs of survivors such as financial compensation, therapy and education?

- Does it respond to the needs of families, communities, and peoples?

- Does it contribute to public education and prevention?

As one would expect, none of the existing approaches evaluated by the Commission was revealed to be ideal at fulfilling all of these criteria. Nonetheless, in one or more respects every process had something positive to offer. A criminal trial is a powerful vehicle for determining accountability and imposing consequences on those found liable. But given the high standard of proof imposed on the prosecution and the presumption of innocence of the accused, a criminal trial can be lengthy and stressful for those who have already been victimised. Also, the criminal justice process does not normally provide compensation to survivors.

Civil actions similarly permit courts to attribute accountability and to correlate burdens placed on wrongdoers with benefits awarded to those they harmed. However, civil actions often take a long time to complete, especially in cases where there is an appeal. They can also be costly and stressful for those who claim damages, even if their claim is ultimately successful.

Public inquiries and Ombudsman investigations are well-suited to exploring individual instances of abuse and systemic sources and causes of abuse. They can, therefore, draw a more complete picture of the factors that contribute to institutional child abuse. These processes may also result in recommendations that a prosecution be launched, a compensation be paid, or that an institution be redesigned or closed. While these recommendations have moral authority that might put pressure on governments to act, neither public inquiries nor Ombudsman offices have any power to enforce the remedies that they feel are necessary or appropriate. Moreover, these types of investigations can be costly, and are often seen by those under investigation as unfair, especially in cases where they are eventually cleared of wrongdoing.

Criminal injuries compensation schemes and *ex gratia* payments can be effective in providing timely, though limited, financial compensation to survivors. Normally, however, they contribute little to generating accountability or to promoting apology and reconciliation. Their goal is not to assign blame, whether individual or collective. Nor is it to provide counselling or therapy.

Finally, some processes are meant to focus primarily on prevention, and on recommending improvements to systems so that similar harm does not occur to others. They do not find facts about historical abuse; nor do they seek to assign blame. Most notable among these are children's advocates and commissions.

In view of these differing strengths, the Commission favours maintaining a variety of approaches to redress. It does not believe that legislation directing survivors to pursue only one or two recourses is appropriate. The diversity of needs and preferences of survivors also argues in favour of maximising the options available to them. For example, some may prefer to seek formal accountability through the prosecution of alleged offenders and are willing to undergo the burdens that the criminal justice system may impose upon them. Others may be prepared to endure a civil trial in order to obtain the validation that comes from a judicial pronouncement of responsibility for wrongful conduct and the award of damages against offenders and those responsible for the institution in question.

The Law Commission has made several recommendations for improving existing legal processes. It believes that implementing these recommendations would not only benefit survivors of institutional child abuse but others who turn to these processes as well. Anyone who is trying to pursue a civil claim, or to have a prosecutor bring criminal charges relating to an incident that happened years ago, will encounter many difficulties similar to those faced by adult survivors of institutional child abuse. The same is true for those seeking redress for child abuse that has occurred recently, or for abuse that took place outside an institution. By pointing to the structural features of existing processes that have caused problems for adult survivors of institutional child abuse, the Commission hopes to contribute to a more general improvement of these processes.

There are, however, limits to how much these different processes can be retooled to meet the special needs of survivors of institutional child abuse. This point is important, especially in relation to the two most commonly invoked legal processes: criminal and civil trials. Both are adjudicative processes intended to handle all kinds of claims, but their internal procedures make it much easier to pursue certain types of claims. In some cases, these same features may make the process a re-victimising experience for those who have already suffered. The uncertainty of outcomes can also undermine the confidence of those who must overcome many hurdles just to bring a claim or instigate a prosecution.

Civil, and especially criminal, trials are well-suited to dealing with wrongdoings between individuals. Abuse in institutions is, however, rarely just a matter of a single act or the acts of a single person. Even where only one person is alleged to have committed offences, there are usually a number of victims. Where one or more perpetrators have operated within an institution over a period of years, justice usually requires bringing to account not only the actual perpetrator(s), but also those who may have had knowledge of the abuse and could have reported, or put an end to it. In these cases, justice for survivors involves coming to an understanding of the systemic causes of abuse, or the factors that made possible its commission. As the proliferation of specialised administrative tribunals such as human rights commissions attest, sometimes, alternative processes are needed in order to respond effectively to systemic weaknesses or breakdowns.

Again, adversarial trial processes work best when the power, knowledge and resources of parties are reasonably balanced. This is not always the case. For criminal matters, it is assumed that the person accused of a crime is at a disadvantage vis-à-vis the State, so an elaborate system of rules is in place to counter that disadvantage. The civil dispute system does not have similar built-in balancing mechanisms. Ironically, the effects of the harms suffered by former residents of institutions are among the very factors that make access to justice difficult for them. Many former residents may have low incomes and low levels of literacy. Some may have had to battle with substance abuse and their own criminality. Conversely, the people they wish to sue are often those who have a certain social status in the community: as teachers, social workers, psychologists, priests and nuns, for example. The disparity in status is even more striking when a former resident brings a civil action against the government or church that employed abusers. Overcoming this imbalance of power and resources is a key to improving the civil justice process in cases involving institutional child abuse.

The above considerations suggest ways that the criminal and civil justice systems can be adjusted so that they are more responsive to the needs of survivors. Remedies may be expanded, rules of evidence may be modified, the trial process may be subjected to greater judicial control through case management, and so on. But however much these systems are adjusted, the root assumptions upon which they have been developed over the centuries and the constitutional values that have been incorporated into their structure and functioning preclude the kind of comprehensive redesign that would be necessary to respond to the survivors' full range of needs.

This is why governments, and others who feel a responsibility for addressing the harms done to children in institutions they sponsored, are now exploring a number of non-traditional alternatives. Some provincial governments have implemented *ad hoc* administrative compensation programs for former residents of certain institutions. They include, for example, Kingsclear in New Brunswick; Grandview, St. John's and St. Joseph's in Ontario; and Jericho Hill in British Columbia.

Since the fall of 1997, the federal government has been working with representatives of Aboriginal communities across the country and church organisations that operated residential schools for Aboriginal children, to develop programs of compensation for survivors and their communities. The aim is to negotiate settlements that would avoid civil court action, and would expedite the process of validation and payment. In parallel with this initiative to settle claims at the community level, the federal government also presented a Statement of Reconciliation to Aboriginal peoples and funded the Aboriginal Healing Foundation. In addition, a number of churches have given specific apologies to Aboriginal peoples and have established funds to support healing initiatives.

The Commission's investigation of how to provide appropriate redress to survivors suggests five fundamental principles that must be respected in any configuration of options. First, former residents must have the information they need in order to make informed choices about which options to participate in. Second, they need support as they proceed through any process or program. Third, those involved in administering or managing any such process must have sufficient understanding of the particular circumstances of adult survivors of child abuse in institutions, and training in how to deal with these circumstances. Fourth, as there is no single response that is adequate for all survivors, ongoing attempts must be made to improve existing programs in order to make them more effective; any new programs that are developed must also be subject to continual re-assessment. Fifth, whatever the process chosen, claimants must be treated with respect throughout, to avoid re-victimisation.

The Law Commission favours promoting choice for survivors. One way in which this can be accomplished is by better accommodating their needs within traditional legal processes. Encouraging, publicising and promoting ground-up community initiatives is another. Establishing *ad hoc* redress programs as a necessary complement to existing responses is a third. The goal in imagining, negotiating and crafting specially focussed approaches is to ensure that the process itself is respectful of those who were harmed, and that the remedies offered are responsive to all of the victims' needs. In each particular case, identifying survivors' needs establishes the central objectives of the redress process. Its features can then be designed with these objectives in mind.

Several arguments favour the negotiation of redress programs. For one, the needs of adult survivors are extremely complex. No existing legal process has developed with these particular needs in view. While nothing prevents adult survivors from simultaneously pursuing a number of different processes, few have the energy, time and resources to do so.

Furthermore, the goals of achieving accountability, apology and reconciliation are often in conflict with the goal of providing financial compensation in existing processes such as public inquiries, criminal trials, criminal injuries compensation schemes and civil trials. Without the possibility of a redress program, survivors are put in the position of having to rank their needs and to choose among them.

Third, some of the procedural features of the criminal and civil justice processes can make these processes a re-victimising experience for adult survivors. Given the constitutional requirement that courts respect the principles of fundamental justice, it is not possible to readjust these processes to fully accommodate the needs of many survivors.

Finally, these specialised programs can exist in addition, and as a complement to, traditional approaches. Existing and new approaches to redress will work in dynamic interaction to meet all the needs of adult survivors of institutional child abuse, their families and communities. The credible threat of civil liability can help lead those responsible for institutions where abuse occurred into entering more comprehensive settlement programs.

Redress programs designed to deal with particular situations are not, however, free from controversy. Three types of objections are commonly made against them: the perception of special treatment; problems of validation; and the additional cost.

Some may ask why a separate process is necessary to provide redress for adult survivors of physical and sexual abuse experienced in institutions as children, but is not needed to redress other societal wrongdoings. After all, survivors are not the only people who have found the civil and criminal justice systems costly, intimidating, lengthy and frustrating. The Law Commission acknowledges this point. Any legal procedure designed to serve the general needs of the population for accountability and compensation cannot perfectly suit the needs of each individual who uses it.

The Commission wishes to emphasise, however, that neither the redress programs it proposes, nor other attempts to negotiate the settlement of civil claims, should be construed as an attempt to create a special system of justice for the survivors of institutional abuse alone. Put more precisely, whenever large numbers of people are harmed in significant ways as a result of the policies, acts or omissions of public authorities or large organisations, the response should not necessarily be restricted to traditional processes. In certain cases, the response must be informed by a sense of what is right and what is necessary, both to mitigate the effects of the harms done (especially where those harms directly affect subsequent generations) and to take steps to prevent their recurrence. This type of approach should apply whenever that combination of circumstances arises. It is not meant to be a response used only in cases involving survivors of institutional child abuse.

Many people are sceptical of non-judicial redress programs because of their perception that there will be insufficient control over fraudulent claims. It is true that the standard of proof for civil, and especially criminal, trials reduces the likelihood of fraudulent claims or charges to succeed. But there are many other, existing compensation programs that do not require claimants to undergo extensive cross-examination in an adversarial setting. The criminal injuries compensation process is an example. Those who hear and determine criminal injuries compensation claims have acquired a level of expertise and experience that helps them to detect unfounded claims. There is no reason to believe that similar processes for filing and supporting claims, and similar techniques for achieving validation cannot be incorporated into any redress program.

In addition, it must be accepted that just as no judicial process is error-free, no redress program will be error-free. Providing compensation to survivors is a quite different objective from ensuring that no person is ever wrongfully convicted. Given this purpose, it is better to err on the side of making payments to some who may not be entitled to compensation, than to exclude legitimate claimants, or to oblige survivors to go through a re-victimising fact-finding process. In all events, survivors themselves have every interest in ensuring that an appropriate validation mechanism is put into place. It will benefit them in that it will ensure that the legitimacy of the awards is widely accepted, and it will mean that whatever resources are made available in a redress program are not dissipated by the payment of fraudulent claims.

Finally, some people have expressed concern about what they perceive to be the costs of comprehensive negotiated redress programs. It may be true, although the evidence is far from conclusive, that more claimants will come forward to participate in a non-adversarial redress program than would launch a lawsuit against perpetrators and their employers. However, the types of settlements that are usually agreed upon within such programs invariably are somewhat less than the sums that would be awarded as damages by the civil courts. In addition, the cost of litigation will always be substantially higher than the cost of negotiating and administering a comprehensive redress program. After all, defendants who are condemned to pay damages are also required to pay a portion of the plaintiff's legal costs, as well as their own lawyers' fees.

But this is not the real issue. Whatever the monetary cost of negotiating a redress program and providing compensation to those who meet the criteria of eligibility, this cost is small when compared to the cost of not acting. The secondary and ongoing damage – to survivors, to their families and to the community – caused by failing to address harms arising from institutional child abuse is incalculable. In view of this fact, it seems misguided and short-sighted to suggest that redress programs are too costly to undertake.

In the final analysis, what matters most is the attitude that governments take toward dealing with this issue. Proposing new resources and advocating adjustments to existing processes will mean little to survivors if officials are not fully committed to redressing the harm done. Whatever particular responses are being pursued by a survivor, governments must respond with candour and integrity: no information should be strategically withheld, and no procedural tactics should be deployed simply to gain an advantage. Governments must also treat all parties equitably: no processes should be undertaken with the idea of preferring communities to individual survivors, or playing off categories of claimants against each other. Also, governments must not seek to defend their interests by exploiting the litigation process: they should not plead a limitation period when this is the only defence, nor should they engage in excessive cross-examination just to induce a settlement. The Law Commission believes that attitudes matter as much as process. It is here that a genuine response to survivors of institutional child abuse must begin.

2. Situating Responses to Institutional Child Abuse: Redress and Prevention

Only recently have Canadians become aware of the full dimensions of past physical and sexual abuse of children in institutions. The fact that this awareness is belated, however, does not justify a refusal to face up to the issue. Nor does it justify responses suggesting that those who were harmed should let bygones be bygones. The devastating consequences of child abuse for survivors, both at the time of the abuse and for the rest of their lives, should put to rest any suggestion that they ought to "just get over it". The havoc that abuse has wreaked on the families and communities of survivors is a stark reminder of how important it is for Canadians to confront and make amends for this dark chapter in our history.

Confronting the past is, however, only a beginning. There are still larger issues that remain ongoing challenges. The fact that physical and sexual abuse was common in many institutions whose purpose was to protect, nurture and educate young people demonstrates a tragic breach of trust by the abusers. It is an indictment of the supervisory processes in place at those institutions, and it is a damning commentary on the casual attitude that society took towards the children it sent there. For generations to come, all Canadians will have to deal with the legacy of the physical and sexual abuse of children. All will have to acknowledge their continuing responsibility to the children who were abused in our institutions.

What is more, this Ministerial Reference must be situated in context. Its relatively narrow scope should not lead us to neglect the other situations within which physical and sexual abuse takes place. The Minister asked the Law Commission to examine and evaluate processes for dealing with the physical and sexual abuse of children in institutions in the past. Each one of these defining features of the Commission's mandate captures only a fraction of those contexts of abuse that society now faces. The broader fields suggested by each of these defining features will be considered in turn, in order to set the stage for the conclusion that public education and prevention must be a central part of any response to adult survivors who were abused as children in government-run or government-funded institutions.

The Minister's letter directed the Law Commission to especially examine the claims of adult survivors of abuse that occurred while they were children. This focus on the past should not be seen as a reassurance that we can put the issue of institutional child abuse behind us. Despite enormous improvements in the design and administration of institutions for children, the training and supervision of caregivers and the systems in place for detecting abuse, child abuse in out-of-home settings continues to this day. Unlike pandemics that may be treated and eliminated by science or technology, whenever harm results from the acts of human beings, ongoing public education and prevention will always be needed.

The Minister's letter also asked the Law Commission to consider abuse that occurred in institutions. The concern was with institutions as bricks-and-mortar locations: training schools, schools for children with physical and mental disabilities, residential educational institutions for Aboriginal children, asylums, sanatoria, and so on. Over the past half century, a wide variety of such institutions have existed: some sponsored by the government, some private; some were total institutions, some not; some were institutions where parents or guardians voluntarily placed children, and some were institutions where children who had been apprehended by the state were placed. It is important not to lose sight of the variety of these institutions and their susceptibility to harbouring those who would physically and sexually abuse children. As Canadian public policy moves towards closing large institutions for children, the potential for abuse does not disappear. The alternatives developed to replace many bricks-and-mortar institutions – foster homes, for example – can also be locations of abuse. So, too, can children's organisations, summer camps, sports leagues, and so on. However much it is possible to design procedures to address and reduce the incidence of abuse in large institutions, public education and vigilance are also important for ensuring that opportunities for the abuse of children in other out-of-home settings are not provided.

The question put to the Law Commission was cast as an inquiry into approaches to redress for adult survivors of child abuse in institutions. The Commission has understood the term "child" as applying to both youths and adolescents. However, it should be remembered that the circumstances in which physical and sexual abuse can flourish, are also present in places where there are no children. Any place where there exists a relationship of unequal power, structured within a context that is not easily opened to public scrutiny, presents an opportunity for a person who is inclined to abuse others, to do so. It is important to keep clearly in mind the conditions within which abuse may flourish, and to direct special attention to minimising the opportunities for abuse that they present.

The Minister also directed the Law Commission to consider processes for handling the physical and sexual abuse of children in institutions. This Report has identified numerous situations where abuse of this kind has occurred. Still, there are many other types of abuse, such as emotional, psychological, racial and cultural abuse. The harm caused by these other forms of abuse is equally devastating. Indeed, there are few occasions when physical and sexual abuse does not, itself, constitute emotional and psychological abuse. The necessary focus on physical and sexual abuse should not be used as an excuse to neglect the deep harms caused by emotional, psychological and cultural abuse. Drawing distinctions between kinds of abuse is, in the context of a report such as this, both unhelpful and invidious.

Finally, the Law Commission was asked to identify and evaluate processes for handling allegations of physical and sexual abuse. This Report has examined existing legal processes and procedures in Canada, such as criminal and civil trials, public inquiries, and so on. But it has also considered international approaches such as truth and reconciliation commissions, community-generated initiatives, and a variety of redress programs that have been negotiated between governments and survivors of abuse. In reviewing these approaches to redress, the Commission was concerned that it not draw a sharp line between process and substance. By focussing on the needs of survivors, it has sought to show the importance of not only thinking about the kind of remedy that may result from a given process, but also considering the effect of the processes themselves on survivors.

For the most part, the approaches to redress examined are oriented towards repairing past harms. They answer the general question "What can be done now to make things right?" But many survivors also express forward-looking concerns on behalf of children who are vulnerable to abuse today. They indicate a deep need to believe that governments in Canada, and Canadians as a whole, have learned from survivors' experiences about the tragedy of abuse, and are prepared to commit themselves to public education and other measures to prevent its recurrence. The Law Commission takes these concerns to heart. It believes that a response to the Minister's inquiry about redress processes is incomplete unless it also examines what is known, and what is being done about, abuse in institutional settings today.

This Report outlines a variety of perspectives on, and approaches to public education and prevention. A culture of abuse requires a ground within which to flourish. Canadians need to develop a better understanding of the nature and scope of child abuse in institutions. A key step is to identify and isolate attitudes that sustain those who physically and sexually abuse children. What do we think about the capacity of residential institutions to improve the situation of children in need of care? Do they afford us the dangerous excuse of simply saying "out of sight, out of mind"? What attitudes about the needs and vulnerabilities of children underlie current policies of child protection? Do these attitudes allow us to discount the voices of children when they raise concerns about abuse? The Commission believes it is essential to establish a better information base for sharing knowledge about child abuse and the ways it can be recognised.

A second dimension of prevention is to carefully investigate the institutional and other out-of-home settings in which abuse has thrived. This process entails gaining a clearer understanding of why certain types of institutions have revealed themselves as more likely to attract people who would abuse children. Conversely, in what kinds of institutions are occurrences of abuse rare, or absent? It is clear that abusers are best able to harm children in situations where the institutional setting reinforces the power imbalance that exists between children and adults. It is also clear that abusers are best able to harm children in institutions where the layout, procedures and routines allow for interactions to take place in isolation. Much of prevention entails putting into place systems and procedures that limit the opportunities for abuse. The Commission believes there are important lessons to be learned from both survivors of past abuse and youth currently in out-of-home care about the structural and procedural conditions in institutions that allow abuse to occur.

A concern with prevention, presented as a complement to a concern about designing respectful and comprehensive processes of redress, highlights a fundamental feature of the Law Commission's understanding of the Minister's request. The reform of law, legal institutions and legal processes can be approached from a perspective that emphasises form and structure. In such a light, recommendations will offer ways of changing the way law looks. Alternatively, reforming law, legal institutions and legal processes can be approached from a perspective that reflects society's needs. In such a light, recommendations will be directed to changing the way law works.

It is the second perspective that animates this Report. It is this perspective which has led the Commission to propose a framework for prevention that includes proper screening of those who are employed in institutions for children, ongoing monitoring and performance reviews, and independent oversight of the operation of these institutions. Furthermore, this perspective has led the Commission to recommend strategies for public education and prevention, and for providing redress to adult survivors of institutional child abuse.

3.   A Continuing Agenda of Law Reform

The Law Commission believes that law is as much the affair of all Canadians as it is the responsibility of legislatures, administrators and courts. It takes the view that all Canadians should be involved in thinking about how law should deal with key social issues. Law provides a link between processes for maintaining an open and democratic society and the values reflected in everyday experience. How we choose to respond to those who have pressing and irresistible claims for redress tells us more about our foundational values than do the abstract declarations of principle in constitutions. For this reason, the Commission does not consider this to be a "final report" on the Minister's Reference. The approach it has adopted and the issues it raises will continue to be pursued in other research projects, under three of the Commission's general research themes: personal relationships, social relationships and governance relationships.

So, for example, the issue of institutional child abuse highlights the need to investigate the causes and the legal responses to abuse and exploitation in all relationships of unequal power. Understanding how the law imagines and structures various relationships of dependence and interdependence, and how it may either reduce or increase power imbalances, are key issues that the Commission intends to explore in developing its personal relationships theme.

Of similar importance are the questions of how children in socially and economically marginalised groups have been, disproportionately, the victims of child abuse, and how devastating the impact of this abuse has been on the social relationships within families and communities. Understanding the way in which the law, in deciding which relationships are worthy of recognition and support, may either reinforce or destroy group identities and communities is another important policy question that the Commission will be pursuing.

There is also a need to reflect on the paradox that today, increased recourse to adversarial processes goes hand-in-hand with increased scepticism about the legitimacy and capacity of courts to resolve conflict. The need to imagine other, more accessible and responsive processes, is a fundamental concern of the Commission under its governance relationships theme.

Developing linkages between this Report and its ongoing research agenda is one way the Commission intends to ensure that the issue of institutional child abuse does not disappear from view. In addition, because law reform must always be judged by how well it succeeds in addressing the concerns prompting the reform, the Commission hopes that Canadians will revisit this Report to assess the degree of success achieved by any of its recommendations that have been implemented.

A primary goal of this response to the Minister's Reference has been to set out the Commission's best sense of the appropriate processes for responding to the needs of adult survivors of institutional child abuse. The Report itself reflects the manner in which the Law Commission understands not only the Minister's request, but also its own statutory mandate. That mandate is to adopt a broad, multidisciplinary approach in order to imagine the kinds of law and legal institutions that are necessary to respond to today's social and economic challenges. Directly involving those most concerned with any issue, through consultations, study panels and participatory research, is a key commitment of the Law Commission.

While this Report is directed to the Minister of Justice, and through her, to the Parliament of Canada, it is written for adult survivors who were abused as children in government-run and government-sponsored institutions. It is meant to give Canadians an opportunity to lean about the harm done to thousands of children, their families and their communities. It is also an opportunity for Canadians to acknowledge this harm and to develop an understanding of the present needs of those who were abused as children in public institutions. The aim is to provide Canadians with the information necessary for them to become fully involved in discussions about how best to meet the challenges presented by past institutional child abuse. Only with broad public knowledge can the policy options concerning possible approaches to redress be publicly debated and justly decided.

Recognising the deep and long-lasting impact of childhood physical and sexual abuse, and the wide range of responses that must be made available in order to provide appropriate redress, is a first step to doing justice to survivors. Putting programs into place to educate the public about the tragedy of abuse is a second step. Committing ourselves, individually and as a society, to preventing its recurrence is a third, and perhaps the most important, step we can take to honour the memory of all abused children – both those who survived, and those who did not.

Recommendations

This Report sets out a number of specific recommendations relating to the improvement of existing processes of redress, the creation of new processes for responding to survivors of institutional child abuse, and the promotion of approaches to prevention. But the Commission's response to the Minister involves more than proposals that can be stated in the form of specific recommendations. To situate and to complete its advice, the Commission proposes six more general recommendations that it feels must frame the way these specific recommendations are read.

General Recommendations

THE LAW COMMISSION BELIEVES that approaches to providing redress to survivors of institutional child abuse must take the needs of survivors, their families and their communities as a starting point.

> Survivors have suffered the harm. They, their families and their communities are best able to articulate the harm suffered. Of all the parties to institutional abuse, survivors traditionally have had by far the weakest voice. Too often the focus of official processes has been on punishing wrongdoers rather than on righting the wrongs done to survivors and on healing their communities.

THE LAW COMMISSION BELIEVES that every survivor has unique needs. All attempts to address these needs should be grounded in respect, engagement and informed choice.

> Survivors must be shown respect. They must be engaged by whatever types of redress processes are put into place to the fullest extent the process permits and they themselves desire. They should have access to adequate and unbiased information about the options available to them. And they must be provided support throughout the process they choose.

Any existing processes for redress should be modified where necessary so as to better achieve these goals. Survivors should be given the time and the information they need in order to make the choices that they feel are best for them individually.

THE LAW COMMISSION BELIEVES that processes of redress should not cause further harm to survivors of institutional child abuse, their families and their communities.

Officials responsible for a redress process should have special training or experience with protocols for assisting survivors. The process should be set within an integrated, coordinated response to survivors, their families and their communities that recognises the full range of harms that have been suffered and the full range of needs expressed. The process should not be a revictimising experience for survivors. It must, however, be fair to all those who are affected by it, including those who are alleged to have committed the abuse.

THE LAW COMMISSION BELIEVES that community initiatives should be promoted as a significant means of redressing institutional child abuse.

Grassroots and self-help initiatives should be encouraged and facilitated. They should seek to build upon community understanding of the types of response that best meet the needs of survivors and their families. Where it is acceptable to survivors, those responsible for institutions at which abuse took place should participate in these initiatives, by providing financial or human resources to help communities to develop and manage these initiatives.

THE LAW COMMISSION BELIEVES that redress programs negotiated with survivors and their communities are the best official response for addressing the full range of their needs while being responsive to concerns of fairness and accountability.

Those responsible for institutions at which abuse took place should demonstrate their willingness to establish optional redress programs with survivors and their communities. The features of these programs should be developed through negotiation. The programs should be designed and operated so as to offer those who wish, the opportunity to be involved in the process. Survivors should have the option of choosing which particular mix of benefits or compensation best meets their needs.

THE LAW COMMISSION BELIEVES that in addition to specific programs designed to meet the needs of survivors, it is crucial to establish programs of public education and to continue to develop and revise protocols and other strategies for prevention.

Canadians need to know more about why children were placed in institutions, what happened to them there and how abuse was allowed to occur. Canadians need to understand that institutional child abuse remains a problem in our society, to which all children in out-of-home care are vulnerable.

Specific Recommendations

The Criminal Justice Process

PEOPLE BRINGING COMPLAINTS TO THE POLICE should be fully informed at the outset of how the criminal justice process works and their role in it.

Considerations:

Governments should prepare, in consultation with interested parties, pamphlets and information kits that describe the character of the criminal process as it affects adult complainants alleging institutional child abuse.

Community service agencies, survivors' groups and other non-governmental organisations should also be given resources to develop their own information kits and pamphlets about how the criminal justice process works when there are allegations of institutional child abuse.

These various information kits should be available at all police stations, social service agencies, hospitals and the offices of health care professionals.

Police, social service agencies, hospitals and the offices of health care professionals should have access to literature or help-line numbers to which they may refer those who may disclose experiences of child abuse.

THOSE INVOLVED IN investigating, prosecuting, defending and judging allegations of institutional child abuse should have special training, expertise or experience and should have access to survivor-sensitive protocols that have been developed for this purpose.

Considerations:

Protocols have been developed to deal with investigations of multi-victim institutional child abuse. Any police force embarking on such an investigation should consult these protocols or those who have developed them.

When approaching potential witnesses, particularly for the first time, there must be respect for the privacy of former residents of institutions.

As a rule, the first substantive interview in an investigation should be conducted by a person with whom a survivor feels comfortable, and this option should be presented to survivors. Where possible, former residents of institutions should have follow-up interviews by an officer with whom they feel comfortable (*e.g.* a female officer or an Aboriginal officer).

Complainants should, however, be informed at the outset that it may not be possible, over long and complex proceedings, to ensure that the witness or complainants will always be able to deal with the same officials.

All major decisions about how the police intend to proceed should be explained fully to the complainant(s), especially any decision not to lay charges or to terminate an investigation.

PEER, PROFESSIONAL AND PRACTICAL SUPPORT for survivors should be available from the commencement of a criminal investigation throughout the trial and beyond.

Considerations:

Those involved in victim witness support programs should receive training or education with respect to the particular needs of survivors of institutional child abuse.

Wherever possible, witnesses for the prosecution should have access to a private area while waiting to testify, so they do not have to wait with the accused.

Support should include access to both peer and professional counselling during a criminal investigation and prosecution.

Financial support should be available to permit a family member or friend of the complainant to attend the trial or to provide the services of a therapist or peer counsellor.

THE EXPERIENCE OF TESTIFYING should avoid revictimising complainants.

Considerations:

Devices to protect witnesses, such as screens in front of the witness box, closed-circuit television and videotaped evidence should be available, in appropriate circumstances, to adult witnesses. Currently, such devices are available only to witnesses under the age of 18, and only where they are complainants in cases involving sexual abuse.

Crown attorneys should have the resources necessary to fully prepare survivors for testifying. Crown counsel who undertake prosecutions of historical child sexual abuse should have the resources to explain issues such as: how the process works, possible outcomes, the role of the complainant, the duration of the process, *etc.*

Efforts should be made to avoid subjecting witnesses to multiple examinations in the course of one criminal proceeding. Such a procedure would require the support and collaboration of the Crown and defence bars. The testimony would have to be videotaped, so that those relying on it and not present when it was taped could assess the demeanour of the witness.

If preliminary inquiries are not abolished, cross-examinations within them should be time-limited, as determined on a case-by-case basis, subject to an extension where this is justified.

The *Criminal Code* should be amended to ensure that all victims of child abuse benefit from the same procedural protections as those who are covered by the 1983 amendments to the sexual assault provisions.

Witnesses' testimony should not automatically be discredited solely because they have spoken together. There should be no presumption that such as evidence is tainted. Defence counsel who wish to establish that testimony is not reliable should have the burden to do so as in other ordinary challenges to evidence.

THE SENTENCING PROCESS should be inclusive and restorative wherever possible.

Considerations:

Defence counsel should exercise discretion and restraint in cross-examining persons who have submitted a victim impact statement.

Family members should be entitled to provide victim impact statements to illustrate the lifelong effect of child abuse and how it affects the relationships of victims with their families.

Where appropriate, courts should promote restorative justice approaches and involve members of affected communities is sentencing hearings.

Civil Actions

PROSPECTIVE PLAINTIFFS should have access to basic information about civil actions at no cost.

Considerations:

Provincial governments, Law Societies, professional organisations and law faculties should continue to develop basic public legal information programmes that provide accessible information about legal options available to survivors of institutional child abuse.

This information should relate to matters such as how to contact a lawyer, the procedure, costs, possible outcomes, and the length of the process.

Community service agencies, survivors' groups and other non-governmental organisations should also be given resources to develop their own information kits and pamphlets on the same topics.

Access to information about the experience of pursuing a civil claim involving institutional child abuse should also be available, and social service agencies or others who work with survivors should set up programs that enable former residents to share their experiences with potential plaintiffs.

PROSPECTIVE PLAINTIFFS should have access to support services to assist them in coping with the stress of civil litigation.

Considerations:

Social service agencies should develop and promote support networks composed of survivors with experience in civil litigation and related processes for seeking redress. They should also compile and publicise a list of community organisations that have experience in assisting survivors. Emotional and psychological support should be available throughout the litigation process.

Professional associations should compile a roster of therapists experienced in working with abuse survivors.

LAW SOCIETIES AND BAR ASSOCIATIONS should continue to organise professional development programs on how to conduct cases involving allegations of past institutional child abuse.

Considerations:

Law Societies may also wish to consider adding civil litigation dealing with child sexual and physical abuse to the list of specialties that may be certified.

Certification should require not only expertise in litigation, but also training in how abuse affects survivors, and the implications for the desirability and conduct of the litigation.

Certification lists should be promoted in appropriate communities, including within therapeutic communities.

LAW SOCIETIES SHOULD REVIEW their *Codes of Professional Conduct* to ensure that appropriate rules are in place to safeguard against the exploitation of survivors of institutional child abuse, especially with respect to recruitment of clients and fee arrangements.

Considerations:

The recent revisions to rule 1602.1 of the *Code of Professional Conduct* made by the Law Society of Saskatchewan could serve as a model.

The potential for exploitation inherent in contingency fees for class actions involving survivors of institutional abuse could also be minimised or eliminated through a variety of means:

- Establishment of a provincially-run class action fund to cover initial disbursements.

- Mandatory taxation of contingency accounts, or a requirement of prior judicial approval of contingency fee arrangements.

- Governments or other institutional defendants could refuse to negotiate settlements where the contingency fee is inflated.

THE NATIONAL JUDICIAL INSTITUTE and other judicial education bodies should promote judicial education programs about the circumstances and consequences of physical and sexual abuse of children in institutions.

Considerations:

These programs should provide judges with basic information about survivor litigants, including:

- information about how survivor symptoms may manifest themselves during litigation, and how they might be misinterpreted.

- information about racial and cultural differences that may manifest themselves in testifying.

- information about the non-financial expectations shared by many abuse survivors, and how the judicial role and the conduct of the litigation may assist survivors to obtain these goals without impeding any other requirements of justice.

LEGISLATURES SHOULD REVISE the principles governing limitation periods in cases of institutional child abuse, and governments should refrain from relying on limitation periods as a defence in such cases.

Considerations:

Provincial legislatures should consider the extension of limitation periods for child sexual abuse through such means as:

- amending legislation so that the limitation period does not begin to run, in the case of certain types of sexual offences in particular those that occurred during childhood or adolescence, until the plaintiff becomes aware of the connection between her or his injuries and the harm inflicted; and

- increasing the limitation period whenever the action is based on misconduct committed in the context of a relationship of dependency.

The federal government should take the lead in adopting a policy that it will not rely solely on a limitation period defence in cases relating to institutional child abuse.

COURTS SHOULD GENERALLY RESPECT the requests of plaintiffs to preserve their privacy over the course of a trial.

Considerations:

In a few recent decisions involving compensation to victims of sexual violence, the courts have respected the victims' wish to protect their privacy by granting a request for authorization to use a pseudonym or initials, seal the file, obtain a temporary order preventing the publication of any information that could identify the victim, or holding the proceedings *in camera*.

Where legislation now protects the anonymity of the parties by requiring civil proceedings in family matters to be held in camera but does not apply to civil proceedings relating to institutional child abuse, it should be amended so that it encompasses any proceedings relating to matters, such as institutional violence, that directly or indirectly affect the family.

GOVERNMENTS SHOULD NOT IMPOSE confidentiality provisions on settlements with survivors of institutional child abuse, or on awards granted pursuant to any alternative dispute resolution process.

Considerations:

It should be up to the plaintiff to decide whether he or she wishes to keep the terms of an agreement confidential.

Settlement agreements that are not confidential could be recorded in the register of the superior court where the case was launched.

Where plaintiffs wish to preserve the confidentiality of their settlement agreements, governments (and other institutional defendants) should nevertheless publish aggregate data about settlements in respect of institutional child abuse cases, so long as the data cannot identify any plaintiff.

WHERE COURTS APPLY statistical data in order to determine lost income for survivors of institutions, they should use the statistics for the Canadian public as a whole, rather than those specific to the population that attended the particular institution.

Considerations:

Statistical averages drawn from among those who were survivors of institutional child abuse offer only a partial indication of how any particular individual would have succeeded had he or she not suffered abuse.

Criminal Injuries Compensation Programs

CRIMINAL INJURIES COMPENSATION programs should explicitly provide for extended limitation periods in cases of sexual or physical abuse committed while the claimant was a child.

Considerations:

Incorporation of the "delayed discoverability" rule or a statutory extension of the limitation period would be consistent with the treatment of child abuse claims in civil actions for damages.

SURVIVORS OF INSTITUTIONAL CHILD ABUSE should not be refused compensation solely because they do not report the abuse to the police or automatically cooperate in an investigation.

Considerations:

Adjudicators should take into account that a claimant's failure to cooperate with the police may result from a distrust of authority originating in the very abuse for which compensation is being sought.

CRIMINAL INJURIES COMPENSATION BOARDS should publish the framework or analytical screen used to determine their awards, as well as their decisions, withholding the names of the claimants.

Considerations:

Publication of awards would promote consistency, especially among provinces with similar ceilings for claims.

This would enable policymakers to assess the adequacy of the program and determine where adjustments should be made.

Ex Gratia Payments

GOVERNMENTS SHOULD REVISE POLICIES on providing compensation by way of *ex gratia* payments to include classes of persons who suffered harm, directly or indirectly, as a result of policy decisions later found to have been inappropriate, even when others are potentially liable in a civil action.

Considerations:

Normally governments are not civilly liable for damages flowing from policy, planning or executive decisions. Where a misguided policy opens the door to, or facilitates the commission of a civil wrong by others, *ex gratia* payments should not be excluded as a means to acknowledge the wrongful policy.

EX GRATIA PAYMENTS should be offered in cases where an otherwise meritorious and provable claim cannot be pursued because it falls outside a limitation period, or where liability is uncertain and it is not in the public interest to defer compensation until litigation has concluded.

EX GRATIA PAYMENT OFFERS to individuals should include reimbursement for the costs of seeking professional advice in order to make an informed decision about whether to accept the offer.

GOVERNMENTS SHOULD REVISE POLICIES on paying compensation so as to provide a mechanism for expedited, interim and "without prejudice" *ex gratia* payments.

Ombudsman Offices

JURISDICTIONS THAT DO NOT now have an Ombudsman's office or similar institution should consider enacting legislation to establish one.

Considerations:

> Where specialised Ombudsman's offices exist in a jurisdiction, but they do not have authority to examine questions of institutional child abuse, either a general Ombudsman office or another specialised Ombudsman (such as, in the case of the federal government, an Aboriginal Ombudsman with authority to investigate abuse in residential schools) should be created.

OMBUDSMAN STATUTES should be amended (where necessary) to require that governments table a response to an Ombudsman report in the legislature within a specified delay.

Children's Advocates and Commissions

JURISDICTIONS THAT DO NOT now have independent bodies to act as children's advocates should consider enacting legislation to establish them.

THE MANDATES OF CHILDREN'S advocates and commissioners should be broad enough to assist children and youth living in residential institutions and other types of out-of-home care settings, as well as those living at home.

CHILDREN'S ADVOCATES AND COMMISSIONS should establish and consult regularly with advisory committees made up of people who are or have been in care, including adult survivors of institutional child abuse.

Considerations:

These committees could advise them generally on how they carry out their advocacy roles and specifically on matters related to education, research and systems reviews.

Public Inquiries

GOVERNMENTS SHOULD WEIGH the following factors when determining whether to launch a public inquiry into allegations of institutional child abuse:

1. Whether individuals have made allegations of multiple abuse affecting several children and authorities have not responded;

2. Whether a primary goal of the inquiry would be to identify systemic weaknesses and failures;

3. Whether a criminal investigation is ongoing or charges have been laid;

4. Whether an Ombudsman or a children's commissioner has authority to investigate; and

5. Whether any other fact-finding process more attuned to meeting the needs of survivors exists.

Considerations:

Even in a jurisdiction with an Ombudsman or a children's commissioner or advocate, a public inquiry may still be appropriate because: (1) the issue involves a private institution; (2) there is need for special resources or expertise; (3) the investigation must be concluded in a short period; and (4) the investigatory powers of a children's commissioner or a children's advocate may be limited to current abuse.

IF A PUBLIC INQUIRY into institutional child abuse is established, the order-in-council should clearly set out its objectives and the key questions to be addressed (*e.g.*, whether the focus will be on determining wrongdoing, or on systemic and organisational aspects of abuse, or both).

Considerations:

The mandate should be communicated to all potential participants; in particular, former residents and employees of the institution(s) being investigated.

The commission should be accorded resources that are sufficient to accomplish its mandate in the time allotted to it.

When a commission of inquiry is established, procedural matters for its consideration should include:

Whether to hold the hearing in public and how to protect the confidentiality of former residents of an institution.

If former residents of an institution are dispersed geographically, how to ensure they are able to attend the inquiry.

How to ensure counselling and peer support is available to former residents during the course of the inquiry.

How to ensure that both the process and the commission's report meet the communication requirements of former residents, including for example, the need for interpreters and the need to publish documents in alternate formats.

IF A PUBLIC INQUIRY into institutional child abuse is established, respect for survivors should be reflected in its membership.

Considerations:

Where an inquiry has several members, the inquiry should reflect expertise not only in law, but also in disciplines experienced in dealing with the impact of institutional child abuse (such as therapists and social workers). The inquiry should demonstrate sensitivity to the specific socio-demographic makeup of survivors.

Truth Commissions and Similar Processes to Address Systemic Human Rights Abuses

A TRUTH COMMISSION HAS the potential to be an appropriate forum for providing redress where large numbers of people spread over a wide geographic area have suffered abuses over several generations, and the goals of fact-finding and healing cannot be achieved without a generalised amnesty for wrongdoers.

Considerations:

The decision whether to establish a truth commission or some other truth-finding procedure is a matter to be determined by governments in cooperation with the affected communities and peoples. If it were agreed to establish a truth commission, then certain issues related to the operation of the commission would need to be considered, including the following:

- A truth commission should have the power to compel production of government and institutional evidence. It must be capable of exploring the evidence left by the institutions in question, and relevant internal records.

- The information-gathering process should be more respectful of survivors and more therapeutic than it is in criminal or civil actions. The process should not force survivors to tell their stories. Those who do participate should be able to testify, publicly or privately, in a safe and supportive environment.

• A truth commission should encourage the presentation of official, public apologies that are meaningful. In addition, the process could create a forum similar to South Africa's "Register of Reconciliation" web page, where individuals can make informal or personal apologies.

Community Initiatives

SURVIVORS AND THEIR COMMUNITIES should be encouraged to experiment with different projects and programs organised and administered at the community level.

Considerations:

A first step is to make available information about other initiatives so that the full range of possible initiatives can be considered.

Existing healing and reconciliation funds, whether established by government or others, should be active in providing seed money for innovative programs.

COMMUNITY-BASED PROGRAMS should be assisted in sharing their experiences so that new programs could be modelled on successful initiatives.

Considerations:

This might involve sponsoring publications, videos and websites or even paying the transportation costs to enable those who are managing successful programs to visit communities that wish to set up their own program.

ORGANISATIONS THAT SPONSORED RESIDENTIAL facilities and governments should continue to make resources available to support local initiatives through which social services are delivered to survivors of physical and sexual abuse.

Redress Programs

A REDRESS PROGRAM should be designed with input from the group it is intended to benefit.

Considerations:

The most credible form of input is negotiation directly with former residents or their representatives.

The circumstances of negotiations should ensure, to the extent possible, that the former residents are on an equal footing with those offering redress. It may also involve funding a survivors' group so that information is disseminated to as many former residents as possible, and they are aware of the progress of negotiations. This should involve ensuring that this group has the means to hire the professional help they require, if they choose, to assist in the negotiations. This may include lawyers, interpreters or others such as survivors from other institutions who former residents feel they need.

Disseminating this information would enable survivors to provide their views to those negotiating on their behalf.

A REDRESS PROGRAM should offer compensation and benefits that respond to the full range of survivors' needs.

Considerations:

In institutions where physical or sexual abuse was pervasive, residents may have suffered psychological and emotional damage as a result, even if they themselves were not victims of such abuse.

In institutions where the culture of the resident population was consistently undermined (*e.g.* in certain residential schools for Aboriginal children or certain schools for Deaf children), residents may have suffered long-term harms as a result.

Deprivation of an adequate education should also be considered as a basis for redress.

REDRESS PROGRAMS should offer a wider range of benefits than those available through the courts or administrative tribunals.

Considerations:

Survivors may require support in the form of services as much as they require financial compensation.

The categories of benefits or services which may be offered through a redress program should not be considered closed. Survivors should have the opportunity of receiving those benefits which are best suited to their needs.

Redress programs should be flexible about how they distribute benefits. The program itself need not provide the benefits directly, but may simply be willing to fund a variety of services in the community so long as they are directly related to survivors' needs.

FAMILY MEMBERS should be entitled to certain benefits of a redress program.

Considerations:

Where a family member has suffered harm as a result of the abuse of a relative in an institution, he or she should be entitled to receive reasonable compensation or to participate in certain of the benefits offered to survivors, in particular, therapy or counselling.

Survivors should also have the option of transferring benefits such as education benefits to a family member.

BEST EFFORTS should be made to contact as many former residents as possible to inform them of the redress program in a timely fashion, while respecting their privacy.

Considerations:

Outreach efforts should protect the privacy of former residents by avoiding direct approaches, for example, through the mail.

General outreach (*i.e.* notices and advertisements) can target settings where survivors are likely to see them, for example, wherever mental health services are provided, Aboriginal friendship centres, community groups, continuing education institutions.

Former residents serving time in prison should be given an equal opportunity to participate in redress programs – outreach to the prison population should therefore be undertaken, and accommodation made to enable prisoners to present their claims. The information provided in outreach letters or advertisements should be in clear and accessible language.

Verbal outreach (*e.g.* via radio or a toll-free 1-800 number) is as important as written communication.

Outreach should commence well in advance of the program itself, to allow former residents the time needed to consider their options and to maximise the number of claimants who apply within the set period.

THE CLAIMS PERIOD should be designed to ensure that the maximum number of claimants has an opportunity to apply.

Considerations:

A claims period should be set for a realistic duration, and should not be terminated prematurely.

Termination of a claims period should only occur with reasonable notice.

A REDRESS PROGRAM must be based on a clear and credible validation process.

Considerations:

The focus of the validation process should be on establishing what harms were suffered at the institution, the effects of those harms, and the appropriate level of compensation.

The standard of proof required should be commensurate with the benefits offered.

Those determining the validity of claims should be impartial decision makers. Members of adjudication panels should have the appropriate professional background, training or life experience to recognise the harms of institutional child abuse. They should have experience with a compensation process, rather than only a fault-finding process.

The onus should be on those organising the redress program to corroborate, to the extent possible, the experiences recounted by those claiming compensation. All possible sources of corroboration should be canvassed, including institutional archives, school performance and attendance records, contemporaneous medical, social service or police reports, and the verdicts of criminal proceedings, if any.

THE ADMINISTRATION OF A REDRESS PROGRAM should have the confidence of both funders and beneficiaries.

Considerations:

Where possible, those administering a program should be independent of those funding it.

An attempt should be made to assure continuity in the administration of the program, both for the sake of efficiency and to facilitate the development of a relationship of trust with survivors.

Adjudication panels should have some members whose backgrounds reflect the backgrounds of the claimants.

BEST PRACTICES IN REDRESS PROGRAMS should be assembled by an independent body, such as a university department or research institute, for the benefits of society as a whole, as well as survivors.

Considerations:

Programs to train survivors or their representatives in the negotiation of redress programs should be established.

Those who negotiate on behalf of governments or churches should also receive training or have knowledge about the circumstances and effects of institutional child abuse.

THERE SHOULD BE A PLACE (OR PLACES) where those who lived in institutions can record their experiences and where historical materials concerning these institutions can be gathered.

Considerations:

The recording of experiences could be done in a variety of formats – tape-recorded conversations, interviews, monologues, original artwork, photographs, written remembrances, videotapes, *etc.* Contributions need not be limited to experiences of abuse, but could include all recollections of life in an institution.

Contributions could come from individuals, groups, and/or communities.

Procedures should be in place to ensure that no allegations or accusations are made against named or identifiable individuals. Where such allegations or accusations are made, they should be deleted or expunged.

Prevention

THE VALUES AND PRINCIPLES set out in the *Convention on the Rights of the Child*, should be the foundation upon which all programs and services for children and youth in out-of-home care are built.

Considerations:

Governmental and non-governmental organisations that deliver programs and services to children outside the home to assist in their personal growth or well-being should review, and if necessary revise, their guiding instruments (such as laws, by-laws, missions statements, policies and standards) to ensure that they clearly and formally articulate and reflect the rights and best interests of the children in their care and are consistent with the values and principles set out in the *Convention on the Rights of the Child*.

GOVERNMENTS, RESEARCH INSTITUTIONS and non-governmental organisations should coordinate their efforts to compile and disseminate an inventory of promising and proven measures to prevent the abuse of children in out-of-home care.

Considerations:

A number of published and unpublished studies and reports have already been produced which relate to the vulnerability and experiences of children and youth in residential and out-of-home care. As a first step, Health Canada could create an inventory of these reports (which have been prepared by provincial Ombudsman offices, children's advocates and children's commissioners, by independent researchers under contract to governments, by non-governmental organisations and by others). The inventory, along with links to electronic copies or information on how to obtain copies of these materials, could be made available online through an electronic resource centre such as the National Clearing House on Family Violence.

The objective in compiling and coordinating information is to raise awareness and provide resources for education. Governments should not control or horde information and a plurality of non-governmental research bodies should be supported.

RESEARCH AGENCIES, non-governmental organisations and governments should compile a comprehensive, inter-disciplinary, and public review of child abuse reporting laws and practices.

Considerations:

This review should explore the reasons mandatory reporting provisions are not working and suggest alternative approaches and frameworks that could lead to more voluntary disclosures, encourage reporting of all types of abuse affecting all children and youth, and produce interventions that are responsive to the young people's needs and serve their best interests.

This review should also examine whether current laws adequately identify the out-of-home care facilities to which they apply, whether they envision licensing and mandatory, independent inspections, and whether they require comprehensive investigations of systemic features of a facility where abuse is reported.

RESEARCH AGENCIES, non-governmental organisations and governments should sponsor research into the most appropriate strategies for healing the harms of institutional child abuse.

Considerations:

The need to understand how to help survivors overcome the negative effects of institutional child abuse is pressing. Traditional legal redress processes have shown their limited capacity to meet the needs of survivors. Newer, more comprehensive redress programs are being established without any clear understanding of the kinds of individual and collective therapeutic needs of survivors and their communities.

Collaborative research funding programs could be an effective means of promoting the necessary research.

Appendix A

Minister's Letter

Mr. Roderick A. Macdonald
President
Law Commission of Canada
473 Albert Street, 11th Floor
Trebla Building
Ottawa, Ontario
K1A 0H8

Dear Mr. Macdonald:

I am writing further to our recent discussions concerning a reference to the Law Commission of Canada. As you are aware, I very much appreciate the role that the Law Commission can play in providing independent advice on reform of the law of Canada and its effects, with a view to ensuring that the legal system meets the changing needs of Canadian society and of individuals in that society.

With this in mind, I ask the Commission to undertake, pursuant to s.5(1)(b) of the *Law Commission of Canada Act*, a report addressing processes for dealing with institutional child physical and sexual abuse.

The federal government and many provincial and territorial governments are confronted with the difficult issue of responding to victims of physical and sexual abuse that occurred in government-run, as well as government-funded and sponsored institutions, in the past. Cases of this nature raise sensitive issues for the individuals involved, for their families and for the communities. Governments are concerned about how best to deal with these issues in a responsible and fair way. While it is clear that lengthy civil and criminal trials are not ideal processes in this context, it is less clear what types of processes would best address wrongdoing, while affording appropriate remedies, and promoting reconciliation, fairness and healing.

As an independent, multidisciplinary agency mandated to consider law and justice, the Law Commission of Canada is well suited to examine processes to deal with institutional abuse. It can provide governments, and Canadians generally, with an inventory and comparative assessment of approaches available.

The Commission is being asked to conduct its research and study in consultation with all interested parties and constituencies. However, the Commission should not address processes that affect Aboriginal peoples until national Aboriginal leadership is closely consulted as to how best to involve Aboriginal peoples in carrying out the reference.

The result of the Commission's study should be analytical, conceptual and non-prescriptive. It should include a discussion of approaches in Canada and elsewhere, but should not be structured so as to pre-empt or derail any ongoing processes in place or under consideration. More specifically, it is not intended to displace, delay or in any way be in lieu of the federal government response to the recommendations of the Royal Commission on Aboriginal Peoples. Nor is this reference to the Law Commission intended to provide a public forum for redress either of general situations or specific cases.

I would suggest that the Commission's work be multi-staged. An initial report, outlining the issues and identifying the required research and studies, including the range of constituencies that must be involved in the process, could be completed by the end of January 1998. A comprehensive analysis of all the facets of the problem could follow in June 1998. The Final Report, reviewing various approaches and their implications, is to be submitted in November 1998.[1]

I look forward to receiving the Report of the Law Commission of Canada on this complex and important issue.

Sincerely yours,

A. Anne McLellan

---

[1] The date for submission of the Final Report was subsequently extended.

Appendix B

Bibliography

Contents

1. Reports and Background Research Published by the Law Commission of Canada

2. Background Research Papers Prepared for the Law Commission of Canada

3. Reports of Inquiries into the Abuse of Children in Institutions (1989 to 1999)

4. Provincial Ombudsman Reports on the Abuse of Children in Institutions (1979 to 1999)

5. Child Advocate Reports on the Abuse of Children in Institutions (1992 to 1999)

6. Other Reports

7. Books and Chapters

8. Journals and Articles

9. Research Studies

10. Press Releases and Speaking Notes

11. Redress Agreements, Program Information and Related Reports

12. Handbooks, Protocols and Models

13. Audio and Video Tapes and CD-ROMs

1. Reports and Background Research Published by the Law Commission of Canada

Law Commission of Canada, *An International Perspective: A Review and Analysis of Approaches to Addressing Past Institutional or Systemic Abuse in Selected Countries*, by M. Gannage (Ottawa: Law Commission of Canada, 1998).

Law Commission of Canada, *Apologising for Serious Wrongdoing: Social, Psychological and Legal Considerations* by S. Alter (Ottawa: Law Commission of Canada, 1999).

Law Commission of Canada, *From Resorative Justice to Transformative Justice [:] Discussion Paper* (Ottawa: Law Commission of Canada, 1999).

Law Commission of Canada, *Institutional Child Abuse in Canada*, R. Bessner, (Ottawa: Law Commission of Canada, October 1998).

Law Commission of Canada, *Institutional Child Abuse in Canada – Civil Cases* by G. Shea (Ottawa: Law Commission of Canada, 1999).

Law Commission of Canada, *Institutional Child Abuse in Canada – Criminal Cases* by G. Shea (Ottawa: Law Commission of Canada, 1999).

Law Commission of Canada, *Minister's Reference on Institutional Child Abuse* (Discussion Paper) (Ottawa: Law Commission of Canada, December 1998).

Law Commission of Canada, *Minister's Reference on Institutional Child Abuse* (Interim Report) (Ottawa: Law Commission of Canada, February 1998).

Law Commission of Canada, *Needs and Expectations for Redress of Victims of Abuse at Residential Schools*, by Claes, R. and Clifton, D. (SAGE), (Ottawa: Law Commission of Canada, October 1998).

Law Commission of Canada, *Redress Programs Relating to Institutional Child Abuse in Canada* by G. Shea (Ottawa: Law Commission of Canada, 1999).

Law Commission of Canada, *Review of the Needs of Victims of Institutional Child Abuse*, Institute for Human Resource Development (Ottawa: Law Commission of Canada, October 1998).

2. Background Research Papers Prepared for the Law Commission of Canada

Corbière, D. and Nahwegahbow, D., "The Mitchikanibikok Inik Experiences" (4 January 1999) [unpublished research report archived at the Law Commission of Canada].

Duffy, L., "Report on the Violation of Ojibwe Laws: The Residential School Experience of Members of The Wabigoon Lake First Nation" (9 February 1999) [unpublished research report archived at the Law Commission of Canada].

Hansen, C. and Lee, T., "The Impact of Residential Schools and Other Institutions on the Métis People of Saskatchewan: Cultural Genocide, Systemic Abuse and Child Abuse" (March 1999) [unpublished research report archived at the Law Commission of Canada].

Hill, L., "Enough is Enough – Report on a Facilitated Discussion Group Involving the Deaf Community, responding to the Minister's Reference on Institutional Child Abuse" (March 1999) [unpublished report archived at the Law Commission of Canada].

Jacobs, B.K., "Rekindled Spirit" (23 December 1998) [unpublished research report archived at the Law Commission of Canada].

Public History Inc., "Children's Residential Facilities Database" (19 March 1999) [unpublished research report archived at the Law Commission of Canada].

3. Reports of Inquiries into the Abuse of Children in Institutions (1989 to 1999)

Australia, Human Rights and Equal Opportunity Commission, *Bringing Them Home: Report of the National Inquiry into the Separation of Aboriginal and Torres Strait Islander Children from Their Families* (Canberra: Sterling Press Pty. Ltd., 1997).

Australian Capital Territory, Law Reform Commission, *The Mandatory Reporting of Abuse of Children*, Series No. 7 (Canberra: Canberra Publications and Public Communication, 1993).

New Brunswick, *Report of the Commission of Inquiry Established by Order-in-Council 92-1022* (New Brunswick: Attorney General, 17 February 1995) (Chair: The Hon. Richard L. Miller).

Newfoundland, *Report of the Royal Commission of Inquiry into the Response of the Newfoundland Criminal Justice System to Complaints*, vol. 1 and 2 (St. John's: Queen's Printer, 1991) (Commissioner: The Hon. S.H.S. Hughes).

Nova Scotia, *Report of an Independent Investigation in Respect of Incidents and Allegations of Sexual and Other Physical Abuse at Five Nova Scotia Residential Institutions* (Halifax: Ministry of Justice, 1995) (President: The Hon. Stuart G. Stratton).

Ontario, *Report of the Royal Commission of Inquiry into Certain Deaths at the Hospital for Sick Children* (Toronto: Ministry of the Attorney General, 1984) (Commissioner: The Hon. Samuel G.M. Grange).

Peterson, K., *Sir Joseph Bernier Federal Day School, Turquetil Hall: Investigation Report* (Yellowknife: Government Leader of the Northwest Territories, 1994).

Québec, *Rapport de la Commission d'enquête portant sur des allégations d'abus sexuels impliquant des enfants résidant dans un centre d'accueil de la région de Montréal* (Montreal: Ministère de la Sécurité Publique,1989) (Chair: Me Jean Denis Gagnon).

Queensland, *Report of the Commission of Inquiry into Abuse of Children in Queensland Institutions* (Brisbane: Commission of Inquiry into Abuse of Children in Queensland Institutions, May 1999) (Chair: L. Forde).

Queensland, *Queensland Government Response to Recommendations of the Commission of Inquiry into Abuse of Children in Queensland Institutions* (Brisbane: Queensland Government, August 1999).

Winter, G.A., *Report of the Archdiocesan Commission of Enquiry into the Sexual Abuse of Children by Members of the Clergy*, Submitted to the Reverend A.L. Penney, D.D., Archbishop of the Archdiocese of St. John's (St. John's, Nfld.: Archdiocese of St. John's, June 1990).

4.   Provincial Ombudsman Reports on the Abuse of Children in Institutions (1979 to 1999)

Ombudsman of Alberta, *A Report on the Westfield Diagnostic and Treatment Centre* (Edmonton: Alberta Ombudsman, 27 November 1979).

Ombudsman of British Columbia, *Public Report No. 32: Abuse of Deaf Students at Jericho Hill School* (Victoria: B.C. Ombudsman, November 1993).

Ombudsman of British Columbia, *Public Report No. 38: Righting the Wrong – The Confinement of the Sons of Freedom Doukhobor Children* (Victoria: B.C. Ombudsman: April 1999).

Quebec Ombudsman, *The "Children of Duplessis": A Time for Solidarity* (Discussion and Consultation Paper for Decision-Making Purposes) (Sainte-Foy: Quebec Ombudsman, 22 January 1997).

5. Child Advocate Reports on the Abuse of Children in Institutions (1992 to 1999)

Ontario, Office of Child and Family Service Advocacy, *Report by the Office of Child and Family Service Advocacy – Care of Youth at Thistletown Regional Centre, Syl Apps Campus*, by J. Finlay (Toronto: Office of Child and Family Service Advocacy, October 1992).

Ontario, Office of Child and Family Service Advocacy, *Exit Report – Summary and Recommendations, Thistletown Regional Centre, Syl Apps Campus*, by J. Finlay (Toronto: Office of Child and Family Services Advocacy, 1995).

Quebec, *The Batshaw Youth and Family Centres – Prévost Campus, La Chapelle Unit, Conclusions of the Investigation* (Montréal: Commission des droits de la personne et des droits de la jeunesse, 4 May 1997).

6. Other Reports

Alberta Children's Advocate, *In Need of Protection – Children and Youth in Alberta* (Edmonton: Children's Advocate and Child Welfare Review Office, July 1993) (Chief Advocate: Bernd Walter).

Alberta, *Task Force on the Criminal Justice System and Its Impact on the Indian and Métis People of Alberta* (Edmonton, 1991).

Alkali Residential School Inquiry Report (Alkali Lake, B.C., 26 June 1997).

Berger, T., *Report of Special Counsel regarding Claims Arising out of Sexual Abuse at Jericho Hill School* (Victoria: Ministry of the Attorney General, March 1995).

Boyer, A., *et al.*, *From Pain to Hope – Report from the C.C.C.B. Ad Hoc Committee on Child Sexual Abuse* (Ottawa: Canadian Conference of Catholic Bishops, 1992).

British Columbia, *Inside Quality Assurance Report – Jericho Residential Program* by B. Smith (Vancouver: Jericho Residential Program, Ministry of Social Services, August 1996).

British Columbia, *Report of the Gove Inquiry into Child Protection in British Columbia – A Commission of Inquiry into the adequacy of the service, policies and practices of the Ministry of Social Services as they relate to the apparent neglect, abuse and death of Matthew John Vaudreuil* by Judge T. Gove (Victoria: Ministry of Social Services, 1995).

Canada, Commission of Inquiry on the Blood System in Canada, *Final Report*, vol. 3 (Ottawa: Minister of Public Works and Government Services Canada, 1997) (Commissioner: The Hon. H. Krever).

Canada, Committee on the Concept of the Ombudsman, *Report of the Committee on the Concept of the Ombudsman* (Ottawa, Government of Canada, July 1977).

Canada, Committee on Sexual Offences Against Children and Youths, *Sexual Offences Against Children*, vols. 1 and 2 (Ottawa: Minister of Justice and the Attorney General of Canada and the Minister of National Health and Welfare, 1984) (Chairman: R. Badgley).

Canada, National Health and Welfare, *The Summary Report of the Special Advisor to the Minister of National Health and Welfare on Child Sexual Abuse in Canada – Reaching for Solutions* by R. Rogers (Ottawa: Canada Communication Group, 1990).

Canada, *Federal Response to Reaching for Solutions – Report of the Special Advisor on Child Sexual Abuse* (Ottawa: Canada Communication Group, 1992).

Canada, *Report of the Royal Commission on Aboriginal Peoples: Looking Forward, Looking Back*, vols. 1-5 (Ottawa: Canada Communication Group, 1996).

Children's Commissioner, *The Children's Commission 1998 Annual Report* (Victoria: The Children's Commission, April 1999) (Commissioner: C. Morton).

Child Welfare League of Canada and Ontario Association of Children's Aid Societies, *Canada's Children ... Canada's Future – Final Conference Report for the Second National Policy Conference on Children* (Ottawa: Child Welfare League of Canada and Ontario Association of Children's Aid Societies, 1997).

Chile, Comision Nacional de Verdad y Reconciliacion, *Report of the Chilean National Commission on Truth and Reconciliation*, trans. P.E. Berryman (Notre Dame, Ind.: University of Notre Dame Press, 1993).

Community Services Council of Newfoundland and Labrador, *Shifting the Focus: Community Discussions on Child Sexual Abuse – Report on Findings* (St. John's: Community Services Council of Newfoundland and Labrador, 1997).

Department of Canadian Heritage, *Convention on the Rights of the Child – First Report of Canada* (Ottawa: Department of Canadian Heritage, Human Rights Directorate, May 1994).

Ireland, *Report on Child Sexual Abuse* (Dublin: Law Reform Commission of Ireland, 1990).

Kirke, G. I., *Players First – A Report Prepared for the Canadian Hockey League* (Toronto: Canadian Hockey League, 7 August 1997).

Lawrence, N., *The Grollier Hall Experience – A Report on the Victim/Witness Support Service of a Multiple Child Sexual Abuse Court Trial in Inuvik, Northwest Territories August 1998* (Northwest Territories: Grollier Hall Residential School Healing Circle, 16 October 1998).

Manitoba, Family Services, *Independent Review of Reporting Procedures in Children's Care Residential Facilities* by P.C. Suche, J. Rogers and P. Vincent (Winnipeg: Manitoba Family Services, February 1992).

Manitoba, *Government Response to the Independent Review of Reporting Procedures in Children's Residential Facilities* (Winnipeg: Manitoba Family Services, 1992).

Manitoba, *Report of the Aboriginal Justice Inquiry of Manitoba: The Justice System and Aboriginal People*, vol. 1 (Winnipeg: Queen's Printer, 1991) (Commissioners: A.C. Hamilton and C.M. Sinclair).

New South Wales, *Systems Abuse: Problems and Solutions* by J. Cashmore, R. Dolby and D. Brennan (New South Wales: New South Wales Child Protection Council and Minister for Community Services, 1994).

Northwest Territories, Ministry of Health, *Medical Patient Search Project – Summary – Final Report* (Yellowknife: Ministry of Health, 1991).

Ombudsman of British Columbia, *Public Report No. 19: The Regulation of AIC Ltd. and FIC Ltd. by the B.C. Superintendent of Brokers (The Principal Group Investigation)* (Victoria: B.C. Ombudsman, 1989).

Ombudsman of British Columbia, *Public Report No. 33: Listening – A Review of Riverview Hospital* (Victoria: B.C. Ombudsman, 1994).

Ombudsman of British Columbia, *Public Report No. 34: Building Respect – A Review of Youth Custody Centres in British Columbia* (Victoria: B.C. Ombudsman, 1994).

Ombudsman of British Columbia, *Public Report No. 36: Getting There – A Review of the Implementation of the Report of the Gove Inquiry into Child Protection* (Victoria: B.C. Ombudsman, 1998).

Ontario, Office of Child and Family Service Advocacy, *Voices From Within – Youth Speak Out: Youth in Care in Ontario* (Toronto: Queen's Printer, April 1998) (Chief Advocate: J. Finlay).

Ontario Law Reform Commission, *Report on Public Inquiries* (Toronto: Ontario Law Reform Commission, 1992).

Ontario Law Reform Commission, *Report on Child Witnesses* (Toronto: Ontario Law Reform Commission, 1991).

Ontario, *Review of Safeguards in Children's Residential Programs: A Report to the Ministers of Community and Social Services and Correctional Services* (Toronto: Ministers of Community and Social Services and Correctional Services, 1990).

Ontario, *Report of the Commission on Proceedings Involving Guy Paul Morin*, vol.1 (Toronto: Queen's Printer, 1998), online: <http://www.attorneygeneral.jus.gov.on.ca/morin/morin.htm> (date accessed: 16 November 1999).

Saskatchewan, Indian Justice Review Committee, *Report of the Saskatchewan Indian Justice Review Committee* (Regina: Indian Justice Review Committee, 1992).

Scotland, Scottish Law Commission, *Report on the Evidence of Children and Other Potentially Vulnerable Witnesses* (Edinburgh: Scottish Law Commission, 1990).

South Africa, Truth and Reconciliation Commission of South Africa, *Final Report* (29 October 1998), online: <http://www.truth.org.za> (date accessed: 16 November 1999).

Sylvester, H., Harry, N., Tom, D. and Sam, L., *The Youth Report – A Report About Youth by Youth* (Victoria. B.C.: The Children's Commission, April 1999).

United Nations Committee on the Rights of the Child, *Consideration of Reports Submitted by State Parties Under Article 44 of the Convention – Concluding Observations of the Committee on the Rights of the Child: Canada* (9 June 1995), Department of Canadian Heritage, The Human Rights Directorate online: <http://www.pch.gc.ca/ddp-hrd/english/rotc/concobs.htm> (date accessed: 9 November 1999).

7. Books and Chapters

Adams, H., *A Tortured People – The Politics of Colonization* (Penticton, B.C.: Theytus Books, 1995).

Armstrong, H., "Victims of Sexual Assault: Psychiatric Profiles" in *Civil Liability for Sexual Assault in an Institutional Setting* (Toronto: Canadian Institute Publications, 1994).

Bagley, C. and Thomlison, R., eds., *Child Sexual Abuse: Critical Perspectives on Prevention, Intervention, and Treatment* (Toronto: Wall and Emerson, Inc., 1991).

Bala, N., "Records, Confidentiality, Disclosure of Information and Reporting Abuse" in *Civil Liability for Sexual Assault in an Institutional Setting* (Toronto: Canadian Institute Publications, 1995).

Ball, J. and Pence, A., "Beyond Developmentally Appropriate Practice: Developing Community and Culturally Appropriate Practice" in *Young Children International* (Victoria: School of Child and Youth Care, University of Victoria, March 1999) 46.

Baudouin, J.L. and Deslauriers, P., *La responsabilité civile*, 5th ed. (Cowansville, Québec: Yvon Blais, 1998).

Bessner, R., "Hearing From The Child as a Witness" in *Wilson on Children and The Law* (Toronto: Butterworths, 1996) 6.28.

Bogart, W.A. and Vidmar, N., "Problems and Experience with the Ontario Civil Justice System: An Empirical Assessment" in A.C. Hutchinson, ed., *Access to Civil Justice* (Toronto: Carswell, 1990) 1.

Branch, W.K., *Class Actions in Canada* (Vancouver: Russell and Dumoulin, 1997).

Bronkhorst, D., *Truth and Reconciliation: Obstacles and Opportunities for Human Rights* (Amsterdam: Amnesty International, Dutch Section, 1995).

Burns, P.T., *Criminal Injuries Compensation*, 2nd ed. (Toronto: Butterworths, 1992).

Carbin, C.F., *Deaf Heritage in Canada* (Toronto: McGraw-Hill Ryerson, 1996).

Canada, Department of Justice, *Building Community Justice Partnerships: Community Peacemaking Circles* (Ottawa: Minister of Public Works and Government Services Canada, 1997).

Canadian Conference of Catholic Bishops, *Breach of Trust, Breach of Faith: Child Sexual Abuse in the Church and Society* (materials for discussion groups) (Ottawa: Concacan Inc., 1992).

Cavanagh Johnson, T., *Sexual, Physical and Emotional Abuse in Out-of-Home Care* (New York: Haworth Maltreatment and Trauma Press, 1997).

Chrisjohn, R.D. and Young, S., *The Circle Game* (Penticton, B.C.: Theytus Books, 1997).

Damaska, M.R., *The Faces of Justice and State Authority* (New Haven: Yale University Press, 1986).

Davison, A., *Residential Care – The Provision of Quality Care in Residential and Educational Group Care Settings* (England: Arena Ashgate Publishing, 1995).

Day, D., "Power and Vainglory: Lessons From Mistreatment of Children at Mount Cashel Orphanage and Other Institutional Settings in Newfoundland" in *Civil Liability For Sexual Assault in an Institutional Setting* (Toronto: Canadian Institute Publications, 1994).

Denis, C., *We Are Not You: First Nations and Canadian Modernity* (Peterborough, Ont.: Broadview Press, 1997).

Des Rosiers, N. and Langevin, L., *L'indemnisation des victimes de violence sexuelle et conjugale* (Cowansville, Québec: Yvon Blais, 1998).

Dyzenhaus, D., *Judging the Judges, Judging Ourselves – Truth, Reconciliation and the Apartheid Legal Order* (Oxford: Hart Publishing, 1998).

Dyck, N., *Differing Visions – Administering Indian Residential Schooling in Prince Albert, 1867–1995* (Halifax: Fernwood Publishing, 1997).

Finkelhor, D., *Child Sexual Abuse: New Theory and Research* (New York: Free Press, 1984).

Fiss, O.M., *The Civil Rights Injunction* (Bloomington: Indiana University Press, 1979).

Fournier, S. and Crey. E., *Stolen from Our Embrace: The Abduction of First Nations Children and Restoration of Aboriginal Communities* (Vancouver: Douglas and McIntyre Ltd., 1997).

Friedenberg, E.Z., *Deference to Authority: The Case of Canada* (Toronto: Random House, 1980).

Furniss, E., *Victims of Benevolence: The Dark Legacy of the Williams Lake Residential School* (Vancouver: Arsenal Pulp Press, 1995).

Goffman, E., *Asylums, Essays on the Social Situation of Mental Patients and Other Inmates* (Garden City, New York: Doubleday, 1961).

Graham, E., *The Ninth Hole: Life at Two Indian Residential Schools* (Waterloo, Ont.: Heffle Publishing, 1997).

Grant, A., *No End of Grief: Indian Residential Schools in Canada* (Winnipeg: Pemmican Publishing, 1996).

Haig-Brown, C., *Resistance and Renewal: Surviving the Indian Residential School* (Vancouver: Tillacum Library, 1988).

Harris, M., *Unholy Orders: Tragedy at Mount Cashel* (Markham, Ont.: Penguin Books Canada, 1990).

Health Canada, *The Invisible Boy: Revisioning the Victimization of Male Children and Teens* by F. Mathews (Ottawa: Minister of Public Works and Government Services, 1996).

Henton, D., *Boys Don't Cry: The Struggle for Justice and Healing in Canada's Biggest Sex Abuse Scandal* (Toronto: McClelland and Stewart, 1995).

Hill, B.H., *Shaking the Rattle* (Penticton, B.C.: Theytus Books Ltd. 1995).

Hodgson, M., "Rebuilding Community After the Residential School Experience" in D. Engelstad and J. Bird eds., *Nation to Nation: Aboriginal Sovereignty and the Future of Canada* (Ontario: House of Anansi Press, 1992) 101.

Hogan, W., *Pathways of Mercy: History of the Foundation of the Sisters of Mercy in Newfoundland, 1842–1984* (St. John's: Harry Cuff Publications Limited, 1986).

Hutchinson, A.C., ed., *Access to Civil Justice* (Toronto: Carswell, 1990).

Knockwood, I. and Thomas, G., *Out of the Depths: The Experiences of Mi'kmaw Children at the Indian Residential School at Shubenacadie, Nova Scotia* (Lakeport, N.S.: Roseway Publishing, 1992).

Kristjanson, F. and Morris, J.J., "Sexual Abuse and Harassment by and of Adults: Institutional Liability Concerns" in *Civil Liability for Sexual Assault in an Institutional Setting* (Toronto: Canadian Institute Publications, 1995).

Kritz, J.E. ed., *Transitional Justice: How emerging democracies reckon with former regimes*, vols. I–III (Washington, D.C.: The United States Institute of Peace, 1995).

Le Dain, G., "The Role of the Public Inquiry in our Constitutional System" in J. Ziegel ed., *Law and Social Change* (Toronto: Osgoode Hall Law School, York University, 1973) 79.

Lewis Herman, J., *Trauma and Recovery* (New York: Harper Collins, 1992).

Linden, A.M., *Canadian Tort Law*, 6th ed. (Toronto: Butterworths, 1997).

Lordon, P., *Crown Law* (Toronto: Butterworths, 1991).

McLean, G.D., "Negligent Hiring & Negligent Supervision" in *Civil Liability For Sexual Assault in an Institutional Setting* (Toronto: Canadian Institute Publications, 1994).

Miki, R. and Kobayashi, C., *Justice in Our Time – The Japanese Canadian Redress Settlement* (Vancouver: Talonbooks, 1991).

Miller, J.R., *Shingwauk's Vision: A History of Native Residential Schools* (Toronto: University of Toronto Press, 1996).

Minow, M., *Between Vengeance and Forgiveness – Facing History after Genocide and Mass Violence* (Boston: Beacon Press, 1998).

Morris, J.J., "Legal and Practical Issues in Representing Plaintiffs in Seeking Damages for Sexual Abuse" in *Civil Liability For Sexual Assault in an Institutional Setting* (Toronto: Canadian Institute Publications, 1994).

Neeb, J. and Harper, S., *Civil Action for Childhood Sexual Abuse* (Toronto: Butterworths, 1994).

Nevitte, N., *The Decline of Deference* (Peterborough, Ont.: Broadview Press, 1996).

Omatsu, M., *Bittersweet Passage – Redress and the Japanese Canadian Experience* (Toronto: Between the Lines, 1992).

Paciocco, D.M., *Charter Principles And Proof In Criminal Cases* (Toronto: Carswell, 1987).

Page, S.J., "Advising and Representing the Institution: Legal and Practical Issues" in *Civil Liability For Sexual Assault in an Institutional Setting* (Toronto: Canadian Institute Publications, 1994).

Page, S.J., "Defending the Claim: Guidelines for Institutional Defendants" in *Civil Liability for Sexual Assault in an Institutional Setting* (Toronto: Canadian Institute Publications, 1995).

Pence, A. and McCallum, M., "Developing Cross-Cultural Partnerships: Implications for Child Care Quality Research and Practice" in P. Moss and A. Pence, eds., *Valuing Quality in Early Childhood Services: New Approaches to Defining Quality* (London and New York: Paul Chapman Publishing and Teachers College Press, 1994) 108.

Raskin, D.C. and Yuille, J.C., "Problems in Evaluating Interviews of Children in Sexual Abuse Cases" in S. J. Ceci, D. F. Ross, and M. P. Toglia, eds., *Perspectives on Children's Testimony* (New York: Springer-Verlag, 1989) 184.

Raychaba, B., *"Pain ... Lots of Pain" Family Violence and Abuse in the Lives of Young People in Care* (Ottawa: National Youth in Care Network, 1993).

Renvoize, J., *Innocence destroyed – A study of child sexual abuse* (New York: Routledge, 1993).

Rindfleisch, N., "Political Obstacles to Reporting in Residential Care Settings" in A. Maney and S. Wells, eds., *Professional Responsibilities in Protecting Children – A Public Health Approach to Child Sexual Abuse* (New York: Praeger, 1988) 54.

Roach, K., "Canada Public Inquiries and Accountability" in P. Stenning ed., *Accountability For Criminal Justice* (Toronto: University of Toronto Press, 1995) 268.

Roach, K., "Fundamental Reforms to Civil Litigation" in *Rethinking Civil Justice: Research Studies for the Civil Justice Review*, vol. 2 (Toronto: Ontario Law Reform Commission, 1996) 383.

Robardet, P., "Should We Abandon the Adversarial Model in Favour of an Inquisitorial Model in Commissions of Inquiry?" in P. Pross, I. Christie and J. Yogis, eds., *Commissions of Inquiry* (Toronto: Carswell, 1990) 111.

Robinson, L., *Crossing the Line – Violence and Sexual Assault in Canada's National Sport* (Toronto: McClelland and Stewart Inc., 1998).

Roche, D., "The Helpline Reconciliation Model Agreement: Historic Breakthrough" in *Civil Liability for Sexual Assault in an Institutional Setting* (Toronto: Canadian Institute Publications, 1995).

The Roeher Institute, *Harm's Way – The Many Faces of Violence and Abuse Against Persons with Disabilities* (Toronto: The Roeher Institute, 1995).

Rogers, R., "Victimization and Its Impact" in *Civil Liability for Sexual Assault in an Institutional Setting* (Toronto: Canadian Institute Publications, 1995).

Ross, R., *Dancing With A Ghost: Exploring Indian Reality* (Markham, Ont.: Octopus, 1992).

Salter, L., "The Two Contradictions in Public Inquiries" in P. Pross, I. Christie and J. Yogis, eds., *Commissions of Inquiry* (Toronto: Carswell, 1990) 173.

Sandiford Grygier, P., *A Long Way From Home: The Tuberculosis Epidemic Among the Inuit* (Montreal: McGill-Queen's University Press, 1994).

Senn, C., *Vulnerable: sexual abuse and people with an intellectual handicap* (Toronto: The Roeher Institute, 1988).

Sheehy, E., "Compensation for Women Who have been Raped " in J. V. Roberts and R. M. Mohr, eds., *Confronting Sexual Assault: A Decade of Legal and Social Change* (Toronto: University of Toronto Press, 1994) 205.

Sky, L. and Sparks, V., *Until Someone Listens* (Work Book) (Toronto: Skyworks Charitable Foundation, 1999).

Stitt, A., Hardy, F. and Simm, P., "Alternative Dispute Resolution and the Ontario Civil Justice System" in *Rethinking Civil Justice: Research Studies for the Civil Justice Review*, vol. 1 (Toronto: Ontario Law Reform Commission, 1996).

Tavuchis, N., *Mea Culpa – a sociology of apology and reconciliation* (Stanford, Cal.: Stanford University Press, 1991).

Tellier, N., "Limitation Issues in Civil Sexual Assault: Overcoming Barriers to Civil Remedies" in *Civil Liability For Sexual Assault in an Institutional Setting* (Toronto: Canadian Institute Publications, 1994).

Thomas, G., "The Responsibility of Residential Placements for Children's Rights to Development" in R. Hanson, ed., *The Institutional Abuse of Children & Youth* (New York: Haworth Press, 1982) 23.

Tucker, R.B. "Alternative Remedies: A Timely Remedy for an Untimely Problem," in *Civil Liability for Sexual Assault in an Institutional Setting* (Toronto: Canadian Institute Publications, 1994).

Vella, S., "Recovered Traumatic Memory: The Need for a Balanced Assessment" in *Civil Liability for Sexual Assault in an Institutional Setting* (Toronto: Canadian Institute Publications, 1995).

Vella, S., "The Healing Package Negotiated by the Grandview Survivors' Support Group: An Example of Alternative Dispute Resolution and Societal Accountability in Action" in *Civil Liability for Sexual Assault in an Institutional Setting* (Toronto: Canadian Institute Publications, 1995).

Wells, M. and Addley, W., "A Religious Institution Responds to the Problem of Child Sexual Abuse" in *Civil Liability For Sexual Assault in an Institutional Setting* (Toronto: Canadian Institute Publications, 1994).

Wells, M., "Fair and Effective Procedures for Institutional Response to Sexual Abuse Complaints" in *Civil Liability for Sexual Assault in an Institutional Setting* (Toronto: Canadian Institute Publications, 1995).

8. Journals and Articles

Beker, J., "Institutional Abuse: The Tip of the Iceberg?" (December 1991) 20:6 *Child & Youth Care Forum* 377.

Belleau, C. and Bergeron, V., "L'accessibilité à la justice civile et administrative au Québec" in A.C. Hutchinson, ed., *Access to Civil Justice* (Toronto: Carswell, 1990) 77.

Berger, T., "Commissions of Inquiry Keynote Address" in "Commission of Inquiry: Praise or Re-appraise" (Inquiries Conference, Faculty of Law, Queen's University, 12-14 February 1999).

Berger, T., "The Mackenzie Valley Pipeline Inquiry" (1976) 83 *Queen's Quarterly* 1.

Bessner, R., "*Khan*: Important Strides Made by the Supreme Court Respecting Children's Evidence" (1991) 79 *Criminal Reports* (3rd) 15.

Bessner, R., "The Competency of the Child Witness: A Critical Analysis of Bill C-15" (1989) 31 *Criminal Law Quarterly* 481.

Bittel, P.T., "Abuse By Caretakers: Arbitral Views on Discipline" (1995) 50 *Dispute Resolution Journal* 66.

Blatt, E., "Staff Supervision and the Prevention of Institutional Child Abuse and Neglect" (1990) 4:6 *Journal of Child and Youth Care* 81.

Blanchfield, M., "Courtroom Warrior Goes to Battle for Accused" *The Lawyer's Weekly* 15:35 (26 January 1996) 1.

Bloom, R., "Institutional Child Sexual Abuse: Prevention and Risk Management" (1994) 12:2 *Residential Treatment for Children and Youth* 3.

Boyle, C., "The Role of Equality in Criminal Law" (1994) 58 *Saskatchewan Law Review* 203.

Bull, L., "Indian Residential Schooling: The Native Perspective" (1991) 18 (Supp.) *Canadian Journal of Native Education* 1.

Cafardy, N.P., "Stones Instead of Bread: Sexually Abusive Priests in the Ministry" (1993) 27 *Studia Canonica* 145.

Centa, R. and Macklem, P., "Securing Accountability Through Commissions of Inquiry: A Role for the Law Commission of Canada" (Inquiries Conference, Faculty of Law, Queen's University, 12-14 February 1999).

Chandry, J.M., Blum, W. M.R., and Resnick, M., "Female Adolescents with a History of Sexual Abuse: Risk, Outcome and Protective Factors" (1996) 11:4 *Journal of Interpersonal Violence* 503.

Christiansen, J.R., "The Testimony of Child Witnesses: Fact, Fantasy, and the Influence of Pre-trial Interviews" (1987) 62 *Washington Law Review* 705.

Chrisjohn, R., "Faith Misplaced – Lasting Effects of Abuse in a First Nations Community" (1991) 18:2 *Canadian Journal of Native Education* 161.

Cipriani, L., "La justice matrimoniale à l'heure du féminisme: analyse critique de la jurisprudence québécoise sur la prestation compensatoire, 1983–1991" (1995) 36 *Cahiers de droit* 209.

Cornwell, J.K., "CRIPA: The Failure of Federal Intervention for Mentally Retarded People" (1988) 97 *Yale Law Journal* 845.

Desbarats, P., "The Independence of Public Inquiries: Dixon v. Canada" (1997) 36 *Alberta Law Review* 252.

Des Rosiers, N., Feldthusen, B. and Hankivsky, O., "Legal Compensation for Sexual Violence: Therapeutic Consequences and Consequences for the Judicial System" (1998) 4 *Psychology, Public Policy and Law Journal* 433.

Des Rosiers, N., "Limitation Periods and Civil Remedies for Child Sexual Abuse" (1992) 9 *Canadian Family Law Quarterly* 43.

D'Ombrain, N., "Public Inquiries in Canada" (1997) 40:1 *Canadian Public Administration* 86.

Doyle, T.P., "The Canonical Rights of Priests Accused of Sexual Abuse" (1990) 24 *Studia Canonica* 335.

Easton, R.E., "The Dual Role of the Structural Injunction" (1990) 99 *Yale Law Journal* 1983.

Ellis, M.S., "Purging the Past: The Current State of Lustration Laws in the Former Communist Bloc" (1996) 59:4 *Law & Contemporary Problems* 181.

Epp, J.A., "Production of Confidential Records Held by a Third Party in Sexual Assault Cases: R. v. O'Connor" (1996-97) 28 *Ottawa Law Review* 191.

Esser, J., "Evaluation of Dispute Processing: We Do Not Know What We Think and We Do Not Think What We Know" (1999) 66 *Denver University Law Review* 499.

Fayant, A., "Love Means Never Having to Say You're Sorry: the Federal Government Expresses Its Profound Regret to Aboriginal People" (22 March 1998) 27 *Briarpatch* 2.

Feldthusen, B., "Punitive Damages: Hard Choices and High Stakes" (1998) *New Zealand Law Review* 741.

Feldthusen, B., "The Civil Action for Sexual Battery: Therapeutic Jurisprudence?" (1994) 25 *Ottawa Law Review* 203.

Feldthusen, B., "Discriminatory Damage Quantification in Civil Actions for Civil Battery" (1994) 44 *University of Toronto Law Journal* 133.

Feldthusen, B., Hankivsky, O. and Greaves, L., "Therapeutic Consequences of Civil Actions For Damages and Compensation Claims by Victims of Sexual Abuse" (2000) 12:1 *Canadian Journal of Women and the Law* [forthcoming in 2000].

Finn, T. and D'Ambra, L., "Lawyering for Children in the Care of the State" (1994) 42 *Rhode Island Bar Journal* 7.

Fiss, O.M., "Against Settlement" (1984) 93 *Yale Law Journal* 1073.

Fleming, J. *et al.*, "The Long-Term Impact of Childhood Sexual Abuse in Australian Women" (1999) 23:2 *Child Abuse and Neglect* 145.

Foté, D.F., "Child Witnesses in Sexual Abuse Criminal Proceedings: Their Capabilities, Special Problems, and Proposals for Reform" (1985) 13 *Pepperdine Law Review* 157.

Galanter, M. and Cahill, M., "'Most Cases Settle': Judicial Promotion and Regulations of Settlements" (1994) 46 *Stanford Law Review* 1339.

Gillespie, N., "Charter Remedies: The Structural Injunction" (1990) 11 *Advocates' Quarterly* 190.

Goldstone, R.J., "Justice as a Tool for Peace-Making: Truth Commissions and International Criminal Tribunals" (1996) 28 *New York University Journal of International Law and Politics* 485.

Grant, P.R., "Settling Residential Schools Claims" in *Aboriginal Writes* (Ottawa: Canadian Bar Association National Aboriginal Law Section, January 1998) 3.

Henderson, J.A., "Comment: Settlement Class Actions and the Limits of Adjudication" (1995) 80 *Cornell Law Review* 1014.

Hodge, B., "Private Prosecutions: Access to Justice" (1998) 4 *New Zealand Law Journal* 145.

Hyman I. and Czumbil, M., "What happens when corporal punishment is legal?" (1998) 12:2 *Journal of Interpersonal Violence* 309.

Jackson, M., "Locking Up Natives in Canada" (1988) 23 *University of British Columbia Law Review* 216.

Jones, D.P.H., "The Evidence of a Three-Year-Old Child" (1987) *Criminal Law Review* 677.

Johnson, J.G. *et al.*, "Childhood Maltreatment Increases Risk for Personality Disorders During Early Adulthood" (July 1999) 56:7 *Archives of General Psychiatry*, online: <http://archpsyc.ama-assn.org/issues/v56n7/full/yoa8212.html> (date accessed: 18 November, 1999).

Kilgore, C., "Abused Children Often Grow Into Sick Adults" (1998) 32:7 *Pediatric News* 10.

Krantz, J. and Frank, C. "Institutional Approaches to Child Abuse" (1990) 4:6 *Journal of Child and Youth Care* 35.

Kritz, J.N., "Coming to Terms with Atrocities: A Review of Accountability Mechanisms for Mass Violations of Human Rights" (1996) 59:4 *Law and Contemporary Problems* 127.

Langevin, L., "Childhood Sexual Assault: – will there ever be a civil remedy" (1992) 10 *Canadian Cases on the Law of Torts* 86.

Langevin, L., "Gauthier c. Beaumont: La reconnaissance de l'impossibilité psychologique d'agir" (1998) 58 *Revue du Barreau* 167.

Levine Powers, J. *et al.*, "Institutional Abuse: A Review of the Literature" (1990) 4:6 *Journal of Child and Youth Care* 81.

Lipez, K.V., "The Child Witness in Sexual Abuse Cases in Maine: Presentation, Impeachment and Controversy" (1990) 42 *Maine Law Review* 282.

Lynch, B. *et al.*, "Unfinished Business: The Mount Cashel Experience" (1991) 6:1 *Journal of Child and Youth Care* 55.

Macdonald, R.A., "Commissions of Inquiry in the Perspective of Administrative Law" (1980) 18 *Alberta Law Review* 366.

Martin, J., "Justice for Victims? The Sentencing of Public Trust Figures Convicted of Child Abuse: A Focus on Religious Leaders" (1994) 32 *Alberta Law Review* 16.

McCauley, J. *et al.*, "Clinical characteristics of women with a history of childhood abuse: unhealed wounds" (1997) 277:17 *Journal of the American Medical Association* 1362.

McEwan, J., "Child Evidence: More Proposals for Reform" (1988) *Criminal Law Review* 813.

Mosher, J., "Challenging Limitation Periods: Civil Claims by Adult Survivors of Incest" (1994) 44 *University of Toronto Law Journal* 169.

Nevin, C., "Staff Training Needs Around Sex Abuse in Residential Treatment" (1993) 11:1 *Residential Treatment for Children and Youth* 63.

Noreau, P., "Accès à la justice: réfléchir autrement les rapports entre la société et l'institution judiciaire" (Colloque sur la déjudiciarisation: une affaire de justice et de société, Palais des congrès de Montréal, 20 January 1999) [unpublished].

Nunno, M. and Rindfleisch, N., "The Abuse of Children in Out-of-Home Care" (1991) 5:4 *Children and Society* 295.

Nunno M. and Rindfleisch, N., "Progress and Issues in the Implementation of the 1984 Out-of-Home Care Protection Amendment" (1991) 16 *Child Abuse & Neglect* 693.

Nunno, M. and Motz, J., "The Development of an Effective Response to the Abuse of Children in Out-of-Home Care" (1988) 12 *Child Abuse & Neglect* 521.

Oates, R.K., "The Effects of Child Sexual Abuse" (1992) 66:4 *Australian Law Journal* 186.

Orentlicher, D.F., "Settling Accounts: The Duty to Prosecute Human Rights Violations of a Prior Regime" (1991) 100 *Yale Law Journal* 2544.

Paulson, J., "The Clinical and Canonical Considerations in Cases of Pedophilia: The Bishop's Role" (1988) 22 *Studia Canonica* 77.

Pierce, R. and Pierce, L.H., "The sexually abused child: A comparison of male and female victims" (1985) 9 *Child Abuse and Neglect* 191.

Reyome Dodge, N., "Executive Directors' Perceptions of the Prevention of Child Abuse and Maltreatment in Residential Facilities" (1990) 4:6 *Journal of Child and Youth Care* 45.

Rindfleisch, N., "Reporting Out-of-Home Abuse and Neglect Incidents: A Political-Contextual View of the Process" (1990) 4:6 *Journal of Child and Youth Care* 61.

Roach, K., "Public Inquiries, Prosecutions or Both" (1994) 43 *University of New Brunswick Law Journal* 415.

Ross, F., "Blood Feuds and Childbirth: The TRC as Ritual" (1997) 6 *Track Two* 7.

Ross, A.L. and Grenier, G.L., "Moving Beyond the Evil Empire of Institutional Abuse – May the Organizational Force Be With You!" (1990) 4:6 *Journal of Child and Youth Care* 23.

Rozell, S. "Are Children Competent Witnesses?: A Psychological Perspective" (1985) *Washington University Law Quarterly* 63.

Russell, D., "Paedophilia: The Criminal Responsibility of Canada's Churches" (1992) 15 *Dalhousie Law Journal* 380.

Siebert, J., "Being Part of the Healing – A workshop outline on Responding to the Legacy of Native Residential Schools" (January 1996) *Mandate* 14.

Sherrott, G., "Foster Care for Abused Children: An Unacceptable Solution" (1993) 57:2 *Saskatchewan Law Review* 479.

Shuman, D., "When Time Does Not Heal: Understanding the Importance of Avoiding Unnecessary Delay in the Resolution of Tort Cases" (1999) 5:4 *Psychology, Public Policy and Law* [forthcoming].

Slobodian, L., "United Church Apologizes for Residential Schools" (22 September 1998) *Catholic New Times* 8.

Stauffer, I. and Bourbonnais, C., "The Sins of the Father: Vicarious Liability of Churches" (1993) 25 *Ottawa Law Review* 561.

Steele, G., "Designing a Compensation Program for Institutional Abuse" [unpublished].

"The Chronicle Interview: Archbishop Emeritus Desmond Tutu" (Spring 1996) 33:4 *The UN Chronicle* 46.

Thomas, G., "Institutional Child Abuse: The Making and Prevention of an Un-Problem" (1990) 4:6 *Journal of Child and Youth Care* 1.

Tite, R., "Detecting the Symptoms of Child Abuse: Classroom Complications" (1994) 19:1 *Canadian Journal of Education* 1.

Trebilcock, M. and Austin, L. "The Limits of the Full Court Press: Of Blood and Mergers" (1998) 48 *University of Toronto Law Journal* 1.

Tyler, T., "The Role of Perceived Injustice in Defendants' Evaluations of their Courtroom Experience" (1984) 18 *Law & Society Review* 51.

Vella, S., "Recovered Traumatic Memory in Historical Childhood Sexual Abuse Cases: Credibility on Trial" (1998) 32 *University of British Columbia Law Review* 91.

Walsh, B., "Resolving the Human Rights Violations of a Previous Regime" (1996) 158:3 *World Affairs* 111.

West, N., "Rape in the Criminal Law and the Victim's Tort Alternative: A Feminist Analysis" (1992) 50 *University of Toronto Faculty Law Review* 96.

Winslow, T., "Reconciliation: The Road to Healing?: Collective Good, Individual Harm?" (1997) 6 *Track Two* 24.

Yates, A., "Should Young Children Testify in Cases of Sexual Abuse?" (1987) 144 *American Journal of Psychiatry* 476.

9. Research Studies

Alberta Law Reform Institute, *Civil Litigation: Judicial Mini-Trial* (Discussion Paper No. 1) (Edmonton: Alberta Law Reform Institute, August 1993).

Alberta Law Reform Institute, *Proposals for the Reform of the Public Inquiries Act* (Edmonton: Alberta Law Reform Institute, 1992).

Alksnis, C. and Robinson, D., *Childhood Victimization and Violent Behaviour Among Adult Offenders* (Ottawa: Correctional Service of Canada, Research Branch, 1995).

Anderson, K.D., "The Ombudsman as an Administrative Remedy" (Occasional Paper #41) (Edmonton: The International Ombudsman Institute, 1987).

Assembly of First Nations, *Breaking the Silence: An Interpretive Study of Residential School Impact and Healing as Illustrated by the Stories of First Nation Individuals* (Ottawa: Assembly of First Nations, 1994).

Assembly of First Nations Health Secretariat, *Residential Schools Update* (Ottawa: Assembly of First Nations, March 1998).

Bernard, C., "L'Obligation de signalement pour les intervenants liés par le secret professionnel" (Québec: Commission des droits de la personne et des droits de la jeunesse, 1996), online: <http://www.cdpdj.qc.ca/> (date accessed: 22 November 1999).

British Columbia, Ministry of Health, *Multiple Victim Child Sexual Abuse: The Impact on Communities and Implications for Intervention Planning* (Victoria: Ministry of Health, 1994).

British Columbia, Ministry of Health, *Dimensions of Multiple Victim Child Sexual Abuse in British Columbia, 1985-1989, and Community Mental Health Interventions* (Victoria: Ministry of Health, Child and Youth Mental Health Services, 1 July 1991).

Canada, Department of Indian Affairs, *The Historical Development of the Indian Act* (Ottawa: Department of Indian Affairs, 1978).

Canada, Department of Justice, *A Survey of the Preliminary Inquiry in Canada* (Working Paper) by D. Pomerant and G. Gilmour (Ottawa: Department of Justice, 1993).

Canada, Department of Justice, *Technical Report: Violence in Institutional Facilities Against Persons with Disabilities – A Literature Review* by The Roeher Institute (Ottawa: Department of Justice, Research, Statistics and Evaluation Directorate, Civil Law and Corporate Management Sector, 1995).

Canadian Ombudsman Association, "A Federal Ombudsman for Canada: A Discussion Paper" (June 1999).

Canadian Conference of Catholic Bishops, *Let Justice Flow Like a Mighty River* (Brief to the Royal Commission on Aboriginal Peoples) (Ottawa: Canadian Conference of Catholic Bishops, 1995).

Canadian Welfare Council, *Indians and the Law – a survey prepared for the Hon. A. Laing*, (Ottawa: Canadian Welfare Council, August 1967).

Correctional Service of Canada, *A Framework Paper on Restorative Justice and the Correctional Service of Canada* (Ottawa: Correctional Service of Canada, 1998).

Daniels, E.R., *How Similar? How Different? The Patterns of Education for Indian and Non-Indian Students in Canada* (Research Paper) (Ottawa: Department of Indian Affairs, 1992).

England, Law Commission, *Limitation of Actions* (Consultation Paper No. 151) (London: The Stationery Office, 1998).

Gibson, J.L. and Gouws, A., *Truth and Reconciliation in South Africa: Attributions for Blame and the Struggle Over Apartheid* (prepared for delivery at the 1998 Annual Meeting of the Law and Society Association, Aspen, Colorado, June 4-7, 1998).

Hart, R., *Beginning a Long Journey*, a research report prepared for the Family Violence Prevention Division, Health Canada, (Ottawa: Minister of Public Works and Government Services , 1997).

Health Canada, National Clearing House on Family Violence, *Canada's Treatment Programs for Men who Abuse their Partners* (Ottawa: Minister of Public Works and Government Services, 1998).

Health Canada, *List of Articles (1986-1996) on Family Violence and Aboriginal Communities indexed by the National Clearinghouse on Family Violence* (Ottawa: Health Canada, National Clearing House on Family Violence, 1996).

Ing, N.R., *The Effects of Residential Schools on Native Child-Rearing Patterns* (M.A. thesis, University of British Columbia, 1990) [unpublished].

Johnston, J.C., *Aboriginal Offender Survey: Case Files and Interview Sample* (Ottawa: Correctional Service of Canada, Research Branch, 1997).

Lane, P. Jr., Bopp, M. and Bopp, J., *Community Healing and Aboriginal Social Security Reform – A Study prepared for the Assembly of First Nations Aboriginal Social Security Reform Strategic Initiative* (Lethbridge: Four Worlds International Institute for Human and Community Development, March 1998).

LaPrairie, C., *Examining Aboriginal Corrections in Canada* (Ottawa: Ministry of the Solicitor General, 1996).

LaRocque, E.D., *Violence in Aboriginal Communities* (Ottawa: Health Canada, 1994).

Law Reform Commission of Canada, *Administrative Law: Commissions of Inquiry* (Working Paper 17) (Ottawa: Law Reform Commission of Canada, 1977).

Loo, S. *et al.*, *Child Abuse: Reporting and Classification in Health Care Settings* (Ottawa: Health Canada, August 1998) online: <http://www.hc-sc.gc.ca/hppb/familyviolence/child.htm> (date accessed: 22 November 1999).

Llewellyn, J. and Howse, R., "Institutions for Restorative Justice: The South African Truth and Reconciliation Commission" (UNESCO Management of Social Transitions Program Conference, Dubrovnik, Croatia, 27-30 November 1997).

McTimoney, D., *A Resource Guide on Family Violence Issues for Aboriginal Communities*, a research report prepared for the Family Violence Prevention Division, Health Canada (Ottawa: Minister of Public Works and Government Services, 1994).

Meston, J., *Child Abuse and Neglect Prevention Programs* (Ottawa: Vanier Institute of the Family, June 1993).

Mussell, W.J., "Institutionalization and Cultural Devaluation – The Effects of Residential Schooling" (Summary of Proceedings) (First Canadian Conference on Residential Schooling, Vancouver, 1991).

National Youth in Care Network, *Into the Hands of Youth: Youth in and from Care Identify Healing Needs* (Ottawa: National Youth in Care Network, April 1996).

National Youth in Care Network, *Treatment Programs for Child Sexual Abuse in Canada* (Ottawa: National Youth in Care Network, 1993).

National Institute of Justice, *Victims of Childhood Sexual Abuse – Later Criminal Consequences* by C. Widom (NIJ Research in Brief, March 1995), online: <http://www.ncjrs.org/txtfiles/abuse.txt> (date accessed: 18 November 1999).

Ontario Law Reform Commission, *Prospects For Civil Justice* (Study Paper) by R.A. Macdonald (Toronto: Ontario Law Reform Commission, 1995).

Osinchuk, S., *Children's Advocate Services in Canada 1998* (Edmonton: Children's Advocate Office, 7 May 1998) [unpublished].

Poirier, M. and Lauzon, L.-P., "Aspects économiques liés à la problématique des "Orphelins de Duplessis" (Chaire d'études socio-économique, Université du Québec à Montréal, Montreal, 1999).

Ryerse, C., *National Inventory of Treatment Programs for Child Sexual Abuse Offenders,* 1996 (Ottawa: Health Canada – National Clearinghouse on Family Violence, 1996).

Sas, L. and Hurley, P., Project "Guardian": The Sexual Exploitation of Male Youth in London, Ontario (London: London Family Court Clinic, 1997).

Sex Offender Programs, *Selected Readings on Sex Offenders: Excerpts from the Research Forum* (Ottawa: Correctional Services Canada, 1995).

Sex Offender Programs, *Towards a National Strategy – A Conference on Intervention with Sex Offenders* (Ottawa: Correctional Services Canada, February 1996).

Statistics Canada, *Family Violence in Canada: A Statistical Profile 1998* by V. Pottie Bunge and A. Levett (Ottawa: Statistics Canada, May 1998).

Statistics Canada, *Family Violence in Canada: A Statistical Profile 1999* by R. Fitzgerald (Ottawa: Statistics Canada, June 1999).

Szandtner, D., "Sexual Assault and The Civil Process: A Proposed Guide for Effective Plaintiff-Side Lawyering" (Master of Social Work and Bachelor of Laws, University of Toronto, 1996) [unpublished].

Wachtel, A., *The "State of the Art" in Child Abuse Prevention, 1997*, a research report prepared for the Family Violence Prevention Unit, Health Canada (Ottawa: Minister of Public Works and Government Services, 1999).

Williams, S., Valée, S. and Staubi, B., *Aboriginal Sex Offenders: Melding Spiritual Healing with Cognitive-Behavioural Treatment* (Ottawa: Correctional Services Canada, August, 1997).

Working Group on Child Sexual Abuse, *It's Hard to Tell – Discussion Paper* (St. John's: Community Services Council of Newfoundland and Labrador, 1996).

10. Press Releases and Speaking Notes

Aboriginal Healing Foundation, Press Release, "Healing Residential School Survivors, Their Families and Descendants: AHF funds first 35 community projects" (23 June 1999), online: <http://www.ahf.ca/english/rel0699.html> (date accessed: 21 December 1999).

Anglican Church of Canada, Press Release, "Church Leader Says Court Rulings Could Jeopardize Church Work – Liability Issues will Force Churches to 'Reassess' Risk of Certain Programs" (17 June 1999), online: <http://www.anglican.ca/news> (date accessed: 16 November 1999).

Canada, Minister of Indian Affairs and Northern Development, "Notes for an Address by The Honourable Jane Stewart Minister of Indian Affairs and Northern Development" (Ottawa, 7 January 1998), online: Indian and Northern Affairs Canada <http://www.inac.gc.ca/info/speeches/jan98/action.html> (date accessed: 15 September 1999).

Canadian Conference of Catholic Bishops, Press Release, "Background Information – Initiative for Reconciliation, Solidarity and Communion" (17 June 1998), online: <http://www.cccb.ca> (date accessed: 15 April 1999).

Canadian Conference of Catholic Bishops, Press Release, "Charting a New Course – Reconciliation, Solidarity and Communion Initiative in the Spirit of the Great Jubilee" (15 September 1998).

Canadian Conference of Catholic Bishops, Press Release, "Fund for Reconciliation, Solidarity and Communion Contributes More Than $100,000 for Aboriginal Community-based Initiatives" (21 January 1999), online: <http://www.cccb.ca> (date accessed: 15 April 1999).

Canadian Ombudsman Association, News Release, "Canadian Ombudsman Association Formed" (24 June 1998).

Crosby, Rev. D., OMI, "An Apology to the First Nations of Canada by the Oblate Conference of Canada" (Edmonton: Oblate Conference of Canada, 1991).

Fietz, M. and Gagné, É., *Reconciliation Process Implementation Committee Workshop Presentation* (Ottawa: Family Service Canada, 20 October 1995).

Nova Scotia, Department of Health, News Release, "Health – Hemophilia Agreement" (27 May 1993).

Nova Scotia, Department of Justice, Press Release, "Retired Judge to Conduct Independent Review" (30 November 1999), online: <http://www.gov.ns.ca/news/details.asp?id=19991201002> (date accessed: 22 December 1999).

United Church of Canada, Press Release, "Supreme Court Decision Has Serious Implications for United Church Groups and Programs" (17 June 1999), online: <http://www.uccan.org/News> (date accessed: 16 November 1999).

11. Redress Agreements, Program Information and Related Reports

Aboriginal Healing Foundation, *Aboriginal Healing Foundation Program Handbook 1999* (Ottawa: The Aboriginal Healing Foundation, 1998), online (2nd edition): <http://www.ahf.ca/engish/handbook.html> (date accessed: 21 December 1999).

Agreement made as of 1994, between: The Grandview Survivors Support Group and the Government of Ontario (unpublished, 1994).

Anglican Church of Canada, "Granting Criteria for Education, Healing and Reconciliation Programs / Events Related to Residential Schools Issues," online: <http://www.anglican.ca> (date accessed: 14 September 1999).

Anglican Church of Canada, *"Residential Schools – Legacy and Response: Summary of Projects 1999, Summary of Projects 1996–1998 and Summary of Projects 1992–1995,"* online: <http://www.anglican.ca/ministry/rs/healing> (date accessed: 19 November 1999).

British Columbia, *Jericho Individual Compensation Program: Terms of Reference* (Victoria: Ministry of the Attorney General, 15 November 1996).

British Columbia, *Report of Special Counsel regarding Claims Arising out of Sexual Abuse at Jericho Hill School* (Victoria: Minister of the Attorney General of British Columbia, 1995). (Special Counsel: T.R. Berger).

British Columbia, *Residential Historical Abuse Program* (Pamphlet) (Victoria: Ministry of Health, revised October 1996).

Canada, Department of Canadian Heritage, *Final Report on the Implementation of the Japanese Canadians Redress Agreement* (Ottawa: Department of Canadian Heritage, 1997).

Council for Reconciliation, Solidarity and Communion, *Charting a New Course – Reconciliation, Solidarity and Communion Initiative in the Spirit of the Great Jubilee* (Pamphlet) (Ottawa: Canadian Conference of Catholic Bishops, 1998).

Helpline Reconciliation Model Agreement, between: Helpline, The Ottawa Brothers, The Toronto Brothers, The St. John's Training School for Boys, The Archdiocese of Toronto, The Archdiocese of Ottawa and the Government of Ontario (unpublished, 1992).

Hoffman, B.C., *The Search for Healing, Reconciliation and the Promise of Prevention – The Recorder's Report Concerning Physical and Sexual Abuse at St. Joseph's and St. John's Training Schools for Boys*, a report prepared for the Reconciliation Process Implementation Committee, Ontario (place of publication unknown: Concorde Inc., 30 September 1995).

Mussell, M.L., *In The Spirit of Healing – Recorder's Report Written for the Survivors*, a report prepared for the Reconciliation Implementation Committee, Reconciliation Agreement between: The Primary Victims of George Epoch and The Jesuit Fathers of Upper Canada (place of publication unknown: October 1995).

Nova Scotia, Department of Justice, *Compensation for Institutional Abuse Program: Guidelines* (Halifax: Department of Justice, November 1997).

Nova Scotia, *Report of the Auditor General, 1998* (Halifax: Auditor General, 1998).

Ontario, Ministry of the Attorney General, *Evaluation of the Grandview Agreement Process: Final Report* by D. Leach (Toronto: Ministry of the Attorney General, 1997).

Ontario, Ministry of the Attorney General, *Wind Down Report: Lessons Drawn By the Abuse in Provincial Institutions Office About the Grandview and St. John's and St. Joseph's Agreement Processes* (Final Report) by D. Leach (Toronto: Ministry of the Attorney General, September 1998).

Provincial Residential School Project, *Information Package* (Vancouver, 1995), online: <http://www.turtleisland.org/healing/brochure1.htm> (date accessed: 18 November 1999).

Protocol for Indian Residential School Abuse Support Service, between: Provincial and Federal Governments and Aboriginal Representatives (21 June 1995).

Reconciliation Agreement, between: The Primary Victims of George Epoch and The Jesuit Fathers of Upper Canada (unpublished, ratified October 1994).

Reconciliation: An Ongoing Process, RPIC Chairman's Personal Report by D. Roche (Ontario: Reconciliation Process Implementation Committee, 30 June 1996).

Roche, D. and Hoffman, B., *The Vision to Reconcile: Process Report on the Helpline Reconciliation Model Agreement* (Fund for Dispute Resolution – Conrad Grebel College of the University of Waterloo, Waterloo, 1993).

United Church of Canada, "The Healing Fund Connection" (9 March 1999), online: <http://www.uccan.org/Healing.htm> (date accessed: 14 September 1999).

United Church of Canada, "Report of the Healing Fund Council Executive" (October 1998), online: United Church of Canada <http://uccan.org/HFCEreport.htm> (date accessed: 18 September 1999).

12.   Handbooks, Protocols and Models

British Columbia, Ministry for Children and Families. *The B.C. Handbook for* Action *on Child Abuse and Neglect* (undated), online: <http://www.mcf.gov.bc.ca/ChildAbuseHandbook/1toc.html> (date accessed: 16 November 1999).

British Columbia, Ministry of the Attorney General, *Help Stop the Abuse: A Handbook for Employers and Volunteer Coordinators*, 3rd ed. (Victoria: Ministry of the Attorney General, March 99).

British Columbia, Ministry for Children and Families, *Standards for Staffed Children's Residential Services Provided under the Child, Family and Community Service Act 1998* (Victoria: Ministry for Children and Families, December 1998).

British Columbia, Ministry for Children and Families, *Standards for Foster Homes Approved under the Child, Family and Community Service Act 1998* (Victoria: Ministry for Children and Families, September 1998).

Canada, Correctional Services, *Standards and Guidelines for the Provision of Services to Sex Offenders* (Ottawa: Correctional Services, March 1996).

First Nations Health Commission, *Proposal of Indian Residential School Study* (Draft No. 4) (May 1992).

Institute for the Prevention of Child Abuse, *Preferred Practices for Investigating Allegations of Child Abuse in Residential Settings* (Toronto: The Institute for the Prevention of Child Abuse, 1992).

McCoy, P.J. and McGrory Manion, S., *The Management and Investigation of Institutional Abuse Cases* (Trenton, N.J.: Department of Human Services, Division of Youth and Family Services, April 1989).

Metropolitian Toronto Special Committee on Child Abuse, *Child Sexual Abuse Protocol – Guidelines and Procedures for a Coordinated Response to Child Sexual Abuse in Metropolitan Toronto*, 3rd ed. (Toronto: Metropolitan Toronto Special Committee on Child Abuse, March 1995).

Prager, B. and Rimer, P., *Making a Difference: The Child Care Community Response to Child Abuse – Resource Manual* (Toronto: The Metropolitan Toronto Special Committee on Child Abuse, 1996).

Protocol for Jericho Hill Intervention (unpublished, undated).

Protocol for the Development and Implementation of a Victim/Witness Assistance Program in Multi-Victim Multi-Perpetrator Prosecutions (January 1996).

Roeher Institute, *No More Victims – A manual to guide the legal community in addressing the sexual abuse of people with a mental handicap* (Toronto: The Roeher Institute, 1992).

Rogow, S., and Hass, J., *The Person Within: Preventing Abuse of Children & Young People with Disabilities – A Handbook* (Vancouver: B.C. Institute Against Family Violence, 1999).

Swanson, S., *Taking Care – A Child Abuse Prevention Manual for Canadian Early Childhood Educators* (Vancouver: Early Childhood Educators of British Columbia, April 1997).

Szabo, A. *et al.*, *Investigative Guide for Sexual Offences* (Ottawa: Royal Canadian Mounted Police, 1997).

13. Audio and Video Tapes and CD-ROMs

Audio:

Apologies (Parts 1 and 2), produced by Patricia Naylor for the CBC Radio program "Tapestry" (Toronto: Canadian Broadcasting Corp., 1998).

Video:

Beyond Survival, produced for the Nuu-chah-nulth Tribal Council (Port Alberni, B.C.: Edward L. J. Lee Video Productions, 1994) 88 min.

Beyond the Shadows, produced for the Cariboo Tribal Council (Vancouver: Gryphon Productions Ltd, 1992) 28:20 min.

Bringing Them Home, produced for the National Inquiry into the Separation of Aboriginal and Torres Strait Islander Children from Their Families, Human Rights and Equal Opportunity Commission (Sydney: Oziris Productions, 1997) 32 min.

Dancing the Dream, produced for the Anglican Church of Canada (Toronto: Anglican Video for the Council for Native Ministries/Anglican Church of Canada distributor, 1993) 29:44 min.

Healing the Hurts, produced for Four Worlds Development Project (Lethbridge: Phil Lucas Productions, 1989) 59 min.

Jericho Walls of Silence, produced by G. Whiting and A. Wilson for the CBC Television program "Witness" (Toronto: Canadian Broadcasting Corp., 1999).

Just Children, produced for the Law Commission of Canada (Toronto: Glen Richards, Indignant Eye Productions, 2000) 24 min.

The Jericho Individual Compensation Program (Vancouver: Rogers Community TV, 1998) 28 min.

The Person Within, produced for the B.C. Institute Against Family Violence (Vancouver: Creative Media Productions, 1999) 28:20 min.

Until Someone Listens: Recovery from Institutional Abuse, produced for the Grandview Survivors Support Group (Toronto: Laura Sky and Skyworks Charitable Foundation, 1999) 120 min.

CD-ROMs:

Absolon, K. and Winchester, T. "Cultural Identity for Urban Aboriginal Peoples (Learning Circles Synthesis Report" (Research paper submitted to the Royal Commission on Aboriginal Peoples) in *For Seven Generations, Pour sept générations* (Ottawa: Libraxus Inc., CD-ROM, 1997) records 110354 to 111945.

Chrisjohn, R. and Young, S., "The Circle Game: Shadows and Substance in the Indian Residential School Experience in Canada" (Research paper submitted to the Royal Commission on Aboriginal Peoples) in *For Seven Generations, Pour sept générations* (Ottawa: Libraxus Inc., CD-ROM, 1997) records 94299 to 122566.

Milloy, J., " 'Suffer the Little Children': A History of the Residential School System, 1830-1993" (Research paper submitted to the Royal Commission on Aboriginal Peoples) in *For Seven Generations, Pour sept générations* (Ottawa: Libraxus Inc., CD-ROM, 1997) records 92370 to 122566.

Nation Series Complete Edition – 96 Census, 4th ed. (Ottawa: Statistics Canada, CD-ROM, September 1998).

Réaume, D.G. and Macklem, P., "Education for Subordination: Redressing the Adverse Effects of Residential Schooling" (Research paper submitted to the Royal Commission on Aboriginal Peoples) in *For Seven Generations, Pour sept générations* (Ottawa: Libraxus Inc., CD-ROM, 1997) records 93980 to 122566.

Thalassa Research, "Nation to Nation: Indian Nation-Crown Relations in Canada" (Research paper prepared for the Royal Commission on Aboriginal Peoples) in *For Seven Generations, Pour sept générations* (Ottawa: Libraxus Inc. CD-ROM, 1997) records 59182 to 61027.